PRAISE FOR *THIN IS THE NEW HAPPY*

"This poignant—yet hilarious—memoir tracks Frankel's lifelong battle with the scale—or, more accurately, with herself. As she diets through good times and bad, Frankel skewers her own weight-loss foibles and a society that teaches women that thin is all that matters."
—Lucy S. Danziger, editor-in-chief, *Self* magazine

"The rueful, zestful, surprisingly funny story of Ms. Frankel's battle reads like a sequel to the adventures of the chubby heroine of Judy Blume's young-adult novel *Blubber*." —*The New York Times*

"Val Frankel is a woman of amazing insight. . . . She takes the step all women who have had lifelong insecurities in front of the mirror must: to face them down and triumph over them. And the fact that she learned how to dress well along the way doesn't hurt either. Read this, weep, and heal."
—Stacy London, cohost of *What Not to Wear*

"I loved this book, as will anyone who's ever looked in a mirror and not always liked what they've seen. Val Frankel's tragicomic memoir of her battle of the bulge is alternately riotously funny and deeply poignant, but always thought provoking. And when ultimately her struggle ends up being less with her belly fat than with her own inner demons, it ends up being downright inspiring."
—Meg Cabot, author of The Princess Diaries and Queen of Babble series

"[A] gritty, funny tale about one woman's quest to jettison a lifetime's worth of hang-ups, not to mention a closet full of Old Navy duds."
—*Entertainment Weekly*

"[F]unny and brutally frank . . . a satiating account of the long road to self-acceptance." —*People* magazine

"Val Frankel's *Thin Is the New Happy* proves that coming to terms with one's body image might not be easy, but is definitely poignant and hilarious. I applaud Val Frankel's bravery and found myself compelled and inspired by her memoir. Doesn't matter what size you are—if you're a fan of a great story, *Thin Is the New Happy* is the perfect fit." —Jen Lancaster, author of *Pretty in Plaid*

"Infused with humor and refreshing candor, the book will resonate with anyone who's counted carbs or tried to subsist on rice cakes and grapefruit . . . a self-aware, witty exploration of a woman's body issues." —*Kirkus Reviews*

"[F]resh, insightful weight-loss memoir." —*OK!* magazine

"I loved *Thin Is the New Happy*, a memoir by a very good, very funny writer about things that aren't funny; it made me laugh, it made me cry, and it made me think. Now I'm telling everybody I know to read it, too; women because we all struggle with body issues, and men so they'll know what we're up against." —Jennifer Crusie, author of *Bet Me* and *Wild Ride*

"If you are what you weigh, read this book. Valerie Frankel's honest account of life on and off the scale is a victorious and funny account of the diet wars." —Betsy Lerner, author of *Food and Loathing*

"[A] funny, smart memoir . . . inspiring in a totally down-to-earth way." —*Parenting*

THIN
IS THE
NEW
HAPPY

Also by Valerie Frankel

NOVELS

I TAKE THIS MAN
HEX AND THE SINGLE GIRL
THE GIRLFRIEND CURSE
THE NOT-SO-PERFECT MAN
THE ACCIDENTAL VIRGIN
SMART VS. PRETTY

FRINGE GIRL
FRINGE GIRL IN LOVE
AMERICAN FRINGE
FRINGE BENEFITS

A BODY TO DIE FOR
PRIME TIME FOR MURDER
MURDER ON WHEELS
A DEADLINE FOR MURDER

NONFICTION

THE BEST YOU'LL EVER HAVE: WHAT EVERY WOMAN
NEEDS TO KNOW ABOUT GETTING AND GIVING
KNOCK-YOUR-SOCKS-OFF SEX (with Shannon Mullen)
PRIME-TIME STYLE (with Ellen Tien)
THE I HATE MY JOB HANDBOOK: HOW TO DEAL WITH HELL AT WORK (with Ellen Tien)
THE HEARTBREAK HANDBOOK (with Ellen Tien)

THIN

IS THE

NEW

HAPPY

Valerie Frankel

ST. MARTIN'S GRIFFIN ☎ NEW YORK

www.stmartins.com

The Library of Congress has catalogued
the hardcover edition as follows:

Frankel, Valerie.
    Thin is the new happy / Valerie Frankel.—1st ed.
        p. cm.
    ISBN 978-0-312-37392-4
    1. Frankel, Valerie.   2. Authors, American—20th century—
Biography.   3. Dieters—United States—Biography.   4. Weight
loss—Psychological aspects.   5. Body image.   I. Title.
    PS3556.R3358Z46   2008
    813'.54—dc22
    [B]   2008020439

ISBN 978-0-312-37393-1 (trade paperback)

First St. Martin's Griffin Edition: October 2009

10 9 8 7 6 5 4 3 2 1

Dedicated to …

THE LAST FIFTEEN POUNDS

I don't miss you,
Not one tiny bit,
You bitches.

ACKNOWLEDGMENTS

So many people to thank, so few letters in the alphabet.

A lot of authors thank their husbands last. Screw that! Thank you, Steve! You're number-one for me, sweetie! My daughters, Maggie and Lucy, give me boatloads of inspiration and motivation. To quote Roger De Bris's solo in a fine musical by Franz Liebkind, "Everything I do, I do for you!"

I ask, where would any writer be without friends she could steal from and bitch to? For all the funny lines, home-cooked meals, snappy e-mails, emotional support, and brutal honesty, I have to thank/give credit to Rebecca Johnson, Judy McGuire, Nancy Jo Iacoi, Daryl Chen, Judith Newman, Liz Brous, Dana Isaacson, and Ann Billingsley.

My parents, Howie and Judy Frankel, take their hits on these pages. That hasn't stopped them from telling friends, acquaintances, and complete strangers on the street to buy the book. Their support has been unflagging. I can only hope to be as tireless a cheerleader to my kids as you both are for me. My sister, Alison Frankel, selflessly talked to me for *hours* during the writing process. She always asked the right questions and pointed my thoughts in the right direction. Just one more time in our lives that Alison helped me get here from there.

Articulate shrinks are a magazine writer's best friends. Ed Abramson and Joan Chrisler submitted to interviews and countless follow-ups, getting nothing in return for their time. They put me on the Not Dieting path, also, for which I can't be thankful enough.

Stacy London: You are incredible! What you did for me was beyond generous. I applaud and admire your determination to spread the joy of personal style, one wardrobe at a time.

My editor at St. Martin's, Jennifer Enderlin, has amazed me with her dedication and commitment. At times, I felt like this book was as important to her as it was to me. She laughs, she cries, she uses a lot of exclamation points (!!!) and CAPS in her e-mails (which I ADORE!!!). Jennifer is the Woody Allen of book editors. Every writer out there would drop anything, and would be honored, to work with her.

I owe a huge thanks to a handful of magazine editors as well. Several chapters started out as articles. Lucy Danziger, Dana Points, and Paula Derrow agreed to let me pose nude for an essay in *Self*, providing me with cocktail party fodder for the rest of my life. Susan Chumsky and Amy Gross hired me to write a piece about bad body image for *O* magazine that proved just how far down the rabbit hole I'd fallen. Without tasting the subject matter in small bites first, I doubt I'd have ever bellied up to the feast.

Nancy Yost, my agent, had represented me for nine years and ten novels when she suggested I try something different for a change. A year and a half later, my life, relationships, body, and thoughts *have* changed, dramatically, for the better. Whatever she tells me to do next, I'm there.

BEFORE

approached the scale. Small, slow steps. I pretended I was walking through water.

"Just get on there," said my mother impatiently.

Exhaling, as if pressing air out of my lungs would make me lighter, I climbed aboard. The numbered wheel spun.

"Oh. My. God," said Mom when the spinning stopped. Tears formed in her eyes; her chin quivered. Her disappointment couldn't have been deeper had I committed mass murder.

I had, instead, committed a serious nonviolent crime. I was chubby. Not fat, mind you. Not large enough to qualify for my own zip code. But I was decidedly big-boned. By 1976 Short Hills, New Jersey, standards, even medium-boned was offensive. My mom, a slim woman (by nature and neuroticism), said, "You're officially on a diet. And I'm going to make you stick to it—for your own sake. You'll thank me one day."

I wasn't feeling the gratitude that afternoon. While Mom

busied herself logging my current weight on her clipboard chart, I looked down at the number on the scale. I was in sixth grade, five feet tall with emerging boobs. I weighed 100 pounds. I'd hit three digits before puberty. Unthinkable! My small-boned sister, Alison, two grades older, hadn't yet crossed the line.

The impetus for Project Daughter Diet was our upcoming family vacation to the Club Med in Guadeloupe. My mom was not going to let me embarrass myself (or her), running around at a tropical resort, a chubby cherub in a bikini. She would spare me the humiliation, regardless of whether I knew I was feeling it. As of that first official weigh-in, my pudge became her heavy burden, one more responsibility she had to shoulder.

And she bore it mightily. Immediately, Mom's crackdown began. Daily calorie counts. Food rationing. Mom colluded with other adults, besides my dad, to monitor my intake. The mothers of my friends would serve me celery sticks after school while giving their own daughters cookies and milk. Teachers discouraged other kids from sharing the contents of their lunch boxes with me. At home, neither Ring Ding nor Twinkie passed between my lips. Crust was cut from Skippy and Wonder Bread sandwiches. Apples replaced chips. I cried, threw tantrums. I hated feeling picked on, scrutinized, deprived. But I couldn't deny that the diet was working. My Sunday weigh-ins proved that I was shedding pounds.

After six weeks, I approached the scale for the final pre-trip weigh-in. Tunnel-visioned, I watched the dial spin until it rested, the needle pointing to the number 88. I jumped into my mother's arms with elation. We hugged and cried big fat sloppy tears of joy.

I'd done it—gone below the goal of 90 pounds. As much as I'd loathed the process, I reveled in the result. I was sleeker, faster, lighter. My clothes hung on me instead of puckering around bulges. My face was bony, my eyes gigantic, like the bug-eyed waifs' on black-light posters. I both resented and soaked up the flattery from the adults who'd conspired against me. I smiled prettily in response to their praise while secretly wishing them dead. My sixth-grade teacher, a fat-assed fan of polyester pantsuits, pulled Mom aside at pickup and said, "Valerie looks fantastic! What a figure! How on earth did you *do* it?"

What a figure. I was eleven freaking years old.

Enforced dieting at that age can certainly skew one's perspective. I developed a premature and acute sense of cynicism. At the Club Med, I ran around in my bikini with the carefree detachment of a girl who didn't care about a number on the scale, fully aware of the cold irony that I'd been that girl two months earlier. Sizewise, I was on a par with my skinny sister and wiry younger brother, Jon. Mom watched me proudly from her beach chaise, pointing me out to the French and German vacationers in neighboring chairs, smiling smugly at what must have been their polite acknowledgment of my attractiveness. By dropping twelve pounds, I'd won the approval of my parents, their friends, teachers, complete strangers, everyone and no one whose opinion carried weight.

I was hooked. The approval was river wide, ocean deep. I became convinced of my own unparalleled beauty. The pounds that once hid my profound loveliness were gone, and now I shone like the sun. My fat-free body was bullet-proof, superstrong, a secret weapon I hadn't realized I possessed. Being thin made me happy. It made my mother happy.

But, sadly, the joy was fleeting. After the trip (I'd gorged on the omnipresent buffets), I stepped back on the scale and was stunned that I'd re-gained four pounds. *But, but, but . . . I am* thin *now,* I thought, as if it were a permanent condition. The blunt and sudden understanding—that if I wanted to continue to shine like the sun, to bask in praise and glory, I would have to eat celery sticks *forever*—gave me a physical pain in the gut. I looked heavenward and screamed, "Noooooo!!!"

The two sources of happiness in my childhood were at odds. I could have food. Or I could have approval. I couldn't have both.

It should come as no surprise to anyone that food won the day, the year, the decades. The quest for approval, however, endured. At age eleven, I became a chronic dieter. A brass ring grasper. A pie-in-the-sky eater. By the numbers, I'd tried approximately 150 distinct diets, every trendy one to come down the pike, as well as scores of my own invention. In my adult life, I'd been as small as a size six and as big as a fourteen. I'd lost and re-gained hundreds of pounds. Dropping weight always equaled victory, validation, the (re)claiming of my rightful status as pretty-on-the-outside. Gaining weight equaled failure, weakness, faulty character, a demotion to really-good-personality. I'd been up and down the diet road so many times in the last thirty years that my footprints were potholes. Monuments dotted the roadside, marking my thinnest periods, my fattest, the ghastly pig-outs, the incredible displays of self-control that appeared blurry as you sped by.

By the way, you like dieting metaphors? Pull up a chair. I could go all night.

A drug addiction. My initial success was like a first hit of crack. Instantly addicting. A high I'd chase forever. I had a chubby monkey on my back. I was hooked on dieting, always looking for the next fix, be it South Beach or French Women. No matter how high (meaning thin) I got, I craved more, never certain where my next hit was coming from.

A gambling addiction. I kept trying to replicate that first big win, but couldn't. I lost my shirt (but not my flab) in the process. The odds were stacked against me. To play, I stared goggle-eyed at a spinning numbered wheel. Unless I hit 21 (pounds lost), the diet was a bust.

A sex addiction. One diet wasn't enough to satisfy me. I needed to try another, and another, and none of them kept me satisfied for long. The harder I tried to deny my lusts, the more inflamed they became, until giving in to desire was all I thought about. My insatiable appetite compelled me to cheat, and cheat again.

Or how about *chronic dieting as psychiatrist Elisabeth Kübler-Ross's five stages of grief*? Denial: "This diet is going to be the one that works!" Anger: "Everyone *else* has cake." Bargaining: "I cheated today, so I'll work out double tomorrow."

Depression: "I can't believe I ate the whole thing." Acceptance: "It's useless. I'll never be thin."

When I finally shuffle off this mortal coil, my tombstone should read: "Here lies Valerie Frankel. She dieted." I might go to my deathbed wishing I'd left a skinnier corpse.

I was gearing up to take my kids to Florida, to Disney World, where I expected to see a lot of people far fatter than me. It was a bathing-suit vacation. With the predictability of the setting moon, I put myself on a prevacation diet. It wasn't as easy to drop weight at forty-one as it was at eleven, but I had to try. I dreaded the appraisal of strangers, people who couldn't possibly care less how much flab spilled over the top of my bathing suit. I dieted for them anyway, like a conditioned lab rat. As I chopped my pretrip lettuce lunch, I imagined I was starring in an absurdist drama that I wrote for myself. Absurd, and ridiculously long. How would my weight obsession end? *Would* it ever end? Would I *really* take my weight obsession to the grave? Scarier still, would it live on after I was gone in future generations?

My mother's fatphobia was instilled in her by my appearance-obsessed grandmother. A vain alcoholic, anorexic narcissist and spoiled housewife with an evil streak, Fay was a true sadist. Nothing amused her more than making Judy—her daughter, my mother—cry and grovel in genuine fear for her safety. As a mother herself, Judy at her worst was a cream puff in comparison to Fay. My grandmother passed down her obsession with looks to Judy. Judy passed down body anxiety to me. It was in my genes, wormed under my skin so deeply it was as much a part of me as the skin itself.

My daughter Maggie was a sixth grader, eleven years old, the age when it all began for me. Lithe and limber, Maggie was spared what Alison and I called "the struggle." Then again, Maggie could thicken up. One never knew what adolescence might bring. She came home from school with stories about the fat girls in her class, kids whose lifelong battles were just beginning. Boys teased them, oinked and mooed behind their backs, asked them out only to laugh in their face when they said yes. When I saw these girls at school, my heart would break for them. I was teased in middle school. I felt their pain. If any boys ever teased Maggie, I'd do to them what I would have loved to do to my adolescent tormentors: corner them, unleash the power of my superior weight, kick the living crap out of them, give them the punishment they deserved.

My younger daughter, Lucy, eight and in second grade, had stretched three inches ever the summer. Formerly soft and round, she became lean and ropy seemingly overnight. The first day back to school, a few mothers at drop-off noticed the change. They cooed over her scrawny legs and sharp collarbone and gave her the "what a figure" treatment. Lucy soaked up compliments with the same greedy lust I had. Never vain before, Lucy started spending hours in front of the mirror. She rambled on and on about "how great it is to be skinny." I disgusted myself by admiring her visible ribs, hoping this wasn't a temporary taste of slimness that she'd hunger for forever.

I didn't tell Lucy my thoughts or compliment her new shape. Before I had daughters—before I'd menstruated, before I'd *heard* of menstruation—I vowed that I'd never harass my future children about their weight. I wouldn't do to them what my mother did to me (what her mother did to her, and so on, and so on). Much as I tried to impart the healthy attitude, the "love yourself for who you are" message, my daughters weren't fooled. They had eyes and ears. They saw and heard what I put myself through: my dieting cycles, anxiety about food, dread of bathing-suit vacations, rising and falling and rising weight. I was a bad example.

Weight anxiety had had me in its grip for thirty years. When I looked at Maggie and her friends and realized how young they were, I was amazed and saddened that I'd been introduced to self-loathing at their age. I mourned for the wasting of my wonder years, the abandon I missed, how lonely I must have been. All the years and hours wasted since then. I wasn't blaming anyone. My problem with body image was my responsibility. As Oprah would say, I owned it. I'd owned it for years. But now, at the age of forty-one, I'd wanted to disown it.

My journey out of the waistland would require confrontations, unlearning, mind sweeping, and cleaning skeletons—and clothing—out of my closet that didn't fit the woman I wished to be. Coming to terms with my diet demons seemed more doable than losing twenty pounds, actually. More worthwhile, too, given what was at stake.

Even more than love, I wished for my daughters a life of comfort in their skin. I had to break our family tradition, ensure that Maggie and Lucy felt superstrong and bullet-proof, no matter what their shape. I had to show them how, but first I would have to figure it out. For me, the struggle started with my mother. For my daughters, the struggle would end with me.

1

DIETS ARE FOREVER

Hello, my name is Val, and I'm a diet addict. I exist on a continuous loop of starting a diet, recovering from one, and planning the next. I'm either counting calories, fat grams, carbs, or the number of days until I begin anew (and it's always "for the last time"). Dieting defines me. It grounds me. If I didn't have a diet to plan or follow, I'd panic. Going cold turkey on dieting would be a shock to my system. I might have delirium tremens. Or go insane and hallucinate scenes from someone else's childhood.

Unlike a lot of other chronic dieters, my compulsion is dieting itself. I'm not an emotional eater, per se. I'm an emotional dieter. Restricting food equals self-righteousness. Exercising makes me feel superior, holy, strong of will and limb. On the other ham—I mean, *hand*—cheating brings on the whiplash of shame, guilt, and disgust. Like numbers on the scale, the emotions of dieting go up and down, up and down.

Although I try to make light of it, the humor of chronic dieting wears thin, even if nothing else does. The alternative to riding the emotional highs and lows? Become what my friend Pam described as "one of those happy, self-accepting fat people." That fantasy—of ordering bacon cheeseburgers with a wink and a cheeky "More of me to love!"—lasted approximately five seconds before I vowed never to give up. Although I've quit dozens of individual diets, quitting dieting, as a way of life, would be the ultimate defeat.

My most recent diet was inspired by *The Biggest Loser,* a reality TV show. The concept was creepy and sadistic and therefore irresistible: Put sixteen grossly obese people of all ages and genders on a ranch in the middle of a desert and make them compete to lose weight for money. As the contestants reduced, they talked to a pantry-cam about feeling reborn, getting their lives back, emerging from a long, lipid-induced waking slumber. Their existential displacement rhetoric was sad as hell. Nearly every contestant cried fat tears of woe or joy, and so did the TV audience (at least, I did). I knew I was being manipulated, but didn't care. Watching the contestants' gradual transformations—physical and emotional—over the course of a few months was downright inspiring.

For the competition part of the show, the contestants were weighed on a livestock scale. Some would routinely shed ten, fifteen, twenty pounds *in a single week*. One guy lost nearly fifty pounds in just three weeks. I'd been struggling to lose twenty pounds for fifteen years. Granted, the contestants started out at 400 pounds. By their standards, I was already an "after." Everyone knew the last twenty pounds was always the hardest. Still, I convinced myself that my Medium-Sized Loser diet would be a snap.

D-day arrived, as it always did, on the first Monday after I got my period after the last major holiday. My inner announcer said, "Start your engines," and I was off and running—or, more accurately, jogging. I was *ready*. I was *pumped*.

I was doomed.

However misguided optimism might be, you can't begin a diet without total commitment. Otherwise, it'd be like marrying a man you hope to grow to love someday. The Medium-Sized Loser Diet (aka The One) would be strict but doable. The rules:

1. Avoid white food (rice, bread, potatoes, sugar, flour, chips, crackers, etc.).
2. Eat at least six servings of fruit and veggies a day.
3. Drink a glass of water every two hours.
4. Run for half an hour five days per week.
5. Do two thousand crunches per week.

In the throes of the early infatuation period, I was sure this diet would be a piece of (Splendafied) cake. For the record, I did achieve perfection for a solid two weeks. But then life interceded, and my diet was, shall we say, compromised. There was a bake sale at my daughters' school. I would have just bought the minimal face-saving number of cookies, but Lucy gave me the sad look and said, "We never bake anymore." Muttering, I mixed the batter, repeating the mantra "I will not sample, I will not sample." Needless to say, when confronted with fresh-baked cookies, mantras were useless. I ate seven cookies in the span of five minutes.

I had a new novel out, and a rash of lunch and dinner offers from friends and editors with expense accounts. A very-tightwad, I never refused a free meal, especially at pricey places I wouldn't go to ordinarily. When you sat down at a two-star New York City restaurant that was famous for its porterhouse, you didn't dare order the garden salad. It was an affront, an insult to the chef.

The final nail in my diet coffin was my actor/musician husband's three-week gig in Alaska. When Steve got work, he took it, wherever and whenever the job might be, regardless of whether it fit into my diet plans. Since Steve was our family's laundry-doer and vacuumer, his absence doubled my housework load. On top of that, it coincided with the kids' spring break and a major deadline for me. When dinnertime rolled around (every frigging night), I was too tired and stressed to bake the flounder and steam the broccoli. Pizza came to the emotional rescue.

If the timing had been better or I hadn't been stressed out, maybe I would have regrouped. Honestly, though, the air went out of my tires during the bake sale debacle. The first cheat created a domino effect (or, I should say, Domino's). After that, I was cheating regularly, at shorter intervals and with increasing quantities of food per incident. I'd already eaten one slice of pizza, I thought. Might as well have three. What the hell?

It'd taken me six short weeks to go from "This diet is The One!" to "What the hell?" As the saying goes, when I was good, I was very, very good, but when I was bad, I was *horrid*. General Tso's chicken for dinner rolled into bacon for breakfast. I said to myself, "Bacon is Atkins friendly!" I had s'mores with the kids and said to myself, "French women eat chocolate!" My own lies were unconvincing—*even to me.*

When you can't lie to yourself, that's depressing.

The guilt and shame of my failure added up more quickly than the calories I was inhaling freely. Did I cut myself slack for erring, being human? No way! I spiraled downhill, despairing. The diet that began with enthusiasm *had* transformed me—into a depressed, frustrated, stressed-out basket case. Who was three pounds heavier.

When the sugar dust settled, I reverted to the familiar reflective between-diets rest period. I called a couple of diet experts I'd consulted with over the years, shrinks with university jobs who'd become my confidants. Joan Chrisler held up perfectionism as my diet undoing. "Very little in life is perfect. If you expect it of yourself on a diet, you're riding for a fall." I denied trying to be Polly Perfect. "But you begin a diet on 'the first Monday after you get your period after a major holiday,'" she replied. "That's really about finding the perfect time to start the flawless diet."

Ed Abramson put some nuance on that analysis. "It's the all-or-nothing mind-set," he said. "You slip once, and it's over. You see a diet as black or white. On or off. And once you go 'off,' it's no-holds-barred."

Both Joan and Ed talked a lot about motivation. "Why was it so important to diet?" they asked. "Why did you structure your day around an eating-and-exercise plan?"

They might as well have asked, "Why have you structured your entire adolescent and adult life around some eating-and-exercise plan or another?"

Big question. Up there with "Is there a God?" and "If you

eat a cookie in the forest where no one can see, does it still have calories?"

Why diet, indeed?

I tried to come up with a decent answer for the eternal question. Was I attempting to lose weight for my husband? Early in our relationship, when Steve and I first fell in love, I was fifteen pounds thinner. Logically, a swing of fifteen pounds wasn't too significant. I was the same person, regardless of the pants I fit into. Irrationally? Fifteen pounds was a gulf. The difference between a job interview and a job offer. Between a first date and a second date. Between being honored by the nomination and winning the Oscar. The chubby kid I used to be will always wonder which version of me—skinny or fat—is more deserving of love. I knew I'd put pressure on myself to be a good dieter while Steve was in Alaska. I wanted to please him upon his return with a slimmer silhouette. I had the fantasy of his finally walking in the door after three weeks away, dropping his suitcase on the floor, laying eyes on me, running into my arms, and muttering ridiculous sap into my ear, along the lines of "I love you beyond measure, every moment apart was sheer agony, your beauty is boundless," etc.

If not for Steve's sake, perhaps I was a chronic dieter simply out of habit. Diet was what I did. It was all I knew. In fact, dieting know-how had been hardwired into my brain since preadolescence. Thanks to recent advances in MRI technology, we now understand that the brain takes shape according to the stimuli it receives. This was a good argument for forcing a kid to take piano lessons. If she learned to play young, her brain's nerves and synapses would retain musical affinity forever. I didn't play piano. Or chess. My teenage brain was honed, forged, and wrinkled for dieting. Reducing was my chief adolescent pastime. I made charts. I logged calorie input and output. I kept food journals. I read diet articles in magazines, ripped through weight loss books (memorably *The Complete Scarsdale Medical Diet,* released in 1979, when I was fourteen). Diet tips and tricks were snaked so deeply into my gray matter, there was no surgical or psychological way to extract them.

Another "why me, diet?" reason? The nagging one that Joan and Ed always brought up, the one that rang loud and clear. Dieting was, as Ed said, "a convenient channel for life's dissatisfactions. Rather than deal with things that make you unhappy, you narrow the focus to eating."

I'd certainly had my share of problems, and at every stage of life, I'd dieted my way through a lot of the bumpy times—even some hard times you'd think would be immune to the cold comfort of losing weight. For instance, when I was thirty-five, I became a widow. My first husband, Glenn, died of lung cancer. He was only thirty-four. It was an unspeakable tragedy for our family—our daughters were five and almost two when he died—as well as for our extended families and friends. The shock of his death was the prelude to the stress of widowed motherhood, of guiding my daughters and myself through grief, supporting our needs on my income. It was a Herculean holding together. I'd managed it, survived. And, yes, I lost weight during those horrible two years, which didn't cure Glenn or ensure my daughter's emotional protection but did give me something to think about when all other thoughts were bleak.

Of course, I re-gained the weight I'd lost, that time, and every other time I'd managed to lose. This predictable outcome raised the same question: "Why?" Why should I, or anyone, diet at all, when many experts in the field believe, and have supportable evidence, that dieting makes you fat? My Medium-Sized Loser Diet was a case in point. I'd starved myself at first; my body's deprivation mode kicked in, resulting in a slower metabolic rate. When I started cheating repeatedly, those excess calories rushed into a body that was burning fuel at a crawl, instantly converting pizza into fat bulges. With each diet I'd tried, I was farther from my goal weight.

My goal weight, since college, had been 135 pounds. At five feet six inches, that would give me a body mass index, or BMI, of 21.8, dead center of "normal" range. I wasn't greedy. I wasn't shooting for a teen-model BMI of 17. My aspirations were for single-digit clothing sizes, bony fingers, a hollow around the cheeks. I'd had that, at brief and glorious periods over the years. Surely I could have it again, or so I'd reasoned a million times, right before starting each new (soon-to-be-failed) diet.

Diet experts would also insist that dieting was futile. Depending on which study you read, 50 to 90 percent of an individual's weight was genetically predetermined. Or you could see it this way: As an egg in your mother's ovary, you were already a size twelve. Now, you might be able to diet your way down to an eight, or even a stretch-fabric six. But you'd never be a two, no matter how bad you wanted it. If you were to stop dieting and eat "normally" (have what you crave when hungry, stop when full), your body would automatically assume its preprogrammed shape, its true size, with virtually no struggle or anxiety on your part.

I had no idea what my true size was. I'd been yo-yo dieting (sometimes so-so dieting; always oh-no dieting) for thirty years. My metabolism and eating had always been erratic. My body hadn't had the chance to automatically assume its preprogrammed shape. My parents were both naturally slim. My sister was small, my brother athletically built. My grandparents on both sides were either slender or athletic. And yet I was a chubby kid. An anomaly? Or perhaps, had I not been a prepubescent diet cycler, I might have burned off my baby fat naturally—and, just as naturally, grown into a slim adult. Slimness might have been my destiny, but only if I was able to let it happen.

On the other hand, it might have been my destiny to be a blimp.

Only one way to find out. I would have to give up dieting. Logically, it made sense. If dieting made you fat and was futile, not dieting should make you thin, effortlessly.

I'd been listing all the reasons for "Why I Should Diet" in my head for thirty years. At forty-one, perhaps the time had come to make a new list, headed "Why I Shouldn't Diet."

I fantasized about the change, both emotional and physical, about the freedom in reach. I painted a mental picture of what a diet-free life would look like—me, in a sundress, running braless, barefoot, through a field of wildflowers. The idea became a hunger. Not a fleeting craving, but a deep, visceral yearning that, I realized, had always been rattling the cage inside.

I would need a plan. (I might be able to stop the diet cycle, but I would never be able to give up planning.) What would be the opposite of chronic dieting? Regular dieting was about the physical, eating and exercise. The Not Diet would be mental, emotional, concentrating on interior conversations, bad memories, the wiring of my brain. The goal of chronic dieting was to shed pounds. The goal of the Not Diet was to shed light on my self-destructive habits and patterns.

The Not Diet (aka The Last One) would be strict but do-able:

1. *Forget everything I already knew about dieting.* That wouldn't be easy. It'd be like tearing out the seams of a dress and wearing it anyway. Trying to be perfect hadn't worked for me, either, so rule number two was . . .

2. *Screw perfectionism.* My wobbly first baby step toward screwing perfectionism was to sit down and eat a bowl of ice cream . . . Okay. Done. And boy, was that delicious. Much easier than I'd thought! I feel confident that I can succeed at imperfectionism. I should call my mother right away and tell her that I've found something I am really good at. Then again, talking (inside my head, or through the lips) about eating hadn't served me well. Ergo, rule number three:

3. *Shut the hell up.* I'd stop the running mental commentary about food, what I see in the mirror, all the things I'm doing/not doing right, comparing myself to other women. I'd silence my mind regarding weight. That'd be tough. Often I didn't even realize I was tallying calories until half an hour had gone by. I resolved to fill my mind with productive thoughts, like getting to the big

bottom of my bad body image. Which dovetails nicely into the final rule of my plan, the whopper:

4. *Do the emotional heavy lifting.* Dieting thus far had been a physical endeavor—and a chronic failure. Perhaps what had been missing all along was the emotional regime, a systematic approach to body image bone picking. Skeleton sweeping. I latched on to the idea that each extra pound I carried on my frame represented a past hurt, an emotional injury that took the physical form of belly fat. If I could let go of the shame, embarrassment, anger, and insult from the past (forgive, forget, whatever worked), my body would release the weight. Into the wind. Like magic!

As I already mentioned, I'm nothing if not optimistic.

"Diets don't *have* to be forever," I said to my sister, Alison. "I've got to stop, or I'll be dieting until I'm too old to feed myself. Knock wood that I should live so long."

The late summer afternoon was sunny and clear. Maggie, Lucy, and I had escaped the Brooklyn heat to spend the day at Alison's home on the balmy North Shore of Long Island.

"Speaking of diets, are you eating bread today?" asked Alison. "I made sandwiches."

Alison could eat bread. Great baskets of it. Except for one fluky, chunky year in high school, she had always been petite. In childhood photos, her legs look like flamingos', stalk thin with knob knees. At five foot three, Alison was small all over. Her feet were a tiny size six, her fingers short. She wore a size two dress. The only big part of her was her thick, curly black hair that pillowed on her bony, narrow shoulders.

Although I was the little sister (fifteen months younger), I'd always been her physical superior—stronger, faster, healthier, *bigger*. Out of the womb, I was inches longer, pounds heavier. Now, I was larger by three inches, four dress sizes, four shoe sizes, and three bra cups. Alison was a pint; I was a pitcher. When we were toddlers, I was considered the pretty sister, and she was the smart one. Now she was both. And I was . . . I was just glad to be here!

If not large, Alison had largesse. Generous as always, she'd laid out a beautiful spread of sandwiches, quiches, and salads for her visitors from the city. Despite our closeness in age and her diminutive size, Alison treated me like a protective big sister would. During the teen years, she'd thrown herself between Mom in full rant and me crying in the corner countless times. Mom's screechy response to her was always, "There's only one mother in this family, and it's not you!" Alison, a mother now, had two daughters (like me; like our mother, Judy). Our four girls, the cousins, were outside while Alison and I talked in the kitchen.

I took a tuna sandwich off the platter. Including the bread. "I've been toying with an idea. Batting it around like a cat with a hair scrunchie," I said. "What would happen if I were to stop dieting? Besides the earth crashing into the sun."

"You mean give up?" she asked.

"I mean stop walking the walk," I said. "Stop talking the talk, thinking the thoughts. I'll probably need a lobotomy."

She nodded. "There's your answer."

"Get a lobotomy?"

"You'll never stop wanting to be thinner," she said. "Every woman wants to be thinner. It's part of the human female condition."

"Okay, yes. That's a given. But I've been going about that quest—thinking about it—the wrong way. What if I did the opposite of what I've been doing all along? Stopped dieting. Stopped obsessing. Go cold turkey on broiled chicken."

"You'll gain," she warned.

"Or maybe, if I purged my bad habits, the bad body image, and the bad memories, the extra weight would disappear."

"Purge the bad memories?"

I said, "Get to the root of my body image problem, and thereby expunge it."

"So you're going to talk to Mom?" she asked, shuddering. "Give me advance warning so I can be five states away."

I'd never had the big talk with Judy about the emotional damage her fatphobia caused me. We avoided that conversation. It seemed pointless, given how much water was under the bridge. We got along famously now, had since my mid-twenties. We enjoyed each other's company and actually looked forward to seeing each other, which we did often. Both my parents were heroic when Glenn was sick and after he died, for which I would always be grateful. There hadn't been a good reason for Mom and me to rehash our ugly past. Maybe our relationship hadn't been strong enough to handle a major confrontation until now.

"Why do you want to do this?" asked Alison.

"I've spent the first half of my life dieting, vacillating between hating myself, depriving myself, and disappointing myself," I said. "I don't want the second half to be more of the same. Anything else would be an improvement. I think it's possible to let go of the obsession without letting yourself go, in terms of weight."

Alison nodded. She saw the logic. "Not dieting, and getting thin in the process," she said. "It's worth a try."

"I've got nothing to lose," I said. Except the self-loathing—and the excess weight.

2

WELCOME TO HELL

grew up in Short Hills, New Jersey, an affluent suburb of New York City. I went to Deerfield Elementary School. After sixth-grade graduation, some parents sent their children to private schools like Newark Academy or Pingry. Most residents of the Millburn–Short Hills township sent their kids to the highest-ranking public secondary school in the most densely populated state in the nation—Millburn Junior High. My class had three hundred kids. Three hundred lucky, entitled, gifted little shits.

Unlike the almost exclusively pasty-white Jewish kids at Deerfield, the larger student body at MJHS was a real mix. I was introduced to a wider spectrum of white—ecru, eggshell, bone—kids from Irish, English, and Italian families. Lots of new faces. New boys. I started seventh grade with confidence. Despite my extra pounds, I'd been popular at Deerfield, one of only two girls asked on a date in sixth grade. Even though I'd gained weight over the summer and was rotating a fresh crop of zits on my forehead, I assumed I'd be popular in junior high, too.

Within a week of stepping off the bus, I realized how wrong I was.

My downfall was lightning fast. I "floated word" that I had my eye on a certain boy named T., an irresistible green-eyed, sinewy gentile from another elementary school. He didn't crush on me back, though. On the contrary. My attraction was an affront to him, so much so that it called for a hasty, public refusal. He had another boy start a conversation with me during recess. While I was diverted, T. crouched on all fours behind me. He gave the signal, and the other boy pushed me backward. I flew over T.'s back and onto the dusty playground yard. As I lay there, stunned, T. and his cohort high-fived each other and ran away laughing. I heard later that T. explained himself by saying, "I'd never like Valerie. She's too fat."

The tone was set from that day forward. I was *that* girl. Every seventh-grade class had one. The target of cruel, heartless twelve-year-old boys. The transformation from "pretty and popular" to "outcast and ugly" was so abrupt, it took a while for my change in status to sink in. I thought I still had some residual clout. So, unlike the dozen other kids who were harassed for a variety of physical abnormalities, including but not limited to buck teeth, shortness, and thick glasses, I was not going to take it without fighting back. I might have been chubby, but I was not then, nor would I ever be, a wimp.

Granted, if I'd accepted the abuse quietly, the junior sadists probably would've gotten bored with me and moved on to any number of girls who were far fatter than I was. But I just couldn't keep my mouth shut. "Cocksucker," "dick-breath," "douchebag," "motherfucker" flowed from my twelve-year-old lips like sweet nectar. I learned quickly which buttons to press. Interestingly, nothing got a boy more riled up than being called a "faggot." I flung whatever shockingly offensive slurs popped into my head. Words were my only defense.

Unfortunately, foul language wasn't enough. I was alone against a cabal of hyperactive boys. They egged each other on, ganged up, boosting their status with each other by escalating their vituperation on me. Insulting me became a quick and easy way for any kid to gain favor with the popular boys. The fattest, ugliest, stupidest kid in the class could walk up to me, say "pig," and, for a nanosecond, be "in" with the assholes.

My comebacks started to sound as desperate as they were. About six months into seventh grade, I gave up. I absorbed the blows without retort. But my acquiescence didn't stop the abuse. By now, boys teased me out of habit.

When I'd talked as an adult about my junior high career as a human target for slings and arrows, people always asked, "What about the girls?" Junior high girls were, without a doubt, as a population, the most savage, cannibalistic, cruel subgroup in our nation. However, in my pathetic case, the Mean Girls, the Queen Bees, and the Wannabes left me alone. I wasn't a challenge to their social status. I was hardly competition for cute boys. Certainly, if my name came up in their private conversations, I was assailed or written off. Some girls laughed along when the boys teased me. By and large, however, I was a hapless victim—already wounded—and not a threat. I probably grossed them out, if anything. I barely registered on their radar.

But when *boys* smelled the fresh blood of the emotionally wounded, they became more excited. Thumbnail sketches of my three chief tormenters:

X.'s style was as subtle as a sledgehammer. He'd race up to me and knock the books out of my arms. When I bent down to pick them up, he'd say, "Look at that fat ass." He'd moo and oink. The scariest times were when he'd corner me in the hallway, and hiss *"fat!"* right into my ear. He was in the C track, which was for borderline special ed students. Among all my repeat abusers, X. seemed genuinely unhinged, a powder keg waiting to blow. The rumor mill had him arrested for vandalism as well as breaking and entering. I'd heard gossip his dad beat him up. X. was a notorious beer guzzler, starting in eighth grade. I'd seen him once in the twenty-plus years since graduation, at a mutual friend's wedding. Even though he'd done nothing with his life and looked like a hollow shell of the vicious whelp he used to be, X. terrified me just by standing there.

Y. was a scrawny, lizard-faced rich boy. He seethed with rancor at me and the other targeted kids as if he were personally insulted by our very existence. If he'd been born in another time and place, Y. would have been a crackerjack teenage Nazi. Unattractive, uncoordinated, of average intelligence, Y. had fantastically wealthy parents who gave him everything he wanted, including a BMW when he turned seventeen. Spoiled and rotten, he was just smart enough to be truly hurtful. Y. and I were in the same eighth-grade homeroom. He chose to sit in the desk immediately to my right. My abusers always wanted to be near me, in a twist on the Stockholm syndrome. Anyway, Y. muttered insults across the aisle for the first fifteen minutes of the day, every day. One memorable morning, he said, "When I grow up, I'm going to fuck every beautiful woman I want. I'm going to drive the fastest cars, wear the best clothes. I'm going to live in a big house and have people wait on me. I'm going to be the president of my own company and have millions of dollars. And all you're ever going to be is fat." I was shocked by his delusion. This was an okay student. He didn't play sports or have girlfriends. And yet he knew he'd always be better than me.

Z. was the smartest jackal in the pack. He was also a gifted athlete and a charismatic leader. He was cute, in a suburban New Jersey sense, big hair, big smile, thick gold chains around his neck. His abuse style came close to clever, which, despite my misery, I appreciated. One example: The DJ at a bar mitzvah party started a game of Name That Tune by playing a few notes of "She Loves You" by the Beatles. Z. stood up and said, "That's Valerie's favorite song: 'She Loves Food.'" Humiliating! But sort of funny. Another time, the whole grade was in the school auditorium, watching an educational film. I was seated on the side, with a couple of my friends. Z. and his cronies piled into seats directly behind me (see above, re: sick Stockholm syndrome). I tensed, waited for it. On the screen, a shot of the quarter moon. Z. said loudly, "Look, Valerie took a bite out of the moon." Uproarious laughter, drawing the attention of the entire class, forcing the AV technician to stop the film and a teacher to demand to know what was so flipping funny, etc. Unlike most of my tormentors, Z. was A track, like me. Out of class, he made fun of me. Often, during class, he spoke to me respectfully, even affectionately. I was convinced that, on some level, Z. thought we were friends. Boys trash-talked each other to bond. Z. might've believed that abusing me, which he not only did but encouraged others to do, was a way of saying, "You're one of us." For this reason, I hated him the most of all.

I existed in a state of constant anxiety. The fear was mainly anticipatory, like how people feel about terrorism today. Although each embarrassment was horrible, waiting for the next was worse. The constant guesswork—When would it happen? Where would they strike?—shifted the bedrock of my personality. Since I was perpetually braced for an insult, I felt relieved when it came. It always came.

A couple of teachers joined the fun. Men. The type who were the ass-kissing followers when they were in middle school, the grown-up boys who sought the approval of the X.s, Y.s, and Z.s of the world.

A math teacher, considered creepy and lecherous by all the girls, made a special announcement one day: He'd noticed a lot of negative attention was being paid to one particular girl, and teasing from a boy really meant that he had a secret crush. This comment brought on a tsunami of abuse that lasted for weeks. Any idiot could have easily predicted it. I was sure that math teacher knew exactly what he was doing.

A science teacher, a former wrestler with a menacing posture, made a point of calling on me in class to answer questions about food. For a lesson on the unit measure of heat called a calorie (at fourteen, I already possessed doctoral-level knowledge on the subject), he wanted to know what students had for breakfast. I didn't raise my hand. He called on me anyway. I fumbled for a response that sounded sufficiently Spartan, but not self-consciously so, and eventually stammered out the word "bread." The teacher mocked me. "Bread? What do you mean, *bread*?" It was an open invitation, the granting of permission, which X. and a few other boys in class jumped on as if it had been a drunk cheerleader. "A loaf," said X. "Two loaves." "A dozen bagels," "five cakes," etc. While the boys competed to shout out the most outrageous quantity of carbs I was to have consumed in a single meal, I stared at the science teacher's face. I kept staring, for the remainder of that class, and every other to follow. He was spooked by my unblinking glare of pure hatred, and he never made eye contact with me again.

Unlike a lot of harassed kids who took their lumps at school, I did not, alas, have a supportive, nurturing safe haven at home. School was the frying pan; home was the fire. After enduring the agony of the junior high day, I'd get home and sink into the living room couch. It was exhausting, keeping the game face on for hours upon hours. I just wanted ten minutes to decompress. But then Mom would walk into the room, look at me sprawling, and say, "Go run around the block, for Christ's sake. Don't just sit there. Do *something*. Who gave you permission to have a snack? You can't eat that. The Ring Dings and Twinkies are for your brother. Give it to me now. Give me that Ring Ding!"

I broke down only in private, music blasting in my room to cover up the violent adolescent sob fests, flailing on the bed, pummeling my pillow. In public, I was unshakable. I learned to feign indifference so well, it became instinctual.

To this day, when I receive bad news, my eyes go flat. My face loses any hint of expression—what forehead-to-chin Botox probably looks like. I show nothing. I give nothing away. A boss fires me from the first real job I ever had and won't give me a reference? Okay, I say, see you never. An editor gives me a massive revise memo on a novel I'd worked on for a year? No problem, I shrug, whatever. Even the worst possible news, the moment it was delivered, failed to ripple my exterior. When the oncologist arrived in Glenn's hospital room late one evening and told us what the biopsy had revealed, stage IV lung cancer, I merely nodded, flat-eyed. The doctor repeated himself. Did I hear what he just said? Did I understand what this meant? Was I even paying attention?

For the record, I've heard every syllable of every horrible thing that's been said to me, in junior high and since. My ears prick up to catch the slightest intonations, the smallest hint of negativity, even in a seemingly benign comment. I was, am, a connoisseur of insult and criticism. My word-for-word analysis reveals the deeper meaning of what wasn't said. Down to the pumping core of my heart, when a boy spat, "This hallway isn't big enough for you," I knew he was confessing to me (and only me), "I'm desperately insecure and have to boost my ego by insulting you." I possessed secret knowledge, an intuitive power of observation and understanding that pretty girls lacked. Like alienated teenagers everywhere, I wrote down my revelations and thoughts, since they were important, real, and deep, and had never been thought of by another person before, nor would they ever be in future.

I kept a journal. A blank book with a red corduroy cover. On the pages, I wrote angsty poetry ("Caverns of darkness/ dungeons of punishment/palisades of cruelty/the light of happiness never shines here"), and I wrote stories. My main character was named Sal. She had an evil mother who said, "So what if you got an A on the Spanish quiz? You'll just fail the next one. Jesus H. Christ, Sal, I'm just teasing. Stop that pathetic sniveling." Sal was an adequately pretty girl with a "fat layer that had to go." She was routinely belittled by her overachiever older sister and hostile younger brother, misunderstood by her friends, and mistreated by her parents and everyone else. But—Sal had a secret. When she retreated to her attic room after a wretched day of torment, she lay on her pallet bed of straw and mud and meted out justice. Sal had magic powers. Anything she imagined came true.

Sal was a wee bit bloodthirsty. X., Y., and Z. died a hundred times on the pages of my blank books, each death more grisly and savage than the last. They were eaten alive by dogs (Sal said, "Slow down, puppies, or you'll get tummy aches!"), pulverized by a speeding garbage truck ("Don't bother bagging them," said Sal to the driver), skateboarded into a sinkhole (Sal said, "Did I say turn *right*? I meant *left*. Oops."). Drowning, dismemberment, suffocation. Their female cohorts—girls who laughed along—met similar sorry fates. Complicity was just as bad, by Sal's rule of law. If a girl stood by and watched Z. verbally assault Sal, well, she deserved to die ignominiously, too. Oddly, Sal never used her magical, deadly thoughts against her family. Even for someone with the questionable morals of a killing machine, murdering one's own blood seemed wrong.

I remember cackling wildly to myself when I wrote these stories. It helped to vent. Back in the 1970s, misunderstood and mistreated kids didn't go around shooting their bullies with AK-47s. Nowadays, when I read about another school rampage, about the awkward, unstable kid with a gun, how he just couldn't take one more day of humiliation and how he'd long fantasized about revenge, I deplore it. I'm saddened and sickened by it. But I understand it.

Of course, for every kid who goes ballistic, there are a hundred thousand teens who suffer in depressed silence. Some find ways to mitigate their suffering. I scribbled bloody comedies in a journal and laughed at my own jokes. Lo and behold, I grew up to be a comedy writer who still laughs at her own jokes. Humor is a coping mechanism for dealing with pain.

What doesn't kill you only makes you funnier.

I rehashed this theory to my friend Rebecca at Teresa's, a Ukrainian diner on Montague Street in Brooklyn Heights, where we both live. We were having breakfast. I was not-dieting, but also not-hungry. Talking about junior high made me feel a little queasy.

"You have to eat the rat," she said.

"Excuse me?" Make that a lot queasy.

"You never heard that phrase? It's from G. Gordon Liddy."

"The Nixon stooge?" I asked.

"He had a lifelong fear of rats," said Rebecca. "So one day, he decided that the only way to overcome his fear was to consume it. So he cooked a rat and ate it."

"Gross," I said. "Bet it tasted like chicken."

"Your goal is to get rid of your weight obsession. Part of your obsession is connected to these assholes from junior high," said Rebecca. "You have to track one of them down. Make contact."

"And eat him?" I asked. "Chew him up and spit him out?"

"Just call him," said Rebecca.

"No way," I said, a cold chill instantly creeping up my spine at the very idea of confronting X., Y., or, especially, Z.

"You must," said Rebecca. "And you will."

Over the coming days, the images of their acned teenage faces kept floating into my consciousness. I wondered what they might look like now. Ideally, they were bald, *fat,* divorced, unemployed, friendless, loveless, depressed, suicidal, one-legged, and living with their parents—correction, homeless.

Tentatively, I did some light Googling. This yielded zero useful information. I was relieved. If I had turned something up, I would've had to use it.

For tenth grade, students left the junior high building and went to the high school down the road. The move was a welcome change. In the new building, the evil boys seemed to forget about me. I was still a loser, but I wasn't attacked hourly anymore. I struggled to fit in, to blend, to be just another girl walking the hallways. I befriended other girls like myself. Many of these friendships lasted as long as the diets we'd start together (with enthusiasm!) and then abandon (in defeat).

You could share only so many rice cakes before the friendship itself tasted stale, flavorless, a substitute for something substantial. I also hung out with other A trackers. But due to their (our) big brains, free-floating geekiness, Jewishness, and/or eccentricity, they (we) were ignored by the Sassoon-jeans-wearing, gum-snapping, blue-eye-shadowing, blond girl jocks who ruled the school.

The Official Preppy Handbook came out in 1980, the year I was a sophomore. Lisa Birnbaum's humor book became my survival guide for living in WASP-dominated Short Hills. My mother was relieved I'd taken a sudden interest in my outward appearance, and my closet filled up with Fair Isle sweaters, corduroy skirts, grosgrain belts, handbags with wooden handles and removable canvas pouches. With a panting determination, I flung myself into preppiness (which, I should have known, given my ample chest and frizzy hair) was yet another impossible dream. I signed up for the JV field hockey team, the epitome of preppy sport.

We had practices every day after school. My mother encouraged my participation. If I were running laps around a field, I couldn't be at home, shoving Ring Dings into my piehole. Although most of the girls on the team sat at the popular table and, therefore, had associative revulsion for me, they treated me politely. Their niceness caused me some guilt. A number of these girls had died painfully under Sal's swinging axe. The coach, a megalomaniac, encouraged team bonding. She chose the first-string lineup and team captains—power positions that popular girls lusted for. We did what Coach wanted, and that meant maintaining a perpetual state of "Psyched!" on the field.

I didn't have ambition to be a first stringer, or a captain. I just wanted to be one of them, another rosy-cheeked pretty girl in a kilt with a stick. I was suspicious of Coach, who seemed overly serious and intense about her team. This was New Jersey, not Texas. The Friday night lights in Short Hills were at the mall, not the football stadium. The town's pride and glory did not rest on the shoulders of the girl's JV field hockey team. Nonetheless, Coach acted as if every practice were a matter of life and death. Granted, some of the gifted players would go on to varsity and possible scholarships to college. Or they came from athletic families and felt the pressure of expectation. Not me. I just wanted to be a player.

But players weren't cynical. I'd had cynicism beaten into me during the junior high years. My snide little comments and sarcastic observations weren't considered insightful or witty by the other girls. I was never initiated into the unofficial team sorority. On the bus to games, I watched the girls get "pumped" and "rowdy" while singing "We Are the Champions," smashing their sticks to the beat on the floor, their faces contorted in competitive fury. I though they looked like escapees from a juvenile prison. I didn't get it. It was only a game.

At the time, I thought of Coach as a middle-aged bachelorette gym teacher who ruled her tiny fiefdom with an iron whistle in order to give her lonely life meaning. The years since have softened my opinion of her. She took herself and her job seriously. She showed pride in her work and had more insight than I gave her credit for. For example, Coach could tell I had selfish reasons for being on the team: to fit in, get out of the house, and try another weight loss strategy. I lacked "heart" and "spirit." Once, Coach said to me, "Frankel! There's no 'I' in team." I said, "No, but there is a 'me.' Also 'at,' 'eat,' 'met,' 'meat,' 'tame,' 'mate,' and 'meta.'" Coach was not amused or impressed by my anagram ability. "Ten laps around the field, Frankel," she barked. "Go!"

My father, Howie, a nephrologist, came home one evening during my field hockey season with a few boxes of a prototype protein powder supplement called Optifast. Protein supplements in liquid or powder form are now available at any supermarket, but back then, replacing solid food with protein shakes for rapid weight loss was a radical treatment that required the supervision of a licensed physician. Optifast was not yet available to the general public. I was to be a guinea pig for the product, under my father's care.

Pause to ponder the wisdom of putting an adolescent, only ten pounds overweight, on an experimental medical protocol for aesthetic reasons only.

Okay, we're back.

Not to cut Dad too much slack about the Optifast initiative, but I believe he brought the box home because he was desperate for peace. Although the evil boys had matured enough to leave me alone, my mom was stubbornly one-noted. She beat the weight loss drum constantly. I heard it in my sleep. Whenever I entered the house, she was there, tall and slender, a stalking dark-haired, dark-eyed menace, monitoring my after-school snack. At dinner, she commented on my rapid chewing, request for seconds, daring grab at a dessert. On weekends, the stress of being around me and my fat accumulated for two days. It was too much for her. She'd explode on Sunday nights and scream at me for purposefully antagonizing her by eating. "You're so fat!" she'd shriek. "Why are you doing this to me?" Alison continued to defend me, which led to more fighting and yelling. I'd hide in my room, crying in fits, blasting music to cover the sound. Not traditional Sunday-night family fun. When Dad got wind at the hospital about the promising new product for weight loss, the lightbulb must have burst into flames over his head. He must've thought Optifast would be the answer to all our family's turmoil. So Optimistic. And so wrong.

The unflavored powder, mixed with water, tasted chalky and gritty, nothing like the chocolaty Slim-Fast shakes you can get today. I choked it down each morning for breakfast. My lunch was a banana and a yogurt. Dinner: another shake. For two weeks, I was perfect (hence, doomed), essentially fasting, and working out like a dog at field hockey practice. As advertised, I enjoyed "rapid weight loss." Fifteen pounds in two weeks. According to weight charts for someone my gender and age, I was officially one pound underweight.

My parents acted like they'd discovered religion, praising the Lord, thanking God, declaring a miracle. I can picture my mother on the phone with her friends, crowing about her success. I reveled in the change, too, as I always did when I dropped weight. I strutted around school, cocky and arrogant, my clothes baggy. My few friends were full of compliments. Mom had to adjust my kilt's snaps, since it kept falling down during laps. I was tired on the field, slower, but Coach, along with everyone else, liked what she saw. She seemed more tolerant of me.

High on downsizing, I was smug and, therefore, vulnerable

to attack. One morning, a boy, P., got bawled out by our homeroom teacher for being late to school. I looked over at him, a couple of desks behind me to the right, his face bright red with embarrassment. I knew exactly how he felt, having been singled out back in my heavy days, which were, thanks to Optifast, now gone forever. I shot P. a look of sympathy, which he must have interpreted as gloating. Narrowing his eyes at me, he said, "Fuck you, Frankel. You're fat."

Simple, clean, plain. Unadorned abuse from a kid on the spot, lashing out defensively at a usual target. Three weeks before, I would have considered it my due. But . . . but . . . couldn't he see that I was officially underweight now? I'd lost fifteen pounds. I'd consumed liquid chalk and baby food for two weeks straight. I'd been starved by my own parents, one of them a doctor, and yet this kid P., an A tracker, not blind or stupid, said "fat" as if I hadn't suffered and changed. He, and probably everyone at school, would always see me as fat. I'd have to go full-blown anorexic (like a couple of other formerly overweight girls) to be considered normal by my classmates.

I was devastated. I'd been off Optifast for less than a week. That afternoon, I started making up for lost snack time. I skipped practice three days in a row. When I finally showed up, I smoked in the locker room before and after. I blew smoke rings at the popular girls with cinched waists and blond hair, none of whom were my friends. I bolted as quickly as possible each afternoon, and I missed a team announcement. The homecoming game against our bitter rival was a week hence. On that day, the rookie JV players, in an initiation tradition, were to wear their kilts to school with high heels.

When I showed up in jeans, I was yelled at by the other players, who all looked pretty good in their kilts, heels, and giraffe-thin legs. I called Mom and asked her to drive over my skirt and the earth-toned platform shoes with Naugahyde straps across the arch and ankle. I changed as soon as I could. I'd been eating at will for a week since P.'s comment, and I'd regained most of the weight. The kilt, with its resewn snaps, was now supertight around the waist, making the hem ride up, revealing as much leg as I had. My panties showed when I bent even slightly. My bloomers, alas, were still in my underwear drawer at home, and I didn't dare call Mom again and ask her to bring them down to the school. I put on my platforms, tugged my kilt down, and went on with my day.

As if. Boys followed me through the halls, laughing at my bulging belly and visible underwear. I walked into the cafeteria at midday as slyly as possible and tried to hide in a corner. A friend said, "Everyone is staring at you." I glanced around the room. Table to table, all eyes were on me. I felt faint. My friend walked me out of there and into the nearest girls' bathroom, where I puked up my nerves and lunchroom fried chicken.

I went to the nurse's office, said I was sick. Mom came to get me and, for once, showed mercy by not asking questions or making comments. I found out later that the girls on JV told everyone I was a wimp for leaving, that I couldn't take a joke, that I didn't have team spirit, that they knew I wasn't really sick, that if I puked it was because I was bulimic, that I smoked in the locker room, which made all of them want to puke, on me, and that I sucked as sweeper, because I couldn't run fast enough, because I was fat.

In the movie version, I would have proved them all wrong. I'd have dug in my cleats, doubled up on practice, kept running around the field in the pouring rain when everyone else had already gone home. I'd have saved the big game in the last second and been redeemed, forgiven, accepted, beloved by my teammates and the entire school.

In the reality version, that day marked a turning point for me. It was the day I said "fuck this" about trying to be accepted.

Almost immediately, I was cut from the team. I forced the issue with Coach when I refused to leave school early for an away game. I'd have had to reschedule an exam. I told her that academics were more important than sports, and if she didn't agree, she was wrong and, for that matter, irresponsible in her position as a "teacher," albeit a gym "teacher." I actually used finger quotes. It was the most flagrantly disrespectful and rude thing I'd ever said to an authority figure. I was sixteen. It was an exciting new beginning.

There was bitterness in triumph. In my journal, I wrote, "I was cut from the team today. I felt like crying but I kept it bottled up in school. As soon as I got home, Mom said, 'You're not good at sports anyway. I knew this would happen. How could you expect to keep up with those other girls?' I stared at her for a while, and then ran to my room to cry."

Instead of heeding Mom's suggestion that I try candy-striping, I spent my afternoons scribbling frantically in my blank book. Sal had an extended field day on the field hockey team. And then I shoved every grosgrain belt, Fair Isle sweater, and duck print skirt into the back of my closet, never to be worn again. "Preppy" became synonymous with "assholey" to me, an opinion that has not evolved much. Whenever I see a grown woman in a velvet headband, I automatically distrust her.

Fitting in, being part of a whole, finding my place in the social order, being appreciated by my peers was suddenly, blissfully, irrelevant.

Along with the clothes, I shed any semblance of mainstream ambition. I'd been a stealth smoker since the eighth grade. I would walk a mile to the nearest restaurant and put seventy-five cents into the vending machine for my Marlboro Lights and smoke them on the roof or behind our house. Cigarettes curbed appetite, after all. If I got caught, I would use that as my defense. Except for my provocative puffing in the locker room, I hid my habit because popular kids didn't smoke. Once I'd accepted that I would never be popular, let alone tolerated by our school's Ruling Class, I lit up whenever, wherever I could. High school students were permitted to smoke on the Patio, an outdoor slab of concrete with a few benches by the cafeteria. The Patio and its undesirable residents—the punks and freaks—quickly became my new home and family. Pot came next, great billowing purple clouds of it. Too bad, the munchies counteracted the appetite-suppressing powers of cigarettes. To my bliss, stoners and punks couldn't care less about size. We cared about getting more pot, going to rock shows in the city, driving aimlessly around town, and sharing our intellectual superiority and deep thoughts about meaningful shit, like life, the universe, and the Clash.

I embraced my outcast status. I shaved my hair into a

Mohawk and dyed it orange; I wore safety pins in my ears, spiked dog collars around my neck, black lipstick, black nail polish, black jeans, shirts, trench coats, leggings. I wanted to look as tough as I felt (I had, after all, committed epistolary murder hundreds of times), and so scary that no one would dare mess with me. Punk rock lyrics about isolation, frustration, and alienation described my feelings perfectly. I doubt any of those skinny Brit heroin addicts could possibly have imagined that their lyrics would ring the bell of an upper-middle-class chubby Jewish girl from suburban New Jersey. I seized the message—"Anger can be power, d'ya know that you can use it?" preached Joe Strummer—and made it my mantra, my mien, my modus operandi.

Mom's rants weren't so monotonous once I gave her more notes to play. "That outfit is disgusting!" she'd screech. "You reek of cigarette smoke! I hate your juvenile delinquent friends. You're not doing your schoolwork! Turn off that horrible music! And put down that Twinkie!" Mom did approve of one change. My new black wardrobe was slimming.

Rebellion became my cause. Anything that pissed off my mother and entrenched me as an outcast was my pleasure. My punk friends and I drove to clubs in New York—CBGB's and Great Gildersleeves—to see hardcore shows. We'd stay out until 2:00 A.M., then drive back to New Jersey drunk on Meisterbräu. I'd stumble home, steal into the kitchen, and inhale the contents of the fridge. I shoveled it in, every bite a "fuck you" to my mother. She always heard, too. Over the years, she'd developed a sixth sense that told her whenever I ate anything with calories (aka anything except celery). The crunch of a single potato chip would awaken her in the middle of the night as if it were a dozen air raid sirens. She'd yell from her bedroom upstairs, waking up the neighborhood, "The kitchen is closed!"

Then I'd go to my room, put on my headphones, sink into the sounds of Public Image Ltd. and the Ramones, and write in my journal. Not that old red one. I'd filled it up stories ago, and had retired many others, too. By eleventh grade, my entries had evolved thematically. My later teenage stories were less violent but equally passionate. They starred Sal as the misunderstood heroine, unloved and unwanted, until a handsome ("cute") hero saw beyond the cigarette smoke, black lipstick, spiked collars, and stomach flab. Instead of Sal slaying the dragons, a conquering hero would do it for her. He'd ride up in his Mustang convertible, vanquish her enemies, cherish her unconditionally, and make mad, hot, gooey love to her.

My romantic fantasies gave me hope. My steady diet of "fuck this and/or you" had brought me adventure, friends, fun, terrible sex. But it hadn't brought me love. That would come later.

3

THE MOTHER LOAD

My mom told me a story the other day about her neighbors in Short Hills. The couple had a son and a daughter. The girl, age ten, was overweight.

I'd seen this kid. She didn't look that fat to me—plump, perhaps—but I was generous about other people's extra weight (so *not* generous about my own, goes without saying). Mom went on to tell me that the chubby girl's mother had been advised by their pediatrician not to talk about weight at home and, instead, outsource the job to professionals. They'd signed her up for weekly sessions at nearby St. Barnabas Hospital for nutritional counseling and exercise tips.

"Let me get this straight," I said. "A healthy ten-year-old girl is going to a *hospital,* where people are sick and dying, to learn how to eat and run."

Mom said, "This is what they do with overweight kids these days. My neighbor said, 'Instead of me riding her, now it's their job.' Children aren't receptive to what their parents tell them."

"You realize you're talking to me, right?" I asked. "You must see the relevance."

"Relevance to what?" she asked.

I should have railed at her, explaining just how receptive I'd been to her homespun version of nutritional counseling ("If I let you make your own sandwich, you'd be big as a house!") and exercise plan ("For Christ's sake, go run around the block!"). Instead, I made up an excuse and hung up. Decades have passed since Mom was in her neighbor's shoes. Back when I was a chubster, overweight kids were a blight, a disgrace, an embarrassment. Nowadays, they are emblematic of our self-indulgent instant-gratification on-the-couch culture. Parents of old were enforcers, will-breakers and disciplinarians. Today, parents are their children's secretaries, enablers, and praise delivery systems.

I felt a wave of envy for this little girl. I would have given my teeth for Mom to leave me alone about my weight and send me to counseling instead.

My only institutional weight intervention was when Mom sent me to Weight Watchers when I was fourteen. She carpooled with the mother of another heavy kid, my sister's friend W. The moms would drop us off at the church entrance for the meeting. W. and I would go inside, get weighed, have our progress marked in booklets (a quarter-pound loss week one, a half-pound gain week two, etc.). For the first few weeks of meetings, we stayed to listen as the fat adults with greasy hair and gray clothing talked about the frustration of hitting a plateau and the bitter triumph of resisting their kids' candy bags at Halloween. The Weight Watchers rep would give an inspirational pep talk about losing a hundred pounds, and I found it sad that, years later, her life was *still* defined by how she was once fat. I don't remember who first suggested that we blow off the post-weigh-in part of the meeting. Probably me. By our fourth week, at our first opportunity, W. and I would sneak out the back door, go to the supermarket across the street, buy junk food, and eat it on the church steps until one of our moms showed up an hour later to drive us home. Many candy wrappers were hidden in the church bushes. After a couple of months of this, W. and I had each gained five pounds. I tried to manipulate the scale by sneaking a toe on the floor during my weigh-in, but the monitors caught me every time. They knew all the tricks. Mom demanded to know why I wasn't losing weight on the program. We had a big fight. In my anger and spite, I flung out the truth of how W. and I spent our inspirational evenings. Mom yanked me out of the Watchers, thereby ending my experience in group dieting.

According to a 2006 Stanford University study, there is a direct link between parental weight criticism and bad body image. Of the study's 455 adult female subjects, 80 percent of those with body-related anxieties (including eating disorders, chronic dieting, and/or appearance preoccupation) reported being teased or criticized by their parents about their weight during adolescence. The study's conclusion: Teenage girls are acutely sensitive about their weight, and a parent's negative comments exacerbate that sensitivity *permanently*. Sure, some criticized girls will grow up to have good body image (whoever they are, I'd like to buy them a Diet Coke), but they are rare exceptions. For the majority of kids with fatphobic parents (roughly one in three, says the American

Obesity Association), an adolescence of enforced diets, weight charting, and harassment will mess them up but good forever. When I read the article about this study in the newspaper, I e-mailed it to Mom. She said, "I saw the article, too. I knew you'd make a big deal about it."

Judy believes that whatever she dished out to me was a trifle compared to what Fay, her alcoholic, manic-depressive, narcissistic mother, did to her. And she is right. I cringe from the stories. When Judy was in ninth grade, she would come home from school and find Fay drinking and smoking in the sunroom of their South Orange, New Jersey, home. Mom was then ordered to sit down and listen to Fay list everything that was wrong with her—hair, weight, height, clothes, manner, the way she sat, the way she spoke, what she said— until Fay was too hammered to continue. At that point, Mom was responsible for undressing her drunk mother, cleaning her up, and putting her to bed.

Judy told me, "She just didn't like me. She told me many times that she started drinking when she was pregnant with me because she was depressed about having another baby." The first child, a son, my uncle, had the responsibility of upholding the family name. In the 1940s, in the Jewish suburban subculture, the boy child was expected to go to college, be a success, make something of his life. A girl child? She was supposed to look pretty and marry well.

Going by what I've seen in old, weathered photos, Judy was a solemn, lovely, delicate child, but she wasn't up to Fay's impossible standards. Petite and feminine, Fay was a legendary beauty on her patch, the Jews-only Mountain Ridge Country Club in West Caldwell, New Jersey. Milton, her husband, was considered an exceptionally handsome, virile, athletic man. As a couple, Fay and Milton were envied and popular. They had full social lives and left their two kids at home under the care of live-in housekeepers.

"Fay was a seductive person," said Judy. "She flaunted her attractiveness and flirted outrageously with other men. I was always embarrassed by that, how she dressed and what she discussed. We'd drive home from the club, me and my brother in the backseat, Fay and Milton in the front, and she'd tell a long story about how some man at dinner propositioned her and asked her to visit him in his apartment in New York. My father liked it. He encouraged her. He took pride in other men's interest in her."

Indeed, Fay and Milton's relationship was overtly sexual. For wedding and anniversary gifts, Milton would routinely give his wife flimsy unmentionables from the local lingerie store. Being a busy dentist, though, he didn't have time to pick out the garments himself. "He gave me money and sent me down to the boutique," said Judy. "Two or three times a year, I had to pick out sexy underwear for my father to give to my mother, starting when I was ten. My mother knew Milton sent me on his gift errands. One year, she was so enraged about it, she threw the box at me."

Fay was jealous of any female who came within five feet of Milton, including Judy. "I was in my midteens when she showed me a photo of Milton I hadn't seen before. He was by the pool, wearing a very tight bathing suit. Fay said, 'I bet this is a real turn-on for you, isn't it?'"

"She was threatened by your relationship with your father?" I asked, sickened and embarrassed on Mom's behalf.

"I suppose," said Judy. "At the time, I counted it as just one more bizarre way for her to humiliate me."

I started to get a disturbing picture of what my mom's childhood in that crazy house must have been like. Fay and Milton behaved like the stars of their own psychosexual soap opera. My mom was their prop girl, criticized when something went awry and ignored otherwise. At the same time, although Fay treated her like an invisible girl, she was relentless about Judy's physical appearance. Even if Mom herself was insignificant, her looks still mattered—as a reflection of Fay. A tall, plump child was out of the question. Fay—the social butterfly, the petite beauty, the fashionable flirt—couldn't stand my mother's height, her dark features, her awkward manner. Mom spent much of her childhood in a protective crouch. I feel for her; I know what it must have been like.

Mom repeated Fay's hypercritical parenting style, to a degree. Fay attacked Judy about everything, including all aspects of her appearance. Judy focused her harassment specifically on my weight. In this regard, Judy showed supreme restraint. She did criticize my hair, posture, clothes, manners, walk, talk, etc., too, but rarely. By my grandmother's standards, Judy let me off easy. In a way, I'm grateful.

During the height of my teen years, when my belly bulge was 24/7 on Mom's mind, she restricted our family's exposure to Fay and Milton. Even before then, we hardly spent time with them. The memories I have of my maternal grandparents are few, but vivid. They took Alison and me to see Carol Channing in *Hello, Dolly!* on Broadway. While walking to the theater, Milton stopped us on the street to show us the bowie knife he had strapped to his forearm under his sleeve. He told us that if anyone tried to mug us, he was ready. The gesture was meant to calm us, but it was terrifying. I never felt comfortable with him after that. As for Fay, I could recount the many disastrous Thanksgivings when she'd start okay and then, after the second drink, mutate into Cruella de Vil before our eyes and lay into everyone and everything until she stormed out of our house in a wild rage to cry in her car, her forehead pressed against the steering wheel.

The classic story was when Fay showed up at our house unexpectedly to take Alison, Jon, and me to a restaurant for lunch. My brother ordered a BLT. The waitress brought the sandwich. My brother, who was five, said he didn't like mayo and refused to eat it. Fay insisted he did like it, that everyone loved mayo. Jon held out for unsullied bread. Fay proceeded to throw a shit fit to rival the most tempestuous two-year-old, screaming at Jon, calling all three of us ungrateful brats, accusing us of hating her, being stooges for our mother. It was shocking to me that an adult could behave that way, be publicly, wildly out of control. All the while, she was puffing like mad on her Vantage cigarettes, the ice clinking in her tumbler of Scotch.

Judy does not drink. She has never smoked a cigarette in her life. My first cigarette was pinched from Fay. She used to keep them stacked in a gold case on her den table. Stealing a handful of smokes was the only plus of going to her house. I'd put them in the pocket of my windbreaker, walk in the woods behind the house, and smoke the ones that hadn't broken.

If Fay barely tolerated Judy when she was under her control, she completely lost her crackers when Judy fled. My parents married very young. Howie was twenty-three; Judy was barely twenty. "Fay hit on all my boyfriends, including Howie," said Judy. "He refused to flirt back. When we got married, Fay decided that he was beneath me and that she hated him. She called me a slut when I got pregnant the first time. When Howie was in the air force, we moved to Texas. Fay and Milton showed up at our house uninvited. I was pregnant with Jon; you and Alison were toddlers. Fay walked in the door and started in immediately. 'Look at your hair, look at your dress. The roast is overcooked, the house is a dump.' We got in a big fight, and my parents turned around and left, flew back to New Jersey. They'd been in Texas less than an hour.

"Fay called the next day," Judy continued. "She said, 'You're a fuck, a shit. You're a whore for getting pregnant three times in four years. You're a slut.' Not that it's ever appropriate to call your daughter a whore, but this was in 1966. It was off the charts. I had a friend of Howie's, a psychologist at the air force base, come over and listen in to my next phone conversation with Fay. When it was over, I asked him, 'So, what can I do about her?' He said, 'Don't speak to her again. Ever.'"

For the record, although she has called me fat and lazy, Judy has never called me a whore or a slut, though I might've deserved such a description circa 1990 in a postmodern, owning-it, sex-positive way. Judy described my punk outfits as "trashy." Mom has called me a bitch often. She's told me to fuck off and described me and/or my behavior as shit. I've called Judy a bitch too many times to count. I've advised her to fuck or screw herself, characterized her as a pile of and/or full of shit, and once, after she'd screamed at me for something totally unfair (can't remember what), called her a cunt. I was seventeen at the time and had been lying on my bed in the dark listening to the Sex Pistols on headphones for, like, thirty hours straight (maybe that was what the fight was about). The English really throw the c-word around. It's like a casual term of endearment to them. No different than an American saying, "Hey, lady."

Judy said, "I don't remember you using the c-word."

"I didn't scream it. It was sotto voce. Even when you were tormenting me and I had to resort to calling you a cunt, I did it with hushed reverence."

"Bullshit!" said Judy, laughing. "You bitch."

"Howie heard me say it," I added. "He looked like he wanted to slap me."

"What would you do," asked Judy, "if Maggie or Lucy glared at you and said, 'You cunt'?"

"I'd say, 'Yes, I can!'"

Despite (because of?) our history, Mom and I are quite close. We're bonded like war buddies. Whenever I have news, good or bad, my instinct is to always call her first. Only Mom can soothe some hurts and say the one thing that'll restore my confidence. I don't sugarcoat my life with Judy; our relationship has never had a rosy paint job. As tirelessly as she dogged me about my weight, she has been an exceptional grandmother. She's been an ardent fan of my novels, bragging to her friends, applauding my efforts, laughing at all the right places, going into bookstores and demanding that they stock multiple copies, sneaking in later to turn them face front on the shelves. During Glenn's illness and after his death, both of my parents excelled, above and beyond, in their emotional support and practical assistance, putting their lives on hold for a year to help in any way. They took Glenn to chemo and physical therapy. Mom babysat, driving to our apartment at a moment's notice. They took turns sleeping over after Glenn died and I wasn't strong enough to be alone. I wonder how the kids and I would have survived those bleak months without them.

Now that I'm a parent, I deeply appreciate all the little things parents do that are overlooked and unappreciated. The lunches Mom packed, the carpooling and schlepping, the birthday parties. She never missed a single recital or match—or, in later years, book reading or public appearance. For the last ten years, Mom has taken her beloved golden retrievers to hospices, pediatric wards, detention centers, and geriatric homes to let the sick, despondent, and old enjoy the warmth and companionship of friendly animals. For such work—it's called pet-assisted therapy—Mom has won awards, including one from the New Jersey Veterinary Association when she brought some joy into the depleted hearts of dozens of New Jersey families who lost loved ones on 9/11. Fearless, Judy ventures into some pretty dicey neighborhoods in Newark to provide four-legged furry affection for those in need.

And yet, for all the love, respect, and appreciation I feel for her now, the fact remains: When I was at a tender, formative, vulnerable age, she was ghastly.

"When *I* was a teenager," she said, "no one expected anything from me. I was a throwaway. A nonentity. I expected a lot from you and Alison. I wanted you to expect great things of yourself."

"What if I'd gotten bad grades?" I asked. "Would you have shifted your focus away from weight and railed about my grades instead?" I asked.

She said, "No, I would have gotten on you about the grades, too."

Judy *was* a martinet about grades, though. Both my sister and brother were class valedictorians, Merit Scholars, Presidential Scholars, award-winning grade-getters. I hovered near the top of my class, but definitely not the tippy-top. I had a reputation, after all. Punks were not geeks. Black leather and straight A's did not go together. I was definitely the only kid in AP biology with a Mohawk. I agreed with my parents that grades were important, learning was essential, the mind was a terrible thing to waste. I worked hard enough. My marks and scores were good enough. God knows, it was a hell of a lot easier to get an acceptable GPA than to lose twenty pounds. My parents' academic pressure was a pain in the ass at the time, but it didn't leave a lasting residue on my psyche. And why would it? My high school class rank and test scores became irrelevant the second I got accepted to Dartmouth. My weight, however, has remained relevant. Plenty of emotional residue there.

If Judy had been born in 1971 instead of 1941, she would have logged a dozen years of therapy before considering marriage and children. Instead, she raced to escape her parents by marrying my dad when she was ridiculously young, finishing college but forgoing a career, popping out kids she would live through vicariously. I sympathize with what she went through. Three kids under four at age twenty-five? It's a miracle she didn't put her head in an oven. Her childhood was stolen by her mother. Marriage and children swallowed her young adulthood. My hardworking dad was largely absent. Mom must have been lonely. As a mother, she was obviously frustrated with me. Maybe if she'd been a drinker, she wouldn't have been so laser-focused on my weight. My friends' parents smoked and swilled like good suburbanites.

Part of me feels ambivalent about blaming Mom for anything that's wrong with my psyche now. She never hit me or chained me to the radiator. She did try to starve me, but only of junk food. Considering the devastating parental abuse so many kids face and have to process as they grow up, I had an easy ride. And if the parenting proof is in the pudding, the truth is, I turned out okay. I'm not an emotional cripple. I have a family, a career, pets, a life. I'm stable and happy.

But. The obligation of a parent—*my* obligation as a parent—is to provide unconditional love as well as discipline and structure. Judy, not a huggy, affectionate person, must've felt unconditional love for her kids, but she sure didn't show it. To my teenage eyes, her love seemed conditional upon my losing weight. She installed body anxiety into my hard drive (*permanently,* you bitch!). She was relentless and degrading to her most sensitive, insecure child. At forty-one, I had a few questions for her about that. And I'd get to them, when the moment was ripe (and I had the nerve).

4

THE FORTY-POUND MARRIAGE

Although I'd been stacked since ninth grade, I'd never been comfortable with my big boobs. They were familiar, *in titu,* reliably there where I left them. They floated in the bathtub, and that could be mildly entertaining. I could smuggle pencils underneath them. They also won the attention of a certain kind of man—not necessarily a good thing.

Women who envy large breasts are not hip to their major drawback: Big tits make you look fat. There are exceptions. Skeletal porn stars with whopper implants look like aliens from Planet Hooter. Dolly Parton long ago achieved the rare and freakish tits-on-a-stick silhouette. By and extra-large, though, women with plus-size breasts project volume. Bird-watchers identify species by gauging the "general impression of shape." Should they catch a fleeting glimpse of a large, flying rectangle with pointy triangle ears, they think "owl." Should girl-watchers catch a fleeting glimpse of a curvy, rounded female with a lot of junk in the front, they think "fat."

I met my first husband, Glenn, at a party I threw to celebrate the release of my first novel. A mutual friend brought him along. We were introduced, shook hands, and then I moved on, performing my hostess duties. The party was a blast, a huge success, talked about by many factions for weeks. But it was a disappointment for me in a crucial regard. Despite my inviting half a dozen ex-boyfriends and a handful of guys I had crushes on, I went home alone.

The next day, I sang the single girl's lament to my friends, one bitter phone call at a time. I was lonely and depressed, I said. There was no one for me. One friend disagreed. He said, "I've got a guy for you." I vaguely remembered meeting this Glenn that he'd invited to my party.

"He liked me?" I asked softly.

He said, "When I asked him what he thought of you, he said, 'I got the impression she's chubby.' And I told him, 'She's not chubby! She's busty!' And Glenn said, 'In that case, hook me up.'"

I wasn't charmed by this anecdote. It took me back to junior high. Still, I agreed to take Glenn's call. We set up a meeting at a club. He showed up with five friends. I brought two and stayed for half an hour. It was long enough to show him that in the hourglass that was my figure, most of the sand was on top. I was chubby in only the right places. He must have been satisfied by what he saw. We started going out.

Glenn didn't know it, but he stumbled into my life during a brief and shining slender period. I was twenty-six and wore a size six dress. My jeans had a 28-inch waist. Glenn was twenty-four. He had the classic male Y-shape: broad shoulders, muscular arms, narrow hips, and long legs. I didn't know that I'd stumbled into *his* life during his one and only buff period. So we met when we both looked our best. Appearance was all that mattered to guys in their midtwenties. To me, too. If Glenn hadn't been working out, if I hadn't been skinny, maybe we wouldn't have started dating, and our lives would have gone in completely different directions.

But we did start dating. Our courtship was a blur of bars, bands, and blowjobs. Glenn was the drummer in a rock band (by night—by day, he worked at a publicity firm). I was his number-one groupie and burned many calories having sex in bathrooms all over the Lower East Side. I chain-smoked, annihilating appetite. In the first flush of infatuation, I wasn't hungry anyway. New Relationship Diet #14 was working wonders. Without any strain, my weight dropped during our first year together. I ran five miles a day and spent a goodly portion of my biweekly paycheck at salons. I wish I had more photos from this era. Despite the fact that I'd never looked better, I was still anxious about cameras and stuck with a lifelong tradition of avoiding them.

Glenn and I got serious. We'd come to rely on each other the way couples do for support, company, sex, fun, friendship. I trusted him, I believed in him. And vice versa. When I looked at myself, I cringed at my flaws. When I looked into Glenn's eyes, I basked in his pure unconditional love. After we got engaged, I wrote a short story for a mystery anthology about a woman whose fiancé left her because she gained fifty pounds. Glenn assured me that he would never leave me, no matter what I weighed. When we signed the ketubah, a Jewish marriage license, before our wedding ceremony, we were told by the rabbi to stand facing each other, holding hands. "Look at each other," said the rabbi. "Is this the person you want to spend the rest of your life with? The person you want to grow old with? The person you vow to love from this day forward?" We said yes, yes, yes. It was one of the few times I saw Glenn cry.

I submitted to being photographed at the wedding. I looked decent. I wore my sister's wedding gown. It had to be let out for me, of course, but it fit well. Glenn fit me well. We meshed. The engagement and honeymoon years were bursting with the activity of starting a life together. Glenn switched jobs and worked hard to prove himself. I was editing articles at *Mademoiselle* magazine by day, writing mystery novels at night. We played house in our Brooklyn Heights apartment (only a few blocks from where I live now). I relished my new role as wifey, cooking elaborate meals for Glenn and our frequent dinner guests. On request, I baked the secret-recipe chocolate chip cookies he craved. For a Valentine's Day gift, Glenn encouraged my culinary talents, giving me two hundred dollars' worth of cookware from Williams-Sonoma. I wasn't particularly motivated to lace up the sneaks and go running, not with a loving hungry husband waiting for dinner in our cozy apartment. I served him on our wedding registry stoneware.

Blessed with a fast metabolism, six-foot-tall Glenn could eat anything and remain slim. When we went shopping together at Key Foods, he threw Doritos and packaged cupcakes into the cart casually, guiltlessly. He'd never dieted a day in his life. If anything, he'd struggled to *gain* weight. That was his rationale for buying junk: If he didn't eat it, he'd get too skinny. If I removed some junk food product and put it back on the shelf, Glenn would toss it back in the cart and say, "If you don't like it, don't eat it." Spoken like a true clueless rube. Naturally, I ate more than he did from those boxes and bags with the crinkly wrapping. Embarrassed by my lack of willpower, I'd sneak a cookie here, a handful of chips there. Presto, the bag would be empty, and I'd have to replace it on the sly before Glenn realized he'd married a hypocrite.

It became a family tradition to go to a nearby sprawling Greek diner for brunch on weekend mornings. Glenn would order fried eggs with bacon, extracrisp home fries, lots of butter on toast. He'd eat all of it, then order pie for dessert. I watched in mock horror and genuine envy. He didn't realize how blessed he was, eating at will.

We'd had opposite childhoods. His mother used to cry and beg and yell at him to eat *more*. He told me stories about secreting food into the napkin on his lap to dump in the trash later, or feeding the dog under the table. His mom tempted him with Hostess snack cakes, literally waving them under his nose. I gave Glenn a detailed account of Judy's fatphobia, how she'd cried, begged, screamed at me to eat *less*. We'd both had bumpy adolescences, bodywise. Me for being fat, Glenn for being pencil thin. We shared our sad and funny tales while we ate those greasy diner brunches. There were a lot of stories, and brunches to match.

Many married couples adopt each other's habits—good and bad. Glenn got me to quit smoking—good. He stopped pumping iron, and I stopped running—bad. I adopted his casual consumption of junk food. With no cigarettes or exercise to keep my weight in control, I gained quickly. Glenn didn't notice that my shirt buttons were straining, my skinny jeans on the shelf, my girth hidden under sweaters. Or maybe he did notice but chose not to mention it.

Within two years of the wedding, I was up fifteen pounds. I rationalized that I didn't have time to diet. My previous diets were elaborately planned and charted. They ate up hours of my time. I didn't have that kind of leisure anymore—the full-time job editing, my part-time job writing novels, being a well-seasoned wifey.

Glenn was in professional disarray. He'd left his publicity job to work at an indie record label, only to leave there for a position at a music wholesaler. At that company, he jumped from department to department. Finally, he resolved to get an MBA at night. That meant Kaplan classes, applications, testing. He spent a lot of nights away from home. I cooked less often, so we ordered Chinese, Mexican, pizza. Neither one of us had seen the inside of a gym for years. We moved to a different apartment, then moved again a year later.

We always made time for love. At thirty—we'd been married for two and a half years—I got pregnant with Maggie. In my second month, we had a scare. It turned out to be nothing. My doctor assured me the baby was fine. Even so, I decided to stay in bed as much as possible, just to be on the safe side. I ate according to the advice books, meeting my daily requirements for protein, fat, and carbohydrates. To make the baby sweet, as I frequently espoused, I ate plenty of sugar, too. I topped 200 pounds by my ninth month, a gain of sixty. One of my most comfortable pieces of maternity clothing was a pink dress with black buttons. A coworker told me I looked like a watermelon.

I dieted after Maggie was born. *The Zone* by Barry Sears had just come out, and everyone at *Mademoiselle* went on the high-protein diet plan. I lost weight, but not enough. The net gain of the Maggie pregnancy was twenty pounds. Predictably, it was impossible to stay in the Zone long term. With a new baby, a full-time job, a husband in grad school, and book deadlines, I ordered in dinner every night. I chose food I could eat while holding the baby. Pizza, dumplings, falafel. Glenn's classes were at night. The lonely hours were passed feeding Maggie every few hours and feeding myself almost constantly. I got pregnant with Lucy when Maggie was two. I tried harder in that pregnancy to be careful with food. I swam laps, avoided sweets. Nonetheless, the net gain of that pregnancy was another five pounds. For those not keeping score, that was a grand total, thus far, of forty pounds.

The night Glenn and I met, I wore a size six backless minidress. Seven years later, at Lucy's first birthday party, I wore size fourteen stretch jeans.

Forty pounds and four sizes in seven years. If I heard this tale of woe (and "whoa!") about another woman, I'd assume something was horribly wrong with the marriage. No woman would be that self-destructive if she were happy. Overeating was really a cry for help. It was a slow, polysaturated suicide attempt. On the other hand, perhaps a massive swelling was the sign of deep contentedness in a secure marriage. As the old saying goes, fat=happy. Or perhaps my girth increase had nothing to do with the marriage itself. I was just overworked and overwhelmed, so I overate.

Being in the thick of life (as it were), I had little time for introspection. I was too harried to analyze what was happening to my body while it was happening. Perhaps I could turn an analytical eye to that period of my life now. It had been six years since the marriage ended. My kids were older, and therefore easier to parent. I wasn't working at an office anymore. I had time to think and the will to do it. Considering the way our marriage ended (which I'll get to in a minute), critical thinking about it was emotionally impossible for years afterward. Our wedded union was preserved in the amber of memory as special and beautiful and tragic. Until recently, the very suggestion that the marriage was less than ideal would have been blasphemous.

But our marriage—like all marriages—wasn't perfect. Glenn and I were happy more often than we weren't. We argued plenty, usually about negative forces outside our relationship (jobs, families, friends). We were in sync about money, travel, long- and short-term goals, how to raise the kids. I was taxed by Glenn's peripatetic career and by his frequent "What am I doing with my life?" complaints. I wished he'd do more around the house and with the kids. He was irked by my bluntness and impatience. We had children before any of our friends, and we were jealous of their freedom. We envied our single friends and loved hearing details about their sex lives. The night two friends called from their Caribbean vacation to tell us they'd gotten engaged, I cried for an hour, mourning that the thrill of new love was behind me forever. Glenn chafed at the isolation of young parenthood,

relief. In our marriage, for the first time in my life, I had room to breathe, to eat what I wanted, to be as lazy as a cat in the sun, without fear of scrutiny or abuse. I believed he loved me, would never leave me. I relied on Glenn's distaste for conflict. I took advantage of his benevolence and indulged myself heartily, wantonly, selfishly.

Both theories could be true. I pray Glenn was also too busy and overwhelmed by life to analyze our marriage. I hate the idea that he knew, even subconsciously, that my explosive growth was an attempt to either test him or take advantage of him. It was probably a little of both. For that, I am deeply sorry.

The new millennium arrived with resolutions. On New Year's Eve 1999, I vowed to get serious about dieting. No more of my usual on-for-two-weeks, off-for-two-months diet cycling. Maggie, four, and Lucy, one, deserved a healthy mother they could be proud of. Glenn deserved to get in bed each night with the slender bride he married, not the behemoth I'd become. Turning thirty-five that year, I was still young enough to get back in shape. It wasn't too late for me to improve myself.

But it was too late—for Glenn. In the winter, he'd switched jobs yet again. He thought the stress was responsible for his increasingly severe back pain. In the spring, he saw a doctor about it and went through a series of X-rays and MRIs. He checked into a hospital for more tests to confirm the worst. The back pain was caused by a malignant metastasis on his spine. He also had multiple brain lesions, too many to count. The diagnosis was lung cancer, stage IV. Glenn was a nonsmoker; his doctors called the cancer a fluke, not his fault, which provided zero comfort. In the summer, he had surgery, radiation, and chemo. Nothing worked. He died in the fall, November 3, 2000. He was thirty-four.

In the five months between diagnosis and death, Glenn relived his childhood struggle to gain weight. He dwindled to skeletal proportions. Watching the ravages of his disease was soul- and appetite-killing for me. I lost interest in food. I dropped twenty-five pounds, and two dress sizes, seemingly overnight, effortlessly.

And I was thrilled about it.

Yes, my husband was dying. I was on the verge of widowhood at thirty-five. My daughters were losing their father. I was lonely, frustrated, heartbroken, horrified by the toll illness took on Glenn and everyone else who had a front row seat. Still, despite the sorrow, I took supreme joy in my increasingly roomy clothing. With giddiness in my heart, I'd reach for the thin clothes in my closet. I'd worn a pair of red jeans on our honeymoon and hadn't been able to squeeze myself into them for years. A few weeks postdiagnosis, I was able to get them over my hips. A month later, I could zip them halfway. Another month, I could zip them—and breathe. Another few weeks, they were loose. I smiled dreamily as I beheld my shrinking self in the mirror. Glenn had half a dozen painkillers and antidepressants to ease his suffering. Weight loss became my Vicodin, my Prozac. The red jeans were my delivery system. It took the edge off my pain. Shrinking calmed me, pleased me, gave me something to feel good about.

I shared my secret joy with no one. Who would understand that I could find any reason to be cheerful, given the grim reality of disease that loomed over us and defined our days? There was ordinary life, schlepping the kids to school and playdates, working, shopping, cleaning. Then there was cancer life, the blur of appointments, driving to hospitals and doctors' offices for chemo and transfusions, reading about treatments and therapies, organizing visits so Glenn wasn't exhausted by too many people at once, dealing with insurance companies, explaining haltingly to Maggie why Glenn had lost his hair, his energy, his appetite, apparently his interest in her. Lucy was still in diapers, a baby, not yet talking. Cared for by our beloved babysitter, Lucy was more or less ignored by me during those five months. I'm sure that'll come back to haunt me.

Most of all, I spent hours in bed with Glenn, talking to him, watching TV and movies with him, feeding him when he could eat, helping him stretch his weakened muscles, reassuring him that he'd beat the disease after every test revealed that the tumors were growing, had spread. We tried guided visualization together, lying flat, imagining a magic blue light had entered his body to wash away the cancer. He went along because it relaxed him. Rationally, he thought the practice was stupid; tumors wouldn't shrink just because you willed them to. Glenn had often said that willpower alone wouldn't be enough at a job or at school to achieve success. Willpower alone had failed me on diets a hundred times. But we held on to hope. Which, in this crisis, was another word for denial.

The glittering blue magic light didn't shrink Glenn's

tumors. But he shrank, as did I, almost at the same pace. Cancer Diet #1 was a success, almost *against* my will. For once, I lost weight without trying. I had conscious thoughts about it, along the lines of "Be careful what you wish for" and "So *this* is what bittersweet tastes like."

I had conscious thoughts, also, that the weight loss would help me when I started dating again. At first I could imagine a life without Glenn only theoretically. But as his cancer spread, my self-preservation instinct set in. I would live, after all, even if Glenn didn't. I was thirty-five years old. A loveless, celibate rest-of-my-life was unthinkable. Instead, I imagined the highly thinkable: that one day a man would come into my life, sex me up, fall in love, marry me, and be a stepfather to the girls. This rosy vision helped me get through some grim moments as Glenn got worse. Losing weight, in part, made my survivalist daydreams possible—or I should say *credible*. It was true when I was single a decade ago, and it would be true a decade from now: Men prefer to date slender women. My slimmer silouette would be a huge plus, whenever I was ready to take advantage of it. Glenn and I never discussed whether he wanted me to marry again or to be his widowed bride for eternity. I was sure he'd expect me to at least try to be happy. I wondered at the time if my subconscious was hard at work during Glenn's illness, killing my appetite to shrink me, leading my thoughts up the rosy path of future love, to prepare me and make me strong for an uncertain future.

Everyone noticed my increasingly bony face and tightened belts. My sister asked, "Have you stopped eating, too?" My friend Rebecca, she of "eat the rat" fame, asked, "Do you find it ironic that as your husband's health declines, you're getting back in shape?" I waved away the comments, discouraged them. I didn't want to agree and thereby reveal myself to be the monster who took pride in her appearance when her husband was dying.

The one person who didn't comment on the change in my body was the man who knew it best. Granted, Glenn was drugged most of the time, and he was grappling with larger issues than my stomach bulge. When he was awake, we talked about anything, everything, no matter how small and insignificant. Glenn had always been a fantastic talker, a great gossip, which I appreciated so much in a man. We laughed about how some visitors to the Apartment Ward were undone by awkward attempts to act sufficiently reverent to the cancer patient. We theorized about our friends' relationships—how would they handle it if one of them got sick?—in minute detail. We strolled around the neighborhood, me pushing Glenn in the wheelchair, and gabbed about ugly clothes in shop windows, the high price of contact lens solution, a restaurant closing. We had lengthy conversations about Ben Stein and Jimmy Kimmel, the duo who hosted Glenn's favorite game show. We talked about us, and how great our lives would be once he recovered. We never talked about loss of life. Or loss of weight. And he didn't comment on my shrinking body, just as he hardly spoke of my expanding one.

With the perspective of years, I realize that my size, bigger or smaller, simply didn't register to him. Whatever it was he saw in me, it had nothing to do with my weight. If I had issued a subconscious test of his unconditional love by gaining weight, I hadn't been paying close enough attention to his marks. Glenn passed the test. He passed it over and over again, with flying colors. If I failed to see it then, I do now. And for that, I'm deeply grateful.

At the funeral, I wore a size ten ankle-length black skirt that Alison picked out for me. Everyone said I looked good, considering. Over the coming months, I continued to lose buckets of water weight through the tear ducts. The weight of guilt clung to me. I learned in my grief books that surviving spouses often feel guilt for being healthy, for not getting sick and dying.

My fantasies about having a happy—if distant—future were useful during the illness, but I had to put them away after the death. No matter how much I'd prepared for it, Glenn's absence from our home was shocking and huge. Maggie rightly said that her friends who'd lost grandparents couldn't understand. When you lose someone who lived in your house, you hurt more. You missed more. I felt like I'd lost, was lost, was left with loss. Losing—formerly the opposite of gaining—was now the antithesis of winning.

I spent night after night in a misery of loneliness and self-pity, alone in my bedroom with the TV on. This was the reality of widowhood. The fantasy had been a lot better. I had the sneaking suspicion I'd find those lost pounds again, probably sooner rather than later. And I feared that true love had vanished from my life forever.

5

SEX AND THE SKINNY

M yth or Fact? Fat girls . . .

1. Use their fat layer to hide from sex.
2. Are so hard up, they'll say yes to anyone—or anything.
3. Only do it in the dark.
4. Overeat because of sexual frustration.

Regarding Point #1, that fat girls hide from sex behind a layer of flab, I'd have to go with Fact. When I was a teenager, sex scared the hell out of me. I was intimidated by the physical intrusion. Learning to use tampons was traumatic enough. The emotional consequences seemed even worse. Based on my observations of girls who actually had a sex life, as soon as they put out, they were either dumped or gossiped about. "Slut" was not a sexually self-actualized term back in 1980s suburban New Jersey. As for how these girls *felt* about being sexually precocious, I came to this conclusion: More tears were spilled over having sex than over being a virgin. I decided

I would wait. Not that anyone was breaking down the door to get at me.

My libido simply hadn't kicked in. I didn't have explicit sexual fantasies, just fuzzy romantic ones. I didn't masturbate. I didn't have an orgasm until college. My sexual education— academic and anecdotal—was ridiculously inept. Everything I learned about teen sex was from movies like *The Last American Virgin* and *Fast Times at Ridgemont High*, with the themes of abortion, STDs, premature ejaculation, and betrayal. We all read Judy Blume's *Forever,* which starred a romantic hero who named his penis Ralph. *So* not a sexy name.

I had the physical maturity for lust, but not the will for it. I got crushes, safe ones on guys I barely knew, faces at assembly, bodies leaning against lockers in the hallways. The few times a boy hit on me at a keg party, I'd get so flustered, I'd break out in a flop sweat and retreat into the nearest bathroom to hide.

I believed, as bushmen in Africa do vis-à-vis photographs, that if I had sex with a boy, he'd steal my soul. So much of my dignity had been peeled away already, I was fiercely protective of the scraps I had left. Sex equaled vulnerability. Losing my virginity at seventeen had been an exercise in getting it over with. Emotionally, I felt nothing, during or afterward, except relief that the deed was done. I'd achieved my modest goal. I would not go to college a virgin.

I went to Dartmouth, a small college in New Hampshire where (it'd been said) the men were men, the women were men, and the sheep were nervous. As soon as I arrived on campus, I felt like an alien. A punk rock Jersey Jew who went to public school? I was like a rare endangered animal among all those New England WASP boarding school preppies. The preps of Short Hills were like babies learning to crawl compared to the kids I met from Exeter, Andover, and St. Paul's. They'd been shipped off to school, many of them, at age thirteen, returning home only for holidays. I was insanely jealous of them. I wished I'd been sent away!

These boarding school kids awed me. They were smarter, wittier, and better educated than scrubs like me. One beautiful boy, E., a graduate of a New England prep school, entranced me as if I were a cobra and he the charmer with a pot pipe. He was also a "writer," and we spent hours in his dorm room, listening to the Grateful Dead, having deep talks, and passing the bong. E. had a red lightbulb in his desk lamp, and it bathed his Indian blankets and Communist wall posters in a seductive glow. We also shared short stories, what we considered "genius" snarls of prose scribbled in notebooks.

He was my first friend who was a boy. But our friendship was also a lie. He thought we were having a meeting of minds—and we were. I was madly in love with him, though, and every second in his presence was an excruciating knife twist of sexual longing. I wanted him, bad. The attraction was visceral. My guts tightened when I was around him. I wasn't sure if he knew. Some signs pointed to yes. He was an exhibitionist and often removed his shirt, tried on another, took that one off, and so on. He had the habit of rubbing his palm in lazy circles over his taut tan belly and the down that covered it. I asked him once if he realized he was doing it. And by "it," I meant driving me insane with lust, inflaming my urge to touch him, the craving for him to touch me. He asked, "Doing what?"

We were best buds for a year. We talked and talked. Then, for a change of pace, we talked some more. We smoked pot, snorted coke, ate mushrooms, dropped acid. Somewhere in there, we took a few English lit classes together, read books, wrote angst-dripping short stories we'd show only to each other. His were often about his own sexual longings, which I fantasized were about me.

I didn't dare make a move. Although I finally understood what lust was, I hadn't a clue what to do about relieving it. I watched dozens of cute girls flow in and out of his life and bed. Each, in turn, complained to E. about me. They wanted to know why he gave his body to them but saved his soul for me. Of course, I would have gladly traded places with them, but at least I had the small pleasure of making the pretty girls jealous. Once or twice, E. told me that his girlfriend theorized that he was actually in love with me and didn't realize it. How we'd laugh and laugh at such an absurd notion. Thank God for the red lightbulb, or he'd have seen my cheeks glow.

After E. dumped a girl, the adorable, conical-breasted ex would seek me out. She'd show up at my dorm room, or track me down in the commons, and ask, "Where did I go wrong?" and cry about her loss. I could only imagine how hard it must have been, to get next to him, to be touched by his beautiful hands, and then abruptly be denied access. I sympathized, honestly. I tried to help the dumped girl, and gave sound and useful advice about moving on. But I had to go now, because I was meeting E. for dinner. My friendship with him, the consistency of it, was my revenge against the girls who got from him what I most wanted. True, I was the fat friend, not the girlfriend. That would have to satisfy, if nothing else did.

I *was* happy to be three hundred miles away from home. No one told me what to eat or do. I could smoke my cigarettes, pile my tray high at the cafeteria. I put on the freshman fifteen by midyear (at Dartmouth, it was called the Thayer Layer, named after the student dining hall). Maybe if I'd had a boyfriend instead of pining for E., I'd have burned the excess calories by having sex. Maybe I pigged out because I couldn't have E., but I could have dessert (see Point #4—fat girls overeat due to sexual frustration—also Fact).

I'd matured enough to handle the (confounding but consistent) sexual attention of other guys. A few times a month, I'd bring a guy back to my dorm room, have sex with him, and pretend to be asleep when he snuck out in the middle of the night. On the phone, my mother would ask if I was seeing anyone, and then she'd say, "Oh," when I told her I wasn't. I knew her "oh" was a truncated "I told you s-oh." Indeed, one of her main "reasons I want you to lose weight" was that boys didn't like dumpy girls. Her delivery system had been wrong, not to mention *loud,* and so was her message. A lot of boys did want me. Just not the ones I wanted.

My sexual interludes gave me grist for conversations with E. One sunny afternoon, we were sitting on rocks on the bank of the Connecticut River, talking about a boy I'd had a weeklong fling with. We'd driven out to the secluded spot to smoke a joint, watch the river flow, gaze at the green mountains in the distance. E. seemed distracted. He started rubbing my back and gave me the misty, half-lidded blue-eyed stare I'd seen him use on countless cuties.

He said, "I feel really close to you, Val."

I said, "That's nice. We should be getting back."

And then we got in the car and left that place—literally and figuratively—never to return.

It was my one and only opportunity. I'd been offered my heart's delight, in a romantic setting, and I refused. When I told my other friends what happened, I acted insulted. How dare E. try his cheesy seduction ploy on me—*me!*—the one girl who knew his soul. I was indignant, offended. The truth? I was a chicken. A coward. E. and I were outdoors, under the bright sun. In the two seconds between offer and refusal, I pictured that sun shining on my imperfections, E. seeing my body in unforgiving light and struggling not to recoil. On the silent drive back to campus, regret already settling in to stay, I hated myself for a whole new reason: I didn't have the guts to take what I wanted. I was so filled with disgust at my own cowardice, I could barely look at E. It got weird. We started to drift.

Looking back at that moment, as I have many times, I understand rationally that getting what I wanted was way outside my comfort zone. I had sex with guys I didn't care about. I cared about E. I'd always soothed my longing by telling myself sex with him would spell doom for our friendship. As it turned out, *not* having sex with him had the same result. I'd romanticized unrequited love. If love was requited, would it be nearly as exquisite? Was love equal to pain? And what, if anything, did this have to do with my relationship with my mother?

E. and I rediscovered each other by senior year. I was over him, sexually speaking. By then, I had a boyfriend of my own. I met K. at the end of sophomore year. He would become my on-again, off-again boyfriend for the remainder of my college career. K. and I started the usual way, a drug- and alcohol-soaked one-night stand. We were at my place, an off-campus apartment. K. was my roommate's friend. We had our fling. Then I couldn't get rid of him. One night rolled into another, and before I knew it, he was living with me. He was a Dartmouth student, too, a senior on a year's personalized curriculum. Every few months, he'd go on some kooky trip tangentially related to his thesis research, driving cross-country in a van or flying freight to Europe. His frequent travel was the reason it took him six years to graduate. But it also made him seem mysterious and romantic—and unavailable, which I was enthralled by.

My relationship with K. was all about drama. We fought constantly, usually about how he was emotionally withholding. I'd throw a "You don't really love me" tantrum. He'd take off on one of his trips. I'd break up with him and spiral into Breakup Diets #1 through #17, during which time I burned a lot of calories by having sex with his friends. I'd beg K. to come back. When he returned, I'd confess about all the guys I'd slept with, cry, and beg his forgiveness, he'd accept my apology ("You're with me now," he said, filling me with pride in his ownership), and we'd start the cycle anew. Along the way, we'd smoke mountains of pot, talk about philosophy, and listen to Bob Dylan. I respected his intellect, and he would read anything I wrote. K. gave me valid criticism. He made me question my ideas, and refused to stroke my ego as E. and I had done for each other.

Although I was shy about getting on top with the lights

on (see Point #3—fat girls only do it in the dark—Partial Myth), I was bolder with K. than I'd been in my previous flings. He was a crunchy, organic, earthy guy. I thought of him as a mental giant, supercerebral, suspicious of superficial ideals of female pulchritude. He did tai chi. He meditated. He wore voluminous hippie clothing. "All bodies are beautiful," he said. I went with that.

For the record, at twenty, I was heavy. I'd adopted the Deadhead style of drawstring-waist baggy pants and peasant shirts that were one-size-fits-all. K. was slim and hairless. His body was beautiful, but I preferred the lights out and covers up whenever possible. He didn't object, so I assumed he'd rather not see my naked truth. He thought of sex as a mental/physical practice, like yoga or meditation. I wanted fiery passion, to feel ravaged by his uncontrollable lust. He wanted to gain insight into himself via sex with me.

Now, I realize our biggest problem was a clash of sexual styles. We should have broken up after two months. Instead, we limped along for over two years. I compulsively tried to seduce him—three, four times a day—to assure myself that my first and only boyfriend craved me desperately, or at least as desperately as I needed to feel craved. If he refused, I'd start a fight. Fights led to make-up sex, which temporarily quieted the insatiable beast within. But the victory was hollow. I knew I'd manipulated him into it.

There was no bliss in victory, either. Of the 300 sexual encounters we had, I faked orgasm 299 times.

No, that's an exaggeration. I faked 298 times.

Seriously, my faking depended on what we did. Certain

acts would guarantee an orgasm. Others were assured to fail. An honest estimate: I faked half the time.

Not K.'s fault. He was an experienced lover. He did what would have worked for any other woman (one who wasn't completely messed up about her body). And he rightly thought his techniques *were* working. I was a good faker. *Very* good. I served up Academy Award–winning performances, night after night. After a particularly nuanced display of my acting chops, as I lay next to him in bed, I wondered if I'd missed my calling, if I should've pursued a career on the stage.

As I later came to understand, bad body image and anorgasmia (not having an orgasm) went together like peanut butter and jelly. I came across this info while researching magazine articles: Two-thirds of American women have some degree of sexual dysfunction that is related to body image. One dysfunction is to think about their perceived body flaws during sex—fat thighs, for example—or to become fixated that their partner is turned off by the flaw. If women get locked in their heads during sex, their nerve endings fail to process the sensual stimulation. No processing, no progression along the sexual response cycle. They stall in the arousal phase, if they get that far, and fall way short of climax. Another common dysfunction is a behavior called "spectatoring." The anxious lover is so concerned about how she looks while having sex, she mentally watches herself doing it. In effect, she floats above her body, observing what's happening to her without actually feeling it.

A woman's feeling of attractiveness and desirability *defines* the quality of her sex life. Doesn't matter whether you're fat or not. What matters is that you *think* you're fat, during sex. Forget about having fun in bed. Forget about orgasms. Say hello to frustration, disappointment, guilt, and shame (incidentally, the same emotional hits triggered by diet cycling).

During sex with K., I was a spectator, mentally watching what was happening, as well as a thespian par excellence! I acted out the sexual rewards I wished I were having. I eventually told K. the truth, but not until I graduated and left Dartmouth. I was living in Cambridge, Massachusetts, to attend the Radcliffe Publishing Course, a summer program for aspiring editors and writers wanting to learn about the book and magazine business. K. came down from New Hampshire to visit me one weekend. We were broken up, but not completely severed. I remember sitting in my dorm room, him in a chair, me on the bed. It was early afternoon. The light came in through the window, illuminating the room in a calming way. He smiled at me with what appeared to be genuine trust, affection, pleasure in my company.

I said, "You know how I scream and thrash around in bed? I was kind of faking a little."

"A little?" he asked.

"A lot."

"You mean to tell me that for two years you've been lying to me?" he asked. "In the most personal way possible?"

"Not to be mean," I said. "I did it to be nice."

He was furious. Quickly, on the heels of that whopper, I told him that I was done with bedroom theatrics forever (indeed, I never faked again). To prove my point, I added that, just the other night, I screwed this Republican from the *Harvard Lampoon,* and I barely grunted for him. "For the record,"

I said, "I didn't find out he was a Republican until the morning after, and then I kicked his ass *out*."

Needless to say, K. was not reassured. He left Massachusetts within the hour. I called him a few days later, and he said, "For the rest of your life, no man will feel as comfortable with you as I did." That was his prediction and his curse. I believed it. The karmic boomerang of lying to K. would surely strike me right between the eyes. His words played into my deepest insecurities, those that he knew so well. I didn't deserve comfort. Trust wasn't feasible. I could never believe, beyond a shadow of a doubt, that any man would truly want me and love me.

The epilogue to the K. story: Shortly after 9/11, he tracked me down and called me in Brooklyn to make sure I was still alive. Life had taken him far. Postgraduation, he'd traveled the world and wandered for a decade. He'd finally settled down and was in law school in California. He was still single, but he sounded solid, happy. I told him my story, that my husband had died less than a year ago, and that I had nervously started to date again. He said, "Don't worry, Val. You're the whole package. Any guy would be lucky to have you." It was the nicest thing he'd ever said to me, at a time when I desperately needed to hear it. He lifted the curse.

During one of our extended breakups, the winter of my senior year at Dartmouth, K. left campus for a few months, and I moved into a house with several other students, one of whom was a coke dealer. The change of venue and free drugs made Breakup Diet #14 my greatest success yet. I dropped twenty-five pounds in two months. Thanks to my newly svelte body and a steady flow of traffic through our house (see above, re: coke dealer), I was deluged with sexual invitations. I accepted as many as I could.

If I were to chart my sexual activity along with my weight, the graph would show an inverse relationship. The smaller my pants, the bigger the number of men that got into them. One guy, a gorgeous just-a-friend from my sophomore dorm, saw me at a party and said he didn't recognize me at first. "You're just another pretty girl now," he said. I might have taken that the wrong way, but his hand was sliding deliciously down my back toward the curve of my ass. Men started to stammer when they spoke to me. They'd bring me beers and light my cigarettes. They tried to impress me with long boring stories about how they humiliated other men. They asked me to be their lucky charm at the pool table. When they said they'd be right back, they came right back. Several times, I realized with a start that two or three men were vying for my attention, clashing antlers over who'd get to take me home.

One of them surely did. That was guaranteed. The others would lash out. At me. That was the flip side of being an object of desire. If a woman gets rejected, she hates herself. If a man gets rejected, he hates the woman who turned him down. I flirted with one guy and then slipped away with another. The runner-up came by our house the next day, and pushed me hard into the refrigerator when I said I'd left the party with someone else. I juggled two friends, and circumstances led the three of us to have dinner together. During the main course, the guys fought over me like two lions over a scrap of meat. By dessert, they'd teamed up against me, accusing me of trying to ruin their friendship. They walked out on me. I'd started out with two guys and ended up with the bill.

Male desire became my drug of choice. Not *sex*. The sex itself was okay, sometimes good, sometimes awful, but being the object of lust became a new high, better than drugs or dieting. I got all the approval of being thin, all the ego boosting. I also got drinks, smokes, meals, strokes, jealous looks from conical-breasted blond girls. Having been so savagely negated as attractive by X., Y., and Z. as a teenager, I gobbled up the positive male attention of A., B., C., D., E., F., G., H., etc., like a starved animal. I embraced my sluttiude and made up for lost time. If a guy did me the favor of wanting me, I did him the favor of schtupping him. If my behavior was reckless, destructive, and soul-annihilating, I didn't see it. Or chose not to.

Friends, friends' brothers, colleagues. I racked up the numbers. A dozen in Europe during my semester abroad. Half a dozen my senior year at Dartmouth. Four of the seven male students at the Radcliffe course. Dozens of editorial assistant and junior editor types came in and out, as it were, of my first apartment in Brooklyn. I had a job, an income, my own place, much to prove, an unquenchable lust to be lusted after, and millions of New York City men at my disposal.

For the record, I had some standards. I didn't bed down with just anything. A guy had to be funny and smart. Cute. I had only one black ball: I wouldn't do fatties. A bitter rejection of my former fat self? You betcha. Superficial and hypocritical? To be sure. I knew it, too. It was right there, on the surface. Some of Mom's fatphobia had rubbed off on me.

Promiscuity went hand in hand (or *beep* in *beep*) with thinness. Counterintuitively, the more dinner dates I had, the less I ate. I sure did drink a lot, though. Vodka tonics were a staple of Sluttitude Diets #1 through #5. I had one-night stands, two-week flings, three-month affairs. Friends would say, "How's Bob?" And I'd say, "Bob who? I'm with Jim now." The dedication page of my second novel, *Murder on Wheels*, published at the height of my easy years, read: "Dedicated to Whomever I'm Seeing Right Now. Honey, You Know It's You." Which was supposed to be a joke but was also apt. I remember going to visit friends at the *Village Voice* offices, where I'd interned a few summers before. (Of course, I'd seduced one of the contributors, who was not there that day, whew.) My former boss, Karen, asked what was going on.

I said, "I'm seeing three guys."

She said, "Don't *brag,* Valerie."

I blinked at her, confused by the criticism. I hadn't thought I was bragging. I was just reporting the news. If I'd been asked what I had for breakfast, I'd have given as accurate and dispassionate a response.

"They'll probably dump me next week," I added humbly.

Guess what? All three *did* dump me. Despite my low weight and revolving bedroom door (see Point #2—fat girls will do anyone or anything—another Partial Myth), I was desperate and lonely—as well as hungry. Quickie relationships gave me a hit of the approval I was addicted to. I was in love with the approval, and, in my early twenties, I thought that meant I was also in love with the man. I lived in fear that I'd lose him, and as sure as chocolate has calories, my anxiety and nagging and demands for assurance would drive him away. Then I'd suffer, wail at the moon, call my friends hourly to give them the feelings update. I took scant pleasure in the relationship itself but was devastated when it ended.

Another of my mom's refrains had been "If you were thinner, you'd be happier."

Again, she was wrong. From age twenty-two to twenty-five, I had visible ribs. I ran miles and miles every day. My hipbones jutted. Yet I was chronically miserable, searching, searching, like a starved wild-eyed wolf in the woods, for love, some fucking (literally) relief from the loneliness and self-doubt.

Then I met Glenn, who saved me.

6

THAT'S RIGHT, I'M TALKING TO *YOU*

Me and the mirror. It's a hate-hate relationship. Doesn't matter if my weight is trending up or down. No matter what shape I'm in, I have a knack for finding the smallest physical flaws. It's a dark gift. One I can't give away.

I have my usual routine when approaching the mirror. I heavily sigh (exhaling makes the stomach flatter), tense my muscles, stand full-frontal before the glass (my most flattering angle), and then appraise. I give myself the once-over thrice. I slap my belly to see how much it jiggles. More than yesterday? Less? I pinch, poke, pull on the flab, and think, "Broiled Chicken Diet #12? . . . Nothing a few thousand crunches won't fix . . . You'll never lose it . . . worthless . . . pathetic . . . Maybe if I hire a trainer . . ." During one incredibly wiggly period a few years ago, I slapped the belly to check for jiggle nearly every hour. I realized how badly off I was when the rug between my desk chair and my closet mirror started to look frayed. One of the drawbacks of working from home.

After consulting a couple of experts and doing some light Googling, I discovered that I suffered from "appearance-checking behavior," or the habitual examination of one's perceived body flaws. Throw in the negative interior body talk, and you've got a bona fide compulsion.

My interior body talk echoed everything my mother ever said to me, plus some new material I came up with on my own. My subconscious playlist, hosted by DJ Inner Bitch, was automatic. The hits kept spinning, whether I heard them or not. "Fat . . . lazy . . . gross," the cerebral sound track of my life.

Perhaps the way to think positive would be to avoid mirrors and reflective surfaces, such as storefront windows, bathroom tile, car chrome, spoons, knives, clean plates, computer screens, framed pictures, windows, puddles, any calm water. I could live 24/7 in a squash court—or, more appropriately, a padded room in the psych ward.

Since my goal was to liberate myself from bad body image, I would have to tackle the mirror problem. I needed a practical approach. The emotional purging thus far had been productive. Crawling through bitter and lonely memories was unlocking a lot of stored-in-the-bones anger. Old rage seemed to be leaking from my pores. To speed the process, I'd been running on the treadmill like a fiend. *But*—in addition to the emotional release, I needed do some interior redesign of the brain. Move around the chairs in my mind. Repaint the skull walls. Break the appearance-checking habit.

As I devised a plan of action, I soon realized that gut slapping was part of a larger problem. My negative body talk didn't begin and end when I bellied up to the mirror. DJ Inner Bitch was in the house 24/7. She cranked out the hits when I looked at myself, but also when I daydreamed about having a flat stomach. When I got dressed. When I got undressed. When I compared myself unfavorably to other women. At meal time, sex time, all the time!

Since there was no accurate way to measure the emotional toll of near constant lambasting, I decided to take another approach. I *could* tally the cost in hours and minutes. I wasted precious time slamming myself. I certainly had better things to do than self-annihilation. Perhaps if I figured out how much of my day-to-day life was lost on negative thought, the terrible truth would spur my conscious mind to overcome my undermining subconscious.

The next day, I bought a stopwatch.

Within a couple of hours, though, I realized my methodology was faulty. When a thought became conscious, the stream didn't flow. I'd focus more on having the thought than on the thought itself, interrupting its duration. Also, I wasn't clear on which thoughts should count toward the total. Choosing a snack? Organizing my day around going to the gym? My thoughts rarely lasted a full minute. Often, I'd have a fat flash (for example, intense envy about how skinny Norah Jones looked on her new CD cover), but it was too fleeting to measure. The flash would end before I had a chance to start the stopwatch.

I had to refine my strategy, think in terms of "instances"

rather than "instants." If I could get a baseline of negative thoughts, I could mindfully decrease them.

The next day, I bought a clicker.

On Monday, I looked at myself 166 times. About ten times per waking hour, or, on average, once every six minutes. Shocking, isn't it? I mentioned the number to friends, and they gasped. The huge total included home mirror visits and catching my reflection in storefront windows, car windows, any chrome or glass surface. I counted everything, even fleeting glimpses if they were long enough to judge myself. The gym is a riot of mirrors. I logged twenty separate instances in an hour of watching myself sweat.

What was even more appalling? Every instance of looking at myself was accompanied by a negative thought. As I already knew, the thought could be fleeting, as long as it took the idea or word "hefty" to flit across my mind. I wanted raw data on how often I had negative thoughts in total, not *only* when looking at myself. I knew cluing into my subconscious would be a challenge. I resolved to try.

On Tuesday, I put the clicker to use counting each instance of negative thought. A flash, a microflash. Since one thought could roll into the next, I wasn't sure if it was one long thought or a series of thoughts that should be counted separately. I decided to apply the logic of multiple orgasm to multiple negative thoughts: If there was a thirty-second break between thoughts, they were to be tallied separately. If one thought led instantaneously into the next (as in, "jeans too bloody tight . . . embarrassment . . . shame . . . that woman's jeans look great . . . she probably eats grilled radicchio," so on and so forth), I'd count it as one solid click.

As it happened, on Tuesday, an unexpectedly warm day, I had to take off my hoodie while doing errands and walk around in a snug T-shirt. I was exceedingly self-conscious about back bacon and the muffin top. If I'd worn yoga pants and a peasant shirt . . . well, no point mitigating the shocking truth. I clicked 263 distinct instances of negative thought on that one day, including random barbs and assessments while looking at myself. I was sure I missed flashes that were too quick, or too deep in the subconscious, to access.

Calculators out: Two hundred and sixty-three hits divided by sixteen waking hours equaled sixteen and a half hits per hour. Or one hit *every three and a half minutes.*

Even on her energetic days, Mom wasn't that relentless.

Imagine what it'd be like to pinch yourself every three and a half minutes.

This was far, far worse than a sharp stick in the eye.

I was my own worst enemy; I was a formidable foe. How on earth could I liberate myself from bad body image when negative thoughts were the glue that held my subconscious together? I wondered what else I thought about. For the next few days, I tallied the rising thought bubbles about other matters.

On Wednesday, I thought about sex thirty-four times.

On Thursday, I thought about my family eighty-seven times.

On Friday, I thought about my work ninety-eight times.

On Saturday, I thought about money sixty-six times.

Looking at the week's raw data, I resisted ranking my priorities according to how often I thought about the subject.

Obviously, I'd be more preoccupied with my family if we were in crisis, but on Thursday, we stuck flawlessly to the usual routine without incident. Regarding the work total, I counted random thoughts during nonworking hours. Obviously, while working, I thought about what I was doing. Family and work thoughts tended to be logistical and practical, not critical or negative. Money thoughts were usually crunching numbers in my head, adding and subtracting, sometimes worrying. Sex thoughts were surprisingly fleeting, such as admiring my husband, Steve, in his new jeans, and thinking they'd look even better on the floor. No lurid daydreams on that busy Wednesday.

The cumulative four-day total of thoughts about sex, family, work, and money was only a bit higher than my one-day total of negative body image blips. This experiment reminded me of Scared Straight videos in high school about drunk driving and the clap. I was horrified and depressed, hating my subconscious. On Sunday, I tallied my negative thoughts about how often I have negative thoughts: 176.

I would never win the body image battle unless I recalibrated my brain, or "did some unlearning," as Susanna, my Krishnamurti-loving former roommate, used to say.

I would become my own thought police, determined to improve my numbers. If I could make a positive turn, logic would have it that my outlook and attitude, generally speaking, would lift.

Redirecting thought was surprisingly easy to do. When I felt compelled to run the hourly check for miraculous deflation of my stomach bulge, I took a deep breath, rooted myself in my desk chair, and played Snood on the computer until the urge passed. When I walked down the street, I'd strap on a set of imaginary blinders, keeping my eyes front and center, thereby avoiding my reflection in car and storefront windows. After a few days, I routinely managed to redirect my gaze—and my thoughts.

Not racking up scores of bad body image thoughts created a vacuum in my mind that desperately, achingly, needed to be filled. Wish I could say a wave of deep philosophical thoughts flooded my brain. Or that I was suddenly drowning in brilliant ideas for novels. To fill the mental hole, as it were, I thought about sex. Day and night. Afternoon and evening. Acts. Positions. Fantasies. What I'd like to do, what I wanted Steve to do to me, and how all that could be physically feasible given the limitations of human anatomy. Thoughts inspired action. Steve didn't know what hit me—or, more accurately, what hit *him*. Not that he was complaining. I was aware that I'd probably replaced one obsessive thought pattern with another, but this felt healthier and far more satisfying.

I wondered if orgasmic relief was the emotional lift I'd been anticipating. It was certainly physically uplifting. Emotionally? Sure! I kept on my imaginary blinders, avoided extraneous mirror use, consciously and subconsciously replaced negative body thoughts with erotic ones. And all was good.

Then it happened. After a month of waiting, the epiphany came unexpectedly. I was walking Lucy home from school. We passed a huge store window by a pharmacy. I used to slow down at that place on the sidewalk to check my profile view in the glass. For weeks now, I'd been intent on looking straight ahead, to avoid the reflection, but on that day, my eyes wandered a bit. I turned them downward, looking at Lucy as she told me a story about school in her eight-year-old excitable way. When she noticed I was looking at her—not at the window, not straight ahead—she smiled up at me, big and beautiful. Looking at her gorgeous face (she is one spectacular kid), I was overcome with gratitude for her being my daughter, for how innately happy she was, how animated and full of life and joy. We locked eyes; energy passed between us. It was no ordinary look. No ordinary connection.

How many of those moments had I missed while frowning at my profile in storefront windows? For years—decades—I'd been mentally trashing myself, obsessing about myself, when the beauty and glory of life was outside of me, my thoughts, my body. It was a horrible, shameful feeling, realizing that myopia and critical self-absorption had defined my existence for quite some time. Worse, my kids had probably noticed.

Naturally, I fell into a spell of myopia and critical self-absorption about the fact that I'd been myopic and . . . you see where this is going.

The time had come to step back, or think in reverse, and ask broader questions of myself, such as "What is the point? Why am I doing this?" One could cut to the heart of existentialism in front of a mirror. Lock in on the eyes—not the stomach, or the thighs—and make a vow to yourself to define existence by generating thoughts, feelings, and actions that increase the amount of joy and happiness in your head, your home, and the world.

Yes, counting negative thoughts on a clicker had come to this. I'd found the big idea, and I aspired to live by it from that moment on the street with Lucy forever forward. Simply put, I wanted to be a better person. And that, as I understood it, had *absolutely nothing* to do with the bulge of my belly.

desperation. In pitch meetings, we frantically grasped for big, splashy ideas. What grabby cover story, we wondered, would hold off Cooper's axing for one more month?

The articles department consisted of half a dozen editors and several assistants—all women in their midtwenties to early thirties. The articles head, M., the woman who hired me, was the oldest, at thirty-five. As a department, we were to supply the magazine with about sixty pages of original editorial content for every issue. When pitching feature articles, we stuck to the three *D*'s—dieting, dating, and diseases of the gynecological variety, as in, "My vaginal discharge smells funny. Help!" We ran arts reviews, advice columns, horoscopes, and celebrity profiles. Also, we'd do the monthly topical feature about a women's issue (rape, abortion, sexual harassment, etc.). At *Mademoiselle,* I learned that women's hot-button political issues were always about the control and protection of our bodies.

The ultimate juicy "get" article was a content trifecta that combined dieting, disease, *and* politics: the eating disorder first-person essay or reported investigation of a clinic that served the emergent needs of the self-starved or self-emetic. Every editorial pitch meeting, we'd collectively rack our brains for a new eating-disorder-of-the-month article.

According to available data, 1 percent of young women are anorexic, 2 percent are bulimic, and 5 percent are chronic bingers (by far the most prevalent eating disorder in America). All other disorders are subcategories of the big three. (Imagine my astonishment when I learned that my bent, chronic dieting, was a subcategory of anorexia! I thought, "If only I could have full-blown anorexia for, like, a month."

Alas, I'd had the JV version for, like, a decade.) It didn't matter that relatively few of *Mademoiselle*'s three million readers actually suffered from life-threatening food-related illnesses. You didn't need to have an eating disorder to feel fascination, disgust, and sympathy for those who did. An anorexic strapped down to a hospital bed for intravenous force-feeding? A bulimic's first purge memory from summer camp or a sorority hazing ritual? The readers lapped it up like pudding. They took these stories as cautionary tales of a run-of-the-mill obsession with thinness taken to horrifying extremes.

In those pre-Google days, we relied on press releases, books, medical newsletters, health studies, and regional newspaper articles to find subjects. Or we'd dip into the vast reservoir of our friends, friends-of-friends, cousins-of-friends, friends-of-cousins. When that well ran dry, we needed only to turn to ourselves. Of the dozen-odd women in the articles department, three-quarters of us had some kind of eating quirk or habit that any shrink alive would diagnose as borderline pathological. We beat national eating disorder statistical averages in a landslide. One assistant ate only a bunch of green grapes and six jelly beans every day. Another traveled with a food scale and weighed every morsel, even at restaurants. Another took twice-daily laxative-tea and high-volume-defecation breaks. Another was a diet product aficionado, swallowing any pill, drink, or bar she could get her hands on (and she got her hands on *everything;* huge shipments of products arrived weekly from companies looking for a mention in the magazine). Still another editor was an exercise-aholic, sweating out hours of her spare time on the StairMaster. A copy editor had full-blown anorexia, which she wrote an essay about in the magazine. A beauty writer was a full-blown bin-ger, which she wrote an essay about in the magazine. We did an article once on what it was like to be really, really fat in Amer-ica. The model we used looked huge to us, but when the issue came out, readers sent in letters complaining that the woman in the pictures wasn't nearly fat *enough*. She was normal, they wrote. At *Mademoiselle,* we didn't know from normal.

My chronic dieting went to extremes at *Mademoiselle.* There was tremendous pressure to look the part, or, as hires were told by the human resources staff, to represent the mag-azine in our personal appearance. Our work ethic: Get thin or die trying (the irony was particularly acute while editing stories about girls who *had* died trying). I certainly quaffed my share of chromium picolinate and Dexedrine. I munched bags of newfangled diarrhea-inducing Olestra-loaded potato chips ("shit chips" we called them). To further stimulate the bowels and curb appetite, I snorted white hillocks of cocaine. I did more blow during my first two years at *Mademoiselle* than in college when I lived with a coke dealer. I would snort before work, after work, and, occasionally, at work. My eyes would start popping, my heart rate zooming, and I'd crank out a story on first-date deal breakers.

If it hadn't been for the blow, I never would've been able to get to and stay at a size eight. Even at that weight, I was the biggest girl in the articles department. I felt acutely self-conscious about my curves. I was sure my job was on the line because I had them. Thinness was just one more way to win favor with the bosses, one more measure of success. It almost didn't matter if I edited twenty pages an issue. The skinniest girls on staff could edit five and get more approval from M., the boss. M. herself was slim but gawky, a former food writer who praised a gourmand lifestyle out of one side of her mouth and trashed her staff for being fat out of the other. With my own ears, I heard her rail against other editors' bodies, hair, clothes, intelligence, tone of voice. When I wasn't around, she gossiped about me to others, brutally mocking my CP Shades clothes and big boobs. Her alleged epithet for me was "the frizzy-haired fat Jew."

I didn't care about the "frizzy-haired" part or the "Jew" part (they were redundant). M. was from a large southwestern state. She'd met maybe two Jews before she moved to New York and was suddenly surrounded by them (us), including Ms. Levin Cooper. I forgave M. her bigotry. But the "fat" comment bothered me. After all, my job hung on my body size. Career advancement ran on a parallel track with weight·reduction. If she considered me fat when I was at a low-for-me 130 pounds, what chance did I have in this business?

As a child, I'd equated slimness with approval and love. As an adult, thinness meant career survival.

Granted, the pressure on the articles department at *Mademoiselle* wasn't nearly as bad as it was on the fashion department. We were word people—supposedly, the brainy girls on staff. Unlike the fashion and beauty teams, articles editors were cut *some* slack about their appearance. But skinny mattered, from the top of the masthead to the lowest ranking assistant (*The Devil Eats Nada*?). I watched from a distance as Cooper, already tiny, got smaller as the rumors of her firing flared up, cooled, reheated, cooled again. An articles editor's fiancé bolted at the altar, and she started scarfing laxatives. Another's father committed suicide; she stopped eating sugar. And bread. And meat. Focusing on weight was a convenient substitute when one's real problems were too big or painful to deal with. For most of the Cooper era at *Mademoiselle,* I was sleeping around, getting dumped, doing dangerous drugs, smoking over a pack a day. Yet I never contemplated the skankiness of my life, or the bleak future that awaited me if I didn't change my ways. Instead, I thought about the number of calories in a tablespoon of diet salad dressing.

An even bigger distraction than weight? Hunger. Back then, we editors were all hungry for job security, advancement, success. We were also hungry for food. Self-starvation was a competitive sport. At staff lunches, the girl who ate the least won. I can't count how often editors would announce, after taking three bites of a sandwich, "Oh, God, I'm absolutely *stuffed*. I couldn't *possibly* eat another bite." Then, in classic control-freak fashion, they'd leave the barely dented sandwich on their desk all day long like a badge of honor, as in, "Look at what I *didn't* eat today!" When we had birthday parties in the office, slices of cake on paper plates would languish on the conference room table untouched (except by that one binger). During downtime, we'd sit in our offices smoking cigarette after cigarette (to quell hunger) and talking for *hours* about who ate what, the calorie counts of our lunches, the latest dieting trends, who on staff looked heavy, who looked thin, what we'd love to weigh, and then, contrarily, how stupid it was to obsess about food and weight when there were so many other, more important things to talk about.

Weight was our world. We couldn't escape it. Even the

staffers with relatively healthy attitudes about food kept a close eye on the expanding and deflating asses on parade in the hallways. It was relentless, the fat talk. Just like home. The editors, my friends, were like a battalion of fatphobic mothers, but younger and better dressed.

Every six months or so, a news story would come across the transom ("heroin chic," for example) and accuse women's magazines of fostering an unhealthy ideal of beauty that no ordinary woman could hope to attain. Were we to blame for eating disorders and drug abuse? Was it our fault designers made clothes the average woman couldn't fit into? Had we created a cultural environment where 99 percent of women had some degree of dissatisfaction with their appearance?

To defend my occupation, I told people, "I don't see how you can go from a pretty picture in a magazine to a girl sticking her finger down her throat." I still believe that there are just too many steps between being born and wanting to kill yourself to lay the blame solely on the media. Editors could certainly attempt to widen the lens of what's considered beautiful. Even slightly. Instead of showing size two models exclusively, editors could shove a size four or six into a bathing-suit fashion spread. You know, in the back row or hiding behind a palm tree.

Speaking of models, six-foot-tall, pencil-thin blonds wandered through the hallways at *Mademoiselle* regularly. We always knew when the fashion department was holding auditions because the reception area filled with refugees from Planet Barbie.

Paradoxically, a particular model kept my body image from sinking all the way into oblivion. One myth that magazines *do* perpetuate is that any woman, given time on the treadmill, beauty treatments, and flattering clothes, can achieve model gorgeousness. I bought that myth completely and blamed myself for failing to come close. Then I met Cindy Crawford. I got to stare at her for two hours while interviewing her for a *Mademoiselle* cover story. She laughed, smiled, was serious, contemplative, bemused, skeptical. No matter her expression, Crawford was—is—unspeakably, dumbfoundingly, jaw-droppingly gorgeous. Otherworldly gorgeous. Not-of-this-species gorgeous. I could lose half my weight, exercise until my brain turned to muscle, and get total face and body plastic surgery, and I would never approach her degree of beauty. Meeting Cindy Crawford made a realist out of me. I stopped comparing myself to models and movie stars. But comparing myself unfavorably to my peers? Business as usual.

After two years at *Mademoiselle,* things took a nasty turn. Cooper started to feel extreme pressure from above to revitalize the magazine. If the layouts were found lacking, a human sacrifice was made in the art department. The fashion was stale? Good-bye, fashion director. An article fell flat? Sayonara, editor. Heads rolled with Henry VIII regularity. It seemed like a colleague quit (fled) or was fired every couple of weeks. When a pregnant editor packed up for maternity leave, vowing never to return, I realized I hadn't a friend left on staff. I should've been applying for other jobs, but my morale and confidence were snake-belly low. I thought I was untalented, useless, inept, but mainly way too fucking *fat* to get hired at another magazine.

M. moved me to the top of the human sacrifice list and

launched a campaign to get rid of me. She sabotaged my work, trashed me in meetings, scorned my frizzy-haired fat Jewishness. Little did she know that I was highly skilled in the art of taking it. My ability to withstand verbal punishment was heralded far and wide (see previous chapters, all of them). M. was tough, but she couldn't hold a candle to X., Y., and Z. Her harsh treatment had reduced other editors to shattered waifs who locked themselves in bathroom stalls to cry. It left me unscathed. Seemingly. Just as in junior high, I appeared unaffected on the outside, but a tempest roiled within. I cried plenty, believe me, in my apartment. At the office, I was dry eyed and stiff lipped.

I could only imagine how frustrating my apparent placidity must have been to M. She used every weapon she had—glaring at me savagely in the halls, writing cruel remarks on pieces I wrote, killing articles I'd edited—but she couldn't break me. The rest of the staff pitied me, but I think they envied my ability to stay cool under fire. Of course, I wasn't *really* cool. I hated M. with a white-hot volcanic fury. I knew her treatment was unfair, but on some level, I felt it was inevitable. I'd been afraid of getting fired since day one. I was, after all, the largest editor in the department. I had the least fashionable clothes, the frizziest hair. I didn't belong.

As it came to pass, I outlasted both M. and Cooper. The rumors finally came true. Cooper was out. The incoming editor, Gabé Doppelt, a South African sprite and a former fashion editor at *Vogue,* dispatched M. and, eventually, every other editor in the department—except me. To this day, I have no idea why Doppelt kept me around. In gratitude, I worked my ass off for her. She was stylish, smart, and funny—plus, she had that accent. I desperately wanted to please her. As per her vision, we turned Cooper's perky college-girl magazine into a grunge-era bible of cool. *Mademoiselle* was suddenly relevant. As the magazine's hot factor rose, so did my self-esteem. As I regained my confidence, I improved my skills, met new people, relaxed into the environment of acceptance and positive reinforcement.

Doppelt hired a few male editors. The Female Zone was suddenly co-ed. We worked long hours; we ate meals together daily, sometimes on weekends. Dieting, food, and weight talk were replaced with gabbing about bands, movies, the war in Yugoslavia, Russian brides, the burgeoning Internet. We lingered over lunches. We munched on brownies at meetings. Birthday party cakes were devoured. We ordered calorie-dense takeout dinners. I barely registered who ate what, or what I ate.

I started gaining—but it didn't appear to matter. At the new *Mademoiselle,* we were judged on our ideas, not our waist-to-hip ratio. It was a dizzying shift. I was happy, satisfied, engaged to be married. For a wedding gift, Doppelt bought Glenn and me way too many items off our registry, and she sent me an enormous bouquet of peonies that made the entire floor smell great. I felt valued and appreciated, which stimulated my appetite for work, praise—and cheeseburgers.

I'll always be grateful to Doppelt for rebuilding my eroded confidence. Unfortunately, she didn't last long at *Mademoiselle.* Like Cooper, she got a lot of pressure from above. Unlike Cooper, Doppelt refused to sacrifice her staff to save herself. After one year as editor, she quit.

Elizabeth Crow would take over leadership of the magazine. A lioness of a woman, Elizabeth was oversized in personality and stature. Under her leadership, *Mademoiselle* tripled in circulation and doubled its page count. With her bottomless energy, enthusiasm, and experience, Elizabeth turned her staff, including me, into worshipful followers of her vision. She believed that young American women were smart and creative, but they could still use a little help with the details of life. That was my operating directive for the seven years I worked with Elizabeth, the most gratifying years of my professional life. If Cooper concerned herself with style, and Doppelt cared about cool, Elizabeth focused on the heart and soul of her readers, and her staff.

My heart had been battered. My soul needed nurturing. Every day at work was like a spa treatment for the spirit. *Mademoiselle* was finally the dream job I'd always hoped it would be. During the Elizabeth years, I had two children, wrote five books, came of age.

I also gained forty pounds, which mitigated the happiness considerably.

8
REAL BUTTER

Diet junkies think of certain foods as "bad" and "evil," equating an inert lump of sugar, fat, and carbs with terrorists and murderers. Putting "cupcake" in the same category as "Osama bin Laden" is just wrong. Yet millions of women do it a dozen times a day. The negative associations with food override the pleasure one derives from eating it. Consider the innocent square of chocolate. A chronic dieter would behold said square and mentally veer from "love" to "loathe" in a nanosecond. If she were to pop it into her mouth, thoughts and feelings would careen around her brain at lightning speed: "Unh, yummy . . . sweet . . . rich . . . fattening . . . a second on the lips, a century on the hips . . . the guilt . . . the shame . . . I have no willpower . . . I suck . . ."

Eating, every bite, becomes an emotional conflict.

The psychological term for this ricochet of conflicted thought is "restrained eating." The phrase might sound benign, but it refers to an insidious tendency to agonize over every bite, even when these bites are coming in rapid succession, at dizzying speed, while standing in front of an open refrigerator. In fact, one might say that the agony over every mouthful fuels the craving for the next bite, and so it goes.

As well as being a chronic dieter, with appearance-checking behavior, I was also a restrained eater. In essence, I'd been eating anxiety for thirty years. Any doctor would tell you: That can't be good for the heart—or the soul.

My friend Nancy is a talented amateur chef. For one of our monthly dinner/card-game nights with two other friends, Nancy prepared an incredible meal of fresh pasta with home-made sauce, salad, and apple raspberry crumble. While we were eating, I asked her what made her sauce so delectable.

"I stew the tomatoes and paste with pork fat," said Nancy.

Pause to picture me, fork hovering just outside my mouth, the piece of pasta upon it suddenly sprouting devil horns and a tail.

Nancy watched me react. "Just eat it, Val," she said. "A little pork fat won't kill you."

Oh, I ate it, all right. Loving/loathing every savory bite. The apple crumble was superb, too. One of the other card players asked for Nancy's secret ingredients for this dish. "Real butter," said Nancy, looking at me, daring me to react. "And real sugar. Which won't kill you either, Val."

Ever the journalist, I decided to investigate Nancy's bold claim. According to the Department of Health, there was not a single incident of death by apple crumble in the United States in the last decade. A one-time use of pork fat in pasta sauce had not claimed the life of a single American citizen.

Nonetheless, in my never-ending pursuit of substituting chemical food product (my *especialité*) for real, whole food (Chef Nancy cuisine), I set out to reproduce Nancy's apple crumble using my own ingredients. I broke out the Smart Balance tub, the Splenda box, and the low-carb flour and baked. When the dessert came out of the oven, it smelled and looked pretty good. Not *as* good, of course, since Splenda doesn't melt crispy like real sugar, and Smart Balance spread doesn't caramelize the apples like real butter. I served it to the fam. My husband and daughters gave me dutiful applause. It was fine . . . but it didn't come close to Nancy's version.

A few months ago, I would have crowed about my accomplishment of replicating real food successfully. I would've felt proud to have sold myself and my family on a subpar dessert. But this "apple crumble" left a bad taste in my mouth. Was my dish really more virtuous and "good" than Nancy's? From a taste perspective, hell no. From an emotional perspective? I realized (aha moment, coming up) that using substitutes was not emotionally healthy. It perpetuated the negative thinking I was trying to break free of. Sugar was not an Osama bin Laden. Butter was not a Kim Jong-Il. I shouldn't be afraid of them.

To eat like an emotionally healthy person, I would have to separate food and fear. Butter shouldn't raise my internal terror alert to orange. I had to embrace it. Take a long luxurious swim in a bath of it. I resolved to associate food with pleasure only and ditch the anxiety.

It would be an adjustment. One forkful at a time. I could pinch myself whenever I thought of food in a negative way. I could break out my clicker (dear old friend!) and count how often I had fearful food thoughts. Instead, I went with a positive approach: to retrieve sense memories of eating for pleasure. Surely there had been a few times in my life when a meal had all the emotional flavor of real butter, whole milk, and raw sugar. Five meals sprang to mind . . .

1. I WAS TWENTY-FIVE YEARS OLD, recently dumped, recently fired, living in a dilapidated apartment in Park Slope, Brooklyn, with two other people. I was running out of money and desperate to find a job, and the manuscript for my first novel had been rejected by twelve publishers. I spent many afternoons sitting in the window, strumming my guitar, singing "Knocking on Heaven's Door" over and over again, watching the hooker who lived on the corner walk up and down the street in her spandex dress. The bright sun made the guitar feel warm in my hands. I played on.

Then the phone rang. It was my agent. The thirteenth publisher wanted to buy my book.

The world turned upside down. The future cracked open. I started shaking. My vision crystallized, and my crappy apartment suddenly looked like a palace. In the span of thirty seconds, I registered a seismic shift of the soul. No matter what was to come, for the rest of my life, I would be an author.

I called my parents first. My mother had always been a staunch supporter of my writing. When I was in second grade, I wrote a poem about love—on construction paper I'd cut into the shape of a heart—that she thought worthy of publication. Anyway, my parents were excited by the news.

Probably relieved, too. Mom gushed on the phone. Dad was almost too proud to speak. They might've been happier for me than I was for myself. Now that I'm a parent, I get that. I can't imagine the immeasurable joy I'll feel when Maggie's and Lucy's dreams come true.

My roommate Susanna soon came home from work, and I told her what happened. She knew how low I'd been lately, and the good news inspired her to scream and throw her arms around me. We jumped up and down together in the living room and then went to the supermarket. I spent almost all the cash I had left on groceries, cheap stuff, box pasta, jar sauce, seven-dollar bottle of red wine. We cooked an absurd amount of spaghetti and baked loaves of garlic bread, swilled the wine, ate until we nearly puked. We celebrated with food and drink, as people had since troglodytes dragged bleeding carcasses back to their caves. As I fell asleep/passed out later, I knew it had been a day, a night, and a meal I'd remember forever.

2. **TWO YEARS LATER, GLENN AND I WERE A COUPLE.** We'd been together for nearly a year, but we had yet to go out for a superfancy meal together. The opportunity arose when, as a reward for busting my ass on a big special project for *Mademoiselle,* my boss offered to pay for a dinner for two, anywhere in New York City. Bouley in Tribeca was, at the time, the most expensive and highest-rated restaurant in Manhattan. I called and made a reservation for the night of my twenty-seventh birthday.

It was a big night for us. We dressed up at his apartment on the Upper West Side. I borrowed a size six black velvet dress from his roommate. It was snug, but I was determined to wear it. I also wore patent pumps, black stockings, and a garter belt. The outfit looked great standing up. Seated, the dress dug into my waist and rode up my thighs, revealing my garter belt straps. I had to tug at the hem all night to keep from flashing my lingerie at anyone who glanced in our direction. In spite of my fidgeting, Glenn grinned at me bashfully as if I'd stepped off the pages of a Victoria's Secret catalog. He was treating our extravagant night out with such sincere gallantry, I was charmed, touched, reminded that in this relationship I could leave my cynicism at home and let myself adore and be adored.

We took in the country French decor, the low candlelight, the three waiters per table. I'd been to four-star restaurants with my parents, but this was a dating first. It felt like we were playing grown-up. When Glenn ordered a fifty-dollar bottle of wine (the second least expensive on the list) and the waiter said, "Excellent choice," we started laughing at the surreality of our being there at all.

As advised by a foodie friend, we ordered the prix-fixe menu, a sampling of twelve tiny courses. The waiters would descend on us with each course, depositing a gorgeous dish before us, explaining in exquisite detail how chef David Bouley had hand-selected this prawn, lovingly, artfully grilled it, whisked the ingredient-packed sauce, wept tears of pride while plating it. We were encouraged to try a certain wine with the fish, another with the beef. Just when we thought the sensory overload might blind and cripple us, we dug deep to make room for more deliciousness to come. The whole time—a four-hour meal—Glenn and I talked about us. How we met. How much fun we'd had so far. How well our lives meshed. Like the food, Glenn and I were comprised of distinct flavors that, when combined, were complementary and harmonic, as if Bouley himself had hand-selected us to blend together.

This was serious romance—rich, heady, and indulgent. By the first of three dessert courses, my dress was incredibly tight around the gut. I'd given up tugging down the hem, and my stocking tops were plainly visible. We were both pretty drunk, too, on our third bottle of wine. Glenn reached into his pocket and withdrew an oblong jewelry box. My first thought was that it had to be a watch. I'd asked for one, after all. He handed it to me and said, "Happy birthday."

I opened the box. Not a watch. In the center of the velvet pillow sat a diamond ring. Underneath that, a label strip with the typed words: "If you've got the time, I've got the years. Marry me, Val."

The honest truth was that I'd kind of seen the proposal coming. There'd been a lot of buildup to this night, a month of anticipation. But even if I'd expected a proposal, I hadn't prepared for it. The waiters hovered nearby. The couples on either side of us were watching. I tried on the ring, which was way too small, and felt touched that Glenn thought my fingers were that bony and delicate.

Glenn was a true romantic, a sap, the kind of guy who wanted everything to be perfect. When we left the restaurant, the last truffle consumed, the huge bill paid with a corporate card, he surprised me again. He announced that he'd taken a room at the Empire Hotel, and his roommate had dropped off overnight bags for us, now waiting in the coat room. Along with clothes and toiletries, Glenn had packed a CD of Frank Sinatra love songs to play in our room on our engagement night.

We stumbled onto the street. The streetlights, once flat and white, now glowed golden. The formerly dirty, dark street had turned slick, shiny, glimmering. Glenn kept a protective arm around his drunk, high-heeled, excruciatingly tight-dressed fiancée while he hailed a taxi. As out-of-body happy as I was, I also felt dangerously overstuffed. I feared the dress would burst open. But I didn't care. My *life* had just burst open, in a dizzying array of flavors. And I knew that our engagement meal had been a sample, just a taste, of the wonders of our life yet to come.

3. GLENN AND I TOOK A TRIP TO NEW ORLEANS with my sister and her husband, Dan, for our fifth anniversary, their tenth. New Orleans was once, will be again, the ultimate destination for authentic American cuisine. Accordingly, Glenn and I planned to eat our way across town, gumbo to beignet, from sunup to sundown. I was six months pregnant with Lucy and in free-for-all eating mode. Add to that the indulge-yourself vacation vibe, plus the ninety-degree heat that made it nearly impossible to do anything *but* go to restaurants.

The highlight of that trip was dinner at Emeril's flagship restaurant in the French Quarter. Emeril Lagasse was, at the time, the most famous chef in America. I couldn't believe our luck, getting a reservation only a few weeks in advance. How I anticipated this meal! I'd sink into a cream-and-cayenne trance, daydreaming about it. The food itself definitely lived

up to the hype. Course after course of revelatory flavor, unlike anything in New York. We each ordered an appetizer,
entrée, and dessert and passed our plates around the table so
we could sample everything. Two memorable dishes blew
my socks off. The oyster stew was so flavorful and spicy, every spoonful was an explosion on the tongue. Also, at that
meal, I had my very first chocolate soufflé. We'd had to pre-
order because the dessert took an hour to prepare. When the
waiter brought it to our table, he poured hot chocolate sauce
into its pillowed heart. Dazzled the senses. I nearly cried
when I had my first bite.

The wine flowed like water. So did the conversation. Although Alison and I had mutual friends in college (she was
two years ahead of me at Dartmouth), we weren't friends
ourselves, per se. Yes, yes, we love each other, best friends for
life and all that, but the two of us were just too different
growing up to be buddies. Let me put it this way: Alison was
a straitlaced, straight-A type. She was a selective dater,
drug-averse, an upstanding citizen. We all know what I was.
Alison deplored many of my adventurous life choices over
the years. In high school, she ratted me out about cigarettes
in my purse, a stash box under the bed, a six-pack of Meisterbräu in the bushes. I'd been with scores of men in half a
dozen countries. Alison had had only one serious boyfriend.
And, reader, she married him! Archetypically, we fit the
models of responsible, superachiever firstborn and rebellious,
free-spirit secondborn. We had little in common, except for
growing up in the same house, going to the same college,
and having issues with Mom. Place meant nothing, though.
We might as well have been living on different planets, given

the widely disparate experiences we had at home and school.

Despite our day/night personalities, somehow Alison and I had wound up in the same stage of life. Since I'd gotten married and had Maggie (and was about to have Lucy), Alison and I had more to talk about. She and Dan had two daughters. We were both journalists and worked at magazines. During that meal, I felt like Alison and I had a "friend" breakthrough. She wasn't my protective, disapproving older sister at Emeril's. At thirty-three and thirty-four, we were finally about to relate to each other as peers, pals who'd chosen to travel together. Seeing Alison as an equal that night was a giant step forward in terms of how I saw myself. I was a fully fledged person now. A mother and wife, a responsible, upstanding citizen, just like her. My druggie slutty life was behind me, and that meal closed the door on it.

4. I WAS THIRTY-EIGHT, AND MADLY IN LOVE. Glenn had died two and a half years before, in November 2000. Ten months later, in August 2001, I met Steve and, in short order, fell in love again. In the spring of 2003, we were still in the infatuation period, thrilling at each other's slightest touch. We took every opportunity to indulge ourselves in each other, and that often included food. One early afternoon, I received the news that one of my novels had been optioned by a famous actress to be the source material for a Hollywood movie. Steve and I made the spontaneous decision to celebrate over lunch at the Oyster Bar in Grand Central Station in Manhattan. The kids were at school until three. Considering travel time, we would have one hour to eat.

We sat at the raw bar, reserved for diners who wanted their lunch served on the half shell on a bed of ice. Steve and I started by ordering two dozen oysters, as well as beers. We were in our own world, sliding the pliant glistening meat onto our tongues, staring into each other's eyes, licking lips, etc. If I were a crotchety prude seated nearby and had to watch a thirty-eight-year-old woman and a forty-nine-year-old man feeding each other oysters in a frankly sexual manner, I'd have thrown down my tiny fork and stormed out of there disgusted. We continued to be disgusting for another dozen oysters, another round of beer. Then we took the train back to Brooklyn to pick up the kids at school.

That lunch—escaping into the city to delight our senses, to visit our private universe of two, and then contentedly return to reality—was emblematic of the thrill of Steve, of the salty sea change he'd brought. My existence as a widowed mother had been lonely, sad, bleak, joyless. Steve rode in and turned my life into a fun, passionate adventure—during off-parenting hours. On-parenting hours, he was great with the kids, making them fall in love with him, too. Steve made me happy again. The movie option? It was a fantastic validation of my work, but an emotional blip compared to the incomparable joy and relief that my heart hadn't stopped beating when Glenn's had. My life with Steve was only just beginning.

5. A YEAR LATER, STEVE AND I GOT MARRIED. We threw a clambake at my parents' farmhouse in Thetford, Vermont. The ceremony itself was lovely. Steve and my dad played a duet of "Aura Lee" (aka "Love Me Tender") on their French horns. Our siblings and friends made funny and tear-jerking

speeches for us. The girls and I wore white. We stood together, as if Steve were marrying all three of us.

Indeed, Maggie had been responsible for our setting the
date for the wedding. We'd been quasi-engaged for a while
already, and then one morning, Maggie asked Steve, "When
are you going to buy Mom the engagement ring you promised her?" Hand to God, I did not put her up to it. The four
of us went to a jewelry store that afternoon after school.

Steve had said before that, had it not been for the girls,
we probably never would have married. Both of us being
middle-aged, we'd decided not to have children together.
We had separate finances, and planned to keep it that way.
There hadn't been any real reason to marry, except the girls
wanted to make it legal. Maggie, eight at the time, was firm
on this point. It wasn't enough that her mom had a boyfriend. She didn't want a stepboyfriend. She wanted a step*father.* Truth be told, I wasn't satisfied with "boyfriend," either.
I wanted "husband."

Second weddings are traditionally small. Ours was only
sixty people. The vows exchanged, the license signed, the
sun came out from behind a cloud (true), and the festivities
continued with a spread of honest food. Lobsters, barbecued
chicken and ribs, baked potatoes, corn on the cob, biscuits.
We'd spent a lot of time in Maine with Steve's family by
then, and my daughters had cracked quite a few claws. At the
wedding, Maggie, nine, and Lucy, six, tucked into lobster
after lobster like seasoned pros. Maggie must have eaten four
whole lobsters that day. Lucy drank straight from the little
cups of melted butter. At one point, she accidentally spilled
some on her white dress. My parents' golden retriever, Jake,

volunteered to help her clean up. One of my favorite wedding pictures is of Lucy standing with her arms at her sides, looking down at Jake licking the golden stain on her dress, his tail a blur. Talk about the joy of real butter; we can learn a lot from our animal friends. Both girls flitted from guest to guest, acting as hostesses, reveling in the attention. Lucy made a speech about how her first father died and, as sad as that had been, now we had Steve, who made us a whole family again. Let me tell you, when a six-year-old grabs the microphone and talks philosophically about death and rebirth, you won't find a dry eye in the house.

As much as that day was about Steve and me, it was about the girls. Despite the hardship they'd already faced in their young lives, they were happy, healthy, socially adept, insightful, wonderful kids. They hadn't been damaged permanently, as I'd feared. On the contrary. They'd rallied, recovered, and recognized our incredible luck when we saw it in Steve.

Looking over this list of meals and memories, it seemed obvious that positive thoughts about food were connected to love and success. Positive thoughts about *life* were connected to love and success. If A equaled C, and B equaled C, then A and B had to be the same.

Food was life.

And all along, I thought food was the Grim Reaper.

Nancy was right. Real ingredients won't kill me. On the contrary, real butter, and real happiness, will only make me stronger.

I called her. "Butter is my friend," I announced. I filled her in on my thought process.

"So you'll throw out the Smart Balance and Splenda?" Nancy asked.

I wasn't willing to go *that* far. "When I cook and bake, I'll use the real thing. With coffee, a little Splenda won't kill me, either."

"Moderation," she said. "A novel concept. Sounds reasonable."

Indeed, as the weeks ticked by, "reasonable" was overriding "irrational" as the mental operating system of choice.

9

THE ALL-CONSUMING STORY OF STEVE

Steve and I began our love affair as disembodied entities, fantasies constructed in part by imagination, and fleshed out with hopes, dreams, biographical details, and the mysterious spaces between typed words. In other words, we met online.

I'd started visiting dating sites after about six months of single motherhood. I was curious about what was out there. I needed to feel hope. I agreed with my family and friends that I wasn't quite "ready" for a serious relationship. But I was definitely ready—*beyond* ready—to have sex. My friend Judith told me early on in my widowhood that she'd read it was common for the grieving spouse to use sex as a life-affirming act, an antidote to the ill effects of months mired in disease. I was desperate for some relief from my grief, and I decided sex was just the ticket. It'd been a reliable distraction—if temporary—in the past. I found myself fantasizing wildly about a few men I knew. When I wasn't dealing with reality—cooking, cleaning, schlepping, digging out from under the avalanche of death-related paperwork—I would lie on my bed and watch XXX-rated movies of the mind, all starring me (thinner) and a fantasy lover.

Fantasy might have been a subconscious protective buffer. I could have used those hours to think about my lonely life and replay horrible scenes from the year before. I decided my brain knew what it was doing. I let it go into the nooks, crannies, and orifices it wanted to go into.

In terms of real sex, I halfheartedly tried to seduce a cute single colleague of Glenn's. I'd always thought he was sexy. This man was responsive to my flirty e-mails at first, but when I suggested we meet for lunch, he freaked out and stopped answering my messages. Poor bastard. I can only imagine how I seemed to him, a desperate, horny widow. Well, I was! I'm not ashamed to admit the truth. I defy anyone who hasn't been a thirty-five-year-old widow to judge. It'd been quite a while since I'd had sex. My weight was at a seven-year low. Although my husband was dead, my libido was very much alive.

I told a friend that when I got back into action, I would screw a different guy every month for a year. After that time, depending on how I liked the variety, I'd either keep going or look for a man with relationship potential.

With that goal in mind, I went on several dates—one fix-up, mostly guys I met online. I could barely stand to have lunch with them, let alone give them blowjobs. I had an almost erotic encounter with (this is so pathetically predictable) a trainer at my gym. He came over to give me a free massage. Afterward, we shared a joint. He was young and sexy. I was stoned and naked under a towel. It was one of the least erotic evenings of my life. I felt nothing. Not the slightest twinge. He was as shocked as I was when I said I had an early morning. He folded his massage table, grabbed his bag of oils, and left. Through neighborhood gossip, I heard that he'd hooked up with another single-mother gym-goer and wound up having an exclusive relationship with her that lasted over a year.

Undeterred by my conflicting impulses (lurid fantasy life, frigid social life), I pressed on with the online search for a lover. I came across Steve's profile, the title of which was "This Ad Is Not Stupid!" Funny. I read his entry and laughed a couple of times at his witty remarks. I sent him an e-mail. He sent one back. We continued to exchange notes and pictures for two months before actually meeting (logistical difficulties; we took turns being out of town or unavailable). Our first date was in August 2001, at a dive bar on Lispenard Street, which, a month later, was deep in the red zone.

With the exception of our e-mailing and first three dates, our entire relationship has been post-9/11. I wonder if that's been relevant, in terms of our instant, intense attachment. You hear a lot about the glut of post-9/11 babies. Sex *is* life-affirming in the wake of tragedy. Maybe I needed double the life-affirmation. And Steve was the man for the job. From our second date on, Steve and I behaved like fornicating bunnies. When the kids were at my in-laws' for the weekend, Steve and I would have forty-eight-hour fuck fests; we'd get out of bed only to use the bathroom or eat sexy food (think succulent, juicy, firm).

I was a size ten. If not thin, I was in great shape, running three or four times a week. I assumed Steve was the kind of guy who loved ample women. He complimented me constantly and made me feel beautiful, irresistible. Everyone could see how happy I was, including the girls. I'd kept them in the loop, told them that I was seeing someone, a musician/opera singer/actor, and that we had afternoon dates when they were at school. I showed them Steve's headshot at his opera company's Web site. Eventually, Steve came over for dinner to meet Maggie and Lucy, then six and three. Shortly after that, I took the girls—and my parents, and Alison and her family—to Carnegie Hall to see Steve star as Ko-Ko in a production of *The Mikado*. When he took his bows onstage, he squinted to locate us in our front row seats and waved at Maggie and Lucy. Steve started sleeping over at our apartment. We introduced each other to our friends. Our sex turned into more-than-sex. I already knew that my plan of sleeping with a guy a month for a year was not going to happen. I laughed with my friends about how the first guy I slept with after Glenn might be the last guy I have sex with ever again. Around our six-month anniversary, Steve and I talked about getting married. We were lazily stroking each other, in a state of physical and emotional bliss.

"I adore every inch of your body," he said. "And it'd be even better if you could get rid of the stomach."

Sound of a needle scratching across a record. That was what I heard in my head when he brought up my bane, my stomach flab. For six months, he'd made me feel like the most beautiful woman alive. I'd had a six-month period of not worrying or caring about my body flaws—because of the way he'd treated me. The subconscious shelf I'd put my bad body image up on came crashing down. All my old fat fears were now scattered across the bed between us. In a rush, I mentally scanned the photos he'd shown me of his ex-girlfriends, dancers and actresses, all of them slim. I was instantly convinced he'd lied about every nice thing he'd ever said to me, that he'd been faking his passion for me. Covering myself, I was too shocked to speak, cry, or defend myself. I was naked, in every way you can be naked.

When I told friends, they were horrified. Rebecca said, "He wants you to lose weight? Tell him to grow a few inches."

In the following weeks, I strived to take his request at face value. Hadn't he proved he loved me and desired me a hundred times over? If I'd had a complaint about his body, didn't I have a right to mention it to him? He hadn't meant to insult me. He didn't know about my complicated issues with body image. One of the things I'd loved most about our relationship was the here-and-now-ness of it. We'd dutifully talked about our childhood (pets, camps, siblings) and old relationships, but we'd skipped deep discussion about our emotional histories of angst, insecurity, and (in his case) depression. I'd wanted to reinvent myself for Steve, and I was not going to dust off the ancient stories about how mean Mom used to be or what a loser I was in junior high. I remembered telling my friends what a relief it'd been, not having to dredge up the past. The mature woman Steve knew was strong, sexy, and secure. Little did he know that when it came to fat, I was a whimpering, quivering infant.

Remembering that night, I can smell my own fear of losing him. No matter how hard you try to ignore your issues, they will creep out of dark corners when goaded by the slightest provocation.

I kicked into "on" diet mode, like the veteran I was. Steve had never seen me on a full-scale diet. He was impressed by my perfectionism, the intensity of my commitment. He thought I was doing it for him. I thought I was, too, and I was motivated by wanting to please him. I started running longer distances, eventually working up to a half marathon of thirteen miles (a feat I have yet to repeat). I stopped eating carbs *completely* (not a mild Zone but full-blown Atkins). After several months of pure perfection, at the age of thirty-seven, I was back to my twenty-three-year-old weight. Size eight jeans were roomy on me. I could fit into the size six backless dress I wore the night I met Glenn. I tried on the dress one night for Steve, amazed I could get into it. I twirled for him. He applauded. I was showing (myself) off, and he was duly appreciative. As well he should've been.

Predictably, the compliments came rolling in. Losing weight—this time, about twenty pounds—was a magnet for public commentary. At school drop-off, mothers said, "You've melted!" and "How'd you get so skinny?" At one of the interminable parent potluck dinners, a father I barely knew came up to me and said, "Wow, you've lost a ton of weight." He turned to his wife. "Doesn't she look great?" His wife was not so impressed. Nor was I by the left-handed compliment. I smiled contemptuously at the idiot husband, and apologetically at the jealous wife. Still, I did walk away with a lightness in my step.

As if I were in a tunnel, I heard the echoes from my sixth-grade teacher and the mothers of Short Hills. The rush of public acclaim for having made less of myself felt exactly the same at thirty-eight as it had at eleven. I was a mother myself now, and as hungry for approval as the needy child I used to be. I'd survived high school, gone to college, seduced scores of men, written a dozen books, made money, bought an apartment, married, had kids, been widowed, but I hadn't really changed at all. Not about this.

And what of Steve? Did my half-marathoner body make him love me more? Make love to me with deeper ardor? Were his kisses extratender, or his whispers sweeter? Not at all. He said he enjoyed my pride in myself. On an aesthetic level, he liked the slimmer silhouette. But he withheld the ultimate reward, what I longed to hear: that he knew I'd scraped and sacrificed *for him,* and he appreciated my hard work. It's sick, I realize, but I desperately wanted him to be pleased that he'd made me suffer.

I owned up to none of these thoughts and feelings. Instead, I pranced around in a lot of lingerie and/or sweaty running shorts and waited for something about our relationship to change as dramatically as my waistline. I might as well have been waiting for the second coming of Christ. By my lights, Steve and I were stalled. I'd done my part. So where was the rush of . . . actually, I don't know *what* big change I was expecting. He continued to ravish me nightly. He professed his love as before. Our home life followed the usual routine. Our professional lives proceeded apace. That was the problem. Steve acted as if nothing important had changed.

My frustration with him was a major cause, but it was inevitable that I'd relax my standards. I started to skip runs on the flimsiest excuse. I became reacquainted with breadstuffs.

I cycled into a new (but, really, so very old) dieting pattern of off-and-on. Whenever Steve went on tour with his opera company, I'd diet frantically, hoping to wow him with a hot bod upon his return. That plan was inherently flawed. Lonely nights were my undoing. When he came home, I'd prepare elaborate meals for us to linger over. I'd blow off the gym to loll in bed with him in the mornings, then simmer all afternoon in silent guilt. Resentment surfaced. Often, I'd willfully eat the kids' junk food in his presence, practically daring him to say something.

In three months, I'd re-gained the twenty pounds I'd lost. Dieter's whiplash. One day I was thin. The next day, my new size-eight wardrobe was suffocatingly tight. Along the way, I complained about the rapid re-gain with Alison. "It's Mom all over again," she said. "You're rebelling."

I didn't completely agree. Mom had tormented me daily. Steve had said, just once, that he'd like to see me without the belly. I had reason to be hurt by Steve's request, but no reason to be spiteful.

"I don't mean you're rebelling against Steve," said Alison. "You're still rebelling against Mom."

Okay, that rang true. Unwittingly, Steve churned up the old toxic dust. He didn't deserve to be punished for his simple request, one that any spouse, male or female, had the right to make. Steve had been only loving to me. He cleaned my apartment, did my laundry, kept me company, made love to me. He'd taken on a widow with two small kids, and saved us all. If he asked me (on gentle wings) to tighten my gut, so what? If that was the worst he could dish out, I should be grateful.

Instead, I'd tried to win his approval by losing weight, just as I had in elementary school with Mom. Then I rebelled against his wishes, just as I had in high school with Mom. Throw in a little "gain weight to test the love" action, as I'd done with Glenn. Would I gain a full forty pounds to test Steve's love?

I asked myself, "Does anything about this have to do with Steve?" It took the better part of a year to get from the night of the belly comment to facing the real issues of our relationship. Yes, Steve had brought joy back into our lives. He was a heck of a lot of fun, a positive influence for the kids. But. Steve was a middle-aged never-married actor who traveled a lot. Would he be the father the girls deserved? Could I be sure he was truly committed to such a huge responsibility? It was entirely possible, once our infatuation wore off, he'd think twice about the life I offered him. Just how devastating would it be for Maggie and Lucy if Steve decided to leave?

I'd spent five months obsessed with an all-consuming diet, and the following three months depressed about falling off the Atkins wagon. Twenty pounds were lost and re-gained. I'd made no progress answering the important questions about our relationship. It was the same old drill, running to stand still.

You know what happened. Maggie pressed the point, demanded that we set a wedding date. Steve and I planned the ceremony and party as a team, which gave me confidence about his commitment. We got married and made everyone cry. I wore a size-ten Nicole Miller dress, sleeveless (although I was anxious about my arms). *The New York Times* covered the wedding for the Sunday Styles section Vows column, and it was exciting to see our photo in the paper and to read the accompanying article. The piece was sweet, sentimental. The reporter hit the right notes. Of course, she didn't mention the parallel story of my weight and how it moved up and down as our relationship evolved.

We'd been married for three years. Our sex life was still wonderful, but it wasn't what it used to be. We'd sometimes go a week without doing it. My friends assured me that this was hardly a cause for concern. But if Steve didn't roll toward me when the lights went out, my immediate thought was "He doesn't want me. He thinks I'm fat." That stomach comment just wouldn't die in my mind. Apparently, some negative thoughts weren't easily controlled. To vanquish it, I'd have to talk to Steve about it. Which I planned to do.

But first, I had a bigger item on the agenda.

10

THE MOTHER LOAD, PART TWO

The Frankels were a family of talkers. Steve thought we were a family of yellers (his family is practically mute by comparison). We scrapped for the last word, used volume like a tool. We repeated, rehashed, diced, and sliced language down to the syllable—was it any wonder Alison and I were both writers? We could talk until blue-faced about nearly any subject, be it politics, movies, books, gossip, philosophy, gardening. When we watched a movie or TV show together, non-Frankels tore their hair out because we talked incessantly over it. Steve refused to watch movies with my family. Can't say I blame him.

I'd probably exchanged more words with my mother than with any other person on earth, many of them swapped at the kitchen table, newspapers strewn around coffee mugs. For all our yakking, however, Mom and I avoided certain subjects, running an obstacle course of conversation to do so. My teenage years. Her obsessive fatphobia. My current weight.

"Why bother bringing it up?" I said to myself. "Judy and I are fine now." There was no point in dragging our skeletons into the light.

Until now. Dragging skeletons into the light had become my day job.

I'd been channeling a lot of old anger into sweaty sessions on the treadmill for six months since I began emotional housecleaning. I'd lost weight, firmed up. A neighborhood friend noticed the change and asked me what my goals were. Ten pounds, fifteen? I shook my head. "My goals are emotional," I said. I hadn't weighed myself since the summer. I hadn't been dieting. No carb was off-limits. The world of food was a cornucopia of availability. I'd eat when hungry, stop when full, sample to satisfy a craving, but I hadn't pigged out on sweets or chips, evidentiary proof that I wanted only what I told myself I shouldn't have.

The Not Diet was working. I was on an even keel with food and exercise. My skips down memory lane had been helping, too. Emotional excavation was painful while it was happening, but a relief afterward. Nonetheless, as the holidays approached, a laziness came over me, like a warm comforter that made it hard to get out of bed. I started to slack off, skipping the gym, waving the banner of not-dieting too often and eating past the point of full for the sake of it. I felt the coming of a low-grade depression, a malaise. I slogged through the last-minute holiday shopping and travel planning. We were going first to Maine to Steve's family and then to Vermont to my parents' farmhouse. I was grouchy about spending hours in the car, the abundance of family, the kids on a nonstop sugar train, the pressure of gift giving. My mood was dark.

What better time for a decades-delayed emotional confrontation?

A few days after Christmas, I got my chance. Alison and her family had left Vermont to return to Long Island. We were leaving for Brooklyn the next day. The kids and Steve were playing outside in the snow. My parents and I were at the kitchen table (where else?) with the newspaper and coffee.

Mom was talking about her volunteer work at pediatric hospitals with her golden retrievers. One cancer kid asked her why she loved dogs so much. "I explained to him that when I was a little girl I was left alone a lot, and my best friend was my German shepherd, Duchess," she said. Mom went on about how Duchess was her confidante. Duchess adored her. When her family ignored her or made her feel worthless, she had her dog to love.

I said, "Did you then tell the cancer kid that when you grew up and had a daughter of your own, you, in turn, made her feel worthless?"

Whoosh. Every window in the house was closed tight, but we all felt the malevolent wind blow through.

Mom braced against the table. "Okay," she said. "We're going to do this now? Let's go." Judy knew I was writing a memoir about body image. I'd already interviewed her about Fay, her mother. She must've suspected this confrontation was coming.

I pointed at a recent photo of Lucy taped to the refrigerator. "Look at her," I said. "That's how old I was when you started in on me. If I snatched a cookie out of Lucy's hand, said she was too fat and wasn't allowed to have cookies again, she'd be crushed. The only thing she'd understand was that I was angry, that she'd done something terrible."

"You ate twice as much as Alison and Jon," said Mom. "You were always asking for food. When you were eight, our pediatrician told us we were going to have to keep a close eye on your weight."

"Did the pediatrician tell you to humiliate me, and yell at me, and punish me for eating? Did he tell you to cry and scream if I ate too much?"

"You were incredibly frustrating," said Mom. "I tried to control you, but you kept eating."

"Did it occur to you that making threats wasn't the best strategy?"

"If I didn't yell, you'd eat *more*," she said. "I'd get more frustrated, and I'd yell more. It's not like I was the only mother who did it. We all did it." She rattled off a few names, moms from New Jersey I'd known my whole life. Among their daughters, I counted an anorexic, a bulimic, a binge eater, and a morbidly obese woman. "We talked about it a lot," said Mom. "We all felt the same way. We didn't want overweight kids."

"So you were all fatphobic," I said. "That doesn't make it right."

Howie jumped in. "We were concerned that you'd grow up to be obese."

"Why would you think that?" I asked. "You're a doctor. You had to know that obesity is mainly genetic. We don't have obesity on either side of the family."

"Look at it from our perspective," he said. "We had three kids. Two of them were skinny, one of them tended to be chubby. We didn't want you to get fat, so we tried to control you. In retrospect, it worked out okay. We kept at you, and your weight stayed in a reasonable range."

"But that wasn't the only thing that mattered. What about my sense of security?" I asked. "You can't believe shrieking at a little kid about every bite of food is good for her."

He said, "I don't remember that."

Why would he? He was a young doctor, working sixty and seventy hours per week. When he was home, late at night and on some weekends, Judy reined it in. She tended to be most explosive when overwhelmed by the demands of daily life. Those demands were lessened when Dad was home to help.

"Just admit that it wasn't about health or fear for my future obesity," I said. "You didn't want a fat kid because she'd be a bad reflection on you."

Dad said, "A lot of time has gone by. I just don't remember. Your weight was just one small part of my life back then."

True. But for Mom, alas, my weight was her number-one concern. I said to her, "I know you remember, Judy. The relentlessness."

"Relentlessness is a part of my personality," she said. "And I admit one hundred percent that it was about aesthetics for me. I was not concerned about your health. I wanted you to be slim because I don't like fat. That's just who I am. It's cultural, part of my own family history growing up. My mother was relentless about my brother's weight. Until the day she died, she was on him about it."

"If you hated her so much, why were you just like her?" I asked.

"When I got frustrated, I couldn't control myself," said

Judy. "You can hate something about the way you were raised and still wind up repeating the mistakes. Yes, I yelled. I screamed. I was not going to give up, and I never got tired of trying to get you to lose weight. I understand you have issues about it and that things are handled differently now. But I did what I felt I had to do."

I knew Judy would never apologize. When I tried therapy in my early twenties, my shrink said these magical words to me: "Your mother is not going to change. You can either fight her to the death, or accept her for who she is and just deal with it." That sentiment was one of my main excuses for not confronting Judy. And now, I was wondering if I should have bothered. What satisfaction was there to be gained, if she refused to admit she'd been wrong?

"Why do you refuse to say it was wrong to terrorize an eleven-year-old?" I asked.

"It wasn't ideal," she said. "But if I could go back, I don't think I'd act differently."

"You made yourself my enemy. You turned my weight into a battle of wills," I said. "It felt like you were trying to break me. To squash my spirit."

"I just wanted you to lose ten pounds!" said Judy. "If you'd've done what I wanted, we wouldn't be having this conversation."

A lifetime of baggage over ten fucking pounds.

"Your love felt conditional," I said. "I questioned whether you cared about me. Whether you even liked me, unless I was thin."

"I wanted you to be thin—I fought for it—*because* I loved you," she said.

I'd run out of questions. I wouldn't get the answers I wanted anyway. I got up from the table, packed the kids and duffels into the car, and we left for Brooklyn within the hour. Dad called the next day and said Mom was upset. She cried all night about how I'd accused her of being a bad mother. I told him that I refused to apologize to her, that she should apologize to me. I had every right to be angry. He said solemnly, "I want you to apologize anyway."

What could I do? I called back in an hour and apologized.

11

THE NAKED TRUTH

I want to pose nude," I told Paula, my editor at *Self* magazine.

We were at lunch. I told her about my vow to rid myself of my fat obsession. I explained that I'd been striving to lay myself bare, strip away the past, cast my body image in a new light. I'd been so focused on the problem areas, I said, I'd lost sight of the big picture. Now, I wanted to see it—see myself, for exactly what I was. The only way to confront reality was to pose naked. Artsy nude. Not beaver shots or flying boobs. Think tasteful, flirty. I had the name of a photographer, Koren Reyes, who specialized in nude portraits of women over forty. I'd do the shoot, then write about the experience in an essay for *Self.*

Paula loved the idea. But . . . "We can't publish the article without running the pictures, too."

I was afraid she'd say that. Hesitantly, I nodded.

Before calling the photographer, I had to psych myself up for months. When I finally made contact, Koren described her philosophy. "Women over forty don't get as much appreciation as they should," she said. "Women of all ages, shapes, and sizes are beautiful."

Yes, well, *of course.* "Have you ever photographed an exceedingly large woman?" I asked.

"I worked with someone who weighed well over two hundred pounds. The pictures turned out great," she said.

That was reassuring. If she could make a plus-size woman look good, perhaps she could make me look like Heidi Klum. "I'm seeing this experience as a final step down the long, long—*really* long—road to self-acceptance," I said.

Koren refused to promise everlasting serenity or to vanquish my demons. She was willing to say this, however: "Everyone I've worked with has had a positive experience." I almost asked for that in writing. We set a date for six weeks hence.

The upcoming shoot loomed on the surface of my consciousness, if abstractly. When I told people of my plans, they thought I was "crazy" or "brave," which I took to be mildly insulting. Nancy made me laugh myself sick one night, demonstrating (dressed) potential poses such as "the Frog," "Rex at the Hydrant," and "Dropped the Soap." The future shoot was a punch line, a lark. And seemingly far, far away. Until it was suddenly right upon me.

A week prior, Koren sent a confirmation e-mail. She'd rented a space, hired a makeup artist and an assistant. I gulped hard when I read the e-mail. The shoot *wasn't* abstract or a lark. It was real and serious—and too late to back out. I was horrified that other people would be there, watching.

I did my level best to make myself presentable on the day

before the shoot. I depilated my legs, arms, belly, chin, lip, eyebrows, and armpits. Should the photos ever be examined under a microscope, not a single unwanted hair would be found. Going for a natural look, I removed toe and fingernail polish. I exfoliated and moisturized. Twice.

Smooth and pink, I arrived at the studio on time, at nine in the morning. I'd skipped breakfast, hoping that would make me appear ten pounds slimmer. Maggie, the assistant, a photographer herself with many artist friends, told me she'd posed nude countless times. "Full body, topless, alone or in groups," she said as if it were nothing. I figured if Maggie, curvy and redheaded, could do it, so could I.

Yuko, the rail-thin hair and makeup artist, was soft-spoken and sweet. She intended to do wonders with my head. Of course, that would still leave a significant amount of flesh unattended.

Koren arrived a few minutes later. Trim and stylish, she gave the immediate impression of professional competence. We talked about poses. I tried to seem cool and comfortable, but inside, I was churning.

When Yuko was done with me, I dashed into the bathroom, stripped, and put on a bathrobe. I returned to the studio, a cavernous space with umbrella lights. A roll of white paper—a "seamless"—was pulled down one wall and across the floor. I started to sweat even though the room was cold. Koren, camera in hand, directed me onto the seamless. Maggie tested the lighting. Then Koren said, "Lose the robe."

This was virgin territory. I had been nude in the presence of women only in fitting and locker rooms. I love locker rooms for showcasing the incredible diversity of the female form. But one didn't linger there. I'd never been fully, flagrantly naked for longer than five minutes in sight of other females. Now, I would be starkers in front of three, for hours.

I took a deep breath, paused, and shrugged off my robe. I wasn't expecting applause, but something other than dead silence would've been nice. When I disrobed for men—especially for the first time—they always said *something* complimentary, even if out of sheer politeness. These women, on the other hand, stared quietly at my nudity. Not stared at—*studied*. They examined me like a specimen, seeing what they had to work with. I nearly said, "Hello! Naked person here! A kind word needed!"

I remembered the *Brady Bunch* adage, "When you're nervous, imagine the audience in their underwear." Perhaps not the best idea, given the situation. Instead, I imagined *myself* in my underwear.

Koren said, "Okay, sit down facing me, cross your legs at the ankle, and fold your arms over your knees."

And, just like my clothes, we were off. While I arranged myself into position, I twisted mentally, too. The lack of flattery bothered me. Then again, convincing me of my attractiveness was not Koren's job. That was *my* job, one I'd failed at chronically.

Concentrating on Koren's directions ("drop the shoulders," "chin down") helped me forget the terror. Yuko and Maggie watched from behind her. Smiley Yuko nodded encouragingly and said, "Beautiful!" over and over again, which I dearly appreciated. Maggie's technical, terse "good" and "nice" commentary also soothed. When I started to loosen up, Koren asked more of me. "You're a *Playboy* model!" she said. "Act like you're caught coming out of the shower!" And "Pout for me." I must have looked like a deranged porn star, because Koren said, "Not like that! On second thought, don't pout. Ever." That made me laugh hard and resulted in, I later saw, some of the day's brightest smiles.

Since we were all working toward the common goal—pretty pictures—nudity started to feel productive and purposeful (as opposed to exposed and vulnerable). The awkwardness of being undressed with women also diminished. Unlike my usual frame of reference, this nudity was decidedly nonsexual. I was reminded of the one time, on Martha's Vineyard, I went to a nude beach and nakedness was free, natural—fun.

I posed sitting, standing, kneeling, lying on my belly and back. Modeling was hard work. Poses that might appear natural were anything but. As I struggled to do what Koren asked, I occasionally paused to think, "I can't believe I'm flat on my back with my tits hanging out *in public.*"

Koren seemed pleased by what she was getting. And, as the day progressed, I became convinced pulchritude was possible. For one pose, Yuko arranged my hair to curl over my shoulder. When I rested my cheek on my knee, strands swept across my back. It felt good; I smiled dreamily. Maggie said an emphatic "Nice!" and I had a veritable "I Feel Pretty" moment. I compared that to my habitual self-annihilation in the mirror, how I zeroed in on the ugly. Artists searched for beauty. I made a vow to look at myself with an artistic sensibility.

The shoot lasted all morning. We ran out of ideas right when lunch arrived. Relieved it was over, I practically inhaled my sandwich. Koren asked what I thought of the experience. I admitted that I'd been tense at first. "But after ten minutes," I said, "I saw the humor of it. How could rolling around on the floor in the buff be anything but comic?"

It could be tragic, if the pictures were awful. Koren showed me some of the images in the tiny box on her digital camera. The size of a postage stamp, they didn't look hideous. She promised to e-mail me the lot tomorrow.

Seeing the portfolio the next day was a revelation. Granted, my belly looked like a deflated beach ball in some shots. Lying on my side squashed my boobs into pancakes. But most of the pictures were quite presentable. In about half of them, I looked downright cute. In a dozen, I would call myself hot. Not thin, of course—but, as I was beginning to understand, thin wasn't necessarily equal to good. Good wasn't necessarily equal to thin. The range of thin was itself narrow. The universe of good was vast and ever expanding.

Steve loved the pictures. "Most nude models look pissed off or mean," he said. "Your pictures are sexy in a completely nonthreatening way. You look like you had a good time." I realized I had. A great time.

I pored over the portfolio for days, hardly flinching at the deflated-beach-ball and pancake-breast shots. I discounted them as bad angles. With so many better angles to choose from, the bad ones hardly mattered.

I was learning to edit, both my photo portfolio and my critical thoughts. My husband suggested we frame some prints, for the posterity of my posterior. I reserved a spot on the shelf next to my bedroom mirror and decided to use the print as rebuttal evidence against the harsh inner monologist, should she speak up again.

Which, actually, she hadn't. Since the shoot, the critical chatter had been barely audible. Apparently, the more you showed of yourself, the less you cared. The photos had turned me away from the negative and toward the positive. Instead of fixating on my flabby gut, my eyes started to go to my strong legs, soft shoulders, pretty face. The photos had shown me what was right before my eyes all along. Beauty had been hiding in plain sight. Now I could see it.

Even my mom agreed that I looked good (in some shots).

I had to wait a few months before the article and photos were published in *Self* (February 2007, check 'em out!). A few days before the issue hit the newsstands, a copy arrived in my mailbox. Steve and I picked up the package on the way out to dinner. We opened the magazine and quickly found the right page. Not one, not two, not three, but *six photos* of naked me accompanied my essay. My stomach flopped. I'd seen the pictures. I'd examined them dozens of times in the last months to reassure myself that I wasn't completely nutso whacko cuckoo to allow them to be published. I could practically draw each image from memory. As I suddenly realized, though, it was one thing to pose for photos, another to look at them in the privacy of my home, and quite another to see them published in a major national magazine with a readership of five million people.

I almost puked, right into the open magazine in the vestibule of our building. Steve said, "Wow. Six pictures. That's ballsy, Val."

He had to hold my elbow as we walked outside. The cold air made me feel less queasy. We went to an Indian restaurant on Montague Street. Steve had the magazine open to my story while we ordered. I watched the waiter glance at the pictures, turn to me to take my order, do a double take, and then blush furiously before he hurried away to get our Taj Mahals.

That made us laugh, and I relaxed. Each time the waiter came to our table, he stammered and fumbled. I started to feel sorry for the guy. Poor bastard was picturing me naked while dishing out the curry. As awkward as it was for him, I liked his nervousness. If I'd known the power appearing nude would give me over men, I'd have done this a lot sooner.

I could tell which of the moms at my daughters' school were *Self* readers by the way they stared at me at pickup. One mother blushed and giggled whenever she saw me. Others congratulated me on my guts (never seen in such a favorable light before), on how lovely I looked (what else could they say?), and on the article itself. The reactions from complete strangers were more satisfying. Dozens of e-mails came in via my Web site, praising my courage and conviction. Several readers made plans to get their own naked photos taken, and I encouraged and thanked them all in reply e-mails that might have been embarrassingly gushy ("Thank you so, so much for writing. You don't know what this means to me. I'm really beyond grateful . . ."). The letters flooded into *Self* also. None were negative, as in, "What, you're photographing walruses now?"

When Lucy saw the piece, she hugged me and told me how proud she was. I felt like a positive role model, an example for her to follow (not by posing nude in a magazine, goes without saying, certainly not until she's forty-one). One day, she had her friend Maria over, and I found the two of them with their heads together, poring over the article and photos. My instinct was to snatch it away, but I resisted. Nudity wasn't shameful. My photos weren't obscene. The whole point was to take pride in myself—Lucy must have been proud of me to show it to her friend—and that was a good message for all women, eight to eighty. Maria looked up from the magazine and said simply, "You look great." No apparent trauma. Her voice was normal. Her mother wouldn't call me later to accuse me of scarring her daughter for life. I thanked Maria, and they went off to play.

Maggie, on the other hand, hated the piece. Of course, she was eleven, on the cusp of her big transformation. She found anything nudity-related to be deathly embarrassing. My parents sent an e-mail applauding the "tastefulness" of the shots. My sister said the story was "well done." (I thought it was "raw.") My friend Judith told me that her online community chat room had been hotly discussing the piece and photos. The point of debate? Whether or not the photos were retouched, and therefore defeating the purpose of laying myself bare. What made them suspicious of Photoshopping? The absence of cellulite on my legs.

For the record, the photos were not retouched. When Judith told me her friends didn't believe my legs were really that smooth, I'd never been more flattered in my life. As I've mentioned, my hindquarters are decent, thanks to genes and twenty years of on-again off-again running. My squishy stomach, obscured in the published portfolio, had dimples enough for both legs, plus a pair of arms. If the women of the Well got a glimpse of some of the deflated tire shots, they wouldn't doubt their veracity.

Would I trade my smooth thighs for a tiny waist? In a heartbeat. I'd trade my curly hair for straight. My fair skin for olive. My big feet for petite. My mannish hands for dainty. Since that wasn't possible, as an alternative, I could accept the things I cannot change, find the courage to change the things I can, and have the wisdom to know the difference.

Body Image Anonymous. An idea whose time has come?

The most out-of-the-blue call post-ultimate-reveal was from two very nice women who organized charity events for a temple in Short Hills. I knew the temple well, an ark-shaped building less than a mile from my childhood home. I'd gone to Sunday school there, attended dozens of bar and bat mitzvahs inside those walls. The women—K. and D.—were on the hunt for a keynote speaker for a spring luncheon fund-raiser, a few months away. It was their association's biggest annual event. Hundreds of women, corporate sponsors, whole ball of kosher wax. D. said she'd been following my work in magazines for years. She'd seen the *Self* article and thought it'd be swell to have me, a native Short Hillian, come talk to the temple ladies about my efforts to overcome bad body image. Plus, they offered to pay me two thousand dollars to do it. Was I available?

First thought: I knew my bad body image would be worth something someday.

Second thought: If I do hardcore Atkins before the luncheon, then I'll . . .

Third thought: *Whoa, girl.* I'd made a vow. There would

be no dieting for specific events. No dieting on deadline. No dieting at all.

Attempting not to sound overeager, I said, *"Two thousand bucks??!* Yeah, baby! That's what I'm talkin' about! I am *there."*

D. arranged for Liz, my oldest friend (we'd done summer camp, the Millburn public school system, and Condé Nast together), who still lived in Short Hills and was a temple member, to introduce me at the lunch. Five minutes after D. and I hung up, Liz called, and we laughed at the heresy of me, a flamingly secular Jew, speaking to the temple women about the self-perpetuating failure of dieting, while we all picked at salads, dressing on the side.

"This is a fancy lunch," said Liz. "Most of the spring selections at Neiman Marcus will be on display."

"So jeans and a T-shirt would be considered dressing down?" I asked, instantly feeling the usual anxiety about having to go shopping, try on clothes, look in a three-way mirror.

"For two thousand dollars, you can buy a new dress," she said.

12

OUR WARDROBES, OURSELVES

You might've heard the axiom: Women wear 10 percent of their wardrobe 90 percent of the time. It was certainly true for me—because I could fit into only 10 percent of mine. My closet didn't contain just fat clothes and skinny clothes. I had the fat-fat selection, the medium-fat, the bordering on average, average, slightly below average, and the skinny items I hadn't worn for over a decade. These pieces had become "goal" clothes. Instead of inspiring me, however, they became wrinkled reminders of my failure.

Most women, at a tender age, learn from their mothers about the joy of shopping and the special satisfaction of finding the perfect outfit. My initiation into the ritual was a nightmare. I still get the shakes, remembering Mom, Alison, and me in the communal dressing room at Bloomingdale's, circa 1975. Alison slipped into pleated wool skirts, ivory silk blouses, and bell-bottoms effortlessly, looking scrawny and stylish. She smiled and twirled, falling in love with shopping, an enduring love for her. While she posed in the mirror, I was over there in the corner, trying to wedge myself into gauchos and lumpy cowl-neck sweaters. Nothing fit right or looked halfway decent. The saleslady sighed heavily and said, "I'll get that in a larger size." Mom frowned disapprovingly. "It's the largest size in juniors," she complained. "We'll have to go to misses." I had to wait for another armful of things that wouldn't fit, quivering kid flesh in white panties in front of the orgy of mirrors.

Alison walked out of that chamber of horrors with a new fall wardrobe, twelve pieces, cute as hell. Me? I got a poncho. And a pair of Mary Janes.

To this day, the words "gaucho," "poncho," and "culottes" make me shudder.

Mom wised up, and left me behind when she and Alison went to Bloomingdale's. Her shopping expeditions with me began and ended at Bill's Army and Navy store for Wrangler jeans, gray or navy hoodies, and crewneck pack-of-three T-shirts in a variety of colors. If I needed a skirt or blouse for an occasion, Mom would shop without me. She'd go to a department store, come home with a few boxes, and pull the items over my head or tug them over my rump. If the pieces fit, we'd keep them. I'd put on the dress as directed, go to the party, wedding, bar mitzvah, Broadway show, or ballet. Fit was all that mattered. Style, cut, and color were not taken into account. Clothes were functional. They covered my nakedness and protected me from the cold. I was relieved not to have to go shopping. Trying on clothes made me feel fat, jealous of Alison, and embarrassed by the saleswomen. It made me feel like a disappointment to Mom.

When I got older, shopping became a leisure sport among my friends in junior high. At first, I'd beg off trips to Lord & Taylor. Later, I took an outright antifashion political stance that reeked of adolescent defiance. "Clothes are superficial. The fashion industry contributes to our consumerist society," I said. I had to eat my words (tasty!) when I went whole hog for the preppy trend. A few years later, like shedding an old skin for a new one, I traded preppy for punk. Then punk yielded to hippie chic in college. I wore the appropriate rock-and-roll uniforms and copied my friends.

When I went to work in magazines and had to dress like a professional, I was at a loss. My stylish friend Tomas took me to CP Shades to buy a few outfits. He did his best, but shapeless cotton-knit duds were not in the same universe as the finer fabrics worn by the editors of the magazine publishing world.

Again, my snotty "clothes are for silly twits" attitude kicked in. I didn't even pretend to follow fashion. I was miles behind my colleagues in my sartorial education; I could never hope to catch up. When we got wind of a designer's top-secret sample sale, all work would stop as the editors raced maniacally to get there. I'd go along to see what the fuss was about. We'd enter a warehouse or a showroom and find racks and racks of skirts, dresses, trousers, and blouses hanging riotously, strewn across the floor, piled in disarray on tables. While the editors picked through the fabric mountains, hunting for gems like miners on crack, I'd stand against the wall and stare in disbelief. A bargain made otherwise rational, intelligent women go bonkers. I simply did not get it. If clothes fit, were black, and were climate appropriate, they were okay by me.

Even clothes that should have had held sentimental value for me didn't. I hadn't personally selected them. The backless dress I wore the night I met Glenn had been picked out for me by an editor at *Mademoiselle*. The velvet dress I wore when Glenn and I got engaged was borrowed from his roommate. My two wedding dresses? The first, a hand-me-down from Alison, had had to be let out (way out) for me. I just stood there for the fittings, barely paying attention. It was white, princessy. It served its purpose.

I did choose my second wedding dress, less than two weeks before the event. Of all the items on my prewedding to-do list, I bought the dress last. If you need to ask why, you haven't been paying attention. I *hate shopping!* For moral support, I begged Steve to go to SoHo with me. He loathed shopping as much as I did and was none too happy to be dragged around the city on a sweltering August afternoon. A fashionable friend gave me a list of stores, all within a ten-block radius. We blew through one shop after another, looked around, saw nothing good, left frustrated. At a few, I tried on a dress that looked good on the hanger, hideous on me. My mood tumbled if a size twelve was tight. I eventually bought a two-hundred-dollar Nicole Miller white sheath dress. Size ten. It fit, was white, and was climate appropriate. The size and price were emotionally and financially acceptable. I exited the dressing room and showed Steve. He said, "It looks fine." I checked myself out in the mirror. The dress met my standard criteria: It didn't make me look too fat. I told the salesgirl that I'd take it. I'd only tried on the one dress.

"It's for your wedding, right?" she asked.

"Yup," I said.

"Do you want to try on a few more dresses? Just to be sure?"

I was sure enough. The frock met my needs. It was hotter than heck outside. Steve was tired. I was hungry. Buying the dress would be a huge load off my mind. Buying *any* dress would have been a relief.

I said, "This'll do, thanks."

The salesgirl said, "But for your wedding, you have to absolutely love it. It's got to be perfect."

She was just like my colleagues at *Mademoiselle*. She loved clothes. She had an emotional connection with what she put on her back, and she wouldn't be satisfied unless I did, too.

I said, "I do! I absolutely *adore* it! I *love* it! I've been searching the city for months. I'm thrilled beyond thrilled to have finally found the one perfect divine sent-from-heaven-on-the-wings-of-angels dress!"

Only then would she take my card and put the dress in a bag.

The only garments I've ever felt close to were, actually, undergarments. I've had a long love affair with underwear. It is a perplexing paradox that someone with my body image problems would be a huge fan of lingerie. Sexy panties and bras have given me what little clothingwise confidence I could claim. Lacy garments held emotional weight because they were associated with my relationships. After Glenn died, opening my underwear drawer and seeing the bras, panties, and nighties he'd loved on me hit me with a wave of grief every day. An important part of my recovery was to throw away the items that reminded me of our sex life and to stock up instead on plain panties and bras, as colorless as I felt.

When Steve and I started dating, I slowly replenished my drawer with Victoria's Secret goodies. Wearing sexy underwear again was like coming back to life. In vivid color. The rest of my wardrobe? As black as midnight.

Since the early days of J.Crew, I'd ordered most of my clothes from catalogues. Or I'd zip into a store and buy a pile of things to try on later, at home. My loathing for dressing rooms has cost me a fortune in clothes that I thought would fit and then didn't. Instead of going through the hassle of returning them, I'd shove them in my closet (more goal clothes to torment me), where they'd hang untouched for years. For my utilitarian clothing needs (i.e., all of my clothing needs), I fell into the Gap. When Old Navy stores arrived in the early 1990s, I went there instead. Same stuff, half the price. Thanks to Old Navy, the stuff I bought that didn't fit or looked bad, never to be returned or exchanged, was far less expensive. I saved hundreds!

I met Rebecca for breakfast. She hadn't seen the naked photo story yet, so I brought the magazine to show her. "Well, you've proven to the world that you can get undressed," she said. "Now you should learn how to get dressed."

I said, "You don't like what I'm wearing?"

"Jeans and a hoodie?"

"My trademark ensemble."

"That's not an ensemble," said Rebecca. "It's grabbing what's clean and throwing it on."

Exactly. "One of the benefits of not caring," I said. "I don't agonize about what to wear."

"You have a beautiful apartment, Val," said Stacy, suddenly off topic. "Where did you get that desk?"

She was referring to my George Nelson art deco desk that I found after years of searching antique stores on Atlantic Avenue in Brooklyn. I told her the story of my joy upon finding it. Stacy asked, "And these rugs. Where'd you get them?"

My Persian rugs were purchased at a warehouse sale at ABC Carpet. I waited months and months for the prices to come down to an acceptable range. I must have looked at three hundred rugs before I chose the beautiful wool and silk magic carpets that cover my bedroom floor. I listened to myself wax rhapsodical about my home decor for a spell, and then I said, "You're trying to trick me, aren't you?"

Stacy laughed. "You obviously care about your surroundings. The first thing you did when I got here was to give me the tour. You take pride and joy in the first impression your home design says about you. Yet you don't care about the impression *you* make?"

"Got it."

"Wouldn't it be fabulous to impress people without having to say something smart or write a single word?" she asked.

It would indeed. "Yes."

"I've done two hundred shows," she said. "I've worked with men, women, and kids of every body type. I've *been* every body type! From being so small I had to shop in the children's section to wearing a size eighteen, and every size in between. I'm guessing you think you can't use the power of personal style because of your body size. Body size has nothing

"You've obviously lost weight. Why not buy some clothes that fit? At least get a pair of nicer jeans. Or a cashmere hoodie with a shape to it," she said.

I cringed, knowing where this conversation was going. I'd had it before, with Rebecca and many others. The "pride in your appearance" conversation. The "dress like an adult" chat. I changed the subject. For once, Rebecca didn't force the issue.

But her point stuck in my head for many meals to come. I'd spent the last seven months purging my figurative closet of emotional skeletons, throwing out the mental clutter, clearing space for a new, healthy way of thinking. What of my actual closet?

I walked into it (yes, my closet is a walk-in, which many people have said was wasted on me) and turned on the light. I flipped through the hangers, examined the shelves and drawers. Ninety percent of the contents were black. That same percentage didn't fit. Black clothes were in sync with the black-and-white dieting existence, but I'd given that up months ago. My wardrobe was lagging behind. To take a further step away from that way of life, I needed to shop and dress more colorfully, too. To truly change the way I thought about my body, I would have to make alterations to its material covering as well.

Clueless how to begin, I needed help from an expert.

I first met Stacy London at *Mademoiselle*. She joined the staff as a stylist during the halcyon Elizabeth Crow years. Before Stacy's arrival, I hadn't befriended anyone in the fashion department, but she and I became instant pals. Her frank sense of humor was irresistible, and she made me howl with laughter in meetings. Since then, Stacy has gone on to well-deserved fame and fortune as the host of the hit TV show *What Not to Wear.* The show's premise is simple: Stacy and Clinton Kelly, her cohost, descend upon an unsuspecting style-challenged target, throw out all her old clothes, take her shopping for new stuff, and, in the process, transform her entire life.

If I were going to accept fashion makeover advice from *anyone,* it'd be Stacy. So I called her up and asked if she'd be willing to take a peek in my closet. "I would *love* to," she said. "It would be my absolute *pleasure.*" I could practically hear her salivating over the phone, all too eager to rip apart my lame wardrobe.

That was when I got a little nervous.

A couple of weeks later—during which time I wore the same four outfits on steady rotation, most of it gym clothes, grubby T-shirts, and jeans—Stacy arrived at my place looking smashing in a black V-neck dress, metallic thong sandals, sparkling jewelry, and a jean jacket that fit her perfectly. After giving her a tour of the rest of my apartment, I drew a deep breath and brought her to my bedroom.

But I didn't let her look in my closet—yet. I needed a little foreplay before the plunder began.

"Why should I care about fashion?" I asked.

"I hear the defiance in your voice," said Stacy, sitting on the edge of my bed. "And I agree with it. Fashion *is* superficial. Following fashion does make you materialistic. The fashion industry definitely takes advantage of the attitude that if you don't get this bag or dress or shoe, you're socially unacceptable."

"Uh, aren't you part of the fashion industry?" I as[ked]

"Not anymore," she said. "What I've learned on fi[ve years] of *What Not to Wear* is that fashion has nothing to [do with] personal style. Fashion makes women feel insecure. P[ersonal] style gives women power. Personal style is derived fro[m you,] not from a magazine or a designer. When you dress ac[cord]ing to your personal style—which we're going to sort o[ut for] you today—you will respect yourself like you can't eve[n be]gin to imagine."

"You, meaning women in general?" I said.

"You, meaning *you,* Val Frankel," she said. "I've kn[own] you for over ten years, and you've never even tried to dre[ss in] a way that reflects who you are."

"I am who I am, regardless of what I wear," I said, soun[d]ing like that defensive adolescent I used to be.

Stacy nodded knowingly. She'd come up against t[he] style-reluctant before. "Why should your daughters d[o] well in school?" she asked. "Because it determines wher[e] they go to college and what kind of job they'll get. It keep[s] their options open. Creating a personal style is exactly th[e] same thing. Your look is visual currency. If you want to look like a slacker in flip-flops"—she pointed at my Old Navy rubber thongs—"that's what the world will assume you are. People make snap judgments. They make subconscious judgments. If you have only one chance to telegraph a message via the way you dress, why not make it a good impression?"

I trotted out an old argument. "The only thing a highly styled person telegraphs is that she cares about clothes more than important things."

to do with it. *Size doesn't matter.* You can look and feel great at any size. You don't have to spend oodles of money. Style has no price points. Grace, personality, and intelligence are the things you love about yourself on the inside—and you can love them about yourself on the outside, too."

I liked what she was saying, in theory, but I still couldn't get over what I'd always thought, that clothes were insignificant. Furniture, on the other hand, was permanent, big, with intrinsic value that could be passed from one generation to the next. Furniture was art.

"You love objects," she said. "Your sparkly kitchen counter. Your acrylic toilet seats. You've found a way to create joy in the everyday. You can look at your red walls and feel good. You can also look at yourself in a flattering red dress and feel good. You styled your home for joy. And you're going to start styling yourself for joy, too. Look, I'm not delusional. Obviously, a great shirt isn't going to end the war. It won't cure disease or stop global warming. But, in general, fashion can make an impact. I talk about style as visual currency. Visual currency is nonverbal communication. When a woman walks out in the morning with confidence—she loves her heels, her dress, she thinks she looks great—her day will be better. She'll be nicer to the people she interacts with. They'll have a better day. And so on, and so on. You're creating joy and spreading it around. Is that insignificant?"

Obviously not. Spreading joy is my usual aim anyway. I write comedy, after all, and strive to make my family and friends happy.

"It has to start with how you feel about yourself," said Stacy. "You've had a lifetime of looking in the mirror and asking, 'Do I look fat in this?' Go out and buy clothes that make you *feel* great. I can teach you techniques for dressing your frame—not Giselle's frame—and finding things that are slimming, that highlight what you like, that camouflage what you don't. But only you know what makes you *feel* great. Mainly, it's about allowing yourself to feel and be beautiful in a way that celebrates your entire person. I can definitely think of a few things that are less superficial than that. People spend thousands of dollars and hours in therapy, but there's a lot to be said for putting on a pretty dress."

My inner feminist reflexes kicked in. I had to question this line of thought. As women, weren't we too complicated to let the simplicity of looking pretty nourish our souls?

A Vassar philosophy major, Stacy had obviously done a lot of thinking about all this. "Women our age are fighting a tougher battle than our mothers and grandmothers," she said. "They fought to be seen by men as more than decorative sexual objects, for the right not to be judged on their looks alone. Our generation is supposed to be CEOs, mothers, wives, expert lovers, have perfect bodies, run marathons, make a million dollars, be gourmet chefs, swing a golf club, never eat, never get tired. Men of any generation have never been asked to do what feminism asks of us. We are multitaskers, but we're not superhuman. The standard for what is expected of us, and what we expect of ourselves, is too high. We're supposed to be all things to all people—and we wonder why we're unhappy. You, Val, have fifteen pounds of guilt and shame for not being who you think you're supposed to be. Those fifteen pounds are an anvil around your neck. You wake up in the morning and feel the heaviness before you get out of bed. It affects your day and your life. I've been there, as you know. What I'm telling you is that personal style, dressing well and caring about your clothes, is one simple way to make you feel better, to lighten the load. Why shouldn't you take advantage? Given how hard life can be, why not do the easy part?"

Hard to argue with that. But enough talking. The time had come to take every scrap of clothing out of my closet and pile it on the bed.

Almost immediately, Stacy recognized one of my big problems. "I can't tell you how many closets I've decimated that were full of cheap crap that people bought without trying on," she said. She saw the telltale tags on a skirt and threw it on the floor. "Trash pile," she said.

She held up an ankle-length linen skirt I'd never worn. I said, "That was a hand-me-down from a friend."

She checked the tag. "It's a size four."

I shrugged.

She balled up the skirt and said, "This is never going to fit you. Why is it here? It reminds you of what you think is a personal failure. It's emotional baggage." Onto the trash pile. "And what's this?"

"A skirt I got at Daffy's," I said.

"It's a size fourteen," she said. "Why have you kept it? To remind yourself of having once been that big? So you'll see it and get that ick feeling? Another reminder of your perceived failure. It's bigger than the size four, but it might as well be the same skirt." It went flying into the trash.

A dress, black. I said, "I bought it for a job interview."

"Never buy something new right before a special occasion,"

she said. "You'll wear it once and never again. Say you need a summer dress for a wedding. You go out the day before and assume you'll find the perfect thing. But you won't, and you have to settle. Take the time to make a list of basics—a job interview suit, a summer dress, a winter coat—and spend an hour a week shopping. You might find a suit at the store where you expected to find the dress. If you have a list and work to acquire what you need, you won't wind up making a snap decision on a mistake. And this dress is a mistake."

"Hey, I like that dress!" I protested. It was ten years old. And I'd only worn it, maybe, twice.

"Val, it's too short!"

"I'm accentuating the positive," I said, patting my thigh.

"Okay, it's a good instinct to emphasize and de-emphasize. You still have to see the whole picture. What you tend to do, Val, is wear tiny miniskirts and big boxy oversized sweaters that make you look like a tomato on a pair of toothpicks."

That made me laugh. She was absolutely right. "Instead," said Stacy, throwing the dress on the floor, "you can even out the top and bottom halves with a longer hemline and fitted tops."

My sweater collection: "Needs to be on antidepressants. Black, black, pilly black, faded black." Fling, fling, fling, flung. "You go for saggy weaves because you think it hides your boobs, but knits are heavy and clingy and make your boobs look even bigger. They're all oversized, which adds bulk and clings at the same time."

A black cashmere turtleneck: "This would look better on Peyton Manning."

A wool crewneck: "This gives brown a bad name."

A sand-colored cable knit. I said, "Hey, my mother bought that for me."

"Your mother hasn't done you any fashion favors," she said. "Keep her out of the shopping equation."

Good point. My mom was hardly style-savvy. We teased her for wearing the same Ferragamo boots for forty years. Both my parents spend hardly any money on clothes, diverting the cash to bigger purchases like houses, cars, antiques, travel. I'd picked up my spending style from them, as well as all my mom's faulty instincts about fashion. Her own wardrobe of low-rent bland neutrals seemed designed to conceal and hide—not trouble areas, but herself, from the world.

One article after another was thrown on the discard pile. Stacy said, "Man, you sure do like Old Navy. This shirt even says 'Old Navy' on the front. Talk about not being invested in your clothes. All this is crap! It has no intrinsic or emotional value. No wonder you don't take care of it. By the way, you need a lint brush. There's no reason things hanging should be covered in cat hair."

Old Navy: No longer the official sponsor of this book.

"You have to invest in your clothes," she added. "Increase the intrinsic value to increase the emotional value. Instead of five shirts from Old Navy, get two from Anthropologie. They'd last longer, look better. Think of it this way: You don't buy stocks because they're cheap. You buy stocks because of their potential increase in value. Do the same with clothes."

A gray short-sleeved knit sweater that I'd worn to Glenn's funeral: "Talk about emotional baggage," she said. "Do you even like it?" Not really. Fling.

A shirt with a high neckline: "Wrong."

A linen striped shirt: "Tugs across the chest, and the stripes make your tits look enormous."

A black print sundress that I wore during both my pregnancies: "You're not pregnant now, are you? Stop wearing maternity clothes. Better than the dress, you have the kids. And the kids are more flattering."

A pair of plaid kilts: "Oh, Gawd! I remember these from *Mademoiselle*. They're way too short! A sixteen-year-old can't wear skirts this mini."

"You remember what I wore *twelve years ago*?"

"I have a photographic fashion memory," said Stacy. "I also had a special fascination with your clothes. You were a high-profile person at the magazine, way up on the masthead, and yet you dressed like an intern."

Ouch.

In an hour of trashing, Stacy threw out everything she'd picked up. Nothing, as she said, had any connection to who I was. I asked, "How do I rate, in terms of being emotionally disconnected to my clothes?"

"Off the charts," she said. "What I see here is someone who has never had a sense of self in how she dresses. It's all beyond utilitarian, lifeless, and it says nothing about you. It's upsetting, really. Not so much that your clothes don't fit and aren't flattering, but they're devoid of any sense of you. Your passion and humor and intelligence. There is no link between who you are and how you dress. I'm guessing the disconnect started a long time ago, when you looked in the mirror and felt unhappy."

Hello, Bloomingdale's communal dressing room. "My hatred of shopping was formed early on."

"That is so sad. You've missed a lot," said Stacy. No ironic tone there. She felt sorry for me. I was starting to feel sad for myself. I *had* missed out on a lot—female bonding over shoes, relating to shopping scenes in books and movies, creating an outer image to match my inner.

The pillage continued. Item after item was deemed off size, a bad color, an unflattering cut, stained, ripped, cheap. She asked, "When you walk into your closet, what do you feel?"

I felt . . . happy?

"You feel like it's a torture chamber of bad memories, personal failings, and sad, ugly options," said Stacy. "Nothing here adds joy to your life. Your closet should make you feel giddy, like you're surrounded by beauty. It should be your happy place, giving you a sense of safety and competence. The same way you feel about your apartment. You can do this, Val. You designed your house as a haven and shelter. Your closet can be a sanctuary, too."

The size ten black leather jeans. I said, "Hold on. I want to keep those. I used them as a weight benchmark."

She mulled it over. "I have a pair of leather jeans, too. By the time they come back into fashion, we'll be too old to wear them. Try them on for me." I did. They fit comfortably. Not tight, but not loose either. I hadn't weighed myself since I'd been not-dieting. Nor had I tried on the leather jeans. Going by fit, I'd lost around ten pounds.

Stacy must've noticed that I suddenly looked pleased when I put them on. "Okay, you can keep them," she said. "But here's how to handle it. You make a choice to hold on to only one thing to use as a benchmark. They're not goal pants. Or a symbol of failure. They're a gauge. These jeans can be the way to track your size, to keep you honest, so you can't lie to yourself. But they can't be used for psychological torture. Let's say you can try them on once every three months."

When the pillaging ended, the trash pile on the carpet was higher than the bed. Only two neatly folded (by Stacy) stacks remained: my jeans and my gym clothes. I had a few tanks left ("for layering"), a couple of dresses ("get them re-hemmed"), and my pj's. We didn't have time to go through coats or shoes, but suffice it to say, I needed to restock the larder in both of those categories as well. A final comment, regarding footwear: "You have six pairs of rubber flip-flops," she said. "Buy some real sandals."

We stuffed the discarded items into large green garbage bags while Stacy rattled off my Basics Shopping List of items and stores.

- Two pairs of dark-wash jeans. Straight leg or slight flare. Lucky Brand, Red Engine.
- Three short blazers. Hip length, short lapel, three buttons to de-emphasize the chest and tummy. Banana Republic.
- New sweaters. Light- or medium-weight wools, preferably cashmere, for layering with tanks and shirts, in saturated jewel tones and soft neutrals like navy, brown, and gray. V-necks. Three-quarter or full-length sleeve. J.Crew.
- Two suits. One skirt, one pant. Brown pinstripe or navy glen plaid. Three-season tropical-weight

wool. Pencil skirt or A-line, to top of knee. Banana Republic, DKNY, Theory.

· Blouses. Cotton broadcloth and silk, yes; knit cotton, no. Empire waist or tunics with V-neck. Side zippers, yes; buttons across the boobs, no. Big, bold patterns, jewel tones, and soft neutrals, yes; tiny prints, no. Anthropologie, Zara.

· T-shirts. Fitted for layering with sweaters and jackets. Bright colors, V-neck, size medium. *Not large.* J.Crew, Banana Republic, Only Hearts.

· Three summer dresses. Wrap dresses, fitted sheaths with V-necks. To knee or just below knee. Soft neutrals or bold, bright prints. Embellishments: beading and embroidery. Ella Moss, Searle, Diane von Furstenberg.

· Three pairs of trousers. Straight leg or slight flare; low or at waist. DKNY, Banana Republic.

Stacy's price points were midrange. I decided to spend two thousand dollars on a new wardrobe, the same amount that had dropped into my lap from the temple ladies (easy come, easy go). I decided to forget about suits and trousers until the fall and get dresses, skirts, and blouses for spring. Along with my shopping list (which didn't include shoes and accessories: "Let's start with remedial stuff before moving to the advanced class," she said), Stacy had some rules of thumb for shopping.

1. **Forget size.** "Focusing on size is psychological torture," said Stacy. "The important thing isn't the number. It's

whether the cut is flattering on your body. Also, there is no consistency with sizes from designer to designer and store to store. A six at one place might be a twelve at another. You haven't gained an ounce, but by walking next door, you've gone up—or down—three sizes. If the six looks great, buy it. If the twelve looks great, buy it. No one can see the number but you. And if it bugs you, cut it out."

2. **Try on everything.** "Even if you get two of the same shorts in different colors, try on *both* pairs. Do not buy anything until you're sure it fits."

3. **Make friends with a tailor.** "Manufacturers produce thousands and thousands of the same item in a factory. It will never fit every single person exactly right. No two human bodies are identical. There is no perfect size eight or ten or twelve. If you spend thirty-five dollars on a shirt and add ten dollars for a tailor, the shirt will look like a hundred bucks. Men always have their suits tailored. Why should women settle for less?"

4. **Trust salespeople.** "You, Val, are in a style rut. More like a ditch, but whatever. You need to break out of it. Ask a salesperson or personal shopper at Saks or Neiman Marcus to steer you in new directions and help you find clothes that are flattering for you. I know you have bad childhood memories about salespeople, but you're all grown up now. Get over it."

We returned the tiny piles of clothes to my closet. I'd have to walk my kids to school naked tomorrow, since I had nothing to wear—literally. We hauled the Hefty bags down the stairs of my building and out to my car. We loaded them into the trunk. Next stop, Salvation Army.

"You better not sneak out any of those sweaters," she said.

I laughed (since I'd been thinking of doing just that). "I have to let it all go. And when I say 'all,' I don't mean just the clothes."

"I promise you, Val, if you can find even one article of clothing that makes you *feel* great, you'll discover a dimension of joy you didn't think possible. I'm not sure you're ready for the depth of emotion. It's big."

"I know you're right," I said. "And I'm so grateful you came over today. Obviously, I needed to do this."

"My pleasure, I mean it," she said. "There are so many people in the world who don't recognize how beautiful they are until someone shows them."

That did it. I cried. Couldn't help it. It'd been building. Thinking about the decades of disconnect, or neglect, realizing how little respect I'd shown myself and the world through my clothes. I suddenly understood why people bawled on *What Not to Wear* every week. Stacy cried, too. We cried together, on the street, by my car with the two huge garbage bags in the trunk.

We composed ourselves, laughing and saying good-bye. Stacy told me to call her with questions. "Remember," she said. "Forget about looking thin. It's not how you look, but how you feel."

The next day, I planned on going to Banana Republic to begin my new shopping life. Maggie insisted on going with me, "to make sure you follow Stacy's rules." When Lucy heard that, she said she wanted to come, too. It'd be a mother and her two daughters in the dressing room all over again, minus the clucking, loaded sighs, and disapproving looks.

By all indications, my bad shopping habits hadn't rubbed off on my girls. They were fashion junkies, almost from birth. When they tried on clothes in dressing rooms, I told them they looked adorable in everything. They did! They're both beautiful, as I remind them all the time. Conventional wisdom dictates that parents shouldn't do that, but I knew there were worse things a mother could say to her daughters in dressing rooms.

As we walked to BaRe after school, I thought, "Here we are. Going shopping. Just like normal people."

We entered the store, and I had to forcibly steer myself away from the sale rack. I was not going to automatically buy the cheapest, blackest, biggest whatever. I was going to browse. We started pulling things off the racks. Twenty items, in Stacy-approved colors and cuts. Then we hauled the lot to a sizable dressing room. Maggie and Lucy sat on the floor as I tried on each piece. If something didn't fit, it was a no, obviously. If Maggie or Lucy was iffy, it was a no. If I was iffy, hell no. If a shirt fit and we all liked it, then I had to decide whether wearing it evoked emotion in my heart. Did it make me feel joy?

This was the tricky part. For the first few tentative yeses, I wasn't sure what I felt, except a smug satisfaction that I was fitting into a lot of size eights (on the bottom), which was a nice surprise.

When I tried on a pair of gray linen shorts, a white tank,

and a cranberry summerweight sweater with a deep V-neck, Maggie said, "Love."

Lucy said, "Totally."

I appraised the outfit. I smiled, liked it. Especially the bright sweater. Then a faint hum rose in my ears. It got louder as I turned for the side view. I said, "Do you hear that?"

"What?" the girls asked.

"Forget it."

I tried on a brown empire-waist dress with embroidery at the hem and a V-neck.

Maggie said, "It's too baggy. What size is it?"

"Large," I said.

"You're not supposed to wear large," recited Maggie. "Stacy *said* medium." I got the feeling I was in for a lot of "Stacy *said*" from now on.

"But the boobs," I said, turning to the sides. Mediums on the bottom were fine, but I needed more room on top.

Maggie stood up and said, "I'm getting a medium."

She left the dressing room and came back with a smaller size. I tried it on. The medium did fit better, even across the chest. I surveyed the image in the mirror, liking what I saw. Loving what I saw. The hum started again in my head. Not as faint.

Lucy said, "Do a twirl."

I twirled. It really did look great. Flattering empire waist, hemline right at the knee. Wide shoulder straps and a bronzy brown that set off my hair and eyes. Okay, the hum was loud in my head now. I would have to recognize it for what it was: an auditory manifestation of emotion. Was it joy? I wasn't sure, but it got louder the longer I wore the dress.

Maggie said, "Definite yes for me."

Lucy said, "Me, too."

The dress cost nearly two hundred bucks. I'd never spent that much on a single item of clothing. I could get three dresses at Old Navy for . . .

Stacy *said* I had to go for quality. One beautiful dress that made me feel good was worth a hundred pieces of crap I'd wear once and never again.

I bought it. And the sweater, the tank, the shorts, a shirt, and a top. I spent over four hundred dollars. Maggie seemed particularly excited that I was slapping down the card. She knew that if I turned into a shopper, it'd mean more clothes for her (she turned out to be right about that). A week later, I went back to Banana Republic to return the top. After the initial enthusiasm for it, I'd changed my mind. And it cost seventy dollars! Over the years, I hadn't returned hundreds of dollars' worth at Target, Old Navy, and Daffy's. I was learning. Stacy *said* I had to think of clothes as stocks. If I bought a bad stock, I dumped it. If I thought twice about a top, I would return it.

A few days later, after dropping off the kids at school, I went into Manhattan, to Fifth Avenue in Greenwich Village, and was amazed to find three of my Stacy-approved stores right next to each other! I wondered if she'd planned that. I went from Zara to J.Crew to Anthropologie and spent five hours (!) trying on scores of blouses, T-shirts, skirts, dresses, jackets, and pants. My buy percentage was about one in four. Since I had an idea of what to look for—stylewise and emotionally—I was very selective. Even if something looked right, I wouldn't buy it unless I heard the hum, felt the love. I didn't get hung up on sizes.

This will seem like stating the obvious to most: Shopping was *fun*! I shopped 'til I dropped. My bags were heavy on my arms. And the salespeople were so nice! At J.Crew, they gave me bottles of water and hung my selections in a reserved dressing room. While I waited in there, they brought me different colors and sizes of dresses and skirts. It was a pleasure, and I found myself feeling pampered, respected, and itching to spend, spend, spend. I knew the girls worked on commission and were paying special attention to me because I had a mad-shopper look in the eye. I didn't care! I dropped over a thousand dollars that day.

I got home and arranged my new purchases in my closet. I modeled all of it for Steve, who said the same exact thing about each one: "Great!" (He really couldn't care less about clothes.) I modeled for the girls later, Maggie gasped when I put on one outfit from J.Crew, a navy flowy skirt and a white tank. She hugged me and said, "Mom, you look so cute!"

That was joy, right there. Not because I looked cute, but because I'd made my daughter proud of me. I'd become more of who she'd like me to be, and who she'd like to be. Why shouldn't role modeling include clothes modeling? And looking cute?

I proceeded to look smokin' cute the whole next day in that outfit. I strutted around Brooklyn Heights like I owned it. At a Montague Street boutique, I bought myself a pair of high-heeled sandals. And a purse to match the shoes. And a pair of earrings. I was in free-spending mode and knew I'd have to stop soon.

Until then, I'd drown in the joy. And once I reached my two-thousand-dollar limit (any minute now), I'd still have all the clothes! Stacy had been right. Two weeks after her visit, I understood what she'd been trying to tell me. Shopping wasn't a values dilemma. By dressing better, I was making a better impression—on strangers, acquaintances, the kids. Mainly, on myself.

I can think of a lot of things less valuable than that.

13

SAVE THE DATE

When Steve and I first started planning our wedding, people asked why I was bothering with the formality when we could just be together without involving the government. A couple of reasons: For one thing, I already knew that marriage was a comfortable, secure, convenient domestic arrangement. Also, the kids wanted us to be legally bound.

So we got married. A year later, Maggie announced that she didn't like the sound of "stepfather." She wanted a "father-father." The girls and I talked about Glenn every day. There were photos of him all over our apartment. We visited Glenn's grave, went to his parents in Florida every year, and saw his brother's family regularly. Maggie knew she had a dead father-father. But she wanted one here on earth as well.

I'd heard stories about people in our circumstances pursuing adoption. As legal procedures go, it wouldn't be too awful. The more we talked about it, the more it made sense. As my husband only, Steve had no legal rights to the kids. He couldn't give approval for an emergency medical procedure if I were unavailable. If I died while the girls were minors, he'd have no claim to them. There could be agonizing complications about inheritance, where they'd live, who would raise them.

My parents and sister applauded the adoption idea, for these reasons and to further solidify us as a family. I brought it up to Glenn's parents when they came to New York for a visit. The conversation went smoother than I thought it would. The idea made them sad, understandably, but they were happy for me to have found a man I trusted enough to adopt the girls.

It'd been two years since that uncomfortable talk, and yet we'd taken no steps toward making it legal. Nothing had happened. Steve hadn't brought it up since the initial flurry of conversation about it. Neither had Maggie, who, in the intervening years, had moved on to middle school with other things (clothes, gossip, the Sims) on her mind. But I still thought about the adoption often—every time I filled out a camp form or parental authorization for a class trip. Even though Steve had been raising the kids for years, he wasn't legally authorized to sign a permission slip.

I had a referral for a lawyer. The info was on a stickie on my desktop. Had been for years. It'd be easy to pick up the phone, set the wheels in motion. It had to be done. And yet, I didn't do it.

What was keeping me from making the call? The girls had thrived under our joint care. Steve was an amazing dad. He was far more involved in the girls' day-to-day lives than any other father I knew. His evening rehearsal and perfor-mance schedules made it possible for Steve to schlep the girls to karate and piano lessons—and he was glad to do it.

A bachelor until he was fifty, Steve had assumed he would

never have children. Now that he was up to his ears in Bagel Bites, sleepover parties, juice pouches, Nickelodeon, and math homework, he appreciated the hectic joy of living with kids more than the average dad. More than the average mom. The girls adored him. Lucy, who was almost two years old when Glenn died, had considered Steve her father for years already. Maggie and Steve bonded over music. For the last two seasons, Maggie had sung in the chorus of Steve's opera company. They gossiped about the other singers and talked in the language of music to each other, which made my tone-deaf heart sing. Steve attended every recital, game, and play. When the second graders recited "The Midnight Ride of Paul Revere," I watched the other dads in suits checking their watches, tolerating the demand on their time, wondering when they could slip away. And there was Steve, in the front row, grinning, hanging on every word, giving Lucy the thumbs-up, applauding the loudest when it was over. He won the gold star for showing up, being there, not losing his patience (as I often did), not yelling (as I did), and enjoying (almost) every minute of the unexpected parental turn his life had taken. He deserved to be their legal father, as much as the girls deserved to be his legal daughters.

Perhaps I'd avoided calling a lawyer due to logistics. The adoption would cost several grand. The paperwork would be abundant. I'd have to go to notaries, find documents, have things sealed and signed, get statements, schedule appointments with court counselors and judges. Then again, I'd faced legal paperwork before, when Glenn died, and when Steve and I got a prenup. I'd made the time and put up the money then. Surely the adoption—a happy reason to bring lawyers into your life—would mitigate the annoyance of paperwork, and the time and money spent.

All marital problems, deconstructed, are about trust. If my hesitation about adoption wasn't about the kids or the hassle, then it had to be about trust.

Steve had had his own trust issues, early on. He refused to sublet his Manhattan apartment, even after we got married. He said he needed a place for all his stuff. We both knew that apartment was a safety net, an escape option for him. For me, it was an affront, an insult, a one-bedroom-sized hole in his commitment to our marriage. And then there was the money suck. He spent thousands a month on his bachelor pad, despite the fact that he was never there. I argued that money would be better spent on the Brooklyn mortgage, on groceries, on *anything*.

Initially, I accepted his decision and found ways to rationalize it as a good thing. Before long, though, his keeping the apartment became a problem. We fought about it. A lot. He had a dry spell professionally and needed a loan to pay his rent. I wouldn't give it to him. He considered my refusal hostile and mean-spirited. I said I couldn't in good conscience flush hard-earned money down the toilet. We reached a stalemate. Our fights drove us into therapy. We auditioned two marriage counselors. As soon as Steve and I explained the root of our problem—that bloody apartment—both of them turned to him and asked, "Why do you think you can't let it go?" We ended up picking a therapist who looked and sounded eerily like Steve's mother. She set him straight. After three sessions, Steve found a subletter, and the apartment conflict was gone.

When he realized how much of an albatross that place—and what it represented—had been, Steve was glad to have been pushed into giving it up. Correspondingly, at the start of our second year of marriage, we had a second honeymoon period. He'd conquered his doubt. But, as my hesitation about the adoption demonstrated, I hadn't dealt with mine. In an ideal world, each spouse would face his or her issues before they said, "I do." Steve and I were both a bit more plodding. I had yet to ease the persistent doubt in my mind about his "lose the belly" comment from years before. Even worse, I'd kept my anxiety a secret.

It bears mentioning that Steve never repeated the criticism, although I certainly invited him to. ("How do I look in these pants?" "Don't you think my stomach looks better?" "My crunches are really paying off, don't you think?") Any sane woman would have forgiven and forgotten. If we went to therapy again over this, the shrinks would surely turn to me and say, "Why do you think you can't let it go?" We'd need more than three sessions to address that.

In the beginning of our relationship, I'd loved reinventing myself. I could portray myself as someone who'd never been harassed about my weight, who was carefree and confident about my body. But that game of pretend was impossible to perpetuate. The streaks of distrust about his attraction ran through my mind like marbling through steak. I couldn't seal our family's future legally via adoption (a vastly bigger commitment than marriage) unless we cleared up this last hanging doubt. Steve would have to get a crash course in my body image history, and he'd have to understand why that comment he made years ago rattled me to the core.

I did not look forward to having this conversation. Since there was no good time to reveal your insecurities to the man you loved, I chose a quiet, peaceful moment. Steve was lying on the bed, resting between homework hour and dinner. I sat at my computer, playing Snood.

"Steve, you asleep?" I asked.

"Not quite," he said, eyes closed.

I loved watching him in this half-conscious state. When he was relaxed, he had the skin of a thirty-year-old. His lips pursed slightly, and I smiled at the sight. Steve was a damned handsome guy, and watching him at ease was one among many small pleasures I took in his presence.

"So listen," I said. "Remember the night we decided to get married?"

He said, "Sort of."

"You were just back from a tour," I said. "We hadn't seen each other in a few weeks. We made mad, passionate love for hours and hours. And then we decided to stay together forever."

He nodded, "It was a midwestern tour."

"Do you remember that you asked me to lose the stomach bulge?" I asked.

"Vaguely," he said.

"You did," I said.

"Okay."

"Well, I didn't like that," I said. "It hurt my feelings."

"Sorry," he said, turning from his back onto his side.

"Don't you feel bad that you hurt my feelings?" I asked.

He groaned and opened his eyes. "We are talking about a conversation from five and a half years ago?"

"It's still relevant."

He sat up, rearranging himself with his back to the head-board and his legs bent at the knee. He said, "I'm sorry your feelings were hurt, but they shouldn't have been. As I recall, I said it nicely enough."

So he did remember. "It's not nice to say 'lose the belly,' no matter how you couch it," I said. "Just mentioning it pushed my personal panic button. It unleashed a lifetime of bad feelings about my weight. My mother used to criticize my belly, too."

"You can't possibly be comparing me to your mother."

Indeed, Steve and Judy were polar personality opposites. "Not that you're like her, but that comment opened up a well of negative associations."

I brought him up to speed about Mom and junior high, college, my early magazine career. Telling him the stories was easier than I expected. He listened quietly but with both ears. Steve didn't make supportive or sympathetic noises. He just took it in.

When I finished, Steve shrugged. "I didn't know all that," he said. "I had no idea about your history. I thought you were happy about your stomach. You seemed to be, because you had it. If you didn't like it, I figured you'd have gotten rid of it."

I blinked in disbelief at his crazy talk. "So millions of people all over the world are happy about their fat because they haven't been able to lose it? Like they're not *trying*?"

"When we met," he said, "you gave me the immediate impression of self-assurance. You walked—you still do—with confidence. When you're working out a lot, you glide, actually. It's fun to watch. So I assumed you were pleased with yourself from top to bottom, or else you wouldn't be so confident."

I could understand his making that assumption. He was a linear-minded guy. A face-value Mainer. And, generally speaking, I did walk with a lively step. I was pretty confident—but only on the surface. Even a blind man could see that! "You must have noticed that I'm a compulsive dieter. That my weight has gone up and down over the years."

"What I notice is that you go through grumpy phases and happy phases," he said. "When you're losing weight, you tend to be cheerful and fun to be around."

"And when I'm gaining?"

"You're kind of nasty," he said. "Terse and humorless. Not at all like a jolly fat person." He smiled mischievously.

Asshole! "You're an asshole," I said. But I grinned, too.

"I'm happy when you're happy," he said. "Like husbands all over the world. What I don't get is why your mood seems to hang on miniscule weight losses. So many times, you announce that you lost five pounds, and I can barely tell. You always look pretty good. I don't have qualms about your belly anymore."

"You cared then, but don't now?" I asked. "Why?"

Steve paused to think. "Well," he said, "a person can get used to just about anything."

Shithead! "You are truly a bastard," I said, but we were both laughing now. "Seriously, what changed?"

"Well, your belly is better now," he observed correctly. "Much firmer. I have noticed that."

"Thank you, but flattery won't get you out of this. You're

going to have to explain yourself. Why did you say what you said that night?"

Steve sighed. "We were in the early stage of being physical. Your belly just got in the way. I was never focused on disliking it, but I thought we could get closer—in a purely physical sense—if it didn't come between us."

Hmmm. That actually made sense. When I was in a thinner phase, Steve really got into the full-body hugs, the frontal pressing and head-to-toe connection, as if we were fused into one four-legged package. A flatter stomach did make the connection closer.

"I get frustrated when I lose weight and you don't notice," I complained.

"Maine is one of the fattest states in the country," he said. "I grew up seeing some really massive people. Three-, four-hundred-pounders. I never considered your weight, even when it's up, to be that bad. There's fat, and then there's fat-fat. You're just not a fat-fat person. You get all excited losing five or ten pounds. It's not dramatic enough to register with me. You say you're down two dress sizes since last summer. I'm sorry, but you don't seem that different. I don't even know what two dress sizes means."

"So you'd notice only if I lost a hundred pounds," I said.

"I had no idea this was such a deep issue for you, with your mom and all this past stuff," he said. "I've noticed that you seem to care a lot about your losses and gains, but I never would have connected it to me, or anything I've said. I think I've been worshipful of your body, haven't I?"

I said, "Yes."

"I'm devoted to you," he said.

"I know."

"Then why have you been obsessing over some minor comment I made years ago when I was probably drunk?" he asked. "And why didn't you say something sooner?"

"I was embarrassed," I admitted.

"You should be," he said.

Being embarrassed about my weight obsession seemed like a step in the right direction.

He said, "Anything I say, take it at face value. I think you're a damned attractive person. When I make love to you, it's because I'm damned attracted to you."

"No matter what condition my belly is in?" I asked, one more time for good measure.

He groaned. "The belly is still here, and so am I."

"But firmer," I said.

"Definitely firmer," he agreed.

When Glenn and I were first married, I started having a recurring dream. Nothing too bizarre. A breakup scene. We'd be sitting at a café, and then he'd lower the boom, tell me he'd fallen out of love and he was leaving. The dream would continue with disjointed scenes from my new life as a divorcée. In bed alone, watching TV. Preparing meals by myself. Missing him and trying to rally my spirits. Being single wasn't so bad. I'd been there dozens of times, and I'd survived. I'd wake up and feel awesome relief to see Glenn in bed next to me. I'd punch him in the arm and say, "In my dream, you were mean to me." Glenn always apologized for the evil-doings of my paranoid subconscious.

After he died, I had vivid dreams of Glenn being miraculously cured, or of our lives before he got sick, as if the cancer and death had been the dream. Maggie also had what we called "Glenn visit" dreams—visions of him descending from heaven to see what we were up to, or of him just walking in the door, whole and healthy, still her dad. The morning after, we were happy to have made a connection with the way things were, but sad that he was gone. I continued to have Glenn-returns dreams, long after Steve became enmeshed in our lives, but my reaction to having them changed. Would I still want Glenn to reappear, to walk in the door, miraculously cured?

Maggie asked, "Is it wrong to want to keep my life the way it is now?"

No eleven-year-old should have to straddle such a dilemma. I assured her that she could love Glenn's memory and still not wish for him to return. That if heaven did exist (and I wasn't saying it did) and Glenn was up there watching, he was glad we'd found someone else to love. I told myself the same thing. Even so, I still felt a twinge of guilt about wanting my life as it was now, with Steve.

I'd had dreams of Steve leaving me, too. They were eerily similar to the Glenn-breakup dreams. I was dumped, and then I'd flash to vignettes of my new lonely life. I'd wake up with a jolt, heart pounding. I'd stare at Steve sleeping next to me until I calmed down. He was still here. I wasn't alone again.

Looking at marital longevity from a practical standpoint, Steve would probably predecease me. He was eleven years older. He had a heart arrhythmia. He drank a lot of beer and never worked out (yet never gained weight, lucky bastard).

The dreams of Steve leaving didn't spring from a paranoid subconscious. They were reality-based. One husband had died on my watch. Another was likely to.

A weight obsession was a convenient distraction from bigger issues.

It was certainly easier to focus on Steve's being turned off by my stomach than to face my fear of death.

The whole point of Steve's adopting the kids was to ensure a continuation of the girls' lives here in Brooklyn in the event of my untimely death. Connecting the dots, I wondered if my legal feet-dragging was related to fear of death—not Steve's, but my own. I'd seen Glenn alive one second and dead the next. I had no idea what was in store for me or Steve. Death could happen to anyone, at any time. It would assuredly come, and it wouldn't be pretty.

That I'd wasted a single second of my time with Steve fretting about one stupid comment suddenly galled me. We had a finite number of years together. And I would be grateful for each of them. If he died first, if I died first, the living spouse had to continue, and strive for happiness for him or herself—and for *our* kids. That was the obligation of a spouse and a parent. If you couldn't meet your responsibility, you might as well be swallowed up by the earth, gone forever, never to return.

Since our talk about the belly comment, Steve started each day by wrapping me in his arms and saying, "Good morning, darling. You're not fat at all today."

When something went awry—the cat peed on Maggie's

cell phone, the kitchen fuse blew—Steve shot me a mockingly sincere look, clasped my hands tightly, and asked, "Do you think it's because of . . . *your fat?*"

When something went right—a great out-of-the-blue assignment, my lilac tree finally blooming after four years— Steve pulled me into a squeeze and asked, "How is all this happiness possible, considering . . . *you know,*" and then he would glance at my midsection.

Maggie caught on to what he was doing and took to teasing me, too. It was weird at first. A sore subject for so long, it'd been co-opted by Steve and Maggie as material for improv comedy. I laughed along. The ability to laugh at yourself is a sign of higher intelligence. So, yeah, I was down with that. I teased Maggie and Steve often about their quirks (Maggie's tendency to spill whatever liquid was within reach; Steve's habit of misplacing his backpack). Why shouldn't my fat obsession be fodder for family fun? Given the choice, to cry about it or laugh, was there any doubt which was preferable? For all of us?

The mood at home palpably lifted. It made me think back to when Steve and I first connected online, crafting perfect jewels in the form of e-mails to send to each other as gifts. I summoned all my skills to sound witty, so he'd laugh and be impressed by my cleverness. In turn, I was blown away by his sense of humor. Writing those funny notes bonded us before we'd laid eyes on each other, before we finally, blissfully, laid hands on each other. Much as we loved to have sex, Steve and I loved to laugh even more. The jokes he served up after I made my big confession erased the doubt and made me fall in love with him all over again.

I realized I'd been twice blessed in marriage. First, with Glenn, an adoring husband who'd been respectful of my insecurities. Second, with Steve, my husband, my equal, who helped me overcome my insecurities by laughing about them.

Three years after we got married, six years after we sent those funny e-mails to each other, Steve and I called Barry M. Katz, Esq., to get the adoption ball rolling.

Steve asked, "Are you sure we're not rushing into this?"

"I should have done it years ago," I said, regarding the adoption, and a few other things.

14

THE PROPER WAY TO EAT A RAT

When we last saw Sal, heroine of dozens of stories scribbled in my teenage journals, she was serving a plate of spaghetti to Z., her number-one nemesis. He waited at a beautifully set table, fork and spoon in his hands, still muddy after a triumphant soccer match. Although he was hungry enough to eat the meat of an entire elephant, he wasn't about to dive into the steaming bowl of pasta Sal had prepared. He wisely asked Y., his henchboy and Sal's number-two nemesis, to be his food taster. Worshipfully devoted to his leader, Y. obediently wound his fork around a saucy strand of spaghetti and tentatively slipped it between his thin, pale lips. He chewed, waited. Nothing happened. The food was safe.

Sal smiled as Y. and Z. greedily consumed every last string of pasta. The meal was delicious, mouthwatering. To enhance the chunky red sauce, Sal had sprinkled it liberally with parsley, oregano—and a slow-acting poison she'd concocted in her underground laboratory. When the poison finally kicked in, twenty-five years from that very moment, Y. and Z. would die instantly in a manner most grisly. Foaming at the mouth, spasmodic convulsions, eyes popping out of their sockets and rolling down the street, or the supermarket aisle, or the green of a golf course, wherever the bastards happened to be at the time. Yet again, Z. had underestimated Sal's deviousness.

The quizzical reader might wonder, why hadn't Sal used a faster-acting poison? Why delay her satisfaction by twenty-five years? Even at the impatient age of fourteen, Sal knew that revenge was a dish that people of taste preferred to eat cold.

Feeling solid after my talk with Steve, enjoying his teasing as much as I'd despised Z.'s, I felt strong and ready to take the next necessary step in my bad body image recovery.

The time had come to eat the rat.

I lost hours of sleep, fantasizing about how an encounter with Z. might go. The fantasies were similar in tone to the overwrought Sal stories from way back when. They wouldn't have been out of place in my red corduroy journal . . .

Sal had had a long night. She was exhausted, but determined to see her plans through, regardless of the potentially destructive outcome. The mission was risky. But she'd been hiding in the shadows for far too long. She knew she had to face her past. Call out her dragons.

She let her head fall back on the car seat. The drive from Brooklyn to Iowa had taken its toll. She flipped down the visor to check herself in the mirror. Even after twelve hours on the road, she still looked pretty good. Fluffing her hair, Sal gave herself a pep talk.

"You can do this," she said. "Just open the car door, walk up to the house, and ring the bell."

The visor snapped back into position, Sal glanced out the car window at the house. Yellow paint peeling, shudders closed, a rusted bicycle upended on the brown lawn. It had taken her weeks of detective work to get this address. In a million years, Sal wouldn't have guessed that life had taken Z. here, to this dead-end street in a nowhere town. Her last look at him had been at high school graduation. He'd been a star that day, most likely to succeed, winning the loudest cheer from the class when the principal put the rolled-up diploma in his hand. Z. had raised his arms, cheered himself, and leapt off the low-rise stage with the grace of a gazelle.

Sal looked in her rearview mirror. Not a soul on the street. For the last five miles of her drive, she hadn't seen a single person outdoors. This was an indoors town. Doors closed, curtains drawn. Z., once a star athlete running on a green grass field, was now locked in a box. It almost made Sal feel sad. But not quite.

She took one last deep inhale, pushed open her car door, and made for the house. No bell. She knocked on the door. The contact made the door open halfway, and she could see into the house's living room. Empty pizza boxes, beer bottles, overflowing ashtrays assaulted her nostrils. She had to take a step back from the smell.

"Who's there?" barked a voice, smoke-ravaged and surly.

"Hello?" asked Sal. "I'm looking for Z. I'm an old . . . friend . . . of his from high school."

The door swung wide open, and a man appeared in the doorway. A savage stench radiated from him, and tears rose in Sal's eyes. She blinked them back and tried to breathe through her mouth.

"Z.?" she asked.

"Yeah?" he replied. Somewhere around the eyes, he looked like

his former self. Everything else had changed. The once charismatic jock with long lean legs and flowing brown hair that bounced when he ran had turned into a bald, bandy-legged troll in a soiled wife-beater T-shirt and plaid shorts belted under a rotund beer belly.

"I'm Sal, from Short Hills. We went to school together."

"Sal," he said, nodding. "Of course, I remember you. BELCH. Oops. Sorry about that."

He seemed genuinely embarrassed. Sal grimaced but asked, "May I come in?"

"Please!" he said, changing from surly to welcoming. "I can't believe this. It's so freaking weird that you're here."

Sal stepped into the house. The stink closed in. The house hadn't been aired out in months, if ever. Z. didn't seem ashamed that he lived in a hole. She said, "I should have called before I came."

"I have to get my wife," he said. "Betsy! Betsy! Get in here! You're not going to believe this."

Z. turned back to her, grinning. His two front teeth were missing. She must have reacted. He said, "Oh, yeah, my teeth. They got kicked out in a college soccer game. It was the last time I played." She detected wistfulness in his voice. But then he yelled, "Betsy! Get your fat ass down here, now."

Sal smiled nervously, looking around the room. Her eyes trailed from one stained, tattered piece of furniture to the next. Spotted gray carpet, water marks on the ceiling, dust-covered lampshades—and, on an armchair in the corner, a person. A girl. A fat girl, around thirteen or fourteen. She sat in the chair, reading a novel, in her own world, ignoring or unaware of the fact that a stranger had entered the room.

"Oh, that's just Tracy," he said. "My daughter."

He spoke without paternal pride, as if his own child were an after-

thought. Sal felt her pulse quicken. She wondered if this was what an anxiety attack felt like. If she fainted on the floor, she wondered, would she get fleas?

"What the hell do you want?" screeched a voice from deeper in the house. And then a female creature appeared in a doorway off the living room. A wild-eyed plus-size filthy blonde. The wife. Betsy. In one hand, she held a greasy turkey leg. In her other hand, she was holding a paperback book.

Z. said, "I fucking told you I knew Sal."

The wife dropped the turkey leg on the floor, where it landed with a squishy thud. She flung herself at Sal, moving across the room with the speed of a woman half her size.

"Holy shit!" squealed Betsy, staring into Sal's astonished face. "I'm your biggest fan!" Betsy held up a tattered copy of one of Sal's novels and waved it overhead.

Sal blinked in astonishment. The fans of her novels were few in number, but fierce in their loyalty. Apparently, Z.'s wife was one of them.

"Z. always told me the two of you were, like, best friends in high school," she said. "I've got all your books. You have to sign them! Come on, this way."

Betsy led Sal into the couple's squalid bedroom. Sal signed the stack of books while listening to the lady of the house explain how she'd always had her doubts that Z. and Sal had been friends, how he'd promised for years to arrange a meeting, and how shocked she was that he'd finally come through.

"He's been a pretty huge disappointment," Betsy admitted to Sal. "I mean, just look at him! He can't hold a job. We're broke. He drinks too much. He's got no friends, so he lies around the house all day long. He's pathetic. I'd leave him today if it weren't for Tracy. I

cry myself to sleep, thinking what I've become living with him. When we first met, I weighed a hundred and twenty pounds. He's such a slob, he turned me into one, too."

Sal nodded sympathetically while Betsy confided her secrets to a complete stranger. When Betsy brought her back downstairs, Sal's heart nearly felt a pang when she saw Z. attempting to clear a space for her on their decrepit couch.

"I've got to go," said Sal.

"You have to stay for just a few minutes," said Betsy, and then, "Tracy! Tracy! Wake up. A friend of your father's is here. Say hello."

The girl's sad eyes drifted toward Sal. Inside them, Sal saw a multitude of hurts and humiliations. She knew that everything Z. and his cronies had done to Sal in junior high had been visited a thousand times upon his daughter. The sins of the father were brought to bear on the child. Sal suddenly felt ill, as if she might hurl.

She turned to Z. and said, "Great seeing you again."

She smiled at Betsy and said, "Thank you for showing me your lovely home."

And then she exited the house, running to her car.

"Wait," called Betsy. Z.'s wife hoofed across the dying lawn to the car just as Sal locked herself inside it. The wife knocked on the passenger-side window. Sal stomped the gas, zooming at seventy miles an hour. Away.

While having these thoughts, I recognized them for what they were: pure, undiluted egotistical fantasy. Building myself up while knocking Z. down. I called Judy (friend, not mother)—my punk rock role model in high school, who'd been just as harassed by Short Hills boys, but for different reasons—and asked, "Am I really this spiteful? Still? Shouldn't I have learned to be kindhearted and generous at some point?"

"That scumbag doesn't deserve your generosity," said Judy. "Once a shithead, always a shithead, I always say."

"That would make a lovely Hallmark card," I said.

If I did manage to get a bead on Z., I knew that the reality of making contact wouldn't be close to the fantasy. The idea of asking, "Why were you so mean to me in junior high?" terrified me. What could he possibly say to justify his cruelty? I hoped he'd stammer and beg forgiveness. I'd unleash some of my time-honed acid articulation on him. He'd probably hang up on me, but at least I'd have had my say.

After weeks of false starts, I started hunting Z. in earnest. I typed his name into a few search engines. His was a common name, the Jewish equivalent of Joe Smith. I wasn't expecting to get a direct hit on Google, and I sure didn't. I must have checked two hundred tags; none were useful. I called Liz, my lifelong friend who still lived in Short Hills, and asked her to tap into her sources for any clue to Z.'s whereabouts. She sniffed around discreetly and came back to me with two nuggets: Z. had gone to law school after college graduation, and he'd moved to a large tropical southern state. I searched that state's bar association, real estate, and police records. Nothing.

On Switchboard.com, I found several dozen listings for his name in the state. I connected to a tracker Web site that, for a fee, would provide active phone numbers and address histories for each listing. The site provided a teaser, the ages and known relatives of the listees. I eliminated all but five of the listings on age alone. Still, that got me only so far. For active phone numbers, I'd have to pay twenty-five dollars. Paying would be too easy. I was determined to find him using only my reporting skills. It'd be all the more satisfying.

A couple of the entries on my short list included a woman's name as a known relative. We'll call her U. I wondered if U. (not Betsy) was Z.'s wife's name and did a Google search for Z. and U.'s names together.

Bingo. I turned up a twenty-three-year-old *New York Times* wedding announcement. That clip provided me with U.'s maiden name—thankfully, an unusual one—and the former address of her parents in Westchester. A Switchboard .com search of that name in Westchester County turned up a listing, along with an active phone number. I dialed. A woman answered, first ring.

"Hello," I said. "I'm trying to find the parents of U."

"I'm her mother," said the woman.

I almost dropped the phone. My first call, a direct hit.

My heart pounded. Stupidly, I hadn't prepared a speech. I stammered, "My name is Val Frankel. I'm a friend of Z.'s from high school, and I'm trying to track him down . . . for a project I'm working on. I'm a journalist."

"Give me your name and number, and I'll pass it on to him," she said briskly. "Hurry up, I'm on the other line."

I gave her my info, and we hung up. My pulse was thundering in my veins. I called Liz and told her what happened. "He won't call," I said. "Why would he? He must know I hate him."

Liz said, "He'll be curious. I bet he calls tonight."

The thought made me queasy—but excited. Steve and the kids arrived home from karate, and I told them I'd found Z.'s in-laws and left my number. They knew I'd been on the hunt, searching for traces of blood in the water. Maggie was behind me all the way about confronting Z. I was her age when he started teasing me. When I told her about my past as a fat loser, she was outraged on my behalf. She seemed to crave my redemption as much as I did.

Maggie asked, "What if he doesn't call?"

"I'll phone the in-laws again in a week, and pester them every day until Z. calls to tell me to leave them alone. When I go after a source, I can be relentless. I've worn down people before, and I will again. I'm committed. I'm on a mission. I'm—"

Ring. My heart leapt into my throat, my hands shook. The caller ID display showed the name of a large tropical southern state.

I said, "It's him." Maggie ran over to me, her eyes and mouth wide open.

I pressed the TALK button. "Hello?" I asked. Casual.

"Hello, Valerie? It's Z. I heard you called my mother-in-law."

"Hello, Z. How's it going?"

"Great," he said. "Sorry about the static. I'm calling from the car."

He was that curious? He couldn't wait until he got home? "Thanks for returning the call," I said, going for gracious.

"It's so weird to hear your voice after all this time," he said.

Yeah. I remembered his voice, too, saying, "Valerie took a bite out of the moon," "She loves food," "Valerie ate the entire bakery."

"Here's the thing, Z.," I said. "I'm a writer now, and I'm working on a project about high school. I'd love to do an interview with you. See what you're doing." I'd start easy, lull him into a state of relaxation—and then go for the jugular.

"Well, I live in [medium-sized town]. I'm a financial adviser, specializing in retirement planning," he said. "I married my college sweetheart and have two sons. My older son just had his bar mitzvah."

"Your 'sweetheart'?" I said. "That's precious. I don't think I've called either of my husbands 'my sweetheart.'"

"We've been married for almost twenty-five years," he said. "She's a beautiful woman, but she spends money like crazy."

"I'm having trouble hearing you," I said.

"Static. I'm losing the signal. Why don't you call me at my office on Monday morning?" he asked.

I took his office number. I felt cold in my guts and hot on the surface of my skin. He'd been unsuspecting to a fault. He hadn't seemed to question my motive.

When I hung up, Maggie said, "Wow. You sounded like you didn't care at all."

"Really?" I asked.

"Totally."

Excellent, I thought, rubbing my hands together, à la *The Simpsons'* Mr. Burns. Nonchalance was the perfect disguise.

Over the weekend, I consulted my panel of advisers about how to handle the upcoming interview. Alison was opposed to the whole thing. "I don't understand what you hope to achieve," she said.

"I'm going to give him the golden opportunity to apologize to me," I said. "Then I'll be able to forgive him and get on with my life."

"You can't get on with your life otherwise?" she asked. "Did Z. really make your life hell, or did you give him the power to upset you? Are you seriously telling me Z. has loomed in your head as Evil Incarnate all this time? He's just some guy! He lives in friggin' [large tropical southern state]. He's a financial planner and complains that his wife spends too much money. Talk about the banality of evil. Part of letting go—which is your ultimate goal, right?—is growing up. Is it the act of a grown-up to start a fight with someone you haven't seen or spoken to in twenty-five years? If you still care about junior high, you're locked at that level of emotional development."

Rebecca had her doubts about a throw-down, too. "God knows, I love confrontation," she said. "The more confrontation the better. From what you say, though, he sounds like a loser, an easy target. Also, you might come off badly."

"How?"

"Consider flipping it," she said. "Say someone you hadn't thought about in twenty-five years called you and said, 'You know, back in junior high? You really hurt my feelings!' *Now* who's the loser?"

That made me spit my coffee laughing. I said, "You're the one who told me to eat the rat."

"You did, by calling him," said Rebecca. "You faced your fear. It's enough."

Judy (friend, not mother) was still in favor of me taking him out. "Look, you've proven that you're courageous. Posing nude? Doesn't get braver," she said. "But this isn't a test of your mettle. It's doing what needs to be done. I was there, Val. I know how much he deserves it."

Judy (mother, not friend) said, "Life is short. We all make mistakes. Don't be mean to Z."

My friend and former *Mademoiselle* colleague Daryl said, "You'll blindside him. He probably doesn't remember harassing you. If you accuse him, you might have to jog his memory about how he treated you, things he said. That would be awful!"

It seemed impossible that Z. wouldn't remember that for three years, approximately five to ten times a day, he'd either make an obnoxious gesture to me, such as puffing out his cheeks and walking like an elephant, or hurl a cutting remark, such as "fat load," "pig," "cow," or, the fantastical favorite, "beast." How could he have forgotten that he'd corralled his worshipful followers to match or best his slurs, and then rewarded them for it by doling out prized high fives in the school hallway? If I hadn't been his target, Z. and I wouldn't have had any social interaction. We had no friends or interests in common. He was a jock; I was a freak. Yet we were glued in my memory by the sticky resin of damage done. I feared Z.'s judgment in the eyes of every man I met, from junior high onward. Men judged women, harshly. That truth was imprinted on my operating system at age thirteen, the year I met Z. and his henchboys. If he remembered me—which he did—how could he not also remember what he'd done to me? He'd taken such apparent joy in cruelty, I assumed he looked back on it with nostalgic fondness—or regret, if he turned out to have a conscience. If Daryl was right, and Z. had forgotten he'd been a huge asshole, then he was an even *huger* asshole, which hardly seemed possible.

Steve shrugged when I asked him how I should handle the interview. "Make the call. Just talk to him, find out what he's like. He was a jerky kid. He's probably a jerky adult. Confirmation of his jerkiness might be all the redemption you need."

Monday morning, Maggie asked at breakfast if I was still going to call Z. I said, "Yes."

"You have to tell me everything," she said, her eyes glowing.

Maybe I *was* locked at the junior high level of emotional development. Maggie, a bona fide middle schooler, was pushing me hard to injure Z. for past insults. She wanted me to do to Z. what she'd love to do to the popular girl who didn't invite her to an exclusive party, or to the boy who called her a shrimp.

"I want details," she said. "The juicier, the better."

I made the call. Not for Maggie, but for me. Blowing it off would've been a total cop-out. Besides, I was curious about his life. I dialed his number, my fingers trembling. I was still undecided about whether I should demand an explanation or an apology.

I understood Alison's point, that I needed to let go and grow up, but I didn't agree that calling was childish. I was erasing my fear by facing it, like an adult. Whether it was right or wrong to view Z. as the symbol of my teenage woe and lasting fear of male judgment didn't matter. That was what he'd become in my mind, and I wanted the weight off me.

"Right on time," he said, picking up.

"Thanks for giving me your time, Z.," I replied. "As I mentioned, I'm doing preliminary interviews for a writing project. Looking back at high school. Seeing where people are now."

"Got it," he said.

"Tell me about your life."

He did. I nearly dozed off after two minutes. He told me about his fantasy football league, his yard work on the weekends, how he dotes on his children, his surprise fortieth birthday party at a cabin in the woods. He said he was in close touch with *thirty guys* from high school and rattled off names I'd completely forgotten. (When I told Rebecca about that, she said, "I guess he's still popular.") I asked if he had friends from other phases of life, and he said, "A few guys from my college soccer team." He had a law degree, but being an attorney was "too demanding," so he quit. His career was "decent." He loved his wife and kids. He was renovating his garage.

In short, he was boring as hell. The golden boy, the charismatic leader who'd seemed destined for greatness, had grown up remarkably unremarkable. He demonstrated zero imagination, ambition, curiosity. Despite the fact that I asked him dozens of personal questions, he failed to ask me a single one. Not even "Do you have kids?" which was pretty much a standard for any reunion-type conversation. Liz said curiosity would make him call me back. Wrong. He'd been motivated by vanity, I realized, not curiosity. He said he wasn't "much of a reader" and didn't follow politics "too closely." He hadn't traveled beyond predictable destinations like Paris and London. He lived in New York City for a few years after grad school, but rejected the epicenter of world culture in favor of his soulless southern state "because I hate the cold." He went on at length about his "best" pals from high school, serving up stories about going to each other's kids' bar mitzvahs, including X.'s (also a financial planner in the same state).

I started to ask questions that probed a bit deeper. About aging, relationships, regrets. He claimed to be immune to all the symptoms of the human condition. No disappointments, no regrets, he said. Finally, I broke out the big guns, a question that would put me on a direct path to his emotional core. "So, you're a married suburban financial planner with two kids," I said. "Is this the life you dreamed about?"

"I never had any dreams," he said.

"Oh, come on! When you were twenty and idealistic and had fantasies about how your life would go, about leaving a mark . . ."

"Honestly, I never had dreams about my future," he said. "I don't care about changing the world or leaving a mark. I just want to be a good friend, father, and husband, and to retire early and play golf."

"That's it?"

"That's it!" he said proudly.

I got off the phone shortly thereafter. A confrontation about our blighted past was beside the point. Why ask for a heartfelt apology from a man who had no conflicted emotions about anything he'd done in his entire life? He didn't grapple with choices. He didn't have anything to prove to the world, let alone to himself. He was content to live out his days and then fade gently, good night.

Naturally, my knee-jerk reaction was to judge him harshly for being so self-satisfied. But I couldn't muster the contempt. The person I'd held up as a monster from my formative years was just a bundle of skin, a thoughtless consumer of the earth's oxygen. Z. had chosen—gleefully—an ordinary life. And that was fine for him. It was fine for anyone.

That life would never be enough for me, though. Not to imply that I was better than him—but at least I had dreams! They defined who I was and who I wanted to be. They spurred me forward, motivated and inspired me to reach higher, prove myself, leave a mark, make an impact on the people close to me, as well as distant strangers in foreign lands. Although my choices had been predictable—college, career, marriage, kids—I'd tried to be extraordinary within (or a few steps beyond) the boundaries of convention. Being a good friend, mother, and wife was paramount. But I wanted—I needed—more.

Strivers are driven to test themselves over and over again. They don't rest on their accomplishments. Success urges them to reach higher, take bigger risks. If they fail, they pull themselves back up. Ambition is the essence of human evolution. Strivers adapt to their changing environment.

I was a striver. My environment—the body I lived in and the mind that controlled the body—was changing. I could feel it. In fact, while I was on the phone with Z., the ground shifted beneath my feet. Not because I understood him—or

THE MOTHER LOAD, PART THREE

Talking and eating. The usual business with Mom. We were at the kitchen table in Short Hills having breakfast the morning of my reading at the temple luncheon. I was going to read excerpts from this book, about chronic dieting, silencing the Inner Bitch, and posing nude. I'd driven out to Short Hills from Brooklyn the night before and slept in my childhood bedroom, the place where I'd scribbled madly in my journal, playing the Ramones at full blast, rattling the windows and frightening the dogs.

I asked, "Who's coming, again?"

Mom recited a list of names. For charity events like this, you have to purchase "a chair" for fifty dollars or "a table" for five hundred dollars. Mom fronted five hundred dollars to reserve a whole table and then gave away or sold the seats to her friends. Some of the spots would be filled by the women who, according to Mom, had been just as relentless about their daughters' weight as Judy had been about mine.

I said, "It's so sweet that they're coming."

"Not to support you," said Mom. "To support me!"

"I'm barely mentioning you," I said.

Was that a flicker of disappointment I saw in her eyes? Probably not. I knew Mom was worried that I'd out her as an imperfect mother. She had a reputation to protect. She'd sent three kids to Dartmouth, after all. Two of us were published authors. The other had a master's in engineering. None of us were rich, alas. By Short Hills standards, Alison, Jon, and I would be considered lower class. To Mom's credit, she always cared more about our accomplishments than our salaries.

"You didn't have to a buy a table," I said. "I could have gotten you a chair for free."

"And go alone?" she asked. "*Never.*"

Mom had a peculiar quirk. Correction, Mom had *dozens* of peculiar quirks, but I was referring to one in particular. Judy had never eaten alone at a restaurant or café, nor gone to a party or function by herself. I learned this about her only last summer. We were sitting (where else?) at the kitchen table in Vermont—reading the paper, drinking the coffee—when Steve called to check in and say that he'd arrived safely at JFK (he was returning from a gig in London) and was going to grab a bite at an airport pub before cabbing home. Mom listened to my end of the conversation and then asked, "He's going to a restaurant?"

I said, "He's hungry."

Mom said, "By himself?"

"He's got a book."

Mom said, "I'd rather die than eat alone in public."

"Why?" I asked, astonished.

"When I see people alone in restaurants—even if they're reading—they look lonely and pathetic. I'd couldn't possibly let myself be seen that way," she said.

"It's official," I said. "You are insane."

"It's just how I feel," she said. The usual "I am who I am" defense.

I reached for my purse and took out my wallet. "I'll give you a hundred bucks to go to Starbucks with the *Times* crossword puzzle and sit at a table with a cup of coffee. For fifteen minutes," I said, slapping twenties on the table.

"I couldn't," said Mom.

"Two hundred."

"Not a chance."

I tore a blank check out of my book and quickly scribbled on it. Holding the check up, I said, "One-time offer: If you go to Starbucks and sit at the counter for five minutes, I will give you *one thousand dollars!*"

"Forget it," she said. "I'm sure you'd dance naked on the counter at Starbucks for half as much!"

"You making an offer?"

"Give me that," she said, taking the check out of my hand and tearing it up.

I knew she wouldn't do it (or I'd never have offered a thousand bucks). Mom could go to a park by herself (with the dogs), or sit in a movie theater, but she couldn't be seen in an *eating* establishment, or at an *eating* event, by herself. This phobia was like another layer of her skewed views about food, eating, and weight. She was in horror at the idea of being thought of as pathetic and lonely by strangers. Interesting, she was so afraid of being judged yet so extremely judgmental herself.

"I find it ironic that you assume a solo diner is pathetic, when the fact that he has the self-possession to eat alone in public proves he's more emotionally stable than you are!" I said.

"Shut up, Valerie," she said, which was her way of changing the subject.

Appearance—make that *appearances*—dominated Mom's thoughts. Being seen eating alone was a sign of weakness or failure to her. Just like having an overweight daughter.

It was setting the bar pretty low in terms of personal accomplishment, but I ate alone at restaurants often. I selfishly grabbed an hour of peace and quiet whenever I got the chance. Solitude had always been a welcomed escape. Mom? I think she had enough solitude when she was a neglected child, and had become an intensely social person to make up for lost face time. She loved to entertain, go out with friends, surround herself with family. She was chatty in the extreme. Nary a silent moment passed by; she would quickly fill it with words. She compulsively crammed empty spaces with people, dogs, furniture, and art. Judy kept herself busy, too. Always chopping, cooking, decorating, doing dog visits at hospitals, organizing, shopping. She rarely had time and quiet to be alone with her thoughts. By choice, I assumed.

Mom's deepest fears, the ones she drowned out with conversation and activity, had to be old, and sculpted sharp by the passage of time. Despite her stabs at therapy, Mom hadn't found a way to conquer her anxieties, or the will to try. She outright rejected psychopharmacology for herself, although she encouraged others to explore it. She had no intention of changing, or even considering whether change might make her happier.

Whereas I sought evolution with the fervor of a convert. This apple had fallen from the tree, rolled down the hill, and made a wild dash out of suburbia, to seed and flourish in the city. My desperate scramble out of New Jersey had been motivated by my impulse to explore—the city and my psyche. I'd been in therapy. I'd tried past-life regression, hypnosis, psychic readings, tarot readings, yoga, hallucinatory drugs, sacral-cranial therapy, energy work, reflexology, and all manner of massage. As a magazine writer, I'd road-tested colon cleansers, lip plumpers, fish oil supplements, and tiny plastic devices to strengthen the muscle tone of the vagina, among many other pills and appliances.

I'd been an intrepid explorer. I'd ventured forth and deep, emotionally speaking, but not that far geographically. Unlike my brother, a neo-Californian, I lived just twenty miles from my childhood home. I was connected to Short Hills, to my parents and the landscape. I visited often, brought the girls to see their grandparents and the dogs. There was comfort to be found in the familiar, even if the familiar had once kicked my ass.

My kicked ass and I arrived at the temple lunch on time. I recognized faces, but I couldn't remember names (see above, re: hallucinatory drug use). Although I hadn't seen some of these women for decades, many looked exactly the same. I hoped I looked half as good as my suburban contemporaries, most of them the wives of wealthy husbands and full-time moms, having quit their jobs when they got pregnant. Merely a statement of fact. I was not judging. If I had a rich husband, I'd probably work a lot less . . . actually, I probably wouldn't. I loved my job! Plus, I had those dreams. But whatever. While talking to the grown-up versions of girls I knew in high school, I flashed backward and saw their faces and hairstyles as they once were. Lauren H. (née L.) brought along a snapshot of a third-grade sleepover party. There I was, on the couch, reading a book. I looked exactly like Lucy does now. And not fat at all, btw.

Liz appeared at my side and stayed there, as she'd promised to do. Her memory was frighteningly sharp, and I needed her to feed me names and make the connections when women came over to say hello. People introduced themselves as the girl who sat next to me in junior high science class, or the friend of a friend from my brother's grade, or a kid I went to summer camp with. They mentioned the titles of my books, specific articles I'd written, TV appearances, reviews of my novels in newspapers and magazines, the Vows column on our wedding in the *Times* Styles section.

Short Hills, a small town, had produced a fair number of well-known authors. Much to my amazement, at least in this crowd, I was among them. The women treated me as if I were a teeny tiny bit famous! That felt *good*. My dress, meanwhile—the brown embroidered empire-waist creation from Banana Republic—felt *great*. In a room packed with rich housewives who considered the Short Hills Mall their daily stomping grounds, I was not a slouch. My chocolate high-heeled sandals matched my new Longchamp purse. I'd blown out my hair. My fingernails and toenails were immaculate and polished. I'd stroked on mascara and lipstick. I was passing for stylish. Stacy London was right. The feeling of being well put together was a powerful tool, an easy way to make an impression without writing or saying a word.

The speeches got under way. Liz introduced me. She gave a brief talk about how I'd always been a misfit in this town (she described it euphemistically as "marching to the beat of her own punk rock drummer"), and how I was continuing to follow my own divergent path on my search for truth. "The naked truth," she said, referring to the article in *Self* that landed me this gig. She also described me as her friend of thirty-five years. Liz had seen me at every stage, every weight. I'd seen her grow up, too, although she'd been consistently beautiful, only her hair changing over the years from Dorothy Hamill to Heidi Klum and most lengths in between. I got choked up when she read her speech. Tingle in throat. Right before I was supposed to start reading. I had to compose myself by pinching my forearm. Then I got up, was applauded by the crowd of 150 women, and started talking about the fear of being fat.

As readings go, it was very good. The women were with me for the entire half hour. During the Q&A afterward, one woman asked, "Do you think body image issues are a particular danger for our daughters in this environment?" She meant affluent suburbs.

I said, "Yes." I spoke the truth, since we were being naked about it, and listed the reasons: pursuit of status, social pressure, sky-high parental expectations, conspicuous consumption, too much free time, too much attention paid to appearances. I didn't dwell on how living in Short Hills had twisted my own body image. I'd been invited to entertain the ladies, not bite the hand. I added, "But bad body image can happen to girls anywhere, in any environment, in any kind of family." I could wind up the greatest, healthiest role model about body image on the planet, and my daughters would still have to contend with their peers, cultural pressure, the media. I said as much to the ladies.

I might've been hoping to have a big redemptive moment, along the lines of "I was a loser here twenty-five years ago, and now I'm standing in front of the microphone!" But that sentiment was irrelevant. I saw the audience as my people, women who'd struggled with body image and were worried about it on behalf of their daughters. I felt only grateful for having been asked to talk, and for being listened to.

Also, as promised, I barely mentioned Judy. Her friend Anita, seated at Judy's right at their table, was disappointed. She said, "I was all ready to jump out of my seat and shout, 'I object!'" That made me laugh.

The lunch concluded, the ladies filed out. The organizers had set up a table where I could sign and sell my books. Mom sat next to me and did the hard work of making chatter. I smiled at the buyers as best I could, but the reading had sapped my energy. Mom picked up the slack, made small talk with everyone, was charming, funny, and "up," as always. Her talk skills probably doubled my sales. Another reason to be grateful.

I asked Mom what she thought. She said, "The women loved it. They were paying attention and seemed to relate. A lot of nodding and laughing at appropriate moments."

"What did *you* think?" I asked.

She pursed her lips. "You seemed confident. I wouldn't have the courage to speak in front of a hundred and fifty people like that."

Although Mom was socially fearless—she could talk to anyone, anywhere, anytime—she shied away from the spotlight. She loved to cook and entertain, but rarely held court at her own fetes, preferring to run back and forth between the kitchen and the service tables, having bite-sized conversations with her guests along the way. I urged her to hire caterers so that she wouldn't be so busy at her own parties, and she insisted she liked to do it her way. "Her way" was to do everything, except be the center of attention. In the dozens of family celebrations we'd been to together, I'd seen her make only one toast—at my wedding with Steve, when she touchingly welcomed him into our family.

"I was surprised by some of what you said," admitted Mom as we walked to the temple parking lot. "I didn't realize you were so preoccupied with weight. I knew you went on diets, but I didn't realize you cared that much."

Visible distortion in the Force. I was dumbfounded. How could my mother be unaware of a dominant theme of my life? Either she'd been selectively blind or I hadn't told her.

Probably both. I hadn't described my diets. She didn't comment on my size fluctuations. Although weight had been the epicenter of our relationship during my adolescence, the subject had been off-limits since I started my independent life in Brooklyn. Once I was self-sufficient, I cut off uncomfortable conversations the same way she did. I'd say, "Shut up, Judy," with a warning tone, and she would. I was willing to talk to her about anything else: dating (well, not sex), my job, books in progress, then Glenn, the wedding planning, pregnancies, etc. I always went to Mom first in a crisis. No one on earth was more reliable than Judy when the chips were down. I'd turned to her for advice on practical matters big and small, parenting to gift giving. She told me the mundane details of her day-to-day life.

Although we'd exchanged millions of words over thousands of cups of coffee, how much had we revealed of our intimate lives to each other? Our conversations were light, practical, logistical. We hardly ever waded into the deeper waters of our emotions. Even during the most emotionally fraught time of my life, when Glenn was sick, Judy was my rock about practical and tactical matters. But about the feelings? My friends heard that part. I'd written articles for magazines that had exposed my soul to anonymous millions, but I hadn't really opened up, not all the way, to my mother. Mom barely knew me, I realized.

And I barely knew her. For all I hadn't shared with her, she'd shared even less with me. We didn't trust each other. On some level, I would always be fearful and defensive about her criticism. She would probably be anxious that I was holding a grudge.

We got in the car. Judy drove out of the temple parking lot, toward home. The familiar, unchanging place.

I'd been able to stop dieting for the last nine months. Would I ever stop distrusting my mom? Moreover, I wondered, would Judy ever really, truly, deeply trust me? As she said, she was who she was. She would not change. Was our relationship also set in stone? I was willing to explore unfamiliar ground, to open up to Mom. Maybe she'd open up to me. Surely *we* could evolve.

Or not. For a relationship to develop, each person in it has to hold up a mirror and look at herself closely and honestly. I was willing to gaze into the mirror and see the reflected (naked) truth, be it beautiful or terrible. Mom? Not so much.

I was going to have to accept her for who she was, and our relationship for what it was, and let sleeping fat dogs lie wheezing in the corner.

I'd asked a lot from Judy in recent months, interviewing her about her childhood, confronting her about our past. It was already July. Steve and I were back in Vermont for parents' weekend at Maggie and Lucy's sleepaway camp. At the kitchen table in Thetford, over berries and scones, I asked Judy for one more thing: to read what I'd written in this memoir.

"I'm not going to do it," she said. "You can believe what you want to believe. You can write what you want to write. But I don't have to have anything to do with it."

I asked Dad if he was going to read it, and he said, "I'm not sure."

Later, in private, Steve and I talked about Judy's response. I said, "Gave me an instant iced-over feeling."

He nodded. "It did seem a bit cold."

Frankly, I was relieved Judy would give this book a pass. Still, her rejection—hard and fast—stung. She wasn't willing or able to face the truth (my version of it), or to experience the difficult emotions that process would evoke. She might as well have wagged her index finger in my face and said, "I will *not* go there."

Thirty years from now, if Maggie and Lucy wrote memoirs that included their grievances against me, of course I'd read them. I'd be dying to read them! I'd be first in line for a peek at the inner workings of my daughters' minds, insight about their thoughts and feelings, and a sense of how they'd experienced their lives—with me and apart from me. I'd use that knowledge to better understand them, and myself, and to strengthen our relationship.

Judy would predictably buy Christmas gifts in May, be available for babysitting, have lots to say about any topic that sprang to mind. She'd be boundlessly helpful, making arrangements, giving advice, offering suggestions. I'd always fill her in on the mechanics of our lives, the comings and goings, the projects and purchases. With exciting news or in crisis, Mom would get the first phone call. As always, we'd be thisclose, and miles   apart.

16
EMOTIONAL MAINTENANCE

Months of not-dieting had come to this: I was, once again, a size eight. A real eight. Not the delusional eight of cramming one's ass into stretch jeans at the Gap and declaring victory. I could walk into just about any store in New York, grab a pair of size eight pants off the rack, and button them comfortably.

I considered myself Test Subject #1. A walking (jogging) contradiction. An American paradox. In eleven months, I'd shrunk two dress sizes without dieting. The weight loss was gradual, physically painless. I had some tough moments along the way, but they were, if unsettling, ultimately constructive. Every so often, Inner Bitch would sneak a barb through my defenses, but I'd learned to squash the negative thought before it ricocheted destructively in my mind. I'd been purposefully imperfect—sometimes eating ice cream while watching TV, or lazily blowing off the gym—without crippling guilt (I'd never eradicate guilt completely; a Jew thing).

I'd admitted mistakes, flaws, and mistreatment to myself and others, which, I hoped, had made me a better, more humble person.

As far as I was concerned, my theory was now proven fact. Excess weight *was* the physical accumulation of past hurts, insults, disappointments, and resentments that, once released from the mind and soul, were freed from the body. I'd purged big-time. The ancient anger, blame, and shame were out of my system. In their place was a glut of self-awareness. I was convinced that any woman—and I do mean *any*—could melt down to her genetically predetermined true weight by (1) stopping dieting today, (2) silencing her negative inner voice, (3) forgiving everyone who'd contributed to her forming a bad body image, and (4) working out four times a week.

I haven't talked much about my exercising (just as appropriate: exorcizing). I'd go to the gym, get on a machine, sweat. The details are freaking boring and didn't fit into the emotional evolution that was far more interesting for all concerned. As it turns out, however, exe(o)rcise has been part of the emotional picture. Good body image and regular exercise have been linked in a spate of recent psych studies in the last couple of years. For a magazine article, I interviewed a grad student from Marymount University about her research. She told me she saw a bump in body image in subjects who worked out only twenty minutes three times a week. Basically, it doesn't take all that much physical effort to shape up your mind.

I didn't want to be obsessive or a perfectionist about workouts. I aimed for four gym visits a week, and pretty much hit that mark. Conventional wisdom dictates that it takes six months for any behavior, good or bad, to become a habit. I'd broken the habit barrier. Now, if I missed two days in a row, I went a little nuts.

Otherwise, I was decidedly sane. My conscience was squeaky clean about my marriage, my mom, my role model behavior for my daughters. I'd come to absolutely *love* walking into my closet and choosing from my piles and racks of superfine new threads. (God, put a blessing on Stacy London's head! She did excellent work!) Catching glimpses of myself in storefront windows used to make me cringe. Nowadays, I paused to admire.

As anyone who's been fat and been thin can tell you, thin feels better. From the moment you wake up in the morning to the second you fall asleep at night. Throughout this process, I'd wanted to stop hating the fat. But I'd also wanted to get thinner. To let go, without letting myself go. To do a reshaping above and below the neck.

So, yeah. I was where I wanted to be. You'd think I'd be ecstatic. I *was* quite relieved and energized. My load(s) had been lightened. I walked with a bouncy step, every day. And yet:

I was terrified.

Another study here, this one not so sanguine. Per national data, only 20 percent of dieters maintained a 10 percent weight loss for a year. Since I hadn't weighed myself, I had no clue what percentage I'd lost. But I did know this: In a far more personal study, conducted over thirty years, I'd regained *at least* 100 percent of the weight I'd lost in 100 percent of the diets I'd tried.

During my glittery, shimmering past periods of size-eight-dom, I'd been cocky and foolish, assuming that, since I was thin now, I'd be able to maintain. I'd overeat, blow off jogging. Then I'd step on the scale and be surprised I'd gained five pounds. I'd vow to crash diet to get back to goal weight. Never worked as planned. I'd rebel against the restriction, regain the rest of the loss, and then suffer an emotional crash. Crash diet, indeed.

This time, I knew enough about my self-destructive patterns and motivations to be righteously afraid. Add to that the huge expense of buying an all-new size eight wardrobe. I really didn't want my snazzy new duds to be my future thin clothes. And I sure as hell didn't want to shell out an additional $3,500 (and counting) to purchase a new fat wardrobe.

Even worse than that, if I were to regain, I'd slide down a shame spiral that I might not return from. The Inner Bitch would come roaring back, and she'd be very, very angry. Steve said I was perpetually "humorless and grumpy" when my weight tracked upward. If I were to gain again, I'd hate myself and be hateful to others.

Also, think of the embarrassment! I'd opened a vein here. I'd dug deep to get *out* of a hole. If I plumped up, I'd be a failure to myself, as well as to my theories. And it'd be a public failure. Along with readings and magazine articles that preached my points, I'd been holding forth about the wonders of not-dieting at dinners and parties and lunches for almost a year. What could be more humiliating than writing a memoir about conquering body image issues, only to allow them to take over my life again?

Well, actually, there was one thing worse. How about appearing on a TV reality show, dropping 122 pounds, winning a $250,000 grand prize, and then putting nearly all of the weight back on in less than a year?

It saddens me to report that Ryan Benson, the season-one winner of *The Biggest Loser,* the show that inspired my last diet, did just that. In a June 2007 *Time* magazine article, Benson said he slipped back into his preshow bad habits, and the weight came back, at lightning (heavying?) speed. Matt Hoover, winner of season two, regained fifty-three pounds of his loss just as quickly. Erik Chopin, season-three winner, regained twenty-two pounds in just a month. God bless him, I hoped Chopin wouldn't put on another ounce, but the guy owned a deli on Long Island, for Christ's sake. He was around food all day long! The one ray of hope in the *Time* article was Kelly Minner, runner-up of season one, who not only kept off the eighty pounds she lost on the show but dropped an *additional* twenty pounds. How? Minner worked out like a fiend, one to four hours *every bloody day.*

Minner was motivated by fear of her former fat. In her office, she kept a life-size photo of herself at 242 pounds. I wondered if Minner walked into her office each morning, looked at her old figure, and tasted the sweetness of her triumph, or if she recoiled at the sight, remembering her years of misery. Minner seemed like a plucky, tough woman. I'd bet she gloried in her success, as she should.

I would rather look at my neat, pretty naked photos for inspiration than at some hideous bloated shot of me at my worst. Ideally, maintenance could be a happy existence, not fraught with fear and guilt. Since my goals for the Not Diet were emotional, I figured an emotionally based maintenance plan stood a better chance of success than my useless crash diet standby.

It seemed wise to check in with Ed Abramson and Joan Chrisler, the shrinks who'd put my feet on the not-dieting path way back at the beginning of my quest. "The emotions of maintenance?" asked Ed. "Frustration comes to mind." He talked about what he sees in his patients, how they struggle with the gap between their expected miraculous life transformation and the reality that life is more or less the same, even after dropping weight. They still don't have sixteen boyfriends and a dream job and feel at ease on the beach in a bathing suit. "It's easy to blame your unhappiness on excess weight. But if the weight goes, the unhappiness might stick around," said Ed. Enter overeating, sedentary mild depression, weight re-gain. The boomerang effect is ruthlessly quick for chronic dieters. Subconsciously—hell, *consciously*—we expect the weight to creep back on. It's always happened before. It's bound to happen again.

Nonetheless, I was always stupidly surprised that my weight losses weren't permanent. I'd reduced to thinness, so didn't that make me a "thin person"? Thin people ate chocolate cake; fat people ate rice cakes. I'd convince myself that being thin made me a thin person. And then I'd relax my standards.

"'Relaxing your standards' is the language of a dieter," said Ed. "It implies all-or-nothing thinking. But you're a nondieter now. You don't have to worry about 'cheating' or 'pigging out.'" I also had the exercise habit going for me. Apparently, among people who'd lost weight and kept it off,

94 percent worked out often. Case in point: Kelly Minner, the woman who purposefully terrified herself with a giant photo of the way she used to be.

I hated the idea of using fear as a motivator for my emotional maintenance plan. I wanted to feel *less* afraid of re-gain, not more. "Good thinking," agreed Joan. "Negative emotions are the hallmarks of diet cycling. Fear, frustration, guilt, shame. They lead to lapses, and then bigger lapses. You have to stop thinking about your past history of re-gaining. What happened to you before won't happen this time. There's a big difference between those times and now."

And that was . . . ?

"You're not-dieting this time!" she said.

Exactly. If I was going to rightfully be afraid of something, Ed and Joan told me, I should worry about lapsing into old destructive habits—like dieting.

What about my nearly pathological habit of chasing the same dream over and over again? My puzzling self-sabotage bent. Logically, the way to go there was, duh, to come up with other goals. Non-weight-related goals. Of which I already had a list as long as my arm. Among them: to finish this book, run another half marathon, cook healthy and nutritious meals for the whole family every night, and take advantage of living in New York City—the museums, theaters, concert halls—more often.

Chronic dieting had exhausted my mind and time. It was oppressing. Perhaps the biggest benefit of not-dieting was the mental space I had cleared to visualize reaching other, more important goals. Joan said, "Women's minds are cluttered with all these tiny details about calories and fat grams. One of the best things a chronic dieter can do for herself is to say, 'I refuse to waste one more minute of my life on this anymore.' You might not get to the exact dress size you want, but you can throw away useless guilt and oppression. Freedom. That's what I'm talking about."

Amen, sister! We shall overcome! Among all oppressed peoples throughout history, we women hold the dubious distinction of being the only group to persecute *ourselves*. We are our own enemies. We chose the battle that we could never win. Call it the Thousand Years War. If every woman on earth were to suddenly release her fat obsession into the wind, the world would change profoundly for the better. The world around us, and the world within.

I would not let fear control my thoughts. The maintenance philosophy I developed reflected that idea. I came up with the plan during the months of summer travel. Travel had always been as much of a journey inward as outward for me. Two trips helped me create a happiness-based maintenance plan I could live with for the rest of my life, as I intended to do.

My policy had two basic tenets. I came up with the first while in San Francisco with the family.

We flew to California right after school ended, in late June. Before we left, I told everyone who'd listen about my plans to run the Golden Gate Bridge. I ran the Brooklyn Bridge often. I loved the idea of jogging across our nation's other famous bridge. It seemed a worthy goal. And since I was setting healthy new challenges for myself, as prescribed by Joan Chrisler, I was pumped. Our hotel was located miles away from the Golden Gate's footpath, not exactly convenient, but I figured I had four mornings to figure out a way to get over there via public conveyance. Steve was happy to spend a few hours alone with the kids while I did my thing. As far as eating went, I promised myself to stick to ordinary Not Diet policy, eating whatever I wanted when hungry and stopping when full.

Almost as soon as my feet touched California ground, the eating plan was out the window. I'd read a Christopher Moore novel in anticipation of our trip, and he wrote about sourdough clam chowder bowls. I mentioned the loaf-'n'-soup dish to Maggie, and she insisted on getting one first thing. Lucy, meanwhile, had heard about the Ghirardelli chocolate shop and was obsessing on a hot fudge sundae upon arrival if not sooner. Since our hotel was located at Fisherman's Wharf, mere blocks from chowder bowl central and Ghirardelli Square, the whole family was drowning in chowder and fudge within an hour of dropping off our bags.

We ate roast pork and fried rice in Chinatown. I consumed copious Boudin bread with creamy fresh butter, using it to sop up the sauce on my empty pasta plate each night. After hiking in Muir Woods, we drove up the coast in our rented convertible and stopped at a beach shack for baskets of burgers and fries. For breakfasts, we went to a bakery for ham and cheese croissants or to a diner that specialized in sourdough French toast, yet another San Francisco treat. We'd been Left Coasters for three days when I realized I hadn't eaten a vegetable or piece of fruit since we'd arrived. And I still hadn't run the Golden Gate.

While walking along the Embarcadero after a fantastic

ferry ride and an audio tour of Alcatraz (where the inmates once rioted for being served spaghetti too many nights in a row), Steve said, "Tomorrow's your last chance to do the bridge."

"Funny how it was so important before we got here," I said. "Now, I don't really care if I do it at all."

"Are you sure?" he asked. "None of that Jewish guilt?"

Honestly, none. About any of it. So I didn't run, or stop eating when full. I was on vacation! We were so busy and having too much fun to waste a single second on negative thought. The kids had finally reached the age when we could expect them to climb a mountain, eat at three-star restaurants, and walk all over town without complaint. They were fantastic, fun co-travelers, excited about our activities, making smart shopping choices, being nice to each other (a pleasant change), grateful, polite, funny. We were a tight little crew, our (almost legal) family.

The adoption paperwork was being processed. It would take a few months before Steve was their legal father, but on that trip I felt the change in status already, a stronger cohesion. We were doing so well together, and I loved the shared experiences of our adventures, including the elaborate meals and street noshing. No way was I going to take off for half a day to pursue a personal goal that seemed less and less important or meaningful.

What did matter on this trip? Our being united in happiness, gluttony, and indulgence. Guilt and obligation didn't fit into the equation. And, upon our homecoming, I realized my new habits *were* entrenched. On the eastbound flight, I started looking forward to hitting the gym and eating lighter.

My body and soul were relieved to return to exercising and green food. And I seamlessly eased back into Not Dieter and gym-goer, as if I hadn't taken the short break at all. Any weight I put on in San Francisco came off within a week of being back in Brooklyn. No harm, no foul. In fact, the break was a help. I was so damn proud of myself for reverting to good habits. The pride spurred me on.

I thought back to previous vacations, for example, our family vacation to Disney World last summer. I didn't work out or eat well then, either. But I felt guilty and crappy about it, which tainted the trip for me. My grousing probably affected Steve's and the girls' time, too. And I sure didn't seamlessly transition back to jogging and salads when we got back. On the contrary. My post-Disney eating was just as bad as it was in Orlando.

The key differences: guilt and regret, negative emotions that brought on bad patterns. In San Francisco, I felt only positive emotions, which inspired me to bounce back into good patterns. Perfectionism really is the enemy of happiness and success.

Hence, Tenet #1: **Live a little.**

Two months later, at the end of the summer, after retrieving Maggie and Lucy from camp, the girls and I flew to West Palm Beach for a short visit with Glenn's parents before school started. They lived in a South Florida retirement community. You had to be at least fifty-five to buy property on the estate, but the average age of the residents was closer to seventy. The community was built less than six years ago. It was pretty-yet-homogenous. Lots of hibiscus plants and tropical landscaping. The terra-cotta-colored houses were identical, lined up in rows on clean streets. Whenever we visited, the girls spent practically the entire time in the pool. I always brought my laptop and tried to get work done. My role there was facilitator, helping the girls and their grandparents bond.

On previous trips, I always brought along my sneakers and sports bras, and swore I'd go to the small air-conditioned gym by the pool while the kids swam. I'd never done it. Not once, in half a dozen trips. Predictably, I'd feel the usual cocktail of guilt and regret as I unpacked my unused exercise clothes upon our return. This year, I brought my jogging gear as always, but I didn't make empty promises to myself. Instead, I took action. Each morning, before breakfast, I excused myself to the in-laws, and I went to the gym.

The place was usually deserted when I arrived, despite the fact that, by eight in the morning, the lounge chairs by the pool were already filling up. The old folk get up *early* in Florida. They eat dinner at three in the afternoon, too, but I digress. A few stragglers arrived at the gym. I was the youngest person in the room by thirty years. I felt like Wonder Woman on the treadmill, next to the ladies on my right who were walking at two miles per hour and yapping about their grandchildren. I realized how pathetic that was, comparing myself to grandmas. Keeping my head down, I did my thing and left.

The next morning, another woman came into the gym. She had to be seventy, going by the folds of skin around her neck. But that was the only area of her body with loose flesh. She was a tight, taut cougar in spandex pants, a black tank top, and the fingerless gloves I'd seen on weight lifters at my gym in Brooklyn.

The biddies on the treadmill waved and said hello to the blonde in black. She returned the greeting. Then she got down to business. As I watched from the treadmill, this old lady started stacking weights onto a bar. Forty pounds on each side. After some stretching, she lay down on the bench and started pressing the dumbbells.

After twelve reps, she stretched and did it again. Then she moved around the gym like a pro, as if she'd done it thousands of times before, which, duh, she obviously had. She went on to perform feats of strength—curls, crunches, and whatnot—that a forty-year-old *man* would crow about. The whole time, this AARP pinup smiled as she moved around the equipment. She glistened with the sheen of accomplishment. She shone with an inner light of strength. I watched her go through her paces openly, awed by the bionic septuagenarian. I might've been gawking. At one point, between crunches, she winked at me.

What did the wink mean? Probably nothing. The habitual act of a friendly person. But I decided that she was trying to send me a message. A covert message, from one exerciser to another: "Be good to your body, because it's the only one you're ever going to get." The alternative? Wind up like those obese women sprawled in groaning lounge chairs who'd driven the three blocks from their houses to the pool because it was too far for them to walk.

I wanted to be that bench-pressing granny. I wanted to be her now, at forty-one. And I wanted to be her at fifty-two and sixty-two and ninety-two, should I live so long. She seemed to represent a conscious choice between (1) a healthy, strong future of thriving and surviving and (2) a slothful existence of inactivity, illness, decline, and dependence.

The choice was obvious. For me, there would be no more fooling around with weight loss and re-gain, or protracted periods of inactivity. At a certain stage in the aging process—and I was well into that—fitness shouldn't be a goal or an obsession. Fitness is life itself.

You have to love your body as a living organism, not hate it as a flawed decorative statue. Only a fool or a child would put a premium on pretty over healthy. Bad body image, I realized, was kid stuff. Mine had kicked in at eleven. I'd dragged a childhood problem into my forties.

That wink was my wake-up call. My *grow*-up call. Which brought me to Tenet #2: **Take care.**

My bad body image, a vestige of the past, was now history. My future would be devoted to strength—of character and muscle. My new role model was that iron-pumping grandma with the fingerless gloves and the frosted blond hair. When the body image demons rattled the cage, as they surely would from time to time, I'd think of her and remember that I had only one body, and one choice. To love it—or leave it. I wanted to stay around long enough to see my daughters' daughters take a big bite out of a cookie and smile with unmitigated pleasure.

So, yeah, I choose love.

AFTER

I stood in front of the mirror, appraising my outfit: a pair of flat-front chinos from J.Crew, a tank top and blazer from Anthropologie. I tried on a different jacket, to see if I liked it better. Then switched to a skirt. Changed my shoes, so I had to go with a different purse. Which made my necklace seem wrong. So I sorted through my burgeoning jewelry collection to find just the right thing.

"How much longer?" asked Steve, suddenly hovering in my closet door. "I liked it better when you took five seconds to get dressed."

"Admit you'd rather be seen in public with me in a skirt and a nice jacket than in jeans and a sweatshirt," I said, fastening my necklace, five interlocking gold circles on a chain, brand-new and not cheap, a gift to myself.

"What answer will get you out of here faster?" he asked.

The girls were now on either side of Steve, wondering what was the holdup.

Maggie said, "You look so cute. I can't go out like *this,* if you're wearing *that.*" She had on the clothes she'd been in all day, cutoffs and a T-shirt. She disappeared into her room to change. Lucy, of course, was compelled to put on a fresh outfit, too.

Steve groaned, walked out of the closet, and stretched out on the bed. "I'll take a nap," he said. "Wake me when you're done."

We were going to Pete's, our usual spot, for a last summer dinner out before the start of the school year the following day. Maggie was entering the seventh grade, the year T. proclaimed me "too fat" to crush on and sealed my junior high fate. Lucy was starting the third grade, the year our pediatrician innocently called Mom's attention to my troublesome weight problem. My girls were still slender. They didn't have any serious complaints about their shapes. Bad body image could still strike them. If it did, I'd recognize the signs and steer them away from self-loathing toward comfort in their skin. I felt adequately prepared to guide them and to be a body-positive role model. I was jogging the jog, more important than talking the talk (which I was also doing, and plenty of it).

After one last look at my outfit, I turned off the closet light. Steve was pretending to snore. I knew he was faking because his real snores are much louder.

"Ready," I said, slapping his ass.

He didn't move. I was hauling back to give him another spank when he suddenly grabbed me and pulled me down on top of him.

I screamed. The girls came rushing in to see what happened. Finding us in a smoochy grapple, Maggie said, "You're disgusting."

Lucy said, "Get a room."

"We're in a room," I said.

Steve pushed me off and stood up. "Can we go now?"

After another twenty minutes of detail work (lipstick, switching purses, feeding the cats), we finally hit the street and walked the four blocks to the restaurant. I already knew what I was going to order: steak tips on a greens salad, and a vodka tonic. I'd had the same dinner at the same place dozens of times.

We sat down at our favorite table. The girls were antic, jittery about starting school again. Steve and I listened to them chatter and held hands under the table.

He leaned over to me. "Early bedtime tonight?"

"For them, or us?" I asked.

"Both."

Before I'd had a single bite, I knew this dinner would be a meal to add to my list. It heralded the ending of one season, the beginning of another. We were whole, happy, and healthy, in mind, body, and spirit. I would treasure this evening as a snapshot, an emblematic still frame from the movie of the rest of my life.

The food was good, too.

Reading Group Gold

THIN IS THE NEW HAPPY

by Valerie Frankel

About the Author

- A Conversation between Valerie Frankel and *What Not to Wear*'s Stacy London

In her Own Words

- Postscript to *Thin Is the New Happy*

Keep On Reading

- Recommended Reading
- Reading Group Questions

A Reading Group Gold Selection

For more reading group suggestions
visit www.readinggroupgold.com.

ST. MARTIN'S GRIFFIN

A Conversation between Valerie Frankel and *What Not to Wear*'s Stacy London

Valerie Frankel: I got dozens of e-mails from readers singing your praises. Did anyone ever mention *Thin Is the New Happy* to you?

Stacy London: God, yes. People called and wrote to me about the book. You made me a lot more sympathetic than I seem on *What Not to Wear*. The way the show is formatted, it's easy to pigeonhole me as the bad guy. In your book, you did such a good job of translating what I'm trying to say in a way that's made me sound nice and not scary at all.

VF: I never think of you as the bad guy on the show. You're funny, not scary. Clinton is a lot meaner than you!

SL: Maybe my sense of humor isn't for everyone.

VF: Are you sticking with *What Not to Wear*, despite all your fancy endorsement deals? Please say yes.

SL: I am absolutely staying with *What Not to Wear*. We've done over 260 shows, and I still think there's more to say about personal style and body image. Bad body image is among the top two or three reasons women reject or fear clothes. Experts talk about body dysmorphia—seeing yourself as having abnormal parts when, in fact, you are not abnormal—as a rare disorder. But I think we've all got a touch of it. You can certainly make yourself crazy about the demands put on women to be attractive. I've been up and down the scale my whole life. And I've blamed the pres-

"I was a walking contradiction and identity crisis."

sure I've felt to be thin on our culture. But the
more you think about it—and you, Val, really
nailed this point in *TITNH*—bad body image is a
symptom, but not the disease. A woman who
doesn't like her body wears sweatpants to be invisible. The shell, the style itself, is evidence of an
identity crisis. That's been my issue for my entire
life. Who do I want to be? How am I failing
myself? Am I too fat, have I gained weight? As I've
gotten older, I've been better. But it's still a challenge. The more I'm in the public eye, the more it's
an issue for me.

VF: My breakthrough, in terms of style and identity, was realizing that clothes aren't superficial.
Feeling special in clothes is a profound emotion.
Dressing well doesn't mean I'm a lemming or a
nitwit.

SL: You do what you can. One of the issues I
feel strongly about lately—and it's the angle I'm
going for more on *What Not to Wear*—is how
style represents a woman's emotional state. It's
amazing how you can look at a wardrobe and see
immediately what she is inherently insecure about.
The layers of defenses she's built up are evident in
her clothes. It's all there in her closet. With women
especially, a terrible wardrobe tells a long story.
We're finding new ways to tap into that on the
show, get to the underlying reasons and forcing
someone to really look at herself. Not just her
clothes, but her life and her sense of self.

VF: That's exactly what you did for me. It's been
two plus years since you cleaned out my closet
and forced me to address my issue: Why was I

dressing in a way that denied the essence of my personality? I was afraid of being judged by my weight, and yet I dressed in a way that made me look even larger than I really was. I was a walking contradiction and identity crisis.

SL: And now?

VF: I've spent more money on clothes in the last couple of years than I have in my entire previous life. So I'm poorer. But you know damn well that I'm a million times happier. My closet is my sanctuary. It's a world of possibilities, just as you said. Getting dressed and picking outfits makes me feel special every morning. My wardrobe and personality match—or, as you say on *What Not to Wear*, they "go." It's the difference between feeling out of whack versus being in sync every minute of every day.

SL: Another life saved.

VF: Amen, sister.

Want to know what Stacy thinks about the personal style of a famous TV talk show host?

What does she think about men and body image?

What would Joan Rivers say?

Visit www.readinggroupgold.com to read more!

"[My hope is] that all of the women who wrote to me have managed to stop the insanity of dieting."

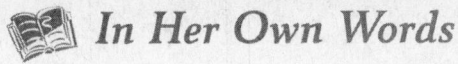 *In Her Own Words*

Postscript to *Thin Is the New Happy*

It's been eight months since the hardcover publication of *Thin Is the New Happy*. Eight fabulous months of bathing in the warmth of acknowledgement and camaraderie. Along with dozens of kvell-worthy reviews (*TITNH* was my nineteenth book—and the first to be reviewed in *The New York Times*), I received hundreds of e-mails from readers who found themselves in my story, got it, totally related to my experiences. Some had fatphobic mothers and found comfort in knowing they weren't alone. Some were fatphobic mothers who were desperate to get a grip on themselves or turn their daughters into, well, me. Fellow diet addicts vowed to try the not-diet. The word "hope" came up a lot, as in, "You give me hope I can conquer my own body-image demons." My fondest hope is that all of the women who wrote to me have managed to stop the insanity of dieting and have silenced their inner bitches once and for all.

Of course, you can't please all the women, all the time. Some readers found my story to be puny, banal, "ordinary" (to that reviewer, I ask, "Is it ordinary to become a widow at 35?"). One angry e-mailer called me an "East Coast snob." I am guilty of being a New Yorker. I'll take "vaguely misanthropic." But snob? I've seen too many of the real thing to accept that hit. An Amazon reviewer accused me of "self-loathing," and said I was desperately in need of intensive psychotherapy. Hmmm, my self-loathing was kinda the point of writing the book. I'm much better now, or didn't she read that far?

The New York Post's Page Six gossip column covered *TITNH*, giving it several paragraphs in an item titled "Mag Editor Dopes to Stay Thin" about my cocaine use in the early 1990s at *Mademoiselle*. Ancient history to some, breaking news to others. The Page Six item was picked up by American Web sites galore, including *New York* magazine, *The Huffington Post, Jezebel,* and *Jossip.* The blog entries caught the eye of producers at *Entertainment Tonight* and *The Tyra Banks Show*. (Tyra, despite what you might've heard, is not-a-bitch. The day I taped her show, she was friendly and smiley, and agreed with the not-diet philosophy completely. I liked her.) *TITNH* was suddenly abuzz.

Surreally, the story of my lifelong struggle with body image jumped across the Atlantic Ocean. Two London newspapers—*The Daily Mail* and *The Observer*—ran excerpts, and reprinted my naked photos along with the text. One morning, I received an urgent e-mail from a British TV producer asking for permission to show my nudie pix on his program, a British version of *The View*, as a launch point for the hosts to chat about body image. By the time I replied ("er, okay, I guess"), they'd already broadcast a slideshow of quivering, unclothed me, and had a hearty discussion about my "bravery." After England, *TITNH* traveled around the world, from Italy and Spain to Australia and South Africa.

Attention memoirists: If you wish to get publicity for your book, display your naked flesh like wallpaper in a foreign country.

I'm recounting the wildfire of media attention for

TITNH not to brag (although, damn, that was exciting!) but to marvel at how profoundly bad body image affects the lives of women all over the globe. My (puny, banal, ordinary, self-loathing) story rang distinct and distant bells from Dublin to Johannesburg. As I mentioned in *TITNH*, my dream as a writer has always been to make an impact on readers near and far, for my ideas and experiences to touch women's lives. Thanks to *TITNH*, I've reached people and been accepted into sympathetic hearts and expansive minds. Not surprisingly, *TITNH* was the first time I'd really put myself out there in print, complete honesty, no holding back about my deepest insecurities.

As gratifying as it has been to connect with readers down the block and across the planet, the book release has caused some trouble here at home. At store signings, book fairs, clubs, and events, one of the most commonly asked questions is: "Has your mother read the book, and what does she think of it?"

My mom has not read a word of the book, nor any of the reviews. You'll recall, when I asked her to read the manuscript, she said she wanted nothing to do with it. Judy has kept her word. She (and my father) pretend *TITNH* doesn't exist. That has been a challenge for Mom, especially when the ladies of Short Hills approach her at the Kings supermarket to say, "How could Valerie do that to you?"

"My friends are outraged on my behalf," said Mom at the time. "You have no idea how hard this is for me."

After an initial flare of resentment ("Since you haven't read the book, you have no idea how hard you made my adolescence," I thought), the guilt settled in. I didn't intend to embarrass Judy in front of her friends, or hold her up as a bad parent. As I said repeatedly in *TITNH*, Judy was a fine mother, except for her obsession about weight. She freely admits she was obsessed. To some extent, she's proud of it. Many of her friends treated their daughters the same way. My great sin was writing about it. I exposed the suburban secret abuse of fatphobic mothers, called them to the empty table, and that was a break from the unspoken rules of discretion and dignity.

"I haven't dieted since the day I started to write [this book]."

Judy feels betrayed. I am sorry about that. According to my friends, my mom's portrayal in *TITNH* was fair. Another generational divide? Mom took her pain like a trooper and kept her trap shut. I come from the heart-on-sleeve, flapping lips era, although it took thirty years of mustering courage to confront Mom about her treatment of me and write about it.

I'll finish up my postscript with the most e-mailed and asked question from readers and book club members: "Are you still not dieting?"

I am a devotee of not-dieting. I haven't dieted since the day I started to write *TITNH*, nearly three years ago. In all honesty, my weight has fluctuated within a small range. I can't say how many pounds up and down since I don't weigh myself (a HUGE relief, meanwhile). If I had to guess, I'd say I've gone up maybe seven pounds max. But then my fabulous clothes start to feel

tight, and it breaks my heart not to wear a
favorite jacket or pair of pants. Instead of getting
depressed, I just increase my workouts. I jog
longer, and/or add an extra gym visit to the week.
I cut back on sugar—if I'd been having frozen
yogurt every night, I limit it to every other night,
for example. A couple of weeks later, my clothes fit
again, and I'm extra happy because, although my
size fluctuated slightly, my mood remained the
same. I have become an emotionally stable
woman, at least about weight.

Does this mean my life is perfect? I wish! I'm still
plenty neurotic about other bêtes—money, my
husband's beer consumption, epidemic brattiness
among the neighborhood kids, my shaky professional standing, the rudeness of cell-phoning assholes in movie theaters, my own shallowness and
impatience as a mother, wife, and human being
(all of which I'll contend with in my next memoir
for St. Martin's, *It's Hard Not to Hate You*). But, as
of this writing on May 1, 2009—and, I firmly
believe, the rest of my life, however long it might
be—I've got body image beat.

Moving along . . .

What do Valerie's daughters think of her book?

How did her husband handle all the publicity?

What ever happened to X., Y., and Z.?

Visit www.readinggroupgold.com
to get ALL the updates!

Recommended Reading

I read widely, jumping genres, fiction, nonfiction, graphic novels, pretty much anything I can get my hands on. I love so many books, it's impossible to make a list. Instead, I'll recommend some of my favorite authors:

Christopher Moore, especially *Fool, You Suck,* and *A Dirty Job*. Many readers of *Thin Is the New Happy* have commented on my sense of humor. Moore's books make me LOFL (I put in the F for fucking). So, if you are looking for amusing, ribald, and clever novels—sex, foul language, supernatural beings, and chock-o-block human emotions—get Moore.

Lindsey Davis. For historical mystery fans, I love Davis's sleuth series set in ancient *Rome*. Her main character, Marcus Falco, is as sexy, charming, and fearless as the best romance-novel hero, plus he's always wearing a toga or tunic for easy access. This series is EIGHTEEN novels strong. I've read 'em all. Loved 'em all. I once corresponded with Davis (slavishly devoted fan drivel), and she was very nice.

Jonathan Kellerman. In a psychological thriller, what better main character than a shrink? Alex Delaware, Kellerman's finest creation, is smart, sympathetic, and erudite, with a voyeuristic dark side that I, for one, find humanizing and appealing. Everything I know of Los Angeles comes from Kellerman novels. Which means LA is populated exclusively with serial murders, sexual predators, and killer cultists. Never a dull moment.

Stephanie Laurens. For Regency romance (and, honestly, is there any other kind???), I get all the twitching, throbbing, heavy-breathing satisfaction

I can stand from Laurens. She supplies ruched nipples, quivering thighs, and shattering climaxes galore, as well as period details and a hoof-clomping, canter-paced plots.

Christopher Buckley. The modern satirist extraordinaire. His most famous novel is *Thank You for Smoking* but I also recommend *Boomsday* and *Supreme Courtship*. Buckley has the rare gift of clairvoyance. His novels come out and then, soon after, real world events unfold uncannily as he'd portrayed them in his books.

Mark Bittman. What, you don't sit down and read cookbooks? What's wrong with you? The *New York Times* columnist is my foodie idol. In *How to Cook Everything*, he makes any recipe seem easy, even the really freaking hard ones. No wonder he calls himself "The Minimalist." I can't cook without him. I feel like I know him. I wish I could meet him! Mark Bittman, if you're reading this, CALL ME!

John Twelve Hawkes. In the sci-fi fantasy category, I love the intense, serious, and creepy Dark River series, about a secret society of sword-wielding Harlequins who live off the grid and thwart the machinations of their ancient enemies. The characters go on trips to hell-like other worlds, such as the land of the hungry ghosts where everyone is starving, but there is nothing to eat (a.k.a. my nightmare). Twelve Hawkes (not his real name) lives off the grid himself. His location and identity are mysteries to all but his agent. Knowing that adds a sharp edge of paranoia to his already disturbing vision of our future.

 *Reading Group Questions*

1. A show of hands: Is anyone on a diet right now? Who has been on a diet during the past year? What kind of success have you had trying to lose weight?

2. Valerie Frankel begins her book by sharing a series of dieting metaphors. A drug addiction. A gambling addiction. The five stages of grief. Do you have any of your own you'd like to add?

3. Did you find the author's tales of chronic dieting humorous or sad? Empowering or self-defeating? Discuss the issues of beauty, body image, and self-acceptance that are raised in *Thin Is the New Happy*. Does the book cover these issues in a unique way? How are they typically discussed—and portrayed—in mainstream American culture?

4. Valerie decided to tackle her dieting obsession once and for all around the time her daughters were reaching puberty. In what ways do you think Valerie's attitudes about her own body changed once she became a mother? Do you think weight is a different issue for children than it is for adults? How?

5. In her postscript, the author mentions that her mother, Judy, never read *Thin Is the New Happy*. Judy's friends did, however—and were outraged on her behalf. What do you think of Valerie's portrayal of Judy in this memoir? Was it fair and balanced? Did Judy emerge as a sympathetic character . . . or a bad mother? And what do you think of Judy now?

6. "I am a connoisseur of insult and criticism," writes the author. "My ears prick up to catch the slightest intonations, the smallest hint of negativity, even in a seemingly benign comment." Another show of hands: Who in the group can recall at least one episode of childhood taunting? (Some of you may want to share your stories.) How can "innocent" teasing have a lifelong effect on one's sense of self?

7. Take a moment to talk about the men, past and present, in Valerie's life. How did they view her? Were they able to see her for who she is on the inside? Also, how did you react when her husband told her: "I adore every inch of your body. And it'd be even better if you could get rid of the stomach." In what ways did this one remark unleash a lifetime of bad feelings Valerie had about her weight? How would you feel in her shoes—or his?

8. After reading the author Q&A in this Reading Group Gold guide, do you agree with Stacy London that bad body image is a symptom, not a disease? Which was it for Valerie? Why?

9. Valerie decided that, with this book, she would finally tell the "naked truth" about her weight obsession. With this in mind, have a look at one of Valerie's nude *Self* magazine photographs (go to: http://origin.www.self.com/health/2007/06/how-nude-portraits-can-help-self-image). What do you think, now that you've seen it? Does it make you think any differently about the author's journey? How?

Keep on Reading

THIS BOOK IS DEDICATED TO
HOWARD WILLIAMS
AND
NORMAN SPRINTHALL.

I CARRY THEIR VOICES WITH ME.

For information on therapists in your local area, please visit www.sexhelp.com. For information on workshops, conferences, and retreats with Dr. Carnes, please call 1-800-708-1796. For information on audio and videotapes as well as other publications by Dr. Carnes, visit www.DrPatrickCarnes.com, call New Freedom at 1-800-708-1796, or write us at P.O. Box 3172, Carefree, Arizona 85377.

CONTENTS

List of Figures   vii

Acknowledgments   ix

How This Book Came to Be   xiii

Introduction: Why Read This Book?   1

1: What Trauma Does to People   21

2: Trauma Bonds and Their Allies   65

3: What Does Betrayal Do to Relationships?   85

4: What Makes Trauma Bonds Stronger?   115

5: What Is the Path of Awareness?   155

6: What Is the Path of Action?   189

7: Further Steps on the Path to Recovery   217

8: What Are the Risks of Recovery?   247

Appendix: Resources   277

Notes   285

Bibliography   293

Index   303

About the Authors   315

LIST OF FIGURES

1.1 Impact of Abuse   36

3.1 Warmth and Intention   92

3.2 Organizational Incest–I   104

3.3 Organizational Incest–II   106

4.1 Intensity vs. Intimacy   132

4.2 Abuse Inventory   138

4.3 The Karpman Triangle   148

4.4 Commonalities for Victim,
     Victimizer, and Rescuer   150

5.1 Role of Trauma in a Life Crisis   163

5.2 Awareness of Victimization Consciousness   167

5.3 Abuse and Addiction Populations   177

6.1 Trauma Bond Recovery Paths   213

ACKNOWLEDGMENTS

As this second edition and its revisions go to press, I am seventy-four years old. Almost two decades have passed since the original was written. At the time, I wrote the "Acknowledgments" section, which said:

> There are many to thank. Pat Mellody, Pia Mellody, and the entire Meadows staff, for their continuous support for my writing and research. I especially wish to thank Maureen Canning, Ray Early, Elizabeth Ewins, Peter Vincent, and Lynda Grange. As primary counselors they helped hone the exercises used in this book. Without Kathy Kelley's support and office skills, this manuscript may have never become manageable. As always, Linda Holman Bentley and the staff of the Phoenix Public Library helped immensely. I relied on two experts, Nancy Hopkins and Jennifer Schneider, MD, whose careful reading of the manuscript helped fill the gaps.
>
> The Health Communications staff experienced a delay in the publishing process because of my transition to The Meadows. They were gracious and understanding in spite of the problems the delay caused. I appreciate the hard work of Bill Chickering, Matthew Diener, and Christine Belleris in shaping and editing the manuscript. I will forever be indebted to Gary Seidler, for he has encouraged my writing, my speaking, and my professional work. I am grateful for his faith in me.

I have a group of friends who watched over the birth of this book. Known as the Woman Lake Gang, they are Ann and Fred Foresman, Phyllis and Lennie Brooks, Skip and Sandy Reiter, and Leslie Myers. Their care meant a lot. My wife, Suzanne, walked every step of the way in the making of this book. It is a lucky man who has a wise woman for a spouse.

Finally, I wish to thank the people whose stories appear in these pages. My hope is that their voices become like a chorus for a new understanding of betrayal.

Today I am struck by how fortuitous it was to write this book while working with Pat and Pia Mellody and The Meadows' staff. They truly were pioneers in underlining the connections between addiction, compulsive attachment, and trauma. I was understood and supported in this original effort.

Note that I also acknowledge that my move to The Meadows caused the original book to be later than expected, causing added stress for Gary Seidler, Christine Belleris, and Health Communications' staff. The irony is that my moving back to The Meadows, along with the Fulbright scholarship, has delayed this revision and added stress to the same talented group of people. Their continued belief in this book has been core to its success, and I appreciate their patience.

In most revisions, I, as an author, often wish to rewrite everything. Out of the twenty-three books I have written so far, only two have I been reluctant to touch: *Out of the Shadows* and *The Betrayal Bond*. While there have been major developments in both addiction and trauma research, the original words still ring true to me. Anybody's writing can be improved, but this is my best effort. You will see, however, that this book has been expanded significantly. We have integrated and updated research from the various fields that intersect each other around traumatic bonding and betrayal. Also, over 50,000 people have participated in our Betrayal Bond Index and hundreds of thousands in the development of our Post-Traumatic Stress Index, and the assessments are reflected throughout.

Again I find myself surrounded by extraordinary expertise. The Meadows has grown dramatically since I left in 2004. With eleven separate campuses, they continue their addiction and trauma treatment. Now they also offer specialty programs serving young adults, eating disorders, and a separate 35-acre campus for sex addicts called The Gentle Path program. The success of all these advances is due to the ceaseless efforts of our CEO, Jim Dredge. His vision, his ability to attract talent, and his capacity to mobilize a herd of cats into extraordinary teams of people is literally transforming The Meadows' business. A new model of helping is emerging out of this blending of extraordinary clinical talents.

I am a senior fellow at The Meadows. Among my colleagues and friends are some of the most influential writers and researchers in addiction and trauma recovery: Pia Melody, Claudia Black, John Bradshaw, Bessel van der Kolk, Shelley Uram, Peter Levine, and John Caldwell. I and the entire Meadows staff regret the passing of John Bradshaw, who brought so much to our community.

My other professional context is the International Institute for Trauma & Addiction Professionals (IITAP®). Started in 2002, the Institute offers specialty certifications in multiple addictions including sex addiction for therapists across the world. Its president, Stefanie Carnes, PhD, is my daughter, and she has heavily influenced the shape of my legacy. She is a gifted clinician, speaker, and author, as well as known for her advocacy for common sense in clinical research and public health matters. She is joined by faculty who are also recognized authors and leaders in the field, including Ken Adams, Alex Katehakis, Rob Weiss, Debra Kaplan, Thomas Tullos, Greg Futral, Jes Montgomery, and Cheryl Knepper.

Inhabiting a community involved in ongoing dialogue and network helps to refine thought and practice. Implementing policy, however, has depended on some key people. Kelly Reece and our office staff have been indefatigable in managing what at points of transition has seemed an overwhelming workflow. Bonnie Phillips' gifted clinical skills, attention to detail, and determined effort provided things I did not even know I needed.

In 2017 I was appointed to be a Fulbright scholar, and no such effort is done in isolation; there are many programs and staff that have united to make this possible, including Pine Grove Gratitude program, Psychological Counseling Services, Gentle Path at The Meadows, Center for Healthy Sexuality, Center for Healthy Sex, Triune Therapy, Kavod Center, Bellevue Christian Counseling University of Southern Mississippi, and the University of Alberta.

Finally, in the first acknowledgment section I spoke of my wife Suzanne; sadly, our marriage ended with her death in 2010. The crucible of widowerhood forged many new insights that were life changing. I often marvel how in many ways I still learn from Suzanne.

Today, I am newly remarried to a woman named Pennie, also a widow and a psychotherapist. People smile at the idea of two therapists being married. That reality is tempered by our losses, which shifted the worldviews of both of us, and certainly that reality changed all of my writing. At the age of seventy-three, the trick is to know when to hold, when to fold, and when to bet. It is a gift to have a partner who understands the fundamentals of those fine lines. My gratitude is that I still get to do the work I love and that I have loving company.

As previously mentioned, in 2017 I was appointed a Fulbright scholar, which I do not believe would have happened without the support of all the people acknowledged here.

The flaws in this book are due to the fact that everything in it goes through the filter of my brain. If we have made this book better, it reflects all the persons mentioned above.

HOW THIS BOOK CAME TO BE

This book started in 1974. I was in graduate school, and I was in love. There was one problem, however. The woman I was in love with was compulsive sexually, acting out with other men. I was putting her through school and trying to be understanding about her behavior. I was totally crazy with the relationship. We went through cycles of agony; I'd discover her behavior, there would be forgiveness and a passionate reconciliation, then I'd make another discovery, and the cycle would begin all over again.

I was working on my doctorate. I had two wonderful advisors in Howard Williams and Norman Sprinthall. The gifts they gave me in my life are uncountable, but none was more important than the day they sat me down and expressed concern about my relationship. I was just on the verge of another passionate reconciliation. Norman Sprinthall looked at me and said, "You remind me of Charlie Brown and Lucy van Pelt with the football." He was referring to Lucy's constant effort to get Charlie Brown to kick the football, which she always jerked away at the last minute. I immediately got the point. Then he added, "There is a cure for this, you know." Pausing for emphasis, he concluded: "No more football!" As far as my personal growth was concerned, it was the most important thing said to me in graduate school.

That conversation opened the door to understanding a part of myself that took a couple of decades to appreciate fully. If it is like other periods of growth in my life, there is more learning still to come. Over time I learned that I bonded with people who were very hurtful to me and remained loyal to them despite betrayal and exploitation. This pattern of insane loyalty affected my professional and business relationships, my friendships, my finances, and my intimate relationships. In my counseling work, I saw my pattern of behavior repeated in others. In my research I documented how that happened for people. Gradually a map emerged for me about what the problem was and how to survive and eventually overcome it.

The problem is called betrayal bonding. Betrayal intensifies pathologically the human trait of bonding deeply in the presence of danger or fear. Writing a book about it became a challenge. First, professionals who work with trauma or post-traumatic stress found very similar things to what addiction professionals found. Yet both fields were largely unaware of the other. Even worse, they used different language to describe what they knew. Within the trauma field, there were those who worked with *object relations* that expanded our understanding of how traumatized persons operated out of a damaged relationship template. Yet their insights were outside of mainstream trauma research. Addiction professionals were also seeing *compulsive relationships* that had all the characteristics of addictive disorders. These relationships, however, were so enmeshed in addictions and compulsive behaviors that they would get lost in the general consequences of the addictions themselves. Professionals knew that there was often a traumatic history in all addictions but were unclear about how that affected these compulsive relationships.

Finally, family and marriage researchers offered an extremely helpful understanding of the systems operating in these relationships. The challenge was how to integrate all of that complex insight into a map most people could understand. Professionals will find a conceptual audit trail in the notes and in the bibliography at the end.

The other part of my motivation to write this book came out of a six-year research project that followed over 1,000 recovering sex addicts and their families. The results of that work were published in a book called *Don't Call It Love.* In that book I reported the stages that trauma victims went through in developing the consciousness to change their lives. As researchers we found it very laborious, tedious work, but the learning was important in that it increased the level of understanding for all those who have experienced betrayal. It is core to this book.

Sometimes I have been accused of writing books that are painful to read at some points. A number of times, I have been introduced to audiences in which the person making the introduction makes the observation that my book *The Gentle Path* should be called *The Brutal Path.* Everyone laughs, including me. We laugh out of identification because we know that to grow and change require courage, honesty, and effort. I have also had people tell me *Out of the Shadows* was at first painful to read. I believe this book on the betrayal bond may also present similar challenges to some readers.

Yet I also profoundly believe that books can be transformative. At times I think we professionals only believe that insight comes through therapy, support groups, and intervention.

All three are important tools, perhaps even indispensable. However, people reading a book in seclusion will admit realities they are not ready to acknowledge to a group or therapist. I wished to write a book that would serve as a map for people seeking some base in reality about their destructive relationships. Such an effort requires an author to join with the reader to map out the emotional landscape.

Every book I have written started with the desire to create what I needed for myself. This book is what I wished I had in 1974.

I dedicate this book to Norman Sprinthall and Howie Williams, with thanks for all their efforts on my behalf.

In the years since the original manuscript was published we have made significant advances in our understanding of trauma, attachment, and how these impact the human brain. It is amazing what we now know about the power and vulnerability of the brain. It has been over twenty years since the original manuscript of this book was published. In that time we have seen an explosion in technological advances. It was just over ten years ago that social media changed the way we make connections in our lives. We are now privy to the everyday occurrences in one another's lives. There are over 1 billion users of Facebook worldwide. Our lives are public in ways never previously imagined. YouTube has 1 billion unique visitors each month with 100 hours of video uploaded every minute.

In 1983 the personal computer became the first non-human nominated for *Time* magazines' person of the year. At that time, there were around 10 million computers at use in the United States. In 2016, there are an estimated 2 billion at use worldwide. The smart phone has drastically changed our mobility and our constant connection to others and to the Internet.

All of these events affect the way we connect and how we feel safe.

At a time in our society where we are increasingly drawn to stories and images that represent emotional, physical, and relational betrayal, this revision is timely indeed. We come face-to-face with these images each day.

Some of the most amazing changes since the original publication have come in the way of neuroscience and what we are continuing to understand about how the human brain grows, changes, and heals following trauma. It has also widened our understanding of addiction and supported the concept of addiction as a brain disease.

For years mainstream science believed that brain anatomy was fixed—after childhood the brain only changed as far as declining through age. In addition, if the brain failed to develop properly, or was injured due to disease, illness, or injury, the brain cells simply died and could not be replaced. What is so exciting about recent developments in neuroscience is we now know that the brain has plasticity to it; it continues to grow, develop, and change. Amazingly, the brain can also heal itself and create new pathways. Norman Doidge beautifully summarizes through science and real-life stories what we are coming to understand about the brain in *The Brain That Changes Itself* (2007). He states, "The idea that the brain can change its own structure and function through thought and activity is, I believe, the most important alteration in our view of the brain since we first sketched out its basic anatomy and the workings of its basic component, the neuron. Like all revolutions, this one will have profound effects" (Doidge 2007, p. xvi). This has immense implications for those who have been affected by trauma and addiction.

There is both good news and bad news related to the plasticity of the brain, and this has significant implications to those who find themselves in compulsive attachments or trauma bonds. The good news is in the hope it provides for those whose brains have suffered injury, disease, or trauma, whether emotional, physical, or through addiction. The knowledge that we can in fact change our brains allows for developments in treatment and opens new pathways for research. The other side, the bad news, is having a deeper awareness that our brains are much more vulnerable and susceptible to variables within human relationships, behaviors, and injury. Awareness of both sides, however, helps us to be more resilient.

In 2010, ASAM (American Society of Addiction Medicine) released an updated definition of addiction, which included the acceptance of process and substance addictions and stated that addiction is a brain disease: "Addiction is a primary, chronic disease of brain reward, motivation, memory and related circuitry. Dysfunction in these circuits leads to characteristic biological, psychological, social and spiritual manifestations. This is reflected in an individual pathologically pursuing reward and/or relief by substance use and other behaviors." This definition is significant in several ways. First, it recognizes that addiction is in fact a disease that affects mechanisms in the brain. Second, the definition recognizes that addiction goes beyond the substance addictions and includes process addictions such as gambling, sex, food, Internet, and so forth. "Alcohol and other drugs have long been recognized as addictive substances and addiction is now generally recognized as a chronic disease of the brain that involves relapse, progressive development, and the potential for fatality if not treated. Developing brain science has set the stage for inclusion of the process addictions, including food, sex, shopping, and gambling, in this broader definition of addiction" (Smith 2012, p. 1).

Like the developments that led to better services, recognition, and treatment of addictive disorders, the recent focus on addiction as a brain disease helps us to understand the nature of addiction and continue to develop more appropriate treatment responses both in outpatient and inpatient settings. "The common pathways in reward circuitry that affect memory and learning, motivation, control, and decision making are also involved in the addictive process. With the more global understanding of addiction come more treatment strategies, such as meditation and mindfulness training, psychosocial interventions, and pharmacologic approaches. Interestingly, our growing understanding of addiction as a disease has not diminished the value of the spiritually driven approaches, such as 12-step-oriented treatments" (Angres and Bettinardi-Angres 2008, p. 696).

Recent research reveals that behavioral addictions (e.g., food addiction, pathological gambling, and video gaming and Internet addiction) and substance addictions share many of the same fundamental mechanisms leading to a collection of shared alterations in brain anatomy and chemistry. "Virtually every study on addiction has demonstrated atrophy of multiple areas of the brain, particularly those associated with frontal volitional control and the reward-salience centers. This is true for drug addictions such as to cocaine, methamphetamine, and opioids, and also for behavioral conditions associated with pathologic overconsumption of natural rewards and behaviors such as food, sex, and Internet addiction" (Hilton 2013).

As we have a more comprehensive understanding of addiction and the brain, we have a deeper understanding of the many ways addiction surfaces and the complexity of relationships involved.

These breakthroughs in neuroscience have also led to a more comprehensive understanding of trauma, attachment, and human relationships, all of which form the context for betrayal.

Freyd has conducted extensive research on the topic of "betrayal trauma," which specifically examines the complexities in which we, particularly children, cannot break from those who have betrayed us as it would be contrary to the drive for survival. This creates an excruciating bind setting up the potential for a lifetime of challenges in differentiating safe and nurturing relationships from those that prove to be dangerous or harmful. "A traumatic experience of love can occur when a child's experience of love, caring and affection collides with an on-going experience of abuse and betrayal. The union of love, trust and safety becomes fractured, while notions of love and betrayal become linked in tragic partnership" (Freyd 1996). Freyd suggests that betrayal is the violation of implicit or explicit trust. The closer and more necessary the relationship for the child, the greater is the degree of betrayal. Betrayal trauma theory explains that "the ability to detect betrayal may need to be stifled for the greater goal of survival. A child who distrusts his or her parents risks alienating the parents further, and thus becomes subject to more abuse and less love or care" (p. 10). Herman (1992) speaks of the double bind of the child of betrayal trauma: "The child faces a formidable developmental task: to find a way to form primary attachments to caretakers who are either dangerous or negligent. She must find a way to develop a sense of basic trust and safety with caretakers who are untrustworthy and unsafe" (p. 101). Research in the areas of attachment, trauma, and relationship continue to help us understand how compulsive attachment occurs.

In *The New York Times*, Dr. Anna Fels wrote a perceptive editorial about the impact of betrayal, stating, "Insidiously, the new information disrupts their sense of their own past, undermining the veracity of their personal history. Like a computer file corrupted by a virus, their life narrative has been invaded" (October, 2013). That insight is the place to begin when examining why to read this book.

INTRODUCTION:
WHY READ THIS BOOK?

Betrayal. A breach of trust. Fear. What you thought was true—counted on to be true—was not. It was just smoke and mirrors, outright deceit and lies. Sometimes it was hard to tell because there was just enough truth to make everything seem right. Even a little truth with just the right spin can cover the outrageous. Worse, there are the sincerity and care that obscure what you have lost. You can see the outlines of it now. It was exploitation. You were used. Everything in you wants to believe you weren't. *Please make it not so,* you pray. Yet enough has emerged. Facts. Undeniable. You sizzle with anger.

Betrayal. You can't explain it away anymore. A pattern exists. You know that now. You can no longer return to the way it was (which was never really as it seemed). That would be unbearable. But to move forward means certain pain. No escape. No in-between. Choices have to be made today, not tomorrow. The usual ways you numb yourself will not work. The reality is too great, too relentless.

Betrayal. A form of abandonment. Often the abandonment is difficult to see because the betrayer can be still close, even intimate, or may be intruding in your life. Yet your interests, your well-being is continually sacrificed.

"Betrayal is the sense of being harmed by the intentional actions or omissions of a trusted person. The most common forms of betrayal are harmful disclosures of confidential information, disloyalty, infidelity, and dishonesty. They can be traumatic and cause considerable distress. The effects of betrayal include shock, loss and grief, morbid pre-occupation, damaged self-esteem, self-doubting, anger. Not infrequently they produce life altering changes. The effects of catastrophic betrayal are most relevant for anxiety disorders, and OCD and PTSD in particular" (Rachman 2010, p. 304). Those who have been victims of betrayal often report feeling that their identity and their psychological well-being have been threatened as a result of the experience as well as at times their physical well-being. These violations of trust through betrayal have powerful effects on relationships (Jones and Burdette 1994; Couch, Jones, and Moore 1999). Psychotherapy's tremendous evolution in the last decades has meant more precise understanding of core concepts. None have been more profound for our purposes in understanding trauma bonding than the redefining of post-traumatic stress disorder, or PTSD. Originally revolutionary in helping to understand the woundedness caused by trauma, its primary focus has been on the anxiety and fear that haunts the life of the exploited or abused victim. Now we are also appreciating the very important role of embitterment. In other words, trauma can leave a legacy of anger, grievance, and rage.

John was a creative visionary and had built a real estate concept that was revolutionary. The company's corporate culture was very ruthless, competitive, and at times corrupt. Yet, his CEO saw the promise of John's ideas and pledged that he would be rewarded with stock options and bonuses for what he had dreamed and planned. While he worked hard and succeeded bringing the project to completion, he—as everyone else in the corporate structure—were never sure where they stood. The CEO would joke that as he would stroll through the corporate complex that he wanted to spread fear. John's idea when implemented was transformative in the amount of wealth it created for the company. The rewards never materialized, his financial life was improved but not as promised. Instead they asked him to do another project and then the original promises would be fulfilled. His life would be a life of "bluebirds and chipmunks" his CEO jokingly pledged.

Eventually, this process was what is called "bait and switch." John would take the bait, desperately wanting his talent to be recognized. Yet others would receive the credit and the money. John spent a decade, with the same process, repeated and he became progressively negative and withdrawn. His therapist explained to him the concept of post-traumatic embitterment disorder (PTED). Unlike PTSD, which focuses on the anxiety caused, PTED acknowledges the residual anger and rage that accumulates with betrayal. The "bluebirds and chipmunks" never arrived, but enough was done to keep him creating. Those gestures were also like the classic "golden handcuffs," in which the rewards required further work and time in the company. John found himself constantly plagued with revenge fantasies in which he gets the rewards deserved and his betrayers suffer. When John talked to his therapist about his anger for the lies that he was told, his therapist observed "but you stayed." His therapist explained how trauma bonding worked whenever there was betrayal. Cults, early childhood abuse and abandonment, and addiction could also create anger at the injustice and exploitation. John had been exploited but he could leave and restore his sense of self and retrieve his spontaneity and creativity.

John is obviously not alone. When the #MeToo movement became a landslide, it had tapped into a reservoir of anger over the abuse of power in an industry built on talent and creativity. The media had trouble sorting some of the stories because there would be examples of loyalty and friendship with men who had sexually harassed and assaulted the victims. Yet they would invite them to participate in their weddings, family celebrations, and philanthropic cooperation.

For people who are traumatically bonded it is often confusing as well. Gestures of caring mixed with exploitation intensifies the bond. Yet, the anger burns and erodes the soul. But they stay.

Michael Linden and his colleagues have defined criteria for PTED (Linden, Rotter, Baumann, and Lieberei 2007). Note that the anger is so intense that it interferes with life functioning just like PTSD does. Both can coexist. Both can be in an environment that has gestures of care and promises to paper over the very real abuses that have occurred. Throughout this book, I will remind our readers of the paradoxes implicit in the traumatically bonded betrayal. Fear and anger can join forces to be debilitating. Also we must not lose sight of the origins of the word "grievance" as well as the word "grief." They both come from the medieval French word for "grip." We hold on to what we need to let go of.

Abandonment is also at the core of addictions. Abandonment causes deep shame. Abandonment by betrayal is worse than mindless neglect. Betrayal is purposeful and self-serving. If severe enough, it is traumatic. What moves betrayal into the realm of trauma is fear and terror. If the wound is deep enough, and the terror big enough, your bodily systems shift to an alarm state. You never feel safe. You're always on full alert, just waiting for the hurt to begin again. In that state of readiness, you're unaware that part of you has died. You are grieving. Like everyone who has loss, you have shock and disbelief, fear, loneliness, and sadness. Yet you are unaware of these feelings because your guard is up. In your readiness, you abandon yourself. Yes, another abandonment.

Attachment research has revealed betrayal and abandonment have long-lasting impact on our development physically, emotionally, and spiritually. When attachment needs are not met, the result is often anxiety, distress, and irrational thoughts, beliefs, and activities. Behaviors can include distancing, dismissiveness, and increased efforts toward emotional connection, preoccupation, and confusion. All of which greatly affects how we relate with others in our lives: "Empirical evidence supports the influence of attachment styles on romantic relationships and the value of close relationship in the development of secure relationships" (Daire, Jacobson, and Carlson 2012, p. 273).

Dr. Allan Schore, who specializes in the integration of neuroscience with attachment theory, highlights the significance of babies who are raised by caregivers who are unable to meet large portions of their needs. Schore states that these children "are at risk for growing into adults who lack resilience and have trouble adapting to life's ebbs and flows. Their brains may be unable to process life's experiences. They appear to have more difficulty making sense of life's events, particularly those that are stressful, and to be more vulnerable to psychological disturbances and disorders, including drug addiction, depression, and PTSD" (Schore 1994).

We have long known the significance of attachment in helping children grow into healthy and resilient adults. As neuroscience has evolved, we are now learning how this process works in the brain and how attunement and attachment in relationships actually promotes integration in the brain. When we are attuned to in relationships, we have the experience of feeling "felt" by another human. This experience happens across the life span in different ways, not just as children. This process happens in a positive therapeutic relationship or in the midst of a therapy group or a twelve-step meeting. When we are understood and attuned to in these relationships, we grow our ability to respond with empathy, and it deepens our resiliency when faced with future challenges.

The reverse is also true; highly addictive attachment to the people who have hurt you can undermine your ability to have secure attachments and respond with resiliency to life's challenges. You may even try to explain and help them understand what they are doing—convert them into non-abusers. You may even blame yourself, your defects, your failed efforts. You strive to do better as your life slips away in the swirl of the intensity. These attachments cause you to distrust your own judgment, distort your own realities, and place yourself at even greater risk. The great irony? You are bracing yourself against further hurt. The result? A guarantee of more pain. These attachments have a name. They are called betrayal bonds.

Exploitive relationships create betrayal bonds. These occur when a victim bonds with someone who is destructive to him or her. Thus the hostage becomes the champion of the hostage taker, the incest victim covers for the parent, and the exploited employee fails to expose the wrongdoing of the boss. Consider the Father Porter case in which hundreds of sexually abused victims maintained their silence. Or remember the loyal residents of Johnstown when 965 of them committed suicide at the request of their charismatic leader. For some, this included murdering their own children—all of this despite years of exploitation, abuse, and terror by their minister, James Jones. Throughout history to the present day, flashpoints across the globe have generated similar stories. Even journalists and war correspondents would see the negative attachments in the shadows of world conflicts. Noted correspondent Chris Hodges, for example, observed how decades of observing war taught him how trauma can be an addictive context for compulsive and negative attachment. Yet the bonds formed in those situations have much in common with the experiences most of us have.

The term "Stockholm syndrome" was first used by a psychiatrist and criminologist named Nils Bejerot to describe the phenomenon that often occurred in a bank robbery in Stockholm in 1973. Hostages were taken in the robbery and were held for five days. During that time the hostages developed strong bonds with their captors and later rejected help from government officials, and even after being freed they defended their captors. The term is now used to describe the psychological phenomenon where captives are placed in a situation beyond their control in the presence of great fear and are forced to depend on their captors. This complex situation can lead to the development of a bond and empathy for their captors. First used to describe victims of hostage situations, it is now not limited to hostage situations. Victims of domestic violence, childhood abuse, incest, and cults as well as prisoners of war can also form these types of bonds with their abusers. In 1991, Jaycee Dugard was lured from a bus stop at the age of eleven by a couple named Phillip and Nancy Garrido. She was held captive for eighteen years at their home. Dugard and her two daughters, born while in captivity, were rescued in 2009. When first questioned, she did not reveal her true identity, claiming a borrowed name, "Alissa," and stated that her captor was a great person and that he was good with her kids. Only after Garrido's confession did she reveal herself as Jaycee Dugard. These stories, while extreme, reveal the complex emotional bonds that can develop out of fear, terror, and the drive to survive.

We typically think of bonding as something good. We use phrases like *male bonding* and *marital bonds*, referring to something positive. Yet bonds are neutral. They can be good or bad. Consider destructive marriages as in the 1989 movie *The War of the Roses* in which the attachment results in a mutually destructive bond that cannot be broken. The bond is so strong that partners cannot leave each other, even when they clearly know the risks. The level of intense and dangerous attachment is depicted in the 2014 movie *Gone Girl*. In turmoil over the loss of their marital bliss, Amy, the wife, hatches a complicated mystery in which she disappears and it seems as though her husband is responsible for the crime. As the story unfolds, the audience is brought into a story of anger, intensity, and betrayal. As she fears for his conviction and possible death sentence, she reveals another plot twist and claims that she was kidnapped and held hostage by an old boyfriend who had been obsessed with her. As this unfolds, Nick, the husband, plans to leave his wife, as he knows none of this to be true. Amy reveals that she is pregnant, and the happy couple announce on television that they are expecting a child; the movie ends with the two of them sitting together in the house. This, too, is another example where the attachment results in a mutually destructive bond that remains intact even after all of the lies, deception, and betrayal. Similarly, adult survivors of abusive and dysfunctional families struggle with bonds that are rooted in their own betrayal experiences. Loyalty to that which does not work, or worse, to a person who is toxic, exploitive, or destructive to you is a form of insanity.

In the 2014 film *Maleficent*, the impact of relational betrayal and the ability for redemption is told beautifully. Maleficent is a powerful fairy that lives in a magical place full of wonder and remarkable creatures known as the Moors. The Moors border the human kingdom, which is focused on conquering and destroying the Moors. When Maleficent is a child, she befriends a young human boy, Stefan, and as they grow older, their relationship, too, grows into one of love, companionship, and friendship. Stefan, however, is not content and is seduced by the thought of power, and over time he visits less and less. In service of the king, Stefan is granted an opportunity to prove his loyalty and ability if he destroys Maleficent. Going to her one final time, he extends a hand of connection and friendship, and Maleficent has no reason to distrust his motives. Stefan is not there to offer friendship but instead drugs her; as she sleeps, he cannot kill her but instead cuts off her wings. As the depth of the betrayal is revealed to Maleficent, she becomes obsessed with revenge, and her heart is filled with anger and embitterment, transforming the Moors into darkness. The story develops and does not end in this darkness but in the beautiful power of forgiveness and love as Maleficent allows her heart to be touched by Stefan's daughter, Aurora. The power of betrayal is significant as is the power of healing and recovery.

Trauma researcher Dr. Peter Levine writes, "Most people think of trauma as a "mental" problem, even as a "brain disorder." However, trauma is something that also happens in the body. We become scared stiff or, alternately, we collapse, overwhelmed and defeated with helpless dread. Either way, trauma defeats life."

This book will help you to understand how these complicated relationships are affecting your life and show you a way to healing and recovery.

A number of signs indicate the presence of a betrayal bond:

1. Everyone around you has strong negative reactions, yet you continue covering up, defending, or explaining a relationship.

2. There is a constant pattern of nonperformance, and yet you continue to believe false promises.

3. There are repetitive, destructive fights that nobody wins.

4. Others are horrified by something that has happened to you, but you are not.

5. You obsess over showing someone that he or she is wrong about you, your relationship, or the person's treatment of you.

6. You feel stuck because you know what the other person is doing is destructive but believe you cannot do anything about it.

7. You feel loyal to someone even though you harbor secrets that are damaging to others.

8. You move closer to someone you know is destructive to you with the desire of converting him or her to a non-abuser.

9. Someone's talents, charisma, or contributions cause you to overlook destructive, exploitive, or degrading acts.

10. You cannot detach from someone even though you do not trust, like, or care for the person.

11. You find yourself missing a relationship, even to the point of nostalgia and longing, that was so awful it almost destroyed you.

12. Extraordinary demands are placed upon you to measure up as a way to cover up that you've been exploited.

13. You keep secret someone's destructive behavior toward you because of all the good they have done or the importance of their position or career.

14. The history of your relationship is about contracts or promises that have been broken and that you are asked to overlook.

Contentious divorce, abusive employee relations, litigation of any type, incest, child abuse, dysfunctional family and marital systems, domestic violence, hostage negotiation, kidnapping, professional exploitation, and religious abuse all are areas that reference and describe the pattern of betrayal bonding. They have in common situations of incredible intensity, or importance, or both. They all involve exploitation of trust, power, or both. They all can result in a bond with a person who is dangerous and exploitive. Signs of betrayal bonding include misplaced loyalty, inability to detach, and self-destructive denial.

If you are reading this book, a clear betrayal has probably happened in your life. Chances are that you have also bonded with the person or persons who have let you down. Now here is the important part: You will never mend the wound without dealing with the betrayal bond. Like gravity, you may defy it for a while, but ultimately it will pull you back. You cannot walk away from it. Time will not heal it. Burying yourself in compulsive and addictive behaviors will bring no relief, just more pain. Being crazy will not make it better. No amount of therapy, long-term or short-term, will help without confronting it. Your ability to have a spiritual experience will be impaired. Any form of conversion or starting over only postpones the inevitable. And there is no credit for feeling sorry for yourself. You must acknowledge, understand, and come to terms with the relationship.

Professional therapists can be so focused on their client's woundedness that they will overlook the betrayal bond that may remain. Why they do this becomes easy to understand.

In addition to insane loyalties, betrayal can bring forth every issue, secret, and unfinished business a person has, all of which are important. Further, fear and crisis are often part of the scene. So the immediate problems come first. As a result, the betrayal bond itself may be ignored.

Finally, consider the context in which betrayal bonds are most likely to occur:

domestic violence

dysfunctional marriages

exploitation in the workplace

clergy exploitation

litigation

kidnapping

hostage situations

cults

addictions (alcohol, drugs, gambling, sex, eating, high-risk behavior)

incest

physical abuse

emotional/verbal/psychological abuse

sexual abuse

sibling relationship struggles

online exploitation

These are all supercharged, complex issues. When a major sports figure batters his wife, or worse, kills her, we can get lost in the legal contest, the race issues, the fate of the children, the grief of the families, and the lifestyles of the wealthy. The fact that the victim stayed in the relationship where violence was predictable underscores an insane loyalty.

When I first published this book, in 1997, the technological world was very different. Now we have instant access to news, media, and the intricate details of one another's lives. Through television, the Internet, and social media we have access to a never-ending stream of instant worldwide news and media coverage. When a crisis happens we know instantly. When there is a celebrity scandal we know all of the explicit details.

We are inundated with stories of celebrities, whether a sports figure, musician, actor, or politician who become embroiled in domestic violence. Just recently we saw the NFL take a stronger stance on the punishment for those who are involved in domestic violence. Often in these very public situations, we can get lost in the many details of the case, whether it is the legal courtroom drama or the grief of the families. One issue that is often lost is related to the victim. These are difficult and delicate issues, and there is a great amount of grief and sadness for all involved, yet there remains the fact that the victim stayed in a relationship where many times the violence was predictable and habitual. This underscores the element of the betrayal bond, an insane loyalty to people who harm us. In 70–80 percent of intimate partner homicides, no matter which partner was killed, the man physically abused the woman before the murder, and less than one-fifth of victims reporting an injury from intimate partner violence sought medical treatment following the injury (National Coalition Against Domestic Violence).

The case of former Baltimore Ravens star Ray Rice brought the issue of domestic violence into the forefront of our awareness.[1] On February 15, 2014, news broke that Rice had been arrested on simple assault charges, along with his then-fiancée, Janay Palmer (though charges against her were dropped), after the two had been in a fight at the Revel Casino in Atlantic City. Palmer later indicated that she did not want to go forward with prosecution. The state however followed up with charges, and on March 27 the charges were changed to aggravated assault, and the case was presented to a grand jury. Just one day later, Rice and Palmer were married. The two held a press conference on May 23. Later that summer on July 24, the NFL responded with issuing Rice a two-game suspension, which brought about a barrage of responses and criticism culminating in the NFL commissioner, Robert Goodell, admitting later that he didn't get it right when he issued the two-game suspension and the NFL making changes to its domestic violence policy. The new policy will apply to all NFL personnel, including executives and owners. On September 8, another video surfaced, which showed Rice punching Janay in the face in the elevator, knocking her unconscious. In response to this video, the NFL suspended Rice indefinitely, and the Ravens announced that they would be releasing Rice.

This case sent the discussion related to domestic violence into a context that has never been experienced before. As the video was watched by millions, many saw domestic violence in a new light, out of the context of report and discussion and into the context of firsthand witnessing. Tania Tetlow, a law professor and director of the Domestic Violence Clinic at Tulane University, stated, "Seeing the video makes such a difference. Even though we knew these facts before, it was easy for the public to minimize the damage done to the victim, to think about domestic violence as vaguely mutual and provoked, and then to dismiss it as a private matter that doesn't matter" (NBC News).

Recently, again we saw this issue take center stage as the Kansas City Chiefs released their star running back, Kareem Hunt. Hunt was involved in a violent altercation with a woman in his Cleveland home. Like Rice, once a video surfaced Hunt was suspended due to the NFL's new domestic violence policy.

Unfortunately, the facts related to domestic violence have been known for some time. The public and personal denial continues to be part of the larger problem. Here are some of the facts related to violence against women:

1. Over 22 million women in the United States have been raped in their lifetime.

2. Every ninety seconds, somewhere in America, someone is being sexually assaulted.

3. Almost two-thirds of all rapes are committed by someone who is known to the victim.

4. Almost three-fourths (73 percent) of all sexual assaults are perpetrated by non-strangers.

5. Sixty-four percent of women who reported being raped, physically assaulted, and/or stalked before the age of eighteen were victimized by a current or former husband, cohabitating partner, boyfriend, or date.

6. One in five adolescent girls becomes the victim of physical or sexual violence, or both, in a dating relationship.

7. Ninety-three percent of juvenile sexual assault victims know their attacker.

8. About one-third of female murder victims ages twelve or older are killed by an intimate partner.

9. Less than half of domestic violence incidents are reported to police.

10. The costs of intimate partner violence against women exceed an estimated $5.8 billion per year.

11. Intimate partner violence causes U.S. women to lose about $727 million in wages from their approximately 8 million days of missed work.

12. One in three women and one in four men have experienced some form of physical violence by an intimate partner within their lifetime.

13. One in five women and one in seven men have experienced severe physical violence by an intimate partner in their lifetime.

14. Intimate partner violence accounts for 15 percent of all violent crime.

Domestic violence is an epidemic affecting individuals in every community, regardless of age, economic status, sexual orientation, gender, race, religion, or nationality. It is often accompanied by emotionally abusive and controlling behavior. It can result in physical trauma, psychological trauma, and even death. The impact can cross generations.

When church figures are exposed for extraordinary sexual misconduct or are conclusively convicted of financial misconduct, for believers to continue to contribute funds and participate in the church community as if nothing had happened is an insane loyalty. Or consider the fact that, on average, a woman will not contact the police until her abuser has assaulted her thirty-five times.[2] There are many reasons for that figure, including insane loyalties.

Nothing in the above list is a simple issue. They are more like a collector's ball of string—years of accumulation tightly tied to one another. An unraveling needs to occur.

This, however, is a simple book. It is designed to be straightforward and direct. Clarity is essential when the situation is complicated. You should read this book to help you clarify what you need to do. There are no magic answers in these pages, only information and guidance that will help you take action. You will find you already know much of what you need to do. You may need assurance that your judgments and intuitions can be trusted.

Unravel the tangled mess slowly, one string at a time. There is great hope for you if you do. You will acquire a depth of substance most people never achieve. This book tells the stories of people who have done it, people who have let their suffering transform them. Names and details have been changed to protect their identities. But their stories are true, much like yours perhaps. Knowing this can reassure you and confirm your judgment, intuitions, and common sense. If you are having difficulty facing these issues, I highly recommend you seek therapy. As this book went through its revision, one of the goals was to be able to offer new resources for those struggling with issues related to healing from betrayal bonds and compulsive attachment. We are excited to be able to share with you two amazing resources that have grown out of this revision.

First, you can access an online assessment tool at *www.drpatrick carnes.com*. The Betrayal Bond Index is created to help you assess and begin to develop an understanding of the core issues related to the specific ways in which you compulsively attach. These will be the building blocks to the development of an effective and appropriate treatment strategy. Along with the assessment you will find a variety of resources from twelve-step groups, research and articles, and suggested readings. It is our ultimate goal that as more individuals complete the index, we will grow in our understanding of compulsive attachment, and in turn we will be able to develop and share resources that will aid in healing and the development of healthy and fulfilling relationships for many years to come. This site will also help you to find and access an appropriate trauma therapist. These therapists are uniquely qualified to provide help as they have been through a specific trauma therapist certification.

Second, we are proud to announce the Betrayal Bond Intensive that will be offered through The Meadows, in Wickenburg, Arizona. For many years The Meadows has been on the forefront of treatment for addiction, codependency, trauma, and sex addiction. Now partnering with Dr. Patrick Carnes, they will offer a weeklong intensive designed on the work in this book. This intensive will allow individuals to work with others in a confidential, safe, and therapeutic environment to identify issues related to compulsive attachment and the impact of unhealthy relationship patterns on their lives. The intensive will be designed to build on the work started as you read *The Betrayal Bond*, and to offer support for your next step, we are providing you with a special offer, which will serve as a discount for the intensive. For more information please visit *www.themeadows.com*.

Also, I recommend the use of a journal as you use this book. It will help you complete the exercises you'll work through in the chapters that follow.

Our world is no longer a safe place. Perhaps it never was.

We are all aware of the shrinking global village. Violence in other lands seems closer than ever before. Terrorism and hatred leak across our borders. No longer can we say that it's not our problem.

There was never a time that this was made clearer than through the events on September 11, 2001. On that day, nineteen men hijacked four commercial airplanes resulting in the loss of thousands of lives. It was the worst terrorist attack in U.S. history but did not just affect the United States. More than ninety countries lost citizens in the attack on the World Trade Center, and it did not end there. Since that day, there have been many more lives lost in battle and due to illnesses such as cancer as a result of the attack. Before the 9/11 attack, the bombing of the Alfred P. Murrah Federal Building in Oklahoma City had been the deadliest terrorist attack on U.S. soil, killing 168 people, 19 of which were children who were in the building day care center at the time of the blast.

On April 15, 2013, we were again faced with unspeakable violence when bombs exploded at the finish line of the Boston Marathon, killing 3 people and injuring at least 264. The bombing, an act of terrorism, turned a celebration and a deep national tradition into an unspeakable tragedy.

Violence has also touched our schools and our children in ways that are still difficult to understand and heal from. On Friday, December 14, 2012, the truly unspeakable happened when a man armed with an assault rifle and two semiautomatic pistols entered Sandy Hook Elementary School. At the end of the tragic event, twenty-eight people had lost their lives: six employees, the gunman's mother, and twenty children under the age of seven. Sadly, this shooting is but one of the deadly school shootings that have been a part of our recent history. Two of the three deadliest school shootings have occurred in the past five years, and five of the seven deadliest in the past fifteen years.

In 2017, our nation saw the deadliest year of mass shootings in U.S. history, with the shooting in Las Vegas at the Route 91 Harvest Festival concert that left 58 dead and over 500 injured, as well as the shooting at the First Baptist Church in Sutherland Springs, Texas, in which 26 were killed and 20 others injured. This deadly trend has continued in 2018. We live in violent and insecure times.

We know what violence does to people. Alice Miller, the famous psychotherapist, described the process in her classic book *For Your Own Good.*

German children in the 1920s and 1930s became acclimatized to physical violence. They saw it in their homes, where physical punishment was routine. By today's standards, this same form of punishment would be abusive. They saw it in the streets. Germany lost a war they felt they should have won. They felt betrayed by their leaders. Political and economic chaos surrounded them. Children learned to split off from the violence. They learned to make it unreal, which is why as adults, Miller points out, they could be in the presence of concentration camps and remain unmoved.[3]

We live in a culture with obvious parallels. A war we felt we could have won but lost. Our nightly news is a chronicle of the day's violence, the latest abductions, and the most recent infidelities of our leaders. There is a feeling of betrayal. If Miller is right, we are currently experiencing the kind of fear and acclimatization that made a Hitler possible.

This violence erodes our sense of safety and trust and betrays our sense of humanity. In a world of instant media, streaming video, and 24/7 news channels we are all touched and a part of this violence. It is a part of our everyday consciousness. We are glued to our televisions, computers, and smart phones. We see instantly those who were injured or perished, we see the face of the perpetrators, we are involved. This is a global phenomenon. We follow these events in ways we did not have access to just a few short years ago. On May 24, 2011, the trial of Casey Anthony began in Orlando, Florida. Anthony was charged in the death of her two-year-old daughter, Caylee, who was reported missing by Casey in 2008. In December of 2008, Caylee's remains were found. The trial of Casey Anthony was the first major trial of the social media age. The case was followed by millions on live-stream video feeds and constant cable-news reports. When the verdict was delivered, it was watched by 5.2 million people on HLN (formerly CNN Headline News) alone. Access to events such as this that happen in real time highlight our exposure. There is a cultural impact. We are on the front row, watching as events unfold and we can't look away. Intensity. Fear. Violence. These are the times in which we live. This fuels cultural pain and fear, possibly leading to secondary trauma. It is the fuel for trauma bonds.

Betrayal makes all of this worse. Betrayal serves as a catalyst. For centuries, cultures took pride in their tolerance. Ethnic groups lived as neighbors and friends. Then there is an isolated act of violence. People suddenly feel betrayed. Feelings escalate. More violence occurs. A vengeful spiral ends in genocide and atrocities. Irretrievable hatred and trauma follow.

Unless we learn how to handle betrayal and the torturous, obsessional relationships that evolve out of treachery, we add to the betrayal of the planet. Trust is restored when we learn to trust ourselves and build trust with others. While we live in insecure and violent times, these very events often remind us of what is beautiful about humanity, life, and connection. Often during these very moments of tragedy, we see the best of ourselves and others. This was true in the aftermath of Hurricane Harvey, which caused unbelievable destruction in

Houston, Texas. We saw the devastation, and we also saw the beauty of the human spirit and the commonality of our humanity as people with boats rescued stranded victims, business owners opened their stores as needed, and communities united for the common good. Trust can be restored through healing. We can reconnect to ourselves and in doing so connect to those around us. Hope. Healing. Connection. There is no other way. By working through whatever prompted you to pick up this book, you help yourself and the rest of us as well.

To start, we need to understand what trauma does to people.

What Trauma Does to People

AFTER A TRAUMATIC EXPERIENCE,
THE HUMAN SYSTEM OF SELF-PRESERVATION
SEEMS TO GO ONTO PERMANENT ALERT,
AS IF THE DANGER MIGHT RETURN
AT ANY MOMENT.

—Judith Herman, *Trauma and Recovery*

A key skill to navigating life's inevitable stressors and challenges is our brains' ability to maintain flexibility and make choices on how to respond when faced with a threat or a challenge. This capacity involves primarily the prefrontal area of the brain and emerges slowly during the course of development.

Those who have experienced trauma may find that they blow up in response to minor provocations, freeze when frustrated, or become helpless in the face of trivial challenges. This inflexibility diminishes the capacity to choose, and without understanding the context of the reactions, their behavior can appear bizarre or out of control.

"Neuroimaging technology has revealed that when people are reminded of a personal trauma they activate the areas of the brain regions that support intense emotions while decreasing activity of brain structures involved in the inhibition of emotions and the translation of experience into communicable language" (van der Kolk, 2006 p. 2). Simply it becomes difficult to choose an appropriate behavioral response in the face of intense emotions. Due to the reality that most traumas occur within the context of interpersonal relationships the problem becomes even more complex. One significant factor in the development of the prefrontal areas of the brain and the ability to respond to emotions effectively occurs as a child is able to develop in the presence of familiar and trusted people in his or her life. These significant relationships are critical to development and later to the ability to emotionally regulate. The child being in distress signals caregivers to respond with an appropriate action. They discover what is troubling the child and how to respond in a way to comfort and help the child to soothe the emotional reactions. This process becomes thwarted when the caregiver is unable to respond to the emotional needs of the child and developmentally the child does not learn the process of self-soothing.

Bessel van der Kolk, MD, is a clinician, researcher and teacher in the area of posttraumatic stress. His work integrates developmental, neurobiological, psychodynamic and interpersonal aspects of the impact of trauma and its treatment. He is a professor of psychiatry at Boston University Medical School and serves as the director of the National Center for Child Traumatic Stress Complex Trauma Network. He states, "Most traumas occur in the context of interpersonal relationships, which involve boundary violations, loss of autonomous action, and loss of self-regulation. When people lack sources of support and sustenance, such as is common with abused children, women trapped in domestic violence, and incarcerated men, they are likely to learn to respond to abuse and threat with mechanistic compliance or resigned submission" (van der Kolk 2006, p. 7).

Interpersonal relational trauma occurs where there is exploitive harm done to one person by another within the context of a personal relationship. This can occur in the context of many human relationships such as marriage, family, parent/child, work, or dating in the form of betrayal, addiction, abuse, violence, or exploitation. There is significant impact on the victim and often results in post-traumatic stress disorder (PTSD).

Trauma can restrict the ability to resolve future stressful and painful situations. Simply put, it undermines resilience. One long-term impact of trauma is the fact that often-traumatized individuals have difficulty recognizing how they are feeling and then fail to respond in an appropriate and helpful way. They become out of touch with their own feelings, bodies, and needs, which in turn makes it more difficult to respond to the feelings, sensations, and needs of others in their lives.

The pathway of healing includes learning to reconnect to our feelings, bodies, and the others in our lives. We learn to be present again with ourselves and the world around us. Being present and paying attention changes our lives. Most cultures and religions have practices that help us in this pursuit. The goal often has been to enrich our personal awareness and knowledge of self. Dr. Daniel Siegel is a clinical professor of psychiatry at the UCLA School of Medicine, where he is on the faculty of the Center for Culture, Brain, and Development and the founding co-director of the Mindful Awareness Research Center. Siegel emphasizes how being fully aware individually helps us to attune to another person, not only changing us but changing the very nature of our personal relationships. Simply put, "attuned relationships promote resilience and longevity" (Siegel 2010a, p. 13). This attunement helps with neural integration, which allows us to be more flexible and resilient as we deal with the curveballs of life. Siegel discusses how our resilience can be undermined by past trauma, addiction, and loss when we begin to respond to life's challenges in a restricted manner. He states in his book *Mindsight* that "when we block our awareness of feelings, they continue to affect us anyway. Research has shown repeatedly that even without conscious awareness, neural input from the internal world of body and emotion influences our reasoning and our decision making. Even facial expressions we're not aware of, even changes in heart rhythm we may not notice, directly affect how we feel and so how we perceive the world. In other words, you can run but you cannot hide" (Siegel 2010, p. 124). This book highlights how attachment can become toxic; these are the underpinnings of trauma bonds. Our bonding in attachment can be undermined by trauma, either in the past or in our present.

WHAT IS TRAUMA?

Throughout our life spans, we are all introduced to trauma in one way or another. Dr. Bessel van der Kolk states, "As human beings we belong to an extremely resilient species. Since time immemorial we have rebounded from our relentless wars, countless disasters (both natural and man-made), and the violence and betrayal in our own lives. But traumatic experiences do leave traces, whether on a large scale (on our histories and cultures) or close to home, on our families, with dark secrets being imperceptibly passed down through generations. They also leave traces on our minds and emotions, on our capacity for joy and intimacy, and even on our biology and immune systems" (van der Kolk 2014, p. 1). Unresolved trauma undermines our resilience and our capacity to connect both to ourselves and to those around us.

At its core, the human response to trauma is about the loss of connection, the loss of connection to our identity, our bodies, our memories, and to the people surrounding us in our lives. The loss of connection can be hard to recognize at times, but the result is recognizable. Trauma has the capacity to undermine our sense of self, feelings of well-being, and connection to life. The world within and around us can become very restrictive, limiting our ability for choice, creativity, and connection.

Dr. Peter Levine, a clinical consultant at The Meadows, developed Somatic Experiencing, a naturalistic approach to the resolution and healing of trauma, defines trauma as "any experience which stuns us like a bolt out of the blue; it overwhelms us, leaving us altered and disconnected from our bodies" (Levine and Klein, 2006, p. 4). When individuals are in the overwhelmed state, their previously held coping mechanisms no longer function, and they can be left feeling hopeless and helpless. The impact of trauma is psychological, neurobiological, and psychobiological. In other words, it affects our mind, body, spirit, and relationships.

This loss of connection to ourselves affects us in many different ways. One of the most pronounced is in our ability to emotionally regulate and in our perception of ourselves and those around us. Often the result is emotional reactions that are under- or overregulated. Dr. Daniel Siegel refers to this process as the window of tolerance in which arousal fluctuates between high arousal and low arousal. In the middle is the optimal arousal zone. Those who have suffered through traumatic situations often have a narrow band of optimal arousal and fluctuate between high and low arousal. At times they may overreact to something relatively minor and underreact when action is preferred. One of the goals in the healing process is to widen this "window of tolerance" and increase the optimum zone. Working in therapy, attending recovery groups, talking with trusted friends, mindfulness, connection to our bodies, and attention to self-care are all ways of increasing our internal integration and promoting connection. In this process the window of tolerance is widened, which allows us to regulate in the presence of stress or intense emotions in a way that we would not have been able to do prior. (Siegel 2010b).

INTERPERSONAL RELATIONAL TRAUMA

This book focuses on the impact of interpersonal relational trauma. We will be exploring the impact of betrayal and exactly what traces are left behind. There are unique qualities when the trauma is by the hand of those who are expected to love, protect, and cherish us. This type of trauma is interpersonal relational trauma. When we are hurt, it is natural to turn to those we are closest to for comfort and healing. However, when these people are also the source of our trauma and pain we are lost in a painfully difficult double bind. It is confusing and difficult to navigate. Before delving into relational trauma, it is important to understand the nature of trauma and its impact. Since the original publication of this manuscript, our understanding of trauma has expanded through the work of neuroscience.

WHAT DOES TRAUMA LOOK LIKE?

Trauma is now often categorized in either "Big T" trauma or "Little t" trauma.

Most of us intuitively understand the concept of Big T traumatic events. These are the extraordinary events such as war, natural disasters, and being a victim of violence that lead to a wide range of symptoms associated with intense anxiety, depression, and shock or numbness. People who have experienced these types of events often suffer with acute stress and PTSD. Big T trauma can involve a single event or a chronic, repetitive series of events, but they are the kind of events that common sense dictates would be hard to handle without some sort of emotional distress.

Little t traumas are the ones that are harder to recognize, as are their impact on you. These are the experiences that might be traumatic for one person but not necessarily another. These are the daily hurts that occur across time and build on each other. These traumas often go undetected not only by others but also often by the person experiencing the hurt. The term "Little t trauma" does not imply, however, that the emotional impact of such an event is insignificant compared to Big T traumas. Each is based on the individual, and the experience and emotional wounds of both types of trauma can be long-lasting.

Relational trauma can be either Big T or Little t trauma that occurred within the context of a relationship and is now triggered by the interactions you have in your current relationships. Relational trauma that is very intense, occurs for long periods, or happened in childhood has a bigger impact and sets the stage for life struggles with depression, anxiety, stress, and relationship and marriage problems.

How vulnerable a person is to trauma depends on many factors, and the vulnerability differs from person to person. Many trauma researchers and treatment providers discuss the impact of childhood events such as traumatic experiences and attachment wounds, which have the potential to leave the child more vulnerable to being overwhelmed in future trauma situations. It is also easy to understand that the younger the child, the more vulnerable he or she is to being overwhelmed by a fearful or hurtful situation. The event itself may not be what labels an experience as traumatic, but rather our response to the event and how we are able to navigate life and connection to resources following the event. When faced with a potentially threatening situation we act to respond in our bodies' natural fight, flight, or freeze responses. When successful, these help us to survive and manage the threat. However, these responses can often become thwarted and can be stored in our nervous systems. When this occurs, as in the case with many situations of interpersonal relational trauma, we can be caught in these responses, with our systems on red alert status.

The younger the age at the time of the relational trauma, the greater the potential impact due to the effect on the attachment, or emotional bond, with the primary caregiver. This is because the quality of attachment actually affects the developing brain of the child. With a healthy attachment, the child comes to expect a sense of security, being valued, and enjoyment from relationships, whereas with an unhealthy attachment, the child comes to expect insecurity, being devalued, and stress from relationships.

These early attachment experiences begin to lay the foundation for our future self-esteem and how to be social with others. It's where we begin to learn about interpersonal boundaries and what our role in a relationship is. It's where we learn how to recognize our social and emotional needs and how to fulfill them. Whether it's with the primary caregiver, family members, teachers, friends, or romantic or marriage partners, it's in relationships that we form beliefs about ourselves and our world. When those relationships are infused with Big T or Little t trauma, our belief systems become distorted.

Attachment and bonding lay the groundwork for our resiliency in life. Trauma researchers through a large body of literature present evidence of how healthy bonding and attachment are critical to brain development, self-soothing, and the ability to cope emotionally throughout life. This process can be significantly interrupted when the attachment bonds are broken through neglect, abuse, abandonment, and betrayal. This is true throughout the life span. When a young child experiences interpersonal relational trauma, he or she often develops unhealthy relationship dynamics.

Van der Kolk (1989) asserted that trauma experiences are often reenacted in some way by the affected people, who are seeking to gain a sense of power over the original traumatic experience. This reenactment is marked by physiological arousal, and consequently, traumatized persons will expose themselves again and again to dangerous situations to get the same arousal feeling, which can look like an addictive pattern (van der Kolk 1989). It has been theorized that sexually compulsive behaviors may be attempts to reenact trauma in different ways with a goal of gaining mastery over the original trauma and turning it into something that gives pleasure (Schwartz 1992). When caregivers are the cause of these traumatic experiences, children often will develop trauma bonds with the perpetrator (Carnes 1997) and may go on to develop an approach/avoidance conflict in their adult attachment relationships.

These traumatic bonds are at the center of this book and often fear plays a central role. The emotion of fear has a very specific neural circuitry etched in the brain, which is paired with physical sensations throughout the body. These physical sensations are familiar, such as elevated heart rate, tense muscles, short and shallow breathing, and sweating. All of these reactions help the body to organize the survival flight-or-fight response. When faced with a trigger of the original threat, we often respond in this same way, even when the threat may not be present. Our bodies are engaged in a survival response often when we are no longer in danger. Many times our survival instinct takes it to the next stage, which is freeze, often present in a situation of traumatic bonding. When we are faced with a threat from someone we trust, love, or depend on for our well-being, our survival instinct is often one of paralysis, the inability to respond. Often we replay the tape in our heads and think of the many ways we could have responded at the time, what we might have said or what we might have done but did not do. These reactions often become the material for intense personal criticism as well as the criticism of others, yet when we understand the nature of trauma and how the body responds to trauma, we gain the beginning of understanding and awareness, which facilitate change.

When the source of the fear is also the person who we are bonded to, these issues become more complex and difficult to break. "We think it is apparent how a dilemma of profound consequences is set up if the people who are supposed to love and protect us are also the ones that have hurt, humiliated, and violated us. This 'double-bind' undermines a basic sense of self and trust in one's own instincts. In this way one's whole sense of safety and stability becomes weakened" (Levine 2010, p. 14).

The good news is that healing is possible. The plasticity of the brain allows for change to occur. Learning to emotionally regulate is essential to overcoming the passivity and fixed reactions, which in turn allows for connected and attuned relationships. The book is designed to be a tool for awareness and recovery.

Trauma and Recovery

When the Jedi Master Yoda began to reluctantly teach the young Luke Skywalker, he stated, "You must unlearn what you have learned."

In the past twenty years, the field of neuroscience has been on that same journey. Just a few years ago, the common wisdom was that after childhood the brain was in a steady state of decline and the brain could not heal or change its structure once there was damage. Dr. Norman Doidge discusses the remarkable advances in our understanding of the human brain and its function and ability stating, "The idea that the brain can change its own structure and function through thought and activity is, I believe, the most important alteration in our view of the brain since we first sketched out its basic anatomy and the workings of its basic component, the neuron" (Doidge 2007, p. xx).

This plasticity can be powerful for healing and growth after events that alter the brain such as traumatic brain injury, illness, and addiction. It provides immense hope where previously there was none. Change is possible. Each experience alters the brain, even as we age. We have the capacity to learn new behaviors, attitudes, and perspectives. Whether in the safety of trusted friendships, therapy, support groups, or challenging ourselves in the development of a new skill, these relationships and processes help to learn new ways of being. "Enriched environments can include the kinds of challenging educational and experiential opportunities that encourage us to learn new skills and expand our knowledge. Higher levels of education, practicing skills, and continued engagement in mental activities also correlate with more neurons and neural connections" (Cozolino 2002, p. 23). These new connections primarily in relationship to others facilitate new growth and integration, allowing for a new personal narrative to emerge.

Lois was only twenty-two. Fresh out of college with a business degree in hand, she had landed a fabulous job with a large printing firm. She was ecstatic. She worked hard. The company gave her a car. She was attractive and fun. Her hard work and enthusiasm made up for her inexperience. Plus, she had support. Her boss, the marketing director, was also young by many people's standards. Nearing thirty, she already had eight years of business experience. The company had grown dramatically, and many chalked it up to her skill and untiring efforts. She took Lois under her wing, and they became good colleagues and friends.

One day the marketing director left the office in tears. A memo came around saying she had resigned. Lois tried to reach her at home, but there was no response to the messages she left. The president of the company asked Lois to come to his office. He talked of his sadness that the marketing director was no longer with the company. He also said that he now had a problem; he had no one to run marketing. He offered Lois the job.

Lois immediately accepted. She had mixed emotions because of the loss of her supervisor and because little was known about why she left, just the tears. Yet Lois knew this was a tremendous opportunity for her. The president told her that he had taken a chance on her previous supervisor being so young and it worked out well. Lois received a bonus and a significant raise. She threw herself into her work.

A week later the president asked Lois to his office to review her first week's efforts. Lois could tell he was not totally pleased with what she had done but was unsure what he wanted. Then he launched into a description of what made her predecessor successful. Critical were her former boss's "special" relationships with customers. In fact, for the buying agents of their key accounts she would perform oral sex. That's how the company kept business. As he talked, Lois went numb with disbelief. She came out of it when he said that their customers liked office sex in certain ways and he would show her how. Then he approached her. Lois stood up and told him that she would not do this for any price. She grabbed her personal belongings and left the company in tears.

She was devastated. Friends and family gathered around Lois. They found her a therapist. The therapist said that she had experienced an assault and would need to work it through or her life would suffer. Lois pulled herself together and responded by saying that it was only a proposition and she would simply forget about it.

The therapist was right though. About a month after leaving her job, Lois started having nightmares about the company president and his office. She had difficulty motivating herself to find work. Interviews went badly. She moved back in with her parents, which added even more stress. She shut down sexually. She was critical of her boyfriend who, in fact, was very supportive. That relationship ended. She found herself continually angry with her former supervisor. She berated herself for being naïve enough to think that the company's success had anything to do with marketing. She was angry with her former employer yet obsessed with what was happening in the company. The betrayal for Lois was that nothing was as it had seemed. None of her ability, hard work, enthusiasm, or creativity mattered. She had believed that people had taken her seriously. In reality management had been grooming her to be the company courtesan. How could she ever trust anyone again?

Lois was also a victim of her own ability to cope. At the time of the betrayal, she felt that it was something she could handle. Calling on ancient family traditions of facing adversity, toughing it out, and forging ahead, she dismissed the significance of what had happened. Only in therapy did she start to understand that she had been victimized and admit that it was traumatic for her. Like many of us, Lois learned that she looked right at it and did not see it.

Stress becomes traumatic when danger, risk, fear, or anxiety is present. For Lois, she lost in a matter of minutes all that she thought she had. Further, the insidious fear was planted that the only way she could be successful was by using her body. Her talent for business didn't matter. Plus, the unwanted advance of someone who had so much power over her well-being placed her in jeopardy. Yet Lois had defenses that helped her cope with the problem. She tended to normalize and minimize. Her body, however, knew.

When in jeopardy, our body mobilizes its defenses. All our physical systems achieve high states of readiness. Adrenaline flows. The electrochemical reactions between synapses in the brain accelerate. It's just like an automobile driven at the maximum possible speed. The sustained, flat-out performance pushes the car's mechanical system past its limits. Pretty soon, things start to break down. Our bodies and minds will react the same way. When pushed past their limits, they begin to fall apart. Unlike a car, however, our bodies and minds can regenerate and recover. Some traumas that occur as a result of betrayal create damage that is residual. That is, we do not see it or understand it until later. Some traumas, especially over time, can alter how our systems operate.

Two factors are essential in understanding traumatic experiences: how far our systems are stretched and for how long. Figure 1.1 helps us understand how these two factors interact. Some events happen only once or just a few times, but the impact is so great that trauma occurs. The experience Lois had with the president of the company only lasted a few minutes, but the impact was significant and enduring. Rape, accident, assault, and some types of child molestation fit this extreme form of trauma. So would being terminated without warning from a job after years of loyal service and excellent performance.

Figure 1.1. Impact of Abuse

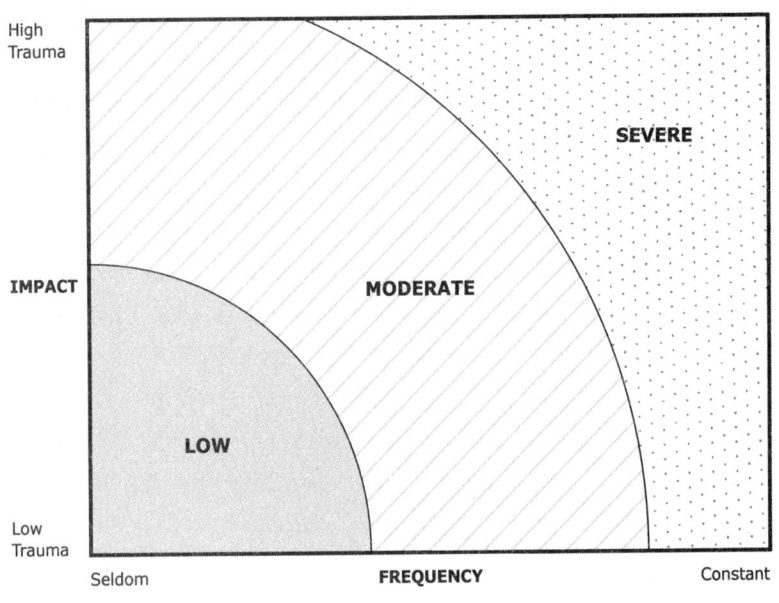

Some trauma experiences are relatively minor, but they happen every day. The hurt accumulates. Many acts of child neglect, for example, in themselves are not that serious. Every parent has moments of not being able to cover all the bases.

A consistent pattern of neglect, however, creates incredible anxiety in a child and leaves serious lifelong wounds. Other examples include living in a toxic marriage or working in a toxic corporation. Little acts of degradation, manipulation, secrecy, and shame on a daily basis take their toll. Trauma by accumulation sneaks up on its victims.

The compromises we make to trauma can deaden us over time. As one man described his recovery from a traumatizing marriage, "It was a full year after we split when I realized that my back felt different. It was relaxed and I could bend without effort. I had spent so many years braced for the next outburst, my back muscles were always tensed up. I never realized that while I was married." It's like walking into a room with a bad smell. The longer you stay in the room, the more the smell will seem to dissipate. Your olfactory system actually adjusts to the offensive odor. It's only by leaving the room that you will recover your sensitivity to the odor. It's the same with high stress, danger, or anxiety; your body and mind will adjust—and pay for it. Only after being away from traumatic circumstances will your sensitivity return.

How does trauma continue to act on us if things return to normal? There are eight predominant ways that trauma continues to affect people over time. They are trauma:

reaction
arousal
blocking
splitting
abstinence
shame
repetition
bonds

While this book will focus on the insane loyalties of betrayal bonding, it is important to understand the other seven dysfunctional options that people have to cope with betrayal. These options often become significant allies of one another. So if you have one, you probably have some of the others as well. In the interest of understanding how these work together, we need to understand each separately.

EFFECTS OF TRAUMA ON THE BRAIN: WHY DREDGE UP THE PAST?

One of the most common questions I am asked is, "Why do I have to dredge up the past? It is over. What good can it do now to bring it all up?" The answer lies in understanding the impact of trauma on the brain.

When people are profoundly frightened, trauma creates a biological alteration of the brain. At birth, only primitive structures like the brain stem (which regulates the fight-or-flight response) are fully functional. In regions like the temporal lobes (which regulate emotions and receive input from the senses), early experiences wire the brain circuitry.

When early trauma/deprivation are present, the circuitry to and within the temporal lobes are profoundly affected, resulting in emotional and cognitive problems. Our primary brain goes into stimulation and is flooded with neurochemicals. When the source of the fear goes away, the chemicals go away. The person experiences cravings. They can become attached to trauma. People become reactive human beings—going from stimulation to action without thinking. PTSD is reacting years later to early trauma events.

Two factors are essential in understanding traumatic experiences: how far our systems are stretched and for how long. Some events happen only once or just a few times, but the impact is so great that trauma occurs. Trauma by accumulation sneaks up on its victims. They become acclimatized. Traumas that are horrendous and long-lasting are the worst. Such was the Holocaust. Or Vietnam or 9/11. Emotional scars can be so severe that generations descended from those surviving will react in ways that still reflect the original trauma. No amount of normalcy makes it safe. Patterns and attitudes evolve far beyond the individual and are incorporated into family and society.

As the brain is shaped by traumatic experiences, primary reactions patterns are developed. There are eight primary trauma reactions discussed below.

TRAUMA REACTION

Definition: Physiological and/or psychological alarm reactions from unresolved trauma experience.

Clinical Patterns: Flashbacks; intrusive thoughts; insomnia; triggered associations; troubling dreams; physical symptoms; hypervigilance; living in extremes; bipolar cycles; borderline personality disorder; victims of violent crimes, soldiers, sexual abuse survivors.

A man finds himself being shaken awake by his wife. He is standing in the hallway outside their bedroom. He has his old army battle fatigues on, left over from his days in Vietnam. He was hearing battle sounds—the chattering of M50s, the dull thuds of mortar fire, earsplitting artillery. He is experiencing all the fear, the sweat, and mindnumbing exhaustion of battle. When his wife wakes him, he is not sure where he is. The battle seemed so real. Yet here he is twenty-three years later at 2:00 AM standing in his home. He has no idea what he was doing in the hallway or how or even why he had put on his fatigues. Scared, stunned, and doubting his reality, he is helped by his wife back to bed. It takes days for him to settle down. He wonders if he is losing his sanity. He drinks heavily to calm himself.

War is a sustained, horrifying experience. In earlier wars we used the term *battle fatigue*. What that meant was that the coping mechanisms of soldiers became overwhelmed to the extent that they could not function. Now remember that the brain, body, and nervous system will adjust. They will acclimatize. So for survival the soldier will continually bury the horrifying experiences into compartments in the brain. Later—sometimes many years—the compartments start to leak. The veteran reexperiences the terror, at times with the same realism of the original experience. Therapists call this post-traumatic stress disorder, or PTSD. The stress of the trauma continues long after the actual traumatic event.

PTSD can occur after any overwhelming and fear-filled event. Survivors of childhood sexual abuse will have nightmares about being sexually assaulted at the same time of night that the original assault took place. Or they will see someone, or something will happen that reminds them of those supercharged events, and it will trigger a flashback—a very real daydream—with all the original feelings. After the flashback it is very difficult for them to function as if nothing has happened. People around the survivor become very confused because something obviously has happened, but they have no idea what.

A much more minor variant of this theme occurs when people dream of taking a test in school for which they are not prepared. This common experience many have had reflects the stress of school exams. These dreams can be triggered by current stress experiences that require preparation. Similarly, the sexual abuse survivor may have difficulty being sexual as an adult because of the feelings that come back about those early terrifying experiences. Or consider how startled veterans can be when you touch them and they did not know you were there. The trigger is surprise contact—of which one type is ambush.

The deeper and more problematic issue with PTSD is how the alarm system of the brain is activated. Fear causes extraordinary changes in your neurological system and your organs—especially the brain. In abused children we know that the actual biological tissues of the brain are altered. Recent research on Vietnam vets also revealed changes in the brain. Sustained or overwhelming fear activates and mobilizes our entire system.

Researchers in human attachment and bonding have long known that neglect and rejection of a child will create anxiety. The child fearfully asks, "What will happen to me?" Even early studies of monkeys who were neglected showed that they became extremely reactive, violent, antisocial, and even compulsive sexually. Therein is the problem. Most people can have an emergency, respond well, and return to normal. But when the trauma is overwhelming and/or sustained, the body's ability to stay in an alarm state is enhanced. The alarm state starts to feel "normal." A metaphor would be an accelerator on a car that sticks. You may accelerate, but slowing down again becomes a problem. And some trauma victims live with their throttles stuck wide open. The result is highly reactive, difficult people who do not want to be the way they are. Their lives are characterized by overreaction (angry outbursts, distrust of others, excessive behavior) and disturbed relationships (short-term relationships, idealizing others until the alarms kick in, and then they hate the same people they once thought were so great). Therapists will talk of *borderline personalities*. Borderline personalities are people who have been hurt so badly they are afraid and on maximum alert—all the time.

Here are some characteristics of PTSD reactivity:

recurrent and unwanted (intrusive) recollections of experiences

periods of sleeplessness

sudden "real" memories (vivid, distracting)

extremely cautious of surroundings

startled more easily than others

distressing dreams about experiences

flashback episodes—acting or feeling as if the experience is happening in the present

distress when exposed to reminders of experiences like anniversaries, places, or symbols

outbursts of anger and irritability

distrustful of others, physical reactions to reminders of experiences (breaking out in cold sweat, trouble breathing, etc.)

Living so reactively takes a toll on the body. For example, women who were sexually abused as children are eight times more likely to have cancer than women who were not abused. Some researchers make a strong case that the impact of trauma is encoded right down to the cellular level. For both men and women, early childhood physical abuse has been linked to an increased risk for cancer (Morton, Schafer, and Ferraro 2012). Between 1995 and 1997, the CDC and Kaiser Permanente Adverse Childhood Experiences (ACE) Study was conducted and is one of the largest investigations of childhood abuse and neglect and impact on health. This groundbreaking study was one of the first to examine the link between adverse childhood experiences and the impact of accumulated stress. The study findings reveal a relationship between the number of these experiences and negative health outcomes and well-being outcomes across the lifespan.

In the case of Lois, who was a secure, healthy adult, betrayal generated such fear and distrust that it took years to overcome the impact. If there is enough time and sufficient fear, the impact can be highly addictive.

CLINICAL STRATEGIES FOR TRAUMA REACTIONS:

- cognitive reframing of trauma experiences
- hypnotic desensitization
- teach PTSD (post-traumatic stress disorder) concepts
- implement relapse prevention and other skills
- controlled breathing
- stress management techniques
- developing meaning from victimization
- therapeutic storytelling
- systematic desensitization
- deep muscle relaxation
- thought-stopping strategies
- guided self-dialogue

- role-playing
- covert modeling
- diaries and self-monitoring
- EMDR (eye movement desensitization reprocessing)
- somatic experiencing
- trauma-informed yoga

TRAUMA AROUSAL

Definition: Seeking/finding pleasure in the presence of extreme danger, violence, risk, or shame.

Clinical Patterns: Sadomasochism; sex offending; prostitution; high-risk experiences; arousal addiction.

Some soldiers in Vietnam used sex as a way to escape the horror of war. They experienced sex in ways that were not reproducible in a peace-time country. High-risk sex became like a drug. It stimulated the system (like amphetamines) and dulled the pain. Coming home meant they could find no parallel experience. So they simply became violent. It was the closest way they could reexperience that rush.

Some girls had their first sexual experiences under scary or even violent conditions. They found it pleasurable and felt responsible for what happened. As adults, the only way they could be orgasmic was when a man was hurting them. Their behavior became supercharged and highly addictive. They may work as prostitutes or hit the S&M clubs. Either way they find willing partners who will revictimize them.

Some executives, in an effort to compensate for horrible experiences as children, find an exhilaration in the climb to power. As CEOs of billion-dollar corporations, they only feel alive when dealing with crisis or huge risk. Leveraged buyouts, takeovers, and acquisitions become the "bets" of just another form of compulsive gambling.

Hooked on the stress of extraordinary power and the risk of losing everything, they cannot leave their jobs. Dealmaking twenty hours a day, they can hardly sleep or be with their families. They play with traumatic possibility and cannot leave it alone. For recreation they love high-speed motorcycles, skydiving, and other high-risk diversions.

Some professionals (clergy, physicians, attorneys) will have sex with those entrusted to their care (parishioners, patients, clients). Some in these professions develop a pattern of high-risk sex that is clearly addictive. Most were sexually abused as children and learned to connect their sexuality with fear. So as adults, they feel most sexual when it is dangerous or risky. One of the characteristics is that with each episode they take a greater risk—until they are inevitably caught.

Addiction specialists talk about the arousal neuropathway of addiction. Gambling, high-risk sex, stimulant drugs, and high-risk activities serve as examples of this category. Stimulation and pleasure compensate for pain and emptiness. In sex alone the possibilities are endless: sex offending, sadomasochism, prostitution, and anonymous sex—all rely on danger and/or fear to escalate the sexual high. Some relationships are saturated with arousal escalators—supercharged sex, violence, dramatic exits, passionate reconciliations, secrets, and threats of abandonment—all in the context of "if anybody ever found out about this, there would be hell to pay." This is why soap operas can be so compelling. They provide vicarious arousal with scripts based on betrayal. As we shall see, high arousal that comes from fear and danger can be an important ally of betrayal bonding.

Trauma pleasure is seeking or finding pleasure and stimulation in the presence of extreme danger, violence, risk, or shame. It is a frequent outcome of betrayal and trauma. Signs of its presence are:

engaging in high-risk, thrill-seeking behaviors such as skydiving or race-car driving

seeking more risk because the last jolt of excitement was not enough

difficulty being alone, calm, or in low-stress environments

using drugs like cocaine or amphetamines to speed things up or to heighten high-risk activities

feeling sexual when frightened or when violence occurs

seeking high-risk sex

loving to gamble on outcomes

difficulty completing sustained, steady tasks

seeking danger

constant searching for all-or-nothing situations

associating with people who are dangerous to you

Arousal accesses a neuropathway that is very compelling. If your brain adjusts to it, you need the stimulation simply to feel normal. Then it can become addictive and interfere with your life. You will not want to give it up. The alarm state induced by trauma becomes the gateway to many forms of addictive arousal. Yet there are other strategies for coping with trauma that also can become addictive, including efforts to block the trauma out.

CLINICAL STRATEGIES FOR TRAUMA AROUSAL:

- conduct assessment for addiction
- initiate addiction treatment
- teach concepts of multiple addictions
- establish a relapse prevention plan
- introduce twelve-step support
- create alternative "high" options
- initiate trauma resolution strategies
- connect addiction relapse with trauma work

TRAUMA BLOCKING

Definition: Efforts to numb, block out, and overwhelm residual feelings due to trauma.

Clinical Patterns: Compulsive overeating; excessive sleeping; alcoholism; depressant drugs; satiation; addictive responses.

Numbing. Comforting. Relaxing. Anesthetizing. Anything to escape the uncomfortable feelings. High arousal? Something to calm the nerves. Slow down. Bad memories? Anything to obliterate the interior world. An analgesic fix to make it bearable. Some use alcohol. Some use drugs. Some do both. Compulsive eating creates comfort and drowsiness. Watching mind-numbing TV wastes time but avoids reality. Excessive sleeping becomes like a butterfly in a cocoon, only there is no intention of coming out.

Cheryl was a domestic abuse victim. She was in court eleven times because her husband had assaulted her. She felt terrible shame. Every time he beat her he screamed about it being her fault because she was so heavy. She felt the accusations were true. She knew she had problems with food and that she needed to do something. But it helped her get through the day. Besides, it was the one thing he could not control. There was an added dividend: Being fat made her sexually unattractive. She hated sex. She was an incest victim. Food was protection. Food was comfort.

Now there was the new crisis. One of the kids had told a counselor at school that her father (Cheryl's husband) was being sexual with her at night. The family had been reported to child protection. Now they were in treatment as a family. Cheryl had to go to a group of new incest moms. The therapist asked about food issues. Nine out of the eleven moms had undergone intestinal bypass surgery. Cheryl got the message. Eating was more than a self-control issue. She made it into a way to keep safe and block pain. As she progressed in treatment, she started to eat differently, and memories of her own childhood experience became clearer as well as memories she had forgotten.

Survivors block their pain. One of the leading factors in relapse for alcoholics is that as they get sober, their memories return. Rather than face the pain, they start drinking again. More and more studies show that alcoholics may switch to other addictions. Addiction becomes a solution to the trauma. The neuropathway involved here relates to a phenomenon called *satiation*. Behaviors and substances that induce calming, relaxing, and numbing create electrochemical reactions in the brain that serve as analgesic fixes. The neurochemical bottom line is anxiety reduction. For the trauma survivor this means avoiding the fear and numbing the pain. Addiction therapists use the term *compulsive* to describe the repetitive efforts to calm the mind. The problem here is that again the brain will adjust, and the compulsive behavior will become necessary in order to feel normal. Then it is hard to stop because it has transformed into addiction.

Trauma blocking is an effort to numb, block out, or reduce residual feelings due to trauma. Signs of satiation or efforts to block include:

excessive drinking

use of depressant drugs or "downers"

using TV, reading, or hobbies as a way to numb out

compulsive eating

excessive sleeping

compulsive working, especially at unrewarding jobs

compulsive exercise

bingeing (with any of the above) when things are difficult

video games

excessive use of technology and social media

difficulty staying awake

always looking for something to do, uncomfortable being at rest

preoccupied with food and eating

feeling anxious and "behaving" to make feelings go away

using drugs to escape

working so one doesn't have to feel

wish to "slow down" one's mind

Any trauma of sufficient magnitude will create this response in your neuropathways. In alcoholism, for example, much research indicates that alcoholics (and indeed, addicts of all kinds) probably are born with an insufficiency of certain receptor sites in the brain. That's why alcoholics can often list other alcoholics in their families, going back many generations. Being raised in an alcoholic home is also traumatic. All these factors are commonly recognized. During the Vietnam War, however, we had young kids with no history of alcohol or drug abuse in the family and a stable history of emotional health who came back from the war drug addicts and alcoholics. Their ability to function became impaired. Simply said, the war overwhelmed them. They used drugs and alcohol to cope, and their brains accommodated. In a recent article, "Compulsive Sexual Behavior Among Male Military Veterans: Prevalence and Associated Clinical Factors," the study found that 16.7 percent of male military veterans struggle with compulsive sexual behavior. This is no surprise as the Internet and sexually explicit material are readily available to soldiers as they serve in dangerous and violent situations. Using sex as a means of trauma blocking is not new, but the access to pornographic material and ways to use high intensity and pleasure as a means to block are. With the explosion of the Internet there is now 24/7 access to pornography in a way that has not been accessible previously. This access allows for the constant search for novelty and intensity, all of which are readily available.

Survivors often use a combination of strategies to cope. A common pattern is to use high-arousal activities of intensity, pleasure, or stress and then follow with blocking strategies to balance the arousal. Drug addicts, for example, will mix uppers and downers. Or consider the man who is having anonymous, high-risk sex with other men in parks and streets. When he returns home ashamed and exhausted but cannot sleep because of the excitement, he has learned to drink a six-pack and eat until his stomach is uncomfortably distended. He passes out, oblivious. Caught up in vicious cycles of arousal and blocking, his behaviors serve as a one-two punch to the painful memories of his childhood sexual abuse. He is caught. His memories will never relent. And his addictions will kill him—one way or another.

CLINICAL STRATEGIES FOR TRAUMA BLOCKING:

- differential diagnosis of addiction
- confront patterns of blocking behavior
- initiate addiction treatment
- teach concepts of multiple addictions
- establish relapse prevention plan
- introduce twelve-step supports
- create alternative ways for anxiety reduction
- initiate trauma resolution strategies
- connect addiction relapse with trauma work

TRAUMA SPLITTING

Definition: Ignoring traumatic realities by splitting off the experience and not integrating into personality or daily life.

Clinical Patterns: Avoiding reality through excessive daydreaming; compartmentalizing parts of self to reduce tension; fantasy addictive responses such as romance addiction or artistic or mystical preoccupation; living double life; extreme procrastination; dissociative disorders including multiple personality disorder.

Escape. Individuals can find another reality to go to if the one they are in is too painful. This is like the *Enterprise* holodeck on *Star Trek*. When members of the crew are distraught or need a break, they go to the holodeck and create a holographic fantasy that seems very real. Many episodes use the holodeck as a counterpoint or even a plot. At the end of each adventure, however, the routine of being on a Federation starship returns, as do the problems. In our technological culture there are endless means to slip into this fantasy world and escape. For some it is through gaming, others pornography, and others through binge-watching television on Netflix. Whatever the method, the goal is often the same, escape.

There are countless similar stories told by children who were sexually assaulted. They recount how they would imagine themselves flying around the room or doing something they liked as they were being fondled or penetrated. They were separating themselves from a reality too painful to bear. At the time it was an important coping strategy. Therapists call this *splitting*—victims learn to split off the uncomfortable reality or dissociate from the experience. They do this by focusing on another reality or by creating an unreality or fantasy. When this coping style becomes a pattern that interferes with living life, it is called a dissociative disorder.

Splitting takes many forms. Sometimes it works as amnesia. The survivor does not remember significant facts about the trauma. Sometimes survivors will find themselves in places and they have no idea how they got there. Or they are in reality but feel detached from their bodies (flying around the room). People will make jokes such as "the lights are on but no one is home" because they have no understanding of the process. When there are different realities, sometimes different personalities will form. We call this either *multiple personality disorder* or *dissociative identity disorder.*

Addiction is an important partner to the dissociative process. Psychedelic drugs and marijuana, for example, are hallucinogenic and create an altered reality. Mystical and artistic preoccupation and some forms of excessive religiosity and spiritual practice create altered mental states and can be highly addictive. Two of the features of addictive disorders to sex, food, drugs, gambling, and alcohol are preoccupation and obsession. These also have a set of neuropathways that are distinct. Addictions here are called the "fantasy" addictions and often accompany arousal and obsession. Some sex addicts, for example, have a pattern of falling in love. As soon as the romance starts to subside, they find another romance. They live for the thrill and borrow endlessly on the promise of "This is the lover that will make the pain go away."

Another example is the compulsive gambler who buys lottery tickets with the family grocery money and obsesses about winning. He fantasizes endlessly about how he will spend the money he will win and how his profound financial difficulties will be behind him. Sadly, he is not able to face his difficulties because he retreats so often into fantasy that he starts acting as if the fantasy was reality. Similarly, the exhibitionist who is cruising and the alcoholic who becomes the wine connoisseur share the ability to go into a trance about their obsessions; they dissociate from their painful realities.

Addicts will talk of the split in realities by saying they feel like two people: the real person who has values and keeps commitments, and the out-of-control addict whose compulsivity destroys everything important to the "real" person. Robert Louis Stevenson wrote the story of Dr. Jekyll and Mr. Hyde (1895) to explain the experience of alcoholism. Addiction and trauma specialists are starting to understand that this *addictive personality shift* is very similar in its processes to multiple personality disorder.

Trauma splitting, then, is ignoring traumatic realities by splitting off the experiences and not integrating them into personality or daily life. Signs of dissociation include:

fantasizing or spacing out during plays and movies that generate intense feelings or are reminders of painful experiences

experiencing confusion, absentmindedness, and forgetfulness because of preoccupation

living in a fantasy world when things get tough

feeling separate from body as a reaction to a flashback

experiencing amnesia about what you are doing or being preoccupied with something other than what needs to be attended to

having a life of "compartments" that others do not know about

living a double life

daydreaming, living in an unreal world

obsessing around addictive behavior

losing yourself in romantic fantasies

the use of marijuana or psychedelic drugs

difficulty concentrating

avoiding thoughts or feelings associated with trauma experiences

inability to recall important details of experiences

procrastinating, interfering with life activities

tendency to be accident prone

a problem with putting off important tasks

All of us seek the holodeck at some point in time. The problem starts when we have been hurt so badly that we wish to stay there.

CLINICAL STRATEGIES FOR TRAUMA SPLITTING:

- assess for multiple personality disorder/dissociative disorders
- assess for fantasy addictive responses
- strategies for integration of realities/selves
- teach how to retain focus within reality framework
- connect trauma issues with dissociative or addictive patterns

TRAUMA ABSTINENCE

Definition: Compulsive deprivation, which occurs especially around moments of success, high stress, shame, or anxiety.

Clinical Patterns: DSM disorders including anorexia nervosa; sexual aversion disorder (sometimes known as sexual anorexia). Additional patterns include compulsive saving; agoraphobia and other phobic responses; poverty obsessions; success avoidance; self-neglect; underachieving; and workaholism.

Sandy was an attractive, extremely creative woman who seemed to wind up with dead-end jobs. Her friends wondered about it since she had such wonderful ideas. Her family wondered about it because she worked so hard in school and did so well. Family and friends alike tended to overlook the issue because Sandy was an incest survivor and also a recovering alcoholic. She had one more secret, however. Sandy went to a self-help group for compulsive debtors.

Compulsive debtors are different than compulsive spenders, who are often extremely successful. Spenders find release and escape with purchases. Debtors may buy things and then return them in a cycle similar to the binge/purge cycle of bulimia. Debtors use debt as a form of impoverishment and self-fulfillment. They cannot move or succeed under their debt burden. They have a core belief about their unworthiness.

One night in group the topic was *poverty obsession*. Some group members suggested that Sandy might have this issue. She was incensed. She was so upset she brought it to her therapist. Her therapist responded that she had been thinking the same thing, since she saw a pattern of aversion and self-discipline. Sandy focused so much on denying herself good things that she was self-limiting. Further, her therapist found it amazing that abstaining from alcohol had been so easy for Sandy. It reminded her therapist of compulsive overeaters who switched to being compulsive dieters or who became anorexics. She encouraged Sandy to look at the issue. Sandy was furious with her therapist as well as her group.

At that time Sandy managed a hair salon. In fact, she had created some shampoo and conditioning formulas that her customers loved. Many encouraged her to market the product and build a franchise system, but Sandy did nothing but continue to eke out a living from her shop. One day she was about to shampoo a client when she noticed that she was out of shampoo. Sandy asked one of her employees if she had an open bottle of shampoo. The employee said "sure" but something in her employee's eyes told Sandy that something was amiss. As she proceeded to work with her client she watched her employee from the mirror as she went to the storeroom and came back with a fresh bottle of shampoo. A realization hit Sandy so hard it was as though her emotional breath was taken away. She never went to the storeroom herself. She always "borrowed" an already open bottle of whatever she needed.

Sandy realized she had a pattern of frugality that made it difficult for her to open a new bottle. Her employees would simply go to the storeroom. It was her inventory and her invention, but denying herself was so ingrained in her she had developed the habit of taking open bottles. As it turned out, this frustrated her employees, who regarded their otherwise well-liked supervisor as pretty idiosyncratic. In an instant Sandy realized the significance of the bottle issue. Her whole life was based on control and deprivation until she could no longer stand it, whereupon she would go out of control as in her drinking or spending. This aversion to good, nurturing things for herself was precisely what her therapist and group were trying to tell her. Like all of us, we get most angry at the truths we do not wish to face. Sandy was like many other survivors, who often are extremely creative people. There is something about suffering that enhances creativity. Yet survivors also experience a bottleneck in their lives by their commitment to deprivation.

Compulsive deprivation or abstinence occurs especially around memories of success, high stress, shame, or anxiety. Most important, deprivation is driven by terror and fear, which we already know have a powerful impact on our brains. In deprivation survivors may:

deny themselves basic needs like groceries, shoes, books, medical care, rent, or heat

avoid any sexual pleasure or feel extreme remorse over any sexual activity

hoard money and avoid spending money on legitimate needs

perform underachieving jobs compulsively and make consistently extreme or unwarranted sacrifices for work

spoil success opportunities

have periods of no interest in eating and attempt diets repeatedly

see comfort, luxuries, and play activities as frivolous

routinely skip vacations because of dedication to an unrewarding task

avoid normal activities because of fears

have difficulty with play

be underemployed

vomit food or use diuretics to avoid weight gain

While there are many faces to traumatic abstinence, common elements do exist. First is the long shadow of family neglect. Neglectful families teach lessons about self-care and self-esteem. The family environment allows children to become comfortable with deprivation. The neglect of children becomes self-neglect in adults. Couple it with high arousal events such as domestic violence or sexual abuse and you have a neurochemical cocktail that is hard to beat. The antidote to being out of control is to be in supercontrol. Maybe the only way to control survival is to freeze like a hunted animal. Ask nothing. Do nothing. Attract no attention. Yet fear mobilizes the body. Adrenaline, cortisol, endorphins, and norepinephrine pour into the body. In a constant state, it can become addictive.

All the conditions are there: obsession, profound neurochemical changes, and a mechanism to manage the fear. Addiction specialists have long recognized the role of addictive deprivations. Anorexia, or self-starvation, has all the characteristics of drug addiction and is regarded as a fear-based, endorphin-mediated process that can be terminal. Even more important is the role of deprivations in serving as a balance to other excessive out-of-control behaviors. One woman described how when she was out of control sexually she would be anorexic with food. Then she would shut down sexually, become sexually aversive, and at the same time become out of control with food. There were one hundred pounds in her life that served to absolutely indicate where she was sexually. Another example is the clergyman who works ninety-five hours a week for an unappreciative congregation, struggling to make ends meet because he is so poorly paid. At the same time he is sexually out of control. It is common among professionals such as members of the clergy, physicians, and attorneys to have excessive, out-of-control aspects of their lives rooted in extreme deprivation. The bottom line is: Wherever addiction is, there will also be deprivation. If not addictive in its own right, the deprivation becomes a life pattern that, in part, is a solution to traumatic experience.

CLINICAL STRATEGIES FOR TRAUMA ABSTINENCE:

- assess deprivation role in other addictions
- teach connection extremes as dysfunctional balance mechanism
- assess compulsive deprivation
- confront disabling beliefs about being non-deserving
- seek patterns of deprivation
- develop incremental "use" strategies
- create relapse prevention strategies
- connect relapse with trauma issues
- learn to play as healing

TRAUMA SHAME

Definition: Profound sense of unworthiness and self-hatred rooted in traumatic experience.

Clinical Patterns: Shame cycles; self-mutilation; self-destructive behavior, expressing self-hatred through suicidal ideation; shame based personality; depression; codependency personality disorder.

A little girl is forced to have oral sex with her father. The father then tells her she is a bad little girl for letting this happen and that she is going to go to hell. The child is not sophisticated theologically and can't make sense out of the experience. All she knows is that she is bad and that she will come to a bad end. When the victim feels defective, or even worse, at fault, there is traumatic shame. Shame in this case is a profound sense of unworthiness and self-hatred rooted in traumatic experience.

Shame does not just originate from a perpetrator blaming the victim, although that happens often. Trauma can also leave a feeling of being defective or flawed. Sometimes victims are ashamed of their reactions to trauma—they are no longer like other people. Shame represents a fundamental break in trust. People who become shame-based have core beliefs that they are unlovable, that if people knew what they were really like they would leave. They believe there is no hope for change. They do not trust anyone to care about them based on their own merits, especially if the trauma was a significant betrayal by a trusted person.

Dr. Brene Brown has written extensively on the topic of shame over the last several years. She defines shame as, "the intensely painful feeling or experience of believing we are flawed and therefore unworthy of acceptance and belonging" (Brown 2007, p. 5). When looking at this definition, you can see how shame is different than guilt. Guilt is about something we have done and regret; shame is deeper and more difficult to combat; it is about our sense of self, who we believe ourselves to be.

"Shame unravels our connection to others. In fact, I often refer to shame as the fear of disconnection—the fear of being perceived as flawed and unworthy of acceptance or belonging. Shame keeps us from telling our own stories and prevents us from listening to others tell their stories. We silence our voices and keep our secrets out of the fear of disconnection. Hearing someone talk about a shaming experience can sometimes be as painful as actually experiencing it for ourselves" (Brown 2007, p. xxv).

Survivors will try to compensate by driving themselves to meet unreachable standards in order to gain the acceptance of others. When they fail, they add to their existing shame. An example would be the dieter on a rigorous diet who binges, feels ashamed at the lack of self-discipline, and tries even harder. Addiction specialists see the whole binge/purge phenomenon as rooted in shameful feelings about self. Trauma specialists also note that one of the changes in brain functioning is that all experiences are processed as extremes. Reactions are totally one way or another. There is no mid-ground, which is what also happens with addiction and deprivation. People lose the ability to operate in a balanced way, which further adds to their shameful feelings.

Shame can result in an obsessive self-hatred, which is more than simply feeling unlovable. It is also more than being depressed. It can become a merciless, unforgiving stance with yourself for which the only ultimate solution is suicide. Much time is taken up in thinking about destroying yourself. Another result of shame is self-destructive behavior—doing things that are bound to damage yourself or doing things that would sabotage any success. Clinicians are struck by how victims of trauma, especially in which there is violence, become violent with themselves. Self-mutilation, cutting or hurting themselves, and placing themselves in high-risk situations—all are rooted in self-hatred. Even their thought patterns can center upon torturous images of self-inflicted violence.

These signs of shame include:

feeling ashamed because you believe trauma experiences were your fault

feeling lonely and estranged from others because of trauma experiences

engaging in self-mutilating behaviors (cutting yourself, burning yourself, etc.)

engaging in self-destructive behaviors

enduring physical or emotional pain that most people would not accept

avoiding mistakes at any cost

feeling that you should be punished for the trauma event and being unable to forgive yourself

feeling bad when something good happens

having suicidal thoughts, threats, and attempts

possessing no ability to experience normal emotions such as sadness, anger, love, and happiness having a deep fear of depending on people

feeling unworthy, unlovable, immoral, or sinful because of trauma experiences

perceiving others always as better, happier, and more competent

having a dim outlook on the future

avoiding experiences that feel good, have no risk, and that are self-nurturing

Consider the story of Ralph, a very successful physician. He learned at an early age to escape his abusive family by being in school. He did not have to be at home as long as he was completely immersed in school activities and was incontestably successful. To outsiders he was the model child. Inside, he lived in emotional shell shock. His father was violent and sexually abusive toward his sisters. In fact, it was Ralph who helped his sisters put locks on their bedroom doors. His efforts to protect his sisters one night resulted in his father badly beating him.

A source of comfort was his mom, who would slip into his bed at night after his dad was asleep in a drunken stupor. He found his mom's body erotic but felt loyalty to his dad. He was confused by his mom's cold demeanor the next day. He never made sense of the cruelty and betrayal he witnessed in his family. He felt embarrassed by his family and empty inside. He compensated by being tops in everything, so no one would know his life was a charade. Yet he was troubled by intrusive thoughts of being cut and hurt. Even minor surgery became difficult. The harder he worked, the less life seemed worthwhile. He started drinking heavily and self-prescribed painkillers to numb the pain and postpone the taking of his own life.

Then he became involved with Emily. She was the wife of his best friend, who also was a physician and one of Ralph's partners. Emily was a clinical social worker who clearly was a sex addict. She had a pattern of high-risk sex with many men, although she preferred high-profile professionals. Best of all, she liked the drama if these men knew of each other and sex compromised their professional and personal situations. Her husband knew of her acting out but agreed to it. This reinforced his own feelings of cuckolded shame and gave him permission for his own sexual activities. Ralph became obsessed with Emily and their extraordinary sex. Their whole relationship was a series of broken promises, high drama, and painful betrayal. He even found himself getting support from Emily's husband. Ralph knew this relationship was destroying him. He could not work or function, yet he could not leave her. Finally, the state medical board intervened because of his drinking, which had become debilitating. When the board admitted him for treatment, he was absolutely suicidal.

His therapist pointed out to Ralph that he was reexperiencing what had happened to him as a child. He was again part of a group of untrustworthy people of which he was profoundly ashamed. His feelings of unworthiness could not be numbed into submission and, in fact, made him vulnerable to chasing moments of pseudointimacy with a manipulative, exploitive person. Emily was like a drug for him. The only alternative in his desperation and self-hatred was to die. His therapist summed it up when he said, "You have re-created your trauma."

CLINICAL STRATEGIES FOR TRAUMA SHAME:

- bibliotherapy on shame
- shame reduction strategies
- teach visualization and affirmation
- intense family of origin work
- restructure faulty or shaming belief
- teach nature of shame cycle

TRAUMA REPETITION

Definition: Repeating behaviors and/or seeking situations or persons who re-create the trauma experience.

Clinical Patterns: Reenactment; efforts to resolve unresolvable; obsessive compulsive disorder; repetition compulsions.

Reenactment. Therapists use the term *repetition compulsion*, which means repeating behaviors and/or seeking situations or persons that re-create the trauma experience. Ralph was reliving a story out of his painful history. Some people will find themselves in the same situation, with the same type of person, over and over again in their lives. Yet like Ralph, they may never link their behavior to the original betrayal and trauma. Reenactment is living in the unremembered past.

Connie is a good example. She was raised with an alcoholic father. Like Ralph's dad, Connie's father was very abusive. So it is no surprise that Connie married three abusive alcoholics in a row. The irony is that Connie left each husband to seek a man who would be better. She wanted an upgrade, yet each successive marriage was worse. Connie did change—she changed husbands. The scenario of living with an abusive, hard-drinking man, however, did not change. Each subsequent marriage was a repeat of the first, which was an echo of her childhood experience.

Some survivors repeat not only the same scenario but also the exact behavioral experience. A nurse was hospitalized many times for depression and suicidal feelings. She kept telling people she had this problem with masturbation. Usually this problem was ignored because it was not seen as relevant to her suicidal intentions. Finally, a perceptive therapist explored what the masturbation was really about, and it was not just masturbation. It was autoerotic asphyxiation.

She would hang herself in her closet while compulsively masturbating. In her art therapy she drew a picture of her father raping her at the age of ten. In the picture the father is strangling her. What the therapist then learned was the whole story of how when this nurse was a child, her father sexually abused her and then locked her in a closet. So all the elements of the original scenario were there: sexual stimulation, strangulation, extreme danger, and the dark closet. She was compulsively reenacting that scene from her childhood. As much as she tried to stop it, she could not. And she was so ashamed, the only way she could ask for help was to be suicidal.

Another form of reenactment is to victimize people in the same way that others victimized you. One incest father related that when he was a kid his parents told him that because he was an uncircumcised child, they needed to stretch his foreskin regularly or he might not be able to be sexual as an adult. This led to the sexual abuse he experienced as a child. As an adult, he reenacted the same abuse with his children. When the grandparents entered therapy, the therapist asked them which doctor had prescribed stimulation of the foreskin. The grandfather responded, "It was not our doctor, it was my father's doctor." This family had received a piece of medical advice in the late 1890s that would become the basis of a sexual abuse history spanning four generations.

Trauma repetition is characterized by:

doing something self-destructive over and over again, usually something that took place in childhood and started with a trauma

reliving a "story" from the past

engaging in abusive relationships repeatedly

repeating painful experiences, including specific behaviors, scenes, persons, and feelings

doing something to others that you experienced as an early-life trauma

inability to stop a childhood pattern

a desire to redo an early trauma experience

reverting to things done as a child

having thoughts and behaviors that do not feel good repeatedly

preoccupation with children of a certain age

In part, trauma repetition is an effort by the victim to bring resolution to the traumatic memory. By repeating the experience, the victim tries anew to figure out a way to respond in order to eliminate the fear. Instead, the victim simply deepens the traumatic wound. Note that repetition, like shame, can draw heavily on the other forms of traumatic impact: reactivity, arousal, blocking, splitting, and deprivation. Shame and reenactment simply intensify the mind-altering experience of trauma. They become allies of one another. They form a devastating combination when they are part of a trauma bond in which there has been betrayal.

Clinical Strategies for Trauma Repetition:

- assessment for obsessive compulsive disorder
- if perpetrator, focus on fixated versus regressed issues
- cognitive restructuring of key experiences and key beliefs about those experiences
- abreactive re-creation of experience through visualization to reduce experience's power
- disrupt systemic cycles that occur in the family system that draw upon this
- experience for power or to empower the trauma

Trauma Bonds and Their Allies

I CAN'T LIVE WITHOUT HIM...
HE MAY BEAT ME, HE MAY CHEAT ME, BUT
I LOVE HIM. AIN'T NOBODY'S BUSINESS IF I DO.

—Porter Grainger and Everett Robbins
"Tain't Nobody's Biz-ness If I Do"

TRAUMA BONDS

Trauma bonds are the dysfunctional attachments that occur in the presence of danger, shame, or exploitation. These relationships are very different from those attachments that occur naturally when we experience a traumatic event with others, and the result is often a pulling together, or a deepening of the bond as a method of survival.[1] These are the stories that resonate following unspeakable tragedy such as the intense bond between WWII veterans, the shared experience between rape victims in a support group, or the way a community can rise to great acts of bravery and shared humanity after horrific events such as natural disasters and terrorist attacks. Trauma bonds on the other hand occur when we are bonding to the very person who is the source of the danger, fear, and exploitation. This type of bonding does not facilitate recovery and resilience but rather undermines those very qualities within us, often with long-lasting impact and often involves seduction and betrayal.

Clinical Patterns: Abusive/conflictual ties like *The War of the Roses, Fatal Attraction,* or *Gone Girl;* systemic setups like Lucy and Charlie Brown; abuse cycles such as those found in domestic violence; misplaced loyalty as in cults, incest, or hostage situations; depression; rage or debilitation resentment; codependency.

Presenting symptoms of trauma bonds:

when you obsess about people who have hurt you and they are long gone (obsess means to be preoccupied, fantasize about, and wonder about even though you do not want to)

when you continue to seek contact with people who you know will cause you further pain

when you go overboard to help people who have been destructive to you

when you continue being a team member when obviously things are becoming destructive

when you continue attempts to get people to like you who are clearly using you

when you trust people again and again who are proven to be unreliable

when you are unable to retreat from unhealthy relationships

when you want to be understood by those who clearly do not care

when you choose to stay in conflict with others when it would cost you nothing to walk away

when you persist in trying to convince people there is a problem and they won't listen

when you are loyal to people who have betrayed you

when you are attracted to untrustworthy people

when you keep damaging secrets about exploitation or abuse

when you continue contact with an abuser who acknowledges no responsibility

CLINICAL STRATEGIES FOR TRAUMA BONDS:

- no contact contracts
- teach strategies for detachment
- support self-help groups that can provide perspective
- teach concepts of "bonds" and systemic repetition
- explore payoffs of bonds
- disrupt beliefs around "uniqueness"
- support grief through ritualization around change
- boundary work

What do the following people have in common?

Joan was petrified. Her best friend was getting married in a Catholic church. She dreaded anything that would remind her of the priest she had been involved with for eight years. She could hardly stand not being with him, yet being with him was worse, especially when she found out she was one of many. To be in a church again would be agony. Perhaps he could change. Perhaps he would be there.

Fred could not believe it. Here he was doing it again. He was helping his ex-wife—a woman who lied to him for years about her affairs, who attacked him viciously both in and out of the courtroom, who lied to the children, his own family, and friends, and who in typical fashion ignored her own attorney's advice and destroyed the company he built. Yet there was a snowblower he saw on sale, and there was snow on the ground. She had no way of dealing with that in her new house, and it felt good to help her this way. Maybe she would notice.

Because of her abuse history, Maxine began therapy. Her therapist, Fran, found out that Maxine was an excellent bookkeeper. Since Fran needed a bookkeeper, Maxine went to work for Fran and also continued in therapy. Maxine discovered that Fran was committing significant Medicare fraud. Fran expected Maxine to cover up the problems because the regulations were so "irrational." Two years after her therapist's indictment and sentencing, Maxine was still troubled about testifying against Fran.

To belong to Reverend Jim Jones's group was to feel at the same time both deeply cared for and deeply afraid. For all the good that was done, little dissent was tolerated. Even moving out of the country did not help. When Congressman Leo Ryan came to investigate, some decided to leave. All of them were shot trying to escape. The rest committed suicide rather than go against the community. Over 950 people died—out of loyalty.

Jan had a secret. Her dad had been sexual with her since she was nine. She knew it was not right, but she also felt very special. Out of all her sisters, she was picked out. And some nights it felt good. And her mom was such a waste anyway, who could blame him. All the talk about child abuse in health class was disturbing. These people did not understand what it was really like.

These people are all struggling with traumatic bonds. Those standing outside see the obvious. All these relationships are about some insane loyalty or attachment. They share exploitation, fear, and danger. They also have elements of kindness, nobility, and righteousness. These are all people who stay involved or wish to stay involved with people who betray them. Emotional pain, severe consequences, and even the prospect of death do not stop their caring or commitment. Clinicians call this traumatic bonding. This means that the victims have a certain dysfunctional attachment that occurs in the presence of danger, shame, or exploitation. There often is seduction, deception, or betrayal. There is always some form of danger or risk.

SOME RELATIONSHIPS ARE TRAUMATIC

I have been increasingly interested in the publishing and box office success of both the *Twilight* series and the *Fifty Shades of Grey* series. I first started to read the *Twilight* series because my granddaughter was also reading the books. The dynamic between the two main characters struck me—a relationship between a young, innocent female and an older, dangerous man. It is all written within a love story, and the messages within the relationship itself can be lost, yet it is similar to so many others that manifest in a trauma bond. Out of this story, another was built in *Fifty Shades of Grey*. Another similar relationship built on a similar storyline—intensity, trauma, fear, and bonding.

The *Twilight* franchise totals over $6 billion when you include book sales, film sales, DVD sales, and DVD rentals. *Fifty Shades of Grey* has sold nearly 100 million copies worldwide, and had a trilogy of high-grossing movies released starting in February 2015. As documented, the stories parallel one another with several similarities between the characters. These stories highlight the intensity of the bonding that occurs in these types of relationships.

Take, for example, the conflictual ties in movies like *The War of the Roses* or *Fatal Attraction*. What Lucy does to Charlie Brown around holding the football every year is a betrayal we have grown to expect. Abuse cycles such as those found in domestic violence are built around trauma bonds. So are the misplaced loyalties found in exploitive cults, incest families, or hostage and kidnapping situations. Those living with a loved one suffering from addiction in its many forms, or who feel trapped in a domestic violence situation or a toxic work environment, may find it difficult to leave despite what their partner or others do, and may have suffered enough to have a traumatic bond.

Trauma and reactions to trauma are the foundation for these dysfunctional relational patterns.

Take Cheryl as an example. Cheryl grew up with a mother who was a compulsive gambler and who supported her addiction by selling sex. The kindest adult in Cheryl's life was a stepfather who eventually left the craziness of living with her mom. But Cheryl always looked for this kindness. What she was exposed to was a series of abusive men. As an adult she had four marriages, each more abusive than the last. She would find men who were kind and brutal. Between marriages she would deprive herself of food, become thin, and would sexually binge. When she was married she would compulsively overeat, add seventy pounds, and become sexually aversive. In every marriage she was beaten. In this last marriage she was sexually tortured. A neighbor had to call the police and storm the door to get her away from her husband. An astute police chaplain got her into treatment. Cheryl was willing to go to treatment because even she could see a clear pattern.

Here was a professional woman with a master's degree. She was the mother of four children—one with each husband. Even in treatment she looked with horror at what her last husband did one minute but in the next minute would come up with some reason to call him. She would do this even though she could clearly see that any contact with him was dangerous to her. This relationship had become addictive.

A song by the artist Pink, "Just Like a Pill," summarizes the nature of compulsive attachment. It talks about being fearful and running fast—to nowhere—and thinking that another person will make her well, like a pill, but that person just keeps making her ill. This toxic attachment is often romanticized in our culture through music and other forms of media, yet it can bring about devastating consequences and is absent of true intimacy. Intensity not intimacy.

What Is Compulsive Attachment?

The concept of compulsive attachment combines the latest research in trauma, attachment, addiction, betrayal, and neuroscience. It is a comprehensive model for treating not only partners of addicts but also those struggling with addiction and for understanding the complexities of unhealthy relationship dynamics and the patterns that are often involved.

The impact of betrayal is well documented. Earlier we discussed the damage done specifically when an individual is involved in interpersonal relational trauma.

How Is This Different from or the Same As Codependency?

Codependency models focus on how a person derives his or her worth from another person with the other person becoming the sole provider of happiness. Healing involves establishing independent worth and setting healthy appropriate boundaries in relationships. Often those who struggle with codependency are involved in compulsive caretaking and in over-giving in relationships in a toxic way. There can be obsession related to the other person and their behavior. The compulsive attachment model utilizes these core concepts from the codependent model and expands to include the many different ways individuals can end up in toxic relationships. The model focuses on the particular aspects of relational betrayal and its impact and on helping break cycles of toxic relationship involvement. There are overlaps between the two, but not all those who fit the model for compulsive attachment also fit the model of codependency. The compulsive attachment model focuses on the ways in which individuals form trauma bonds with others. Compulsive attachment is a lens through which these bonds can be assessed and treated while understanding the unique impact of relational trauma and other forms of unresolved trauma. Attachment research has long revealed the impact of relationships early in life and the foundation, secure or insecure attachment, and the bonds we form later in life. Compulsive attachment, much like insecure attachment patterns, is a form of unhealthy relationship bonding.

How Does the Trauma Model Fit?

The compulsive attachment model incorporates the trauma model in helping individuals understand the traumatic nature of betrayal, loss, secrets, and addiction. Based on the latest resources taken from trauma research and literature, the model provides steps for healing. The model also builds on the foundation from family systems and attachment in order to help understand personal histories and the complexities of human relationships. Not only is there current trauma needing to be faced, there is also often unresolved trauma beyond the current impact from addiction.

Compulsive attachment pairs high intensity with low commitment. It can feel like a very strong bond, yet at its core it is highly volatile, dangerous, and low in intimacy and attachment. In research on domestic abuse, Ferraro and Johnson (2011) found that the lack of options coupled with emotional attachment and loyalty led many women to ignore or rationalize the abuse they were suffering. They found that women in these relationships experience a strong bond but not secure attachment with their partner.

We continue to learn about the long-term impact as well as the underlying issues common to compulsive attachment. In the next section you have the opportunity to assess the impact of trauma on your life by taking the Post-Traumatic Stress Index. You can also access the Betrayal Bond Index online at *www.drpatrickcarnes.com*.

TRAUMA BONDS AND THEIR ALLIES: A SELF-ASSESSMENT

It is important to take stock of what you have learned so far. One way to do that is to see what impact trauma has had on your life. What follows is a series of questions to help you clarify your thinking about your own behavior. There are 144 questions, and it will take approximately forty to sixty minutes to complete them and the accompanying worksheets. Many have found this inventory to be extremely helpful in understanding their behavior. I have placed the inventory here in this chapter because having the results in mind at this early point will help you think about the chapters that follow. Plus, later on in the book we will use the results of this inventory in preparing a recovery plan. I strongly encourage you to take the time to complete the inventory.

POST-TRAUMATIC STRESS INDEX

The following statements typify reactions trauma victims often have to child abuse. Please check those you believe apply to you. Although the statements are written in the present tense, if the statements have *ever* applied to your life, then place a check next to that item. Statements are considered false only if they have *never* been a part of your life. If in doubt, let your first reaction be your guide. Given these guidelines, place a check mark next to the statements you feel apply.

○   1. I have recurring memories of painful experiences.

○   2. I am unable to stop a harmful childhood pattern.

○   3. I sometimes obsess about people who have hurt me and are now gone.

○   4. I feel bad at times about myself because of shameful experiences I believe were my fault.

○   5. I am a risk-taker.

○   6. At times, I have difficulty staying awake.

○   7. I sometimes feel separate from my body as a reaction to a flashback or memory.

○   8. I deny myself basic needs at times, like groceries, shoes, books, medical care, rent, and heat.

○   9. I have distressing dreams about experiences.

○ 10. I repeat painful experiences over and over.

○ 11. I try to be understood by those who are incapable or don't care for me.

○ 12. I have suicidal thoughts.

○ 13. I engage in high-risk behaviors.

○ 14. I eat excessively to avoid problems.

○ 15. I avoid thoughts or feelings associated with my trauma experiences.

○ 16. I skip vacations because of lack of time or money.

○ 17. I have periods of sleeplessness.

○ 18. I try to re-create an early trauma experience.

○ 19. I keep secrets for people who have hurt me.

○ 20. I have attempted suicide.

○ 21. I am sexual when frightened.

○ 22. I drink to excess when life is too hard.

○ 23. I avoid stories, parts of movies, or reminders of early painful experiences.

○ 24. I avoid sexual pleasure.

○ 25. I sometimes feel like an old painful experience is happening now.

○ 26. There is something destructive I do over and over from my early life.

○ 27. I stayed in conflict with someone when I could have walked away.

○ 28. I have suicidal thoughts.

○ 29. I often feel sexual when I am lonely.

○ 30. I use depressant drugs as a way to cope.

○ 31. I am unable to recall important details of painful experiences.

○ 32. I avoid doing "normal" activities because of fears I have.

○ 33. I have sudden, vivid, or distracting memories of painful experiences.

○ 34. I attempt to stop activities I know are not helpful.

○ 35. I go overboard to help people who have been destructive.

○ 36. I often feel lonely and estranged from others because of painful experiences I have had.

○ 37. I feel intensely sexual when violence occurs.

○ 38. My procrastinating interferes with my life activities.

○ 39. I sometimes withdraw or have no interest in important activities because of childhood experiences.

○ 40. I will hoard money and not spend money on legitimate needs.

○ 41. I am upset when there are reminders of abusive experiences like anniversaries, places, or symbols.

○ 42. I compulsively do things to others that were done to me as a young person.

○ 43. I sometimes help those who continue to harm me.

○ 44. I feel unable to experience certain emotions (love, happiness, sadness, etc.).

○ 45. I feel sexual when degraded or used.

○ 46. Sleep is a way for me to avoid life's problems.

○ 47. I have difficulty concentrating.

○ 48. I have attempted diets repeatedly.

○ 49. I have difficulty sleeping.

○ 50. My relationships are the same story over and over.

○ 51. I feel loyal to people even though they have betrayed me.

○ 52. I have a dim outlook on my future.

○ 53. I feel sexual when someone is nice to me.

○ 54. At times I am preoccupied with food and eating.

○ 55. I experience confusion often.

○ 56. I refuse to buy things even when I need them and have the money.

○ 57. I have difficulty feeling sexual.

○ 58. I know that something destructive I do repeats a childhood event.

○ 59. I remain a team member when obviously things are becoming destructive.

○ 60. I feel as if I must avoid depending on people.

○ 61. I sometimes feel bad because I enjoyed experiences that were exploitive of me.

○ 62. I abuse alcohol often.

○ 63. I tend to be accident-prone.

○ 64. I spend much time performing underachieving jobs.

○ 65. Sometimes I have outbursts of anger or irritability.

○ 66. I do things to others that were done to me in my family.

○ 67. I make repeated efforts to convince people who were destructive to me and are not willing to listen.

○ 68. I engage in self-destructive behaviors.

○ 69. I get high on activities that are dangerous to me.

○ 70. I use TV, reading, and hobbies as ways to numb out.

○ 71. I go into a fantasy world when things are tough.

○ 72. I am underemployed.

○ 73. I am extremely cautious of my surroundings.

○ 74. I have thoughts and behaviors repeatedly that do not feel good to me.

○ 75. I attempt to be liked by people who clearly are exploiting me.

○ 76. I engage in self-mutilating behaviors (cutting self, burning, bruising, etc.).

○ 77. I use drugs such as cocaine or amphetamines to speed things up.

○ 78. I put off certain tasks.

○ 79. I use romance as a way to avoid problems.

○ 80. I feel very guilty about any sexual activity.

○ 81. I often feel that people are out to take advantage of me.

○ 82. I revert to doing things I did as a child.

○ 83. I am attracted to untrustworthy people.

○ 84. I endure physical or emotional pain most people would not accept.

○ 85. I like living on the edge of danger or excitement.

○ 86. When things are difficult, I will sometimes binge.

○ 87. I have a tendency to be preoccupied with something other than what I need to be.

○ 88. I have a low interest in sexual activity.

○ 89. I am distrustful of others.

○ 90. Some of my recurring behavior comes from early life experiences.

○ 91. I trust people who have proved to be unreliable.

○ 92. I try to be perfect.

○ 93. I am orgasmic when hurt or beaten.

○ 94. I use drugs to escape.

○ 95. I use marijuana or psychedelics to hallucinate.

○ 96. I sometimes spoil success opportunities.

○ 97. I am startled more easily than others.

○ 98. I am preoccupied with children of a certain age.

○ 99. I seek people who I know will cause me pain.

○ 100. I avoid mistakes at any cost.

○ 101. I love to gamble on outcomes.

○ 102. I work too hard so I won't have to feel.

○ 103. I will often lose myself in fantasies rather than deal with real life.

○ 104. I go without necessities for some periods.

○ 105. I get physical reactions to reminders of abuse experiences (breaking out in cold sweat, trouble breathing, etc.).

○ 106. I engage in abusive relationships repeatedly.

○ 107. I have difficulty distancing myself from unhealthy relationships.

○ 108. I sometimes want to hurt myself physically.

○ 109. I need lots of stimulation so I will not be bored.

○ 110. I get lost in my work.

○ 111. I live a double life.

○ 112. I vomit food or use diuretics to avoid weight gain.

○ 113. I feel anxious about being sexual.

○ 114. There is a certain age of children or adolescents that is sexually attractive to me.

○ 115. I continue to have contact with a person who has abused me.

○ 116. I often feel unworthy, unlovable, immoral, or sinful because of experiences I have had.

○ 117. I like sex when it is dangerous.

○ 118. I try to slow down my mind.

○ 119. I have "compartments" that others do not know about.

○ 120. I experience periods when I'm not interested in eating.

○ 121. I am scared about sex.

○ 122. There are activities that I have trouble stopping even though they are useless or destructive.

○ 123. I am in emotional fights (divorces, lawsuits) that seem endless.

○ 124. I often feel I should be punished for past behavior.

○ 125. I do sexual things that are risky.

○ 126. When I am anxious, I will do things to stop my feelings.

○ 127. I have a fantasy life that I retreat to when things are hard.

○ 128. I have difficulty with play.

○ 129. I wake up with upsetting dreams.

○ 130. My relationships seem to have the same dysfunctional pattern.

○ 131. There are certain people whom I always allow to take advantage of me.

○ 132. I have a sense that others are always better off than me.

○ 133. I use cocaine or amphetamines to heighten high-risk activities.

○ 134. I don't tolerate uncomfortable feelings.

○ 135. I am a daydreamer.

○ 136. At times, I see comfort, luxuries, and play activities as frivolous.

○ 137. I hate it when someone approaches me sexually.

○ 138. Sometimes I find children more attractive than grown-ups.

○ 139. There are some people in my life who are hard to get over, though they hurt or used me badly.

○ 140. I feel bad when something good happens.

○ 141. I get excited/aroused when faced with dangerous situations.

○ 142. I use anything to distract myself from my problems.

○ 143. Sometimes I live in an "unreal" world.

○ 144. There are long periods with no sexual activity for me.

TRAUMATIC STRESS INDEX ANSWER SHEET

Place an *X* next to all statements that are true about you. Count all the *X*s in each column and place the total in the space at the bottom of each column.

1. ___	2. ___	3. ___	4. ___	5. ___	6. ___	7. ___	8. ___
9. ___	10. ___	11. ___	12. ___	13. ___	14. ___	15. ___	16. ___
17. ___	18. ___	19. ___	20. ___	21. ___	22. ___	23. ___	24. ___
25. ___	26. ___	27. ___	28. ___	29. ___	30. ___	31. ___	32. ___
33. ___	34. ___	35. ___	36. ___	37. ___	38. ___	39. ___	40. ___
41. ___	42. ___	43. ___	44. ___	45. ___	46. ___	47. ___	48. ___
49. ___	50. ___	51. ___	52. ___	53. ___	54. ___	55. ___	56. ___
57. ___	58. ___	59. ___	60. ___	61. ___	62. ___	63. ___	64. ___
65. ___	66. ___	67. ___	68. ___	69. ___	70. ___	71. ___	72. ___
73. ___	74. ___	75. ___	76. ___	77. ___	78. ___	79. ___	80. ___
81. ___	82. ___	83. ___	84. ___	85. ___	86. ___	87. ___	88. ___
89. ___	90. ___	91. ___	92. ___	93. ___	94. ___	95. ___	96. ___
97. ___	98. ___	99. ___	100. ___	101. ___	102. ___	103. ___	104. ___
105. ___	106. ___	107. ___	108. ___	109. ___	110. ___	111. ___	112. ___
113. ___	114. ___	115. ___	116. ___	117. ___	118. ___	119. ___	120. ___
121. ___	122. ___	123. ___	124. ___	125. ___	126. ___	127. ___	128. ___
129. ___	130. ___	131. ___	132. ___	133. ___	134. ___	135. ___	136. ___
137. ___	138. ___	139. ___	140. ___	141. ___	142. ___	143. ___	144. ___
TRT ___	TR ___	TBD ___	TS ___	TP ___	TB ___	TSG ___	TA ___

Traumatic Stress Index Worksheet

Score	Characteristics	Therapy Strategies
TRT	**TRAUMA REACTIONS:** Experiencing current reactions to trauma events in the past	Study ways you are still reacting. Write letters to your perpetrators telling them of the long-term impact you are experiencing. Also write amends letters to those you know you have harmed. Decide with therapist what is appropriate to send.
TR	**TRAUMA REPETITION:** Repeating behaviors or situations that parallel early trauma experiences	Understand how history repeats itself in your life experiences. Develop habits that help to center yourself (e.g., breathing, journaling), so that you are doing what you intend, not the cycles of old. Work on boundaries. Boundary failure is key to repetition compulsion.
TBD	**TRAUMA BONDS:** Being connected (loyal, helpful, supportive) to people who are dangerous, shaming, or exploitive	Learn to recognize trauma bonds by identifying those in your life. Look for patterns. Use detachment strategies for difficult people. Use a "first step" if necessary.
TS	**TRAUMA SHAME:** Feeling unworthy and having self-hate because of trauma experience	Understand the shame dynamics of your family. Why was it important to you that you feel shameful? Start reprogramming yourself with affirmations.
TP	**TRAUMA PLEASURE:** Finding pleasure in the presence of extreme danger, violence, risk, or shame	Do a history of how excitement and shame are hooked up to your trauma past. Note the costs and dangers to you over time. Do a "first step" and relapse-prevention plan about how powerful this is in your life.
TB	**TRAUMA BLOCKING:** A pattern exists to numb, block out, or overwhelm feelings that stem from trauma in your life	Work to identify experiences that caused pain or diminished you. Re-experience feelings and make sense of them with help. This will reduce the power they have had. Do a "first step" if appropriate.
TSG	**TRAUMA SPLITTING:** Ignoring traumatic realities by dissociating or splitting off experiences or parts of self	Learn that dissociating is a normal response to trauma. Identify ways you split reality and the triggers that cause that to happen. Cultivate a caring adult who stays present, so you can stay whole. Notice any powerlessness you feel.

Score	Characteristics	Therapy Strategies
TA	**TRAUMA ABSTINENCE:** Depriving yourself of things you need or deserve because of traumatic acts	Understand how deprivation is a way to continue serving your perpetrators. Write a letter to the victim that was you about learning to tolerate pain and deprivation. Work on strategies to self-nurture, including inner-child visualizations.

Match your scores with the appropriate capitalized code. Behind each score is an explanation of what the score measures. Also included are some recommendations for actions that would be appropriate for you to take. If your score is low (0–3), this is not an area of concern for you. If your score is moderate (3–6), you should discuss with friends or a therapist what strategies would now help you. If your score is higher than six, this should be an area of intense focus for you. You may wish to discuss with a therapist a series of target activities to help you with these trauma patterns. Remember, this is only a paper-and-pencil instrument to help you think about the role of trauma in your life. Only you and your therapist can see if the results fit your experience.

For most people, completing the Traumatic Stress Index provides much to think about. First of all, you may have noticed patterns that were clear to you before. This will help lay the groundwork for change. Sometimes people are anxious because they scored high on some of the scales. Take comfort in knowing that you have identified where some of the issues are. Pinpointing the problem means you can take the action your worksheet suggests.

Perhaps you disagree with the results. Or maybe nothing significant or new emerged. That sometimes happens. Remember, this was only a paper-and-pencil exercise to help give you clarity. It may not have been a good match for your experiences. I encourage you to keep reading, however. What is important is to understand what trauma can do to you. In the next chapter we take the next step by examining what betrayal does to relationships.

What Does Betrayal Do to Relationships?

"ANYONE WHO HASN'T EXPERIENCED
THE ECSTASY OF BETRAYAL KNOWS NOTHING
ABOUT ECSTASY AT ALL."

—Jean Genet, *Prisoner of Love*

I t happens every fall. Lucy van Pelt offers to hold the football for Charlie Brown. Every time this happens, Charlie Brown recognizes that this is a ploy to use him. And every time, Lucy comes up with a plausible reason why Charlie Brown should trust her. Charlie Brown sets aside his distrust and takes a risk again. Lucy then does what she always does—jerks the football out of the way at the last second. Charlie Brown always ends up flat on his back. Lucy then makes it clear why he should not have trusted her. We smile because the scenario is so familiar and perverse it is comical. It also contains the basic elements of deception and seduction that are the essence of betrayal.

In real life the scenario ceases to be funny. Here are some examples:

A nationally known physician is approached by a hospital administrator about setting up a program in his specialty. Meetings are held with staff to prepare a proposal for the board of directors. The physician is promised the medical director's position for the program. The proposal is turned down by the board, but the administrator encourages another round of breakfast meetings and work sessions. Again the proposal is turned down, followed by more meetings. The physician starts to distrust the process and drops out of the planning. Six months later the program opens. A staff member confides to the physician that the administrator never intended to use the physician but needed his expertise to train staff and put the program together. The board had never seen the proposal. The administrator simply used the physician with no intention of ever hiring him. When challenged, the administrator says the physician lost hope too early. The staff says this is the administrator's common method for getting free consultation.

A rabbi sets up a special religious education course for adolescent girls. Parents are thrilled with the prospect. Part of the new curriculum involves sex education, however, and some parents withdraw their children because of rumors of the rabbi being "too close" to some of the girls. Other parents steadfastly keep their daughters enrolled. They write the rumors off to temple politics and the sexual rigidity of some of the parents. Nobody in the congregation is prepared for the revelations that the beloved rabbi is, in fact, having sex with a number of the girls in a sex ring.

Carol is a woman in her early forties. She is an investment broker married to a wealthy CEO with his own company. Together they have raised three daughters, all in their early twenties. Carol starts a passionate affair with a man whose source of money is difficult to determine. But the passion is in sharp contrast to the "lifeless" marriage she sees herself in. Her sexual experiences with her new partner are unlike anything she's experienced with her spouse. She leaves her husband amidst much anguish from her daughters and a lot of anger from him. Once living with her new partner, the nightmare begins—beatings and torture to the extent of being hospitalized twice. He is so in control of her life she cannot go to the bathroom by herself. One day while she was sitting in my office, and after she had been pulled out of her nightmare, I ask her why she stayed with this man. Her answer comes from some distant place inside: "The sex was good."

In each example there is a promise. In the physician's case, it was the professional position and recognition he always wanted. In the rabbi's case, it was the promise of a solid religious education that had solid parental support. For Carol, it was a form of sexual redemption that would pull her out of a sterile, emotionless marriage. Common to all was a promise. Those who betray read their victims well. They appeal to the emptiness, the unfinished, and the wounds of others. The promise is designed to fix, to heal, to resolve, or to make up for what has happened.

The promise is so appealing that intuitions are set aside. Even Charlie Brown knows better. In the cartoon on the following page, Charlie Brown sets his suspicions aside because Lucy sounds sincere. He wants to believe so badly that Lucy will hold the football that he persuades himself to take yet another run at it. The promise and his desire to believe the promise are so great that he ignores the obvious and accepts the improbable. And once again, he is sucked back into the inevitable result.

There are five main ways promises are used to betray. They are: betrayal by seduction, betrayal by terror, betrayal by exploitation of power, betrayal by intimacy, and betrayal by spirit. One of these is bad enough, but oftentimes all five are present. To understand traumatic bonding, the reader must understand these separate types of abuse.

The more we develop the Betrayal Bond Index and further understand the vulnerabilities that underlie compulsive attachment, the more we will develop tools and education aimed at helping individuals and families to strengthen their resilience to these specific forms of betrayal. We start with betrayal by seduction.

BETRAYAL BY SEDUCTION

Technology is offering new ways to seduce, and they are extremely difficult to track and monitor. Take for example the case of Shad Knutson, middle school teacher in Omaha, Nebraska, who was caught using technology to lure students into sexual encounters. In one year, Knutson, exchanged 26,986 text messages and phone calls (on average seventy per day) with one of his fourteen-year-old students and as many others with several other thirteen- to fifteen-year-old female students at the middle school where he worked. He would promise good grades if the girls would flash him and threaten discipline if they did not.

PEANUTS reprinted by permission of United Feature Syndicate, Inc.

New York City school officials, for example, reported that the number of complaints involving inappropriate relationships between teachers and students on Facebook skyrocketed from eight between September 2008 and October 2009 to eighty-five between October 2010 and September 2011, according to *The New York Times.*

In the case of the middle school teacher, when several girls made official complaints to the school, the school did not take their report seriously. In fact, keeping up with technology and how it is used to intimidate, abuse, and harass is often difficult for law enforcement, schools, and parents. Seventy-five percent of online abuse is targeted at women. A University of Maryland study revealed that feminine usernames in online forums averaged 100 sexually explicit or threatening messages a day compared to the 3.7 averaged by masculine ones.

Technology has offered ways to be connected we did not dream possible just a few short years ago. We have access to information and opportunities to learn at our fingertips. There is a wealth of positive benefit offered through technology, but with the gifts also comes the potential for harm. We are lured into believing a false sense of safety in regard to what we do online, and this can exacerbate the problems related to unhealthy relationships and the development of compulsive attachments.

Seduction is high warmth with low intention. For example, if a person touches your arm during a conversation, it may simply be a gesture of human kindness. It also could be considered warm and connecting. However, the same touch could also be a sexual overture. If the intention is not clear, you may not know what the touch means. Lack of intention can cover risk. If the person who touched you was indeed testing for sexual interest, when challenged as to what he or she wanted, the person could say, "Oh, I was just being friendly." So communicating and understanding personal intent are incredibly important skills that must be learned.

Figure 3.1 graphically creates contrasts between high and low warmth and between high and low intention. What emerge from these contrasts are four possible combinations.

First there is high warmth and high intention. This can be a very close and rewarding relationship because you know where you stand with a person who wants to be connected with you. Characteristics of this combination are:

relationships are committed and involved

agreements are clear and rewarding

feelings are excited and enthusiastic

trust is high

rewards are immediate or concrete

risk is mutually shared

Figure 3.1. Warmth and Intention

| | | WARMTH | |
		HIGH	LOW
I N T E N T I O N	**H I G H**	relationships are committed and involved	relationships are goal-oriented rather than people-oriented
		feelings are excited and enthusiastic	agreements are clear but disconnected or unemotional
		agreements are clear and rewarding	feelings are disconnected or unemotional
		trust is high	trustworthy
		rewards are immediate or concrete	rewards are specified and reliable
		risk is mutually shared	risk is minimal
	L O W	relationships are manipulative and exploitive	relationships are inscrutable and disengaged
		agreements are ill-defined, unclear, or tentative	agreements are short-term and difficult to negotiate
		feelings are anxious and intense	feelings are absent
		trust depends often on exaggerated or unreal promises	high distrust
		rewards are in the future and often conditional	rewards are minimal
		risk is often one-sided	no risk since little is asked

The second is low warmth and high intention. These are very task-centered relationships in which the primary objective is to accomplish a transaction or do a job. It is simple and businesslike. We all have such relationships because they are very functional. Characteristics of this combination are:

relationships are goal-oriented rather than people-oriented

agreements are clear but emotionally detached

feelings are disconnected or unemotional

there is trustworthiness

rewards are specified and reliable

risk is minimal

The third is high warmth with low intention. These relationships are very deceptive and seductive and are commonly found in traumatic bonding. If the person were clear about his or her intention, the other might not respond or become involved. Characteristics of this combination are:

relationships are manipulative and exploitive

agreements are ill-defined, unclear, or tentative

feelings are anxious and intense

trust depends often on exaggerated or unreal promises

rewards are in the future and often conditional

risk is often one-sided

The fourth combination is low intention and low warmth. These are difficult relationships because there seems to be no obvious purpose for them. It is not about human contact or any specific desire. Characteristics of this combination are:

relationships are inscrutable and disengaged

agreements are short term and difficult to negotiate

feelings are absent

there is high distrust

rewards are minimal

there is no risk since little is asked

The high warmth/low intention combination is often found in betrayal scenarios. The emotional content of the relationship obscures what the partner's true intent is. Warmth can be expressed in many ways:

expression of admiration and liking

expression of caring and concern

indication of long-term relationship

affectionate gestures and touching

positive, upbeat conversation about the relationship

project or challenge at hand

excitement and desire to get to know you better

complimenting and fawning behavior

excessive familiarity

personal revelations and disclosures that may feel inappropriate to the context

But if the real agenda is not expressed, it may be seduction. When the warmth is part of an effort to get you to do something and it is obvious, you distrust it. When the politician seeking your vote or the car salesman pushing a car uses too much warmth, we use words such as "sleaze" or "smooth" because we do not like being finessed or manipulated.

People who come from dysfunctional families in which there was abuse or trauma are particularly vulnerable to seduction. First, because of the intrusion that is part of living in exploitive systems, the boundaries that prevent most people from being deceived are not there. These people have not been taken care of or protected, so they may not know how to protect or care for themselves. Most of us learn not to be easily conned into things that might hurt us. Trauma survivors can be extremely naïve even while being vigilant. Their discernment and common sense have been impaired by living with secrets, denial, deception, and exploitation.

Further, they are vulnerable because of the nature of traumatic shame. The nature of shame creates disconnection with the self and often results in doubting their own perceptions. When a person feels flawed and unlovable, flattery, attention, and kindness can further disarm any concerns. When flattered or fawned over, the person will ignore that voice within that says, "Don't do this." Anybody can be seduced. But if you are shameful, needy, and afraid, you are much more easily led down the trail of exploitation.

Some survivors continually are attracted to people who were like their abusers, people who can re-create the same situations over and over again. These people can seduce them repeatedly because the attraction is so powerful. The phrase sometimes used in treatment is that "the picker is broken." Translation? A person will invariably seek out people who will do them harm or betray them. Healthy people with integrity and appropriate boundaries are boring. There is no adrenaline rush, no dopamine high (the key chemical in "falling in love"), nor is there the mobilization of the endocrine system to cope with crisis.[1] Jack McGinnes, one of the former chaplains at The Meadows, wrote a country-and-western song that captures this process well. When he sings it, there is laughter and shouts of self-recognition. One of the frequent lines is "If you won't leave me I will find someone who will." And the song's refrain is "I am just addicted to emotional pain."

Along with the seduction comes a sustaining fantasy or supportive script. The victim of seduction usually wants so badly for the story to be true that she (or he) will overlook the obvious and accept the improbable. The sustaining fantasy can come in a number of forms:

> **The belief in the story:** There usually is a tale that explains why we are in the situation we are in, why we are taking specific actions, or where we are headed.
>
> **The belief in the person:** The abuser, who may be doing wonderful things for others, is viewed as someone with high credibility whose behavior is beyond question.
>
> **The belief in the dream:** Almost always there is the promise of realizing some cherished goal, be it a personal goal, a state of well-being, or the redressing of some loss or wound.
>
> **The belief in the mission:** Often there is some noble cause or meaningful vision that requires personal sacrifice.

Whatever the script, the victim of betrayal wants to believe it so badly that common sense is abandoned. I know a counselor who made this point in family week very effectively. In a lecture on self-care, she described how she went about buying a new car, a new "vette." The next day she gave a lecture in which she mentioned that a family member of hers used her "Chevette." Of course, everyone had thought she had bought a new Corvette. She challenged the audience as to why they thought she was driving a brand-new red Corvette when she had only said "vette." Family week participants always reply that they wanted her to have a nice, expensive sports car. Then, with a penetrating stare, she tells them that they wanted to believe the story so much that they automatically put her in the Corvette. Then when she asks if anyone has bought a vette lately, there is stunned silence. Everyone knows what she means. Everyone had wanted to believe the addicts in their families so much, they would make leaps to believe their stories, even when they were not true.

To put it another way, Charlie Brown wanted so badly to kick the football, he would misperceive Lucy as sincere when she was not. There will always be the look of sincerity. Seduction always relies on the victim's willingness to trust again. In betrayal bonds, the victim prefers the story over facts, behaviors, and results.

BETRAYAL BY TERROR

If you cannot achieve your goals by seduction, there is always terror. Logic would say that using fear and threat is not a good way to gain cooperation or loyalty. The irony is that in a perverse way it is. Fear immobilizes and deepens attachment. It escalates attraction and arousal. It provides addictive intensity and obsession. It keeps behavior secret. And it is very flexible and can be applied in a variety of situations at varying levels:

the incest daughter who is told that if she says anything, the family will be destroyed and Dad and Mom will go to jail

the corporation that retaliates viciously to any employee who raises issues and therefore keeps a tight lid on sexual harassment problems

the wife who knows in her heart that her husband is right about the fact that he will always be able to find her and kill her

the child of the raging alcoholic who walks on eggshells because he knows that the next out-of-control rage could be deadly

the client who is told by her therapist that unless she complies and continues therapy, the therapist will have to reveal their sexual activities to her extremely jealous, abusive husband

the wife of the physician who has four children and is told she cannot reveal what she knows because her husband would lose his license and there would be no money to support her

Terror works better when coupled with seduction. Even in concentration camps, prisoners who were tortured often experienced a "good cop, bad cop" strategy. False confessions are more likely when there is someone who talks kindly and seems to have some compassion for the prisoner. We have already noted how acts of kindness create traumatic bonding in hostage situations. If the seduction has a powerful story line, the terror can be excused and actually bring people together. The incest daughter might believe the story about Mom's treatment of Dad. Or the client of the therapist might believe him to be the heroic helper of others who was trapped in marriage with a shrew of a wife. Or the hostage might develop sympathy for a rebel with a good cause. If the story is strong enough and well told, the victim of terror can also believe that she or he deserves it, created it, has to endure it, and is part of it.

The classic combination of seduction and terror is used very successfully by modern cults. Studies of organized cults have received national attention because they revealed recruitment processes that are often well-organized, well-funded campaigns built on the twin principles of seduction and terror. They are marketing campaigns that hide behind kindness and opportunity. They offer financial success, happiness, self-fulfillment, and instant family or friends. They come in the form of stress seminars, business opportunities, study groups, and personal growth groups. What lurks behind this curtain of positive activities is an organization that will take over someone's life, exploit the person's resources and energy, and demand an exacting discipline with little tolerance for deviation.

Consider the story of a Texas group whose leader was a woman who promised adolescent girls she could make them into championship horseback riders. She appealed to their love of horses. What they got, however, was day after day of hard physical labor and religious study that was so abusive, police intervened. Or look at the Heaven's Gate cult in Southern California, which ended with thirty-nine suicides. Here you had a charismatic leader, Marshall Applewhite, who at one time in his life was arrested for sexual misconduct but ended his life castrated along with his most devoted followers. (Note the themes of high arousal and traumatic abstinence.) Heaven's Gate was seen by cult specialists as "mainstream" in its outreach campaign. The cult targeted college campuses and appealed to young people who liked computers.[2]

One of the most successful strategies used by cults is the *love bomb*. When a new member joins a group, the person is lavished with praise and attention. Members of the group offer to study with the new member, spend social time, share meals, and spend holidays together. It is an instant community of friends so intensely rewarding, it feels like the "family you always wanted." But when new members raise a question about their loyalty, they quickly feel the withdrawal of support. If emotionally impoverished or from a dysfunctional family, they have a terror of abandonment. They find that the "family they always wanted" exacts a huge price. Sometimes the penance for wrongdoing is harsh (e.g., long hours of work, extra efforts to recruit other members, or sexual favors). This is a convenient way to introduce exploitation and make the member feel responsible.

The love bomb is a great way to enforce group discipline and keep it closed from outsiders who raise disturbing questions (e.g., family members, therapists, media, and police). The love bomb strategy can work in a wide variety of contexts. Victims of domestic abuse describe the initial courtship in love bomb terms. Similar stories are told by incest victims.

If the story is strong enough and there is sufficient terror, the outcome is also guilt and shame. Clear evidence for that can be found in how reluctant victims are to report offenses.

Every two minutes there is a victim of sexual assault in the United States, with 80 percent of the victims being under the age of thirty.

Most of these offenses will never be reported. Most of these crimes are committed by someone who knows the victim. For example, 50 percent of women living in North America will experience sexual assault sometime in their lives. Much of the time, it will be by people that they know. Only 7 percent of those assaulted women will report the offense. Seduction, shame, and self-doubt erode whatever sense of self the person had.[3] The combination of seduction and fear is a potent combination used to distort personal judgment. One of the best platforms for exploiting this relationship chemistry is power.

BETRAYAL BY POWER

It was a story more fitting for the front page of a tabloid than the *Wall Street Journal*. The company was the American division of a huge international pharmaceutical corporation. It was the successful manufacturer of the second-largest-selling drug in the world. *Business Week* broke the scandal. Older women (past forty) were systematically removed and replaced by young, extremely attractive single women. These women were recruited for sex and harassed brutally by the top four executives of the firm. There was also the small problem of the embezzlement of millions of dollars. The result was that the parent company had to make a huge settlement for sexual harassment.

Other victims of sexual harassment do not fare as well. A major airline received complaints of sexual harassment in its Boston office. The woman complaining was a baggage handler. She reported to company officials that after filing the complaint, her life was threatened. The company did not respond. She reported more threats. Finally, the woman was found brutally murdered in the trunk of her car. The company spokesman defended the company, saying there was little they could do.

Sexual harassment is a widespread problem affecting 42 percent of women and 15 percent of men in occupational settings.[4] In past years, movies like *Disclosure, Fatal Attraction,* and *Presumed Innocent* highlighted these issues. In more recent years, we saw the explosion of the #MeToo movement. The Pentagon has already spent in excess of a billion dollars resolving sexual harassment issues in the military.

Below are examples of sexual harassment suits that were paid out in 2013:

The National Guard was ordered to pay a former staffer $231,000 after failing to investigate her complaints of sexual harassment. The worker claimed that her colleague repeatedly harassed her, including slapping her on the buttocks.

A female firefighter was awarded $1.7 million after being fired for complaining about sexual harassment that came at the hands of her supervising lieutenant.

Nearly $200,000 will be paid out to a former Atlanta school district bus driver who claimed her manager exposed himself to her, tried to have sex with her, and then fired her after she refused.

A former public pool lifeguard was awarded a whopping $3.5 million after she claimed her manager propositioned her and ogled her in her bathing suit. She complained to six separate supervisors— none of whom took any action—and then was fired.

Also, in 2012 a physician's assistant at Mercy General Hospital was awarded the largest payout in history for a single plaintiff in a sexual harassment case, $168 million.

One in four women has experienced workplace sexual harassment, an *ABC News/Washington Post* poll found. One in ten men say they've experienced it as well, and a quarter of men say they worry about being falsely accused of sexual harassment. A 2011 study by the American Association of University Women found that 50 percent of middle and high school students were sexually harassed, but girls were more likely than boys to be harassed by a significant margin (56 percent vs. 40 percent). Only 12 percent of girls reported the harassment.

Over the past year we saw the issue of sexual harassment on the forefront as accusations of sexual harassment hit many well-known public figures. As these women came forward, the issue was elevated to public awareness in a new and powerful way with campaigns such as the #MeToo movement. As the stories were unfolding, we were faced with the reality of the ongoing pain related to sexual harassment.

Yet only 1 to 7 percent of sexual harassment victims ever report the crime. There are many reasons for this, but the primary reason is the disequilibrium of power.[5] One of the most famous cases is Anita Hill's complaint about Clarence Thomas when he was being considered for his position on the Supreme Court. One of the many hotly debated questions was why Anita Hill waited so long to report her experience. Some point to the reality that the only person to report the harassment to was the head of the EEOC, Clarence Thomas. Perhaps there is another explanation—traumatic bonding. You can see it in other forms of abuse involving the disequilibrium of power. Take incest, for example. DeYoung and Lowry define trauma bonding as:

> the evolution of emotional dependency between two persons of unequal power—an adult and a child, within a relationship characterized by periodic sexual abuse. The nature of this bond is distinguished by feelings of intense attachment, cognitive distortions, and behavioral strategies of both individuals that paradoxically strengthen and maintain the bond.[6]

Incest survivors may also wait years to report what happened. What incest and sexual harassment have in common is the exploitation by people in power of those most vulnerable to them. If you're not equal in power, then by definition you're vulnerable. And that vulnerability is critical to trauma bonding. The misuse of power, which includes terror and seduction, induces fear, anxiety, and self-doubt—all critical aspects of traumatic reactivity.

Here is how it works. Take the example of the executive director of a social service agency who starts an affair with one of his three department heads. Both are married, so there is lots of fear and secrecy. The department head feels very special but also very precarious. She receives special treatment. In return, she tells her secret partner what the other department heads really say about him. He cannot go to them and acknowledge where or how he heard about their opinions, but he starts treating them differently. The other department heads start to doubt their own perceptions and feel fear. Soon the whole organization feels crazy. The department head involved with her boss no longer can separate her performance from their relationship. Is she well-treated because she is a willing employee or a willing bed partner?

To go one more step, add a further level of authority. The executive director now has an affair with a counselor who works for the department head, who reports to the director. All the above conditions are made worse. The counselor feels even more precarious and protective than a department head would. In pillow talk the counselor tells the director how the staff perceive each of the department heads. And so now the organization is even more anxious. Figure 3.2 depicts four levels of the social service agency, starting with the board on top and counseling clients on the bottom. The more levels of authority crossed, the more problems there are. The worst-case scenario would be if a member of the board of directors was involved with a client being seen by a counselor.

Figure 3.2. Organizational Incest—I

Board Members	XXXXX	
Executive Director	X	
Supervisors	XXX	
	XXX	
	XXX	
	XXX	
	XXX	
Staff	XXX	
	XXX	
	XXX	
	XXX	
	XXX	
Clients	XXX	

Organizational incest is no different from incest in the family, which in reality is no different from sexual misconduct by clergy or health professionals, which is no different from the abuse of physical power in date rape or domestic abuse. They all take advantage of the vulnerable, and they all can result in the dysfunctional attachments we call trauma bonds.[7]

BETRAYAL BY INTIMACY

I was in a large city conducting a workshop. During my stay I was invited to sign books at a bookstore within a large clinic. I was familiar with the clinic's program since the staff had referred a patient to me. I looked forward to meeting the staff and talking about the patient's progress. The book signing went well, and the staff were very engaging, but at the end of a long day I was ready to go back to my hotel. The clinic manager offered to drive me back. We got into the car, and as we were about to leave the parking lot, she burst into tears, pounded her fists on the steering wheel, and said between clenched teeth and tears, "I can't let him do this to you!"

Haltingly and between sobs the story poured out. Her husband was the doctor who owned the clinic. She was his fifth wife. He was charming and very engaging during the first year of their marriage. Then one day, one of the male staff members walked into her husband's office to return a book to his library and found him having sexual intercourse with a woman client. When his wife found out, she was furious and promptly moved out. She then told me that in the six months since this all took place, he had two other young women in their early twenties as lovers. He was in his late fifties.

I interrupted her and asked if anyone had reported him. She said no. I asked why she hadn't. Her story went like this: When she discovered he was sleeping with patients, she immediately asked for a divorce. In dividing up the property, she found he had not paid employment taxes to the IRS for the entire clinic for three years. She knew the IRS to be unforgiving about this type of situation. If you are married to someone who has not paid taxes, you are liable for half. She knew she could not make that amount of money. So she became the clinic manager and started to aggressively pay back the taxes. She concluded that in about four months, all the taxes would be paid, and then she could report him and divorce him. I asked if she knew if he was still having sex with his patients, and she said that it was probably happening.

I stayed over an extra day and met individually with staff members. If they did not report him, I would have to do it. Every person I talked with knew about the problem but was in some incredible bind with this doctor. For example, there was a single-parent mom who was completing her supervised hours for her clinical internship. She was desperate to finish so that she could support her children. She knew that if he was reported, she would have to do the internship all over and go through an additional twelve months of agony. She could not do it to her children. Then there was the counselor who made the initial discovery. He owed the doctor substantial amounts of money. There was also the best friend whom he blackmailed. Everyone had a story. To their credit, they banded together and reported the doctor.

The binds they were in are familiar. In addition to a betrayal by power, you had a betrayal of intimacy. Whatever vulnerability existed, the doctor exploited. His wife and friend were betrayed by their trust. Those who worked for him clinically were betrayed by his power.

To return to our graphic of the hypothetical social service agency, in Figure 3.3 I have added, in addition to levels of power, the intimate partners of those at each level. Thus the executive director could have an affair with the spouse of one of the supervisors who worked for him. Both power and intimacy would be betrayed in that scenario. The doctor in the agency I visited had essentially done both as well.

There is only one thing worse than someone who betrays using seduction, terror, power, and intimacy: someone who betrays by the spirit.

Figure 3.3. Organizational Incest—II

	STAFF	PARTNERS
Board Members	XXXXX	OOOOO
Executive Director	X	O
Supervisors	XXX	OOO
Staff	XXX	OOO
	XXX	OOO
	XXX	OOO
	XXX	OOO
	XXX	OOO
	XXX	OOO
Clients	XXX	OOO
	XXX	OOO
	XXX	OOO
	XXX	OOO
	XXX	OOO
	XXX	OOO

BETRAYAL BY SPIRIT

In Chicago, fifty-four Catholic priests are banned from their pastoral roles because of sexual misconduct with children. Father Porter, a priest in Minnesota, has had over 240 victims come forward and accuse him of sexual abuse. Still another has had 162 counts of sexual misconduct with children filed against him. In that case, the out-of-court settlements thus far exceed $20 million. A religious order has settled a $3.5 million suit and faces imminent bankruptcy because of others yet to be settled. A treatment center that specializes in work with clergy has come under sharp criticism as being little more than a "warehouse" for the bishops that failed to do serious rehabilitation.

In a 2009 article, "The Prevalence of Clergy Sexual Advances Toward Adults in Their Congregations," the researchers found that:

1. Three percent of women reported being the object of clergy sexual misconduct at some time in their adult lives.

2. Ninety-two percent of these advances were made in secret.

3. Sixty-seven percent of offenders were married to someone else at the time of the sexual advance.

4. An average of 7 percent of women in an average congregation of 400 members have experienced clergy sexual misconduct.

5. Eight percent of respondents reported knowing about clergy sexual misconduct in their congregation.

In the midst of all this controversy, a disturbing study of two religious orders for women emerged from Johns Hopkins University. The study documents that over 80 percent of these religious women were sexually abused as children. A new book suggests that only 2 percent of Catholic clergy remain celibate over their careers and that 6 percent are involved with children. Worse, the author documents that some of the cover-ups involve bishops who have also been involved with children.

The pastoral abuse of children has grabbed the public's attention. Yet other stories are emerging, including revelations about compulsive prostitution, exploitation of pastoral counseling clients, and clergy living double lives of public abstinence and private relationships. As the revelations continue, a deep despair grows; something is very wrong—and has been for a long time.

Protestant and Jewish congregations have also suffered devastating stories of sexual transgressions. The most blatant have been the televangelists whose careers and empires have crumbled because of sexual improprieties. One of the most successful went before his faithful and asked for forgiveness, only to be arrested for prostitution several weeks later. He made the news again when it was discovered that after his arrest he went out that same night and procured another prostitute. Another Protestant minister preached nationwide crusades against pornography, only to be arrested for the production and distribution of child pornography. His followers were stunned. Another well-known minister was arrested for bank robbery. Why had he done it? He had $40,000 in credit card charges for using prostitutes. An Episcopalian bishop committed suicide because his sexual misconduct was about to become public.

One temple was driven apart when word spread that a beloved and respected rabbi had been sexual with many women in his congregation. Ironically, down the street in the same suburban community, a Lutheran congregation learned that they had been found liable—as a congregation—for the sexual abuse of a teenager by one of their ministers, thus setting a legal precedent.

One conclusion all these reports share is that what little data we have is but the tip of the metaphorical iceberg. Professionals in general see this in reporting rates. A detailed study of reporting rates suggests that, depending on the category, the actual number of assaults may be from two to twenty times greater than the number of assaults reported by authorities. Studies of offenders also document numbers far in excess of what was expected. An average sex offender commits at least two different types of assaults and will commit many assaults before being caught. For example, child molesters average 281 assaults against 150 victims. Sex offenders, in general, perpetrate over 520 offenses. These figures are for the culture at large. How much more difficult it is to report when our offender is a beloved clergy person.

A few empirical studies of clergy and sexual misconduct do exist. Two general surveys indicate that 10 percent of clergy self-reported sexual contact with congregants.[8, 9] Another indicates 3 percent of Christian therapists have acted on sexual feelings toward clients (Leong 1989).[10] These figures would parallel studies of psychotherapists and psychiatrists, which report results ranging from 5 to 15 percent having had sexual contact with clients.

Even fewer studies exist on the victims of clergy, although it is generally agreed that the impact on survivors of sexual abuse by spiritual leaders is greater than survivors of other forms of power abuse. Since part of coping with trauma is spiritual, sexual abuse by a spiritual leader further complicates the recovery process. Barbara McLaughlin found that as a result of their abuse, victims do not attend church or synagogue, and their ability to trust church officials (and God) is impaired or permanently damaged. She suggests further that the victim's relationship with God may cease to grow developmentally because of the abuse. The victim remains frozen spiritually to the time when the abuse occurred.[11]

In order to make sense of this, we can look at what Viktor Frankl wrote about the Nazi concentration camps. The Nazis had a rule that if you interfered with the suicide of an inmate, you would be shot on the spot. The only way the prisoners could help each other survive was to ask those in despair what gave their life meaning. What Frankl learned in the Holocaust was that those who survived were the ones who could make meaning out of suffering. My experience with survivors of trauma is that every journey or recovery depends on the survivor coming to a point where all that person has gone through means something.

Betrayal by the spirit means that the person who betrays the victim also plays a critical role in the resources the victim has for defining meaning. The victim's spiritual path is blocked. The fundamental question all victims have to answer for themselves is "Why do bad things happen to good people?" It is a far more troubling question when the cause of the problem is supposed to be the resource for the answer. Whether it be a new cult or a traditional religious denomination, people are searching for meaning. That search and the vulnerability it produces may be used as part of the seduction or the promise. Trauma bonding is exponential under these circumstances because it blocks the critical process of trusting anything meaningful and leaves only the option of despair.

At The Meadows, we often see victims of spiritual abuse. As part of their treatment experience they spend some very moving time in the Sonoran Desert, where the program is located. Something about being in an environment so profoundly quiet allows a person finally to hear his or her inner voice, a voice that had been lost. The person is often so moved that tears shut away for decades suddenly flow. And each time it happens, I am reminded of the human capacity to reach beyond suffering, no matter how ill-deserved the pain.

REFLECTING ON BETRAYAL

The starting point for all trauma survivors is a complete acceptance of the betrayal. Without that window on their reality, they will be locked in a circular program—like a computer when it cannot get unstuck. You literally have to reboot the computer to get reality functioning again. Human systems are the same.

This chapter has explored betrayal in all its forms and in stark detail. In the next chapter, I'll focus on our need to understand what makes betrayal bonds so strong.

This chapter ends with a series of activities under the title of "Your History of Seduction." Take the time to read it over in its entirety, and then complete it carefully. At this point, you may want to find a journal, tablet, or folder in which to keep all your work from this book. Some people have actually done these exercises on their computer and placed them in a special file. As the book progresses and you continue to complete more exercises, you will find it extremely helpful to be able to refer to your earlier work.

Take your time. Do not push yourself. Allow the material to guide. If you get stuck or find it difficult, talk to people who know you and support you. Be gentle with yourself. Take breaks, but do not skip the work.

YOUR HISTORY OF SEDUCTION

Reflect on your life and select at least five people (ten if you can) who have exploited you using seduction. Do not restrict yourself to sexual issues, but expand your list to include all forms of exploitation. Write the names of each person. Record after each individual the promise made (e.g., story, fantasy, dream, or omission). After the promise, write the real intent or agenda you now know was true. An example is provided. You can do this in your book or you may wish to use your journal, a computer, or a special tablet. We will be using this information later.

EXAMPLE:

| Gene A. | Pledged that if I met my performance criteria, I would be made partner. When I did, he added that I had to do it for three years. | After three years, I exceeded all my goals, he picked a fight and fired me. He never intended to bring me into the business. |

Individual: **Promise made:**   **True agenda or intent:**

1. _____

2. _____

3. _____

4. _____

5. _____

6. _____

7. _____

8. _____

9. _____

10. _____

ANALYZING YOUR LIST

The following activities will deepen your understanding of the work you have done. Record your answers in a journal, computer file, or dedicated tablet. They will be very important for your later work in this book and for your recovery. The temptation will be to say, "I have the idea" and move on to the next section. Doing this thoroughly—even if painstaking—will substantially lay the foundation for what you now need to do.

1. Place a *T* under the name of each individual who used terror or fear to manipulate you. Place a *P* under the name of each individual who abused his power over you, such as an employer, therapist, teacher, or parent. Place an *I* under the name of each individual who exploited the intimacy of your relationship, such as a friend, spouse, family member, or therapist. Place an *S* under the name of each individual who exploited your values or sources of meaning (spirit) in your life.

2. After you have put the letters under their names, notice if you have any patterns. Are there specific letters that appear over and over again? For example, do you have a lot of *T*s and *P*s? Record in your paperwork what you think this means. Where does this pattern come from?

3. Some individuals on your list may be seducing you in many ways. Perhaps it was even difficult to select which seduction to record. For each individual, make a separate list of all the seductions and what the true intent was for each.

4. Notice if there are any commonalities across the promises made. Is there any common story or promise to which you are susceptible? What is it about that scenario that makes you so vulnerable? What hope or need kept you going?

5. What efforts to stop did you make? What happened to those efforts? In what ways could you have taken care of yourself better?

6. What do the various people on your list have in common? Notice if there are any personality traits, habits, or qualities they share. Does a type emerge? If so, who in your family or early childhood history is similar? Write a description of the "typical" person who can seduce you. What sense do you make of how that came to be?

What Makes Trauma Bonds Stronger?

TODAY, OUR SOCIETY IS CAUGHT
IN THE GRIP OF SUPERFICIAL VALUES—
GLAMOUR, GLITTER, MATERIALISM,
A PATHOLOGICAL EMPHASIS ON YOUTH,
A NEGLECT OF THE ELDERLY AND THE
HANDICAPPED. FAMILIES ARE BEING BROKEN UP
UNDER THE IMPACT OF A FRENZIED DESIRE
FOR SUCCESS. VIOLENCE IS GLORIFIED AND

PARADED IN FRONT OF CHILDREN
EVERY DAY IN THE MEDIA.
WE LIVE IN A TIME OF INSTANT ACCESS
AND STREAMING MEDIA. NOT ONLY DO WE SEE
A CONSTANT STREAM OF CRIME, VIOLENCE,
AND FEAR BUT WE ALSO ARE LIVING IN A TIME
WHERE WE POST EXPLICIT DETAILS OF OUR
OWN LIVES THROUGH ACCESS TO SOCIAL
MEDIA AND TECHNOLOGY.
BASIC HUMAN VALUES, BASIC DECENCY,
KINDNESS, AND COOPERATION ARE LESS AND
LESS EVIDENT. ECONOMIC PRESSURES AND
PSYCHOLOGICAL PRESSURES MOUNT. MORE AND
MORE INDIVIDUALS FEEL UNHAPPINESS—
AND HELPLESSNESS—IN THEIR ACQUISITIVENESS
FOR PLEASURE AND ACCUMULATION IN THIS
SELFISH SOCIETY. THEY TURN TO ARTIFICIAL
STIMULANTS, THEY LOSE TOUCH WITH
THEMSELVES. THEIR PROBLEMS AND THEIR
INSECURITIES MOUNT AND THEY BECOME
DESPONDENT. SUICIDES CAUSE US TO REFLECT
ON THE TERRIBLE TREND.

—Reverend James Jones
Anti-suicidal speech in 1977 delivered from the
Golden Gate Bridge eighteen months before the Jonestown deaths

T he new venture was so exciting. Jan, Phil, and Don were forming a new company based on breakthrough research Phil had done as a biochemist. The idea was to start the company by marketing products based on Phil's work and then build the company by developing other biotechnology products. They would have fun, run their own show, and end up wealthy. Jan and Don were experienced executives at another biomedical firm. Don had been president and CEO, and Jan had been head of product development. Every meeting they had together was filled with laughter and excitement.

They started with Phil signing a licensing agreement that gave the company the right to manufacture and sell the products he developed. That way the company could get started. The partnership agreements were much more complex and not so urgent, since everyone agreed in principle as to what was to happen. What followed was a rush of frenzied activity to get the product to market so that the company could get a cash flow going. Everybody was working so hard that the partnership agreement kept being postponed because of financial pressure.

But some things bothered Phil. It started when he visited Don's former company to discuss a matter unrelated to the new business. The company had been sold as part of an acquisition, which was why Don had left. The remaining employees described their relief at the end of Don's "reign of terror." Anybody who even saw Don reported the "Don sighting." Everyone took turns on the "Don watch" so that nobody would have to run into him. Phil wrote this off to Don having presided over a substantial and unpopular downsizing. In fact, it was a comfort to know Don could make the hard decisions. Still, their comments bothered him.

Another thing that bothered Phil was that shortly after they started production, Jan and Don sat down with him and let him know they were now living together. They were to be married because Jan was pregnant. They wanted to assure Phil that this would not slow down the startup; they just wanted to be up front with him before they signed the partnership papers. Phil was very congratulatory but also very disturbed. Should there ever be a dispute, he would lose.

Other disturbing things started happening. A critical vendor who had worked many years with Phil had done a credit check on Don. The vendor told Phil he would not process orders he had received because Don was on the verge of bankruptcy. Phil gave the vendor assurance that the bills would be paid.

When told of the vendor's response, Don criticized him and then got upset with Phil for selecting the vendor. Other vendors started calling Phil and reporting that Don was losing his temper over really small issues. Jan reassured Phil that it was simply stress and that she would help Don keep cool. Then one vendor became so outraged with Don's tirades that the president of that company gave orders that no one could do business with Phil and his partners. Jan again assured Phil there would be no problem.

Phil finally acknowledged he was in trouble when his bankers called and asked to have lunch. They reported to Phil that Jan and Don had been in to see them about a credit line for the company. In the course of the meetings about the credit line three things became clear. First, they asked to use Phil's assets for the credit line since they had none. Second, they revealed that they would be the principal owners of the company. No plans existed for Phil to be a partner. And finally, they talked disparagingly about Phil. They said his technology was excellent but that they did not want to work with him long-term.

The bankers revealed that by giving Phil this information they were violating Federal regulations about client confidentiality. However, they had known Phil to be a good customer for many years. Phil had also told them how excited he was about the new partnership. The bankers wanted Phil to know that he was about to be swindled out of his hard-won research. They saw his potential partners as dangerous and advised him to sever his relationship with them. Within a day of the lunch, several vendors called to indicate either nonpayment or a serious diversion of funds. His partners were now guilty of fraud. Jan and Don went bankrupt. There were suits, countersuits, and losses to go around.

This story is about much more than a business failure. Some further data creates a much more complex picture. Phil was an incest and sexual abuse victim. The fact that he ignored or discounted warnings that he was being exploited was actually a life pattern and resulted in a lot of hard work and creativity that were all for naught.

Don was a physical abuse victim. He had a significant weight problem because of compulsive overeating, and a compulsive debt problem. But it was his raging that had cost him both marriages and businesses. Jan was a battered wife who could not end the relationship with her violent husband until she started the affair with her boss, Don. Jan was also an alcoholic who dismissed her sponsor and recovery friends when they raised questions about Don. Put these facts together, and it's not hard to understand why the business failed.

There is deception and exploitation in this scenario. Don is sexually involved with a married employee. Don and Jan love-bomb Phil so that he will hand over his technology and overlook their relationship and the absence of partnership papers. The bankers violate legal statutes and deceive Don and Jan in order to help Phil. And there is rescuing. Phil saves the deal by intervening with vendors. Jan intervenes on behalf of Don with Phil over Don's temper tantrums. The bankers work to rescue Phil from being fraudulently deceived. Jan's friends work to rescue Jan from Don. The irony is that Don and Jan had initially presented themselves as rescuers who would save Phil from the big corporations that would take advantage of him. They promised he would be an owner.

Lurking in the background of this scenario is a very large, heavyset man whose rage is legendary. In fact, Phil was to learn that people had a hard time getting over Don. The president of the company that did the leveraged buyout of Don's previous company told Phil years later that he still had unresolved anger relative to the way that Don had handled the merger. Former employees told Phil that it was a long time before they stopped their "Don watches." Years later, vendors would shake their heads about the whole episode. Terror and intimidation were Don's stock in trade. But for him it was simply the coping skill he had learned to deal with the abuse in his family.

You might say, "What a soap opera!" Exactly. Soap operas are intentionally built on betrayal, deception, exploitation, and terror. The intensity created from these ingredients is addictive. That's why there are so many loyal viewers. It is in these soap opera environments that betrayal bonds thrive. It is the same in many of the reality TV shows and other series today. In 2000, television ushered in a new ear as the show *Survivor* introduced the world to reality television. The show is built on deception and betrayal, with the goal to become the final survivor. The intensity and drama pulls us in, and many of the reality shows that have followed are built on the same relational dynamics. They are never simple. Convoluted plots always enliven the script. Or think about other current series such as *House of Cards* or *Game of Thrones*. These plot lines are full of betrayal and intensity, situations where fear and seduction are paired. This is what grabs our attention in our culture. This is also the foundation where trauma bonds are built—the pairing of fear and seduction, betrayal and intensity. These are complex relationships and issues. If it were simple, it would be easy to detach. Phil, Don, and Jan couldn't detach because they were hooked on the drama of it all. Business and personal life dysfunctions overlap.

Betrayal, addiction, and trauma weave a design of continually recycled wounds that create an overarching pattern of compulsive relationships. Whether corporate or familial, the same abuse patterns appear.

While these patterns are not simple, it is possible to discern what makes them so strong. If we break down the patterns into specific component parts, they become clear and then no longer hold any power.

There are eleven ways that betrayal bonds are made stronger. They are when:

1. there are repetitive cycles of abuse
2. the victim and the victimizer believe in their own uniqueness
3. high intensity is mistaken for intimacy
4. there is confusion about love
5. there are increasing amounts of fear
6. children are faced with terror
7. there is a history of abuse
8. exploitation endures over time
9. the community, family, or social structure reacts in the extremes
10. there is a familiar role and script to be fulfilled; and
11. victims and victimizers switch roles of rescuer and abuser

Each of these conditions adds to the emotional bond and deepens addictive attachment.

WHEN THERE ARE REPETITIVE CYCLES OF ABUSE

In domestic abuse there is a predictable cycle. First there is a buildup stage. It combines both intensity and fear. As the tension rises, family members obsess about the outcome. Although it is probably inevitable, there is always the hope that compliant action (the proverbial walking on eggshells) will postpone the perpetrator's rage. For the sake of example, let us say that this stage lasts four weeks. Then the outbreak of violence occurs, and that violence may last only ninety seconds. From my counseling experience, I can tell you that a great deal of damage can be done in ninety seconds.

The violence is immediately followed by what is called the "honeymoon" stage. The perpetrator experiences the relief of tension and then is filled with shame over what he (or she) has done. He apologizes with deep remorse and pledges with all the sincerity he can muster that he will never do it again. Further, he demonstrates his change of heart by starting a new courtship. He showers her with gifts and devotion. He says the things she has always wanted to hear from him. He is tender in the most endearing, lovable ways. He's Lucy van Pelt promising Charlie Brown that this time she will hold the football. Let us say this period also lasts four weeks. This is the time of promise—it is the story, the dream.

In part this is an intimacy disorder, for as soon as she starts to recommit to the relationship, he starts distancing himself. The intensity begins to build again. He feels trapped or jealous or possessive or something else that distances him from her. Imagine that a relationship is a circle. For true intimacy to take place, both must stay in the circle at the same time. In abusive relationships with this type of cyclical nature, neither person can allow him- or herself to stay. She must leave the circle when he is abusive. He can only be abusive when he has left the circle. When the "love bomb" works, she is brought back into the mini-cult of their relationship. The terror and fear begin to intensify.

Notice that throughout this eight-week scenario, there is always something intense and absorbing. In the buildup phase you have the incredible intensity, high risk, and obsession we identified earlier as traumatic arousal. We know that people do become hooked on high risk, especially if it involves sex, romance, or power. The actual violence is not the goal here. It serves to give credibility to the terror and to signal the shift back to the honeymoon stage. Nor is the romance of the honeymoon stage just about reconciliation. It is also the soothing, medicating, and nurturing that are part of betrayal bonding. Both partners are obsessed with whether she is going to accept the promise again. Neither partner has to come to grips with the pain or patterns of their lives. No one can begin to understand the drama of O. J. and Nicole Simpson, or any other couple caught in the domestic abuse cycle, without knowing how that cycle engages its participants.

Traditional patterns of addiction are also present within this cycle. The abuse of drugs, alcohol, sex, and food are commonplace for the participants. Nearly 75 percent of all wives of alcoholics, for example, have been threatened, and 45 percent have been assaulted by their addicted partners. Alcohol and drugs may be used to rationalize violent behavior. Family members and perpetrators will blame their behavior on drug and alcohol abuse.[1] Not true. It is simply one layer of compulsion on top of another, layers that defined and managed betrayal cycles going back for decades, even generations.

Sexual addiction is also part of the drama. Compulsive sexual violence can emerge in many forms:

pressure to use alcohol and drugs before sex

insistence on the use of sexual performance enhancers

derogatory comments during sex

forced involvement in unsafe sex or group sex

forced risk for unwanted pregnancy

requirement to undergo cosmetic surgery

humiliating, degrading practices

some types of dress and role-play

public sex (exhibitionism, voyeurism, swapping)

use of bondage

rape or sexual assault

Similarly, compulsive food use can be something the abuser cannot control, and obesity can be a way to deflect unwanted attention. What follows is a summary of domestic abuse characteristics that underscore the involvement of addictions and the repetitive, compulsive nature of the cycles themselves.

Men who assault female partners are more likely to have witnessed or experienced violence in childhood, abuse alcohol, be sexually assaultive, and be at risk for perpetration of violence against children. In fact, 63 percent of abusers report having seen their mothers abused.

On average, in Canada, a woman will be assaulted 3.5 times before contacting the police. In fact, among battered women who are first identified in a medical setting, 75 percent will go on to suffer repeated abuse.

Many women who make repeated attempts to get help are told the violence must be their own fault and in some cases find that revealing the truth of what happened makes people so uncomfortable that disclosure negatively affects their treatment.

About 50 percent of abusers have a problem with alcohol and 33 percent with illicit drugs.

Nearly 25 percent of women in the United States will be abused by a current or former partner sometime during their lives.

Forty-seven percent of husbands who beat their wives do so three or more times a year.

Thirty percent of women murdered were killed by their husbands or boyfriends, and it is estimated that 53 percent of female murder victims were killed by a current or former partner.

In 45 to 59 percent of child abuse cases, the mother is also being abused.

Of women over the age of 30 who have been raped, 58 percent were raped in the context of an abusive relationship.

Recent statistics reveal information related to interpersonal violence (IPV):

twenty-four people per minute are victims of IPV

35.6 percent of women and 28.5 percent of men in the United States have experienced IPV in their lifetime

29 percent of women and 10 percent of men in the United States have experienced IPV and report a related impact on their functioning

15 percent of women and 4 percent of men have been injured as a result of IPV

IPV affects more than 12 million people each year

females ages 18–24 and 25–34 experienced the highest rates of IPV

most female victims of IPV were previously victimized by the same offender

Notice as well that the engaging elements of the domestic abuse cycle have parallels in other forms of exploitation. Incest also has cycles of abuse, with predictable stages of arousal and relief for both abuser and child. Child researchers De Young and Lowry describe in detail the typical cycle of the incest family. In describing the scenario from the father's perspective, they write: "This pattern of buildup, the act of abuse and relief can become habituated, and the parent's growing dependency on the child for both arousal and relief can preclude his ever seeking other, more appropriate, sexual partners. Traumatic bonding to the child has taken place."[2]

In corporate abuse, the employees who wait for another wave of terror know this cycle. In the case of Don, Jan, Phil, and the failed partnership with which we started this chapter, they each played their parts in the cycle very well. They learned the roles in their respective families and played out the scene in a different arena. If it repeats so that it is a predictable cycle, it adds to the trauma bond.

WHEN THE VICTIM AND THE VICTIMIZER BELIEVE IN THEIR OWN UNIQUENESS

She has been seeing her analyst three times a week for nine years. She has been having sex with him during those sessions for seven years. And she pays for the sessions in which they have sex. On Fridays she comes to his office and types for him. She doesn't know why his wife refuses to meet his needs because he is such a good man. He has been so helpful to so many people and so helpful to her; she cannot be grateful enough. Sometimes she actually enjoys sex with him. But mostly she is content with knowing how special their relationship is. She sees the other women patients in his waiting room and the attractive nurse. They are absolutely gorgeous. And out of all these women, he has selected her to meet his special needs. She knows he would not do it with anyone else, and she gets so much extra help because of their special relationship.

As long as she is convinced of her uniqueness in his life, the secret is safe. When she finds out she is only one of eighty, she is enraged. But until that point, the "promise" works. She believes she is the only one.

The relationship is also secret, which means no one can raise any issues about it. This covenant of betrayal can be found in incest families (Dad picked me out of all the kids), in sexual misconduct by clergy (he picked me out of the whole congregation), or in schools (I was picked out of all of the students). The victim does not see the sexual exploitation as betrayal. The real betrayal is if the secret gets out and Dad goes to jail, Father can no longer be a priest, or the teacher can no longer teach. In the covenant of betrayal, the victim accepts the story and the promise, which justifies the feeling of uniqueness. Telling the secret would betray the dream and the meaning it carries. It is like the science fiction thriller in which an alien has been planted inside the victim. Life can go on if it is not disturbed. But it will destroy its host if awakened.

More than likely the victimizer will believe the story as well. Jerry was a psychiatrist who specialized in family therapy. His abilities were truly extraordinary. He was recognized nationally and internationally because of his ability to articulate family dynamics so quickly and clearly. Patients flocked from all over the world. Therapists filled his seminars to see if they could perform the same kind of magic he did. Unfortunately, Jerry saw himself as unique as well. He believed that he was above the conventions and rules that other therapists had to observe. Jerry was convinced that he was able to take certain liberties with his patients in order to accelerate their progress. If women could learn about how to be sexual with him, he could use his insight and personality to help the patient make a shift in her sexual well-being.

Over one hundred women came forward to testify to Jerry's sexual conduct in the office. As a result, the state board of medical examiners took his license away. For months it was front-page news. Yet amazingly, patients still flocked to see him. It was as if nothing had happened—except that now people paid cash because their health insurance would no longer cover their visits. The patients who now saw him believed that the medical establishment could not tolerate his ability to challenge traditional medical concepts. Jerry, too, believed in his own uniqueness.

When uniqueness means that you are not like other people and do not have human limitations, you enter the arena that the Greek playwrights called *tragedy*. Greek heroes often had the same tragic flaws: *hubris*, or excessive pride. They had set themselves above other human beings. To the Greeks that meant to make yourself unto a god. That was always a mistake. Greek gods were not very tolerant of mortals who looked for godhood. Oedipus, Sisyphus, Tantalus, and Jason all suffered because of their excessive pride and their refusal to accept their own limits. Their myths describe otherwise noble, likable, attractive people who suffered horrible fates because of their tragic flaw of hubris. It's the same with people who victimize. They can be wonderfully gifted and even do many wonderful things. That, in fact, makes the "promise" even more believable. Yet when they fail to accept human limitation, and when they believe they are not subject to the same constraints as others, they enter the arena of tragedy.

Here are some ways such entitlement can develop:

> Some people were so damaged while growing up that they came to trust no one and to regard all rules, laws, and limits as applying to others and not themselves. They are often angry and well disguised. Clinicians define these people as *sociopaths* or *antisocial* individuals.

> Some people had parents who were so obsessed with them that they met all their adult needs by focusing on their child. These children, in turn, became so obsessed with themselves that they do not realize they are having an impact on others. Clinicians term these people *narcissists*.

> Some people were so abused that they manage their anxiety with compulsive use of alcohol, drugs, sex, food, or gambling. Their obsession and preoccupation so distort reality that they rationalize their entitled behavior. Clinicians call them addicts.

> Some people grew up in families of extraordinary wealth, power, and fame, which insulated them from accountability and a healthy sense of human limitation. As adults, they often feel very trepidatious about the loss of their status. At the same time, they feel that the public invades their privacy and that their heritage entitles them to do whatever is necessary to meet their needs and preserve their image.

> Some people, because of great talent and hard work, rise to positions of great power, such as physicians, members of the clergy, or attorneys. They may see themselves as having worked harder, achieved more, sacrificed more, and been smarter and tougher than others. Therefore, they believe that they are more deserving.

The paths to entitlement are myriad. In a recent study of sexual misconduct by members of the clergy, for example, researchers found that over 55 percent were alcoholics or drug addicts or both, 50 percent were sex addicts, and 33 percent were compulsive. The compulsive disorders included eating, spending, working, and a variety of high-risk activities. There were also identifiable personality disorders, including a large number of diagnosable narcissists, but also clergymen who were extremely dependent, obsessive-compulsive, and histrionic (highly dramatic).[3] Not surprising was that they also came from intrusive, abusive families.

Organizations and movements also have their sense of entitlement. Jonestown, the Holocaust, the Japanese followers of those who put poisonous gas in the subways—all shared a sense of uniqueness. Group hubris simply has the effect of making tragedy exponential.

Terrorist groups use similar methods to recruit members. A recent example is the terror group ISIS, which recruits members worldwide through packaging this entitlement and fantasy. John Horgan, a psychologist at UMass Lowell who specializes in terrorism and who has interviewed members of a wide variety of terrorist groups, states that part of their appeal is the call to answer something meaningful in an individual's life while restoring honor and to address some type of injustice. He states that ISIS as compared to other terrorist groups he has studied in the past, such as the IRA, are masters at packaging the fantasy deal, making the real obstacle a geographic one. Many are recruited through a powerful high-tech media campaign while capitalizing on the message of family, unity, and camaraderie.

Elliot Zweig is deputy director of the Middle East Media Research Institute, which has been tracking ISIS on the web, and he states, "You see messages of camaraderie, the focus of these are much more on 'come and join us,' it is not all difficulty and gore and suffering. It is 'come and join us, join me and we'll fight the good fight together'" (Singal 2014).

The point is this: Both victim and victimizer draw energy for their traumatic bonding from a sense of uniqueness. In fact, part of the covenant between them, if it were written down, would start: "Because we are unique…"

WHEN HIGH INTENSITY IS MISTAKEN FOR INTIMACY

When you come from a family in which members showed little emotion or affection, and you meet someone around whom there are lots of feelings, you might perceive this as intimacy. At least there are feelings. But if the feelings are about high drama, betrayal, and passionate reconciliations, it is not intimacy—it is intensity. And it is both absorbing and addictive.

The addiction is about high arousal and high risk. In the mid-1970s addiction specialists were already noticing that people could become compulsive about high-risk situations. Solomon at Brown University described skydivers and race car drivers who would continually put themselves at risk when it was clearly insane to do so.[4] McClelland at Harvard also researched CEOs of large corporations who could not leave their offices because they were so addicted to the high drama of acquisitions and buyouts.[5] In fact, the character Sherman McCoy in the novel *The Bonfire of the Vanities*, by Tom Wolfe, epitomizes this type of executive, the one who sacrifices all for living on the edge.[6] This character is famous for his soliloquy on being a "Master of the Universe" capable of living in high-risk situations. McCoy is a character written in the Greek tradition of hubris. In many ways this type of arousal is similar to the risk of compulsive gambling. In 2013, the movie *The Wolf of Wall Street* was released telling a similar story about Jordan Belfort who worked as a Wall Street stockbroker engaging in high risk through work, sex, and drug use. In relationships, the biggest gamble of all is the high-risk relationship.

Intensity exists in relationships when there are betrayal and victim-victimizer scenarios. Intensity thrives on fear and arousal—especially sexual arousal or the fear of sexual betrayal. Return to our circle of intimacy analogy, where to be intimate, both have to be in the circle at the same time. Intense relationships often have one in and one out of the circle. There is always the prospect of more betrayal and abandonment. High drama becomes a way to manage anxiety. Dramatic exits, for example, act out the anxiety rather than use the tension for healthy problem-solving. Conflict, in fact, is more likely to be resolved through escalation than resolution. Episode follows episode as the cycle repeats.

Intimacy, in contrast, starts with mutuality and respect. There is neither exploitation by abuse of power nor betrayal of trust. Passion flows from vulnerability and care—and is a function of the soul. Intimacy relies on safety and patience. Healthy intimacy usually has no secrets. Intensity requires secrecy and develops from it. Intimacy pushes partners to grow. Intensity serves as a distraction from oneself and limits the possibility of growth. Conflicts that arise in intimacy result in negotiation and a clear understanding about fair fighting. Absent are the fear and anxiety of intensity. Constancy and vulnerability create more of the epic than the episodic. Figure 4.1 summarizes the differences between intensity and intimacy.

Trauma bonds thrive on intensity. I had a woman client describe intensity in reference to her experiences with traumatic bonding. She said, "Intensity is like Styrofoam. It takes up space but has no substance."

WHEN THERE ARE INCREASING AMOUNTS OF FEAR

In almost all beginning psychology courses there is a section describing an amazing phenomenon: People are more sexually attractive to us when we associate them with danger. Psychology professors describe experiments in which they show students pictures of young people in a neutral context and then show pictures of the same people on a swaying bridge. Somehow, these same people are more sexually attractive when on a perilous, swinging bridge than when in a safe, neutral setting.

Figure 4.1. Intensity vs. Intimacy

DIMENSION	DIMENSION	INTIMACY
Roles:	victim/victimizer	mutual, respectful
Feelings:	fear and arousal	passion and vulnerability
Commitment:	one in/one out	involved and enduring
Prospects:	threats of betrayal/ abandonment	safety and patience
Anxiety:	high drama	problem resolution
Problems:	no structure/rules	fair fight contract

Development:	high distraction	high growth
Openness:	built on secrecy	no secrets
Conflict:	escalation	negotiation
Scenario:	episode begets episode	constancy

Actually, it is more than romantic interest that fear escalates. Countless investigations show that fear intensifies all human attachment. In fact, all forms of vertebrate species studied, encompassing birds, dogs, and primates, including humans, appear to have this trait. Fear deepens bonding. Traumatic violence in relationships (especially if moderated by positive episodes even occasionally, as in cycles) greatly increases the intensity of the attachment bond.

A series of neurobiological changes occurs in the body during intense fear. In adults and especially in children, the actual biological strata of the brain can be altered. This results in the reactivity and other trauma options described in Chapter 1. The parts of the brain designed to protect yourself gain dominance and may override other parts of the brain that limit reactive responses. A growing body of evidence indicates a neurochemical "scarring" can occur throughout the body.

This means that severe trauma can leave a mark that can be discerned in every system of the body. That is how pervasive the impact of terror can be.[7] Fear escalates the reactivity of the body, which in turn escalates all the survival options: arousal, blocking, splitting, abstinence, shame, repetition, and bonding. This year marked the forty-year anniversary of the single largest mass murder of American citizens until 9/11, the Jonestown massacre, where 900 Americans lost their lives. They were a mixture of senior citizens, whites, blacks, hippies, doctors, middle-class executives, orphans, and disadvantaged youths whom Jones personally had adopted. They were members of the People's Temple, who had left America to set up a better society in the jungle of Guyana. What they created was a nightmare of terror. Jonestown was more like a concentration camp. Jones controlled all property and income, he worked to weaken family ties, he created a caste system to control what people said, he controlled any possibility of escape, and he worked to control thoughts and emotions. There were beatings. He sexually exploited his members. As one investigator described Jones at the end:

> His paranoia was severe; his megalomania pervasive, insisting all members address him as "Father," and he seemed to be progressively falling victim to disease, a lust for money, power, guns, sex, and drugs. His leadership toward the end was punitive, narcissistic, and paranoid to the extreme.[8]

Congressman Leo Ryan had heard of the plight of some members of the Jonestown community and flew down to secure the freedom of people who wished to leave the community. During the confrontation that ensued, some of the members did want to leave. As they went to board the plane, they were shot, along with Ryan and his aides. Reverend Jones then asked for the supreme sacrifice of his followers to show their disappointment in the American system. Nine hundred thirteen people followed him to their deaths. They were victims of violence, sadism, sexual exploitation, and murder—yet they followed.

Some might say this is an isolated event. Not so. History is filled with such examples. Here is another: Synanon was established as a therapeutic community to deal with drug addiction in 1958. Over the years it became a closed system and evolved into a religious cult. It ended with the founder, Charles Dederich, being arrested for conspiracy to commit murder. Ironically, he was extremely intoxicated at the time of his arrest. William Whyte describes part of that evolution:

> As Synanon moved closer to the status of a cult, Dederich introduced a series of conformity tests that would drive out all but the most committed Synanon members. These tests included mandatory shaving of heads

of all members, mandatory vasectomies and abortions and, in late 1977, Synanon couples were required to "change partners." ... What is amazing in this story is not Dederich's demand to change partners, but the fact that over 700 Synanon members complied with this request.[9]

Control makes the fear. The fear deepens the bond.

WHEN CHILDREN ARE FACED WITH TERROR

Trauma bonding for children appears to be more severe. First, they are experiencing their primary attachments. If they experience terror in those relationships, the mind creates deep patterns and scripts. Relationships with primary caregivers create a relationship template that will be used across a lifetime. Further, children who experience traumatic bonding often exhibit the following characteristics:

They have an all-or-nothing response to emotional stimulation.

They compulsively seek out similar situations to reexpose themselves to similar types of people.

They experience significant biochemical changes in norepinephrine, dopamine, serotonin, and endogenous opioids because of stress depletion, and their needs now exceed their ability to produce.

They respond to further stressors in hyperreactive fashion.

They need caregivers to help modulate their reactivity, but the caregivers instead create more trauma.

They may only remember their emotional reactions and not the actual events because of the insufficient maturation of brain function.

The implications are threefold. First, children have a hard time understanding their own reactions. This in turn creates shame and more anxiety. Second, they have what traumatologists call *addiction to the trauma.*[10] They deliberately seek or re-create the abuse experience. Finally, their initial trauma bond is more intense because of their vulnerability, which makes subsequent relationships of a similar nature more probable. They have difficulty internalizing either moderation or self-protective boundaries.

WHEN THERE ALSO IS A HISTORY OF ABUSE

Let us say there are two current victims of sexual harassment. One is a victim of prior abuse going back to childhood. The other has a history of normal childhood and adult development. Both will suffer symptoms of post-traumatic stress. Both are vulnerable to traumatic bonding. The one with the abuse history, however, will have more severe reactions to stress and an increased potential for traumatic bonding.

Van der Kolk describes the impact of trauma: "Traumatized people become stuck, stopped in their growth because they can't integrate new experiences into their lives ... Being traumatized means continuing to organize your life as if the trauma were still going on—unchanged and immutable—as every new encounter or event is contaminated by the past. After trauma the world is experienced with a different nervous system. The survivor's energy now becomes focused on suppressing inner chaos, at the expense of spontaneous involvement in their lives ... This explains why it is critical for trauma treatment to engage the entire organism, body, mind, and brain" (van der Kolk 2014, p. 53).

The problem is admitting it. With abuse comes loyalty to the abuser. With loyalty come secrecy and denial. The abuser threatens that if there is any disclosure, the result will be tragedy—exile from the family, destruction of the family, severe punishment or death of the victim, or any ultimate threat. Whether the threat is real or simply used to control the victim, it becomes part of the interior world of the victim. The victim starts to take on the views of the perpetrator and uphold the perpetrator's position in the family or organization. William Tollefson describes this loyalty:

> Sexual abuse victims do not view the breaking of the trust bond by the abuser as a betrayal. But if the victim ever discloses the secret, it is then that the ultimate betrayal has occurred, and that cannot be forgiven. If the abuser is not around, the victim will carry out the sentence in any form—from addictive behavior to self-abusive behavior.[11]

As a therapist, I cannot count the times a breakthrough has occurred when the patient faces the question: Who in the family would benefit by your life being such a mess? Oftentimes it is the abuser. The victim, who leads a life filled with relationship failures, addiction, career catastrophes, arrests, and high drama, has no credibility, has taken all focus off the abuser, and has used personal chaos to deflect questions of accountability.

Sometimes it helps simply to review categories of abuse to see if they fit your experiences. I have provided the following Abuse Inventory upon which you can reflect. Completing it will provide you with information that will help you as you proceed with this book. Notice whether you feel as though you are breaking rules by completing it. You may wish to write about it in the notes you are keeping.

ABUSE INVENTORY

Betrayal bonds are more intense when there is history of abuse. Sometimes looking at the categories of abuse can help you broaden your own self-awareness. The following checklist and worksheet will help you assess the extent of your abuse during your childhood. To cope with your own abuse, you may have minimized the impact the abuse had on your life. Now is the time to recognize the abuse for what it was. Know that it was not your fault, and recognize your powerlessness over it.

Read over each of the three categories of abuse (emotional, physical, and sexual). Fill in the information in the spaces next to the items that apply to you. For each type of abuse, record the information to the best of your memory.

These may be powerful memories. You may wish to use your journal pages to record details and memories. You may also wish to consult with your therapist, friends, or support group.

In Chapter 1, we learned that to view trauma, we must look at two factors. First, how significant the impact was; second, how often the abuse happened. So, for example, you could have something happen just a few times, but it may have had a very harmful effect on you. Similarly, something done may not be in itself that harmful, but it may cause severe stress simply because it happens repeatedly. Look at Figure 4.2 to see the relationship between frequency and impact of abuse.

For example, if you experienced touch deprivation occasionally, you may not consider the deprivation very important. However, if you were deprived constantly, you may view your situation quite differently. It is not just the quantity that is important, but how you experienced the abuse.

Figure 4.2. Abuse Inventory

Age How old were you when the abuse started?

Abusing persons Who abused you? Father, stepfather, mother, stepmother, adult person relative, adult friend, adult neighbor, neighborhood children, professional person, brother or sister, stranger.

Frequency How often did it happen? Daily, two to three times a week, weekly, monthly? You may use the following scale: 1=one time; 2=seldom; 3=periodically; 4=often; and 5=very often.

FORM OF ABUSE	AGE	FREQUENCY	ABUSING PERSON
Emotional Abuse			
Example: Neglect	3	5	grandparent, father

FORM OF ABUSE	AGE	FREQUENCY	ABUSING PERSON
Neglect (i.e., significant persons are emotionally unavailable; emotional or physical care is inadequate)			
Harassment or malicious tricks			
Being screamed at or shouted at			
Unfair punishments			
Cruel or degrading tasks			
Cruel confinement (e.g., being locked in closet; excessive grounding for long periods)			
Abandonment (e.g., lack of supervision, lack of security, being left or deserted, death or divorce removing primary caregivers)			
Touch deprivation			
No privacy			
Having to hide injuries or wounds from others			
Forced to keep secrets			
Having to take on adult responsibilities as a child			
Having to watch beating of other family members			
Being caught in the middle of parents' fights			
Being blamed for family problems			
Other forms of emotional abuse			
Physical Abuse			
Example: Shoving	8, 18–30	5	Mother, stepfather, spouse

Shoving			
Slapping or hitting			
Scratches or bruises			
Burns			
Cuts or wounds			
Broken bones or fractures			
Damage to internal organs			
Permanent injury			
Beatings or whippings			
Inadequate medical attention			
Pulling and grabbing of hair, ears, etc.			
FORM OF ABUSE	**AGE**	**FREQUENCY**	**ABUSING PERSON**
Sexual Abuse			
Example: Flirtatious and suggestive language	6, 12–17	4	Stranger, adult neighbor
Propositioning			
Inappropriate holding, kissing			
Sexual fondling			
Masturbation			
Oral sex			
Forced sexual activity			
Household voyeurism (inappropriate household nudity, etc.)			
Sexual hugs			
Jokes about your body			
Use of sexualizing language			
Penetration with objects			

Bestiality (forced sex with animals)			
Criticism of your physical or sexual development			
Another's preoccupation with your sexual development			
Other forms of sexual abuse			

For many of us, denying the pain and reality of the abuse that we endured has been a source of our insanity. Accepting our powerlessness is not saying that it was okay; it is recognizing, maybe for the first time, that the abuse was not okay. Until we can accept the fear, anger, and sadness, we cannot grieve. It is our grieving that helps us accept our powerlessness.

How has the abuse you received as a child affected you? How do you feel when you reflect on these events? How has abuse impacted your behavior?

WHEN IT INVOLVES TRUSTED FAMILY MEMBERS OR TRUSTED FAMILY FRIENDS AND IT LASTS A LONG TIME

The husband shot his wife as she attempted to leave their driveway in her car. When their oldest son valiantly tried to stop the shooting, the father assaulted him. Newspaper reports about this Oregon family described how the fifty-six-year-old man had murdered his wife, who was thirty-six years old. The husband fled into the woods in the midst of one of the worst blizzards to hit northern Oregon. Embedded in the news reports was the fact that this man's wife was also his stepdaughter. They had three children together, including the oldest son, whom the father had assaulted. What the newspapers could not prove, but what everyone in town knew, was that his wife was not his stepdaughter.

Actually, he had married his real daughter after the mysterious death of his original wife, her mother.

While extreme, this story illustrates the worst that can happen to a victim. There is a growing body of evidence that shows the most distress occurs in victims whose family members or family friends have betrayed them. There is further evidence that part of the problem is that these situations can last for many years, which simply deepens the traumatic bonding. "Betrayal is the sense of being harmed by the intentional actions or omissions of a trusted person. The most common forms of betrayal are harmful disclosures of confidential information, disloyalty, infidelity, dishonesty. They can be traumatic and cause considerable distress. The effects of betrayal include shock, loss and grief, morbid pre-occupation, damaged self-esteem, self-doubting, anger. Not infrequently they produce life-altering changes. The effects of catastrophic betrayal are most relevant for anxiety disorders, and OCD and PTSD in particular" (Rachman 2010). Clinicians measure assaults not by the number of events but by over how long they took place. The variable that emerges from this research is that the impact of trauma is greatest not when strangers commit it but when someone who is known and trusted commits it. So to marry that abuser and thereby make permanent an exploitive relationship would be the worst nightmare possible. "The trauma survivor's relationship to the perpetrator is an established predictor of trauma-related psychopathology, with interfamilial or interpersonal traumas being associated with more negative psychological outcomes than extrafamilial or noninterpersonal traumas" (Martin et al. 2013, p. 111). "When the traumatic event is the result of an attack by a family member on whom victims also depend for economic or other forms of security, as occurs in victims of intrafamilial abuse, victims are prone to respond to assaults with increased dependence and with a paralysis in their decision making processes" (van der Kolk 2000).

To provide perspective, in the earlier section of this chapter there is a summary of data on domestic abuse. Note the staggering percentages of women who are murdered by someone whom they know. In the case of the Oregon family, it is clear that there was a betrayal of power and intimacy that resulted in deadly intensity.

Review the Abuse Inventory you just completed. In the sections you completed on the abuser(s), mark the ones who would fit the category of "known and trusted." Record any reflections you have in your notes.

When the Community, Family, or Social Structure Reacts in the Extreme

When denominations of various religious traditions had to confront sexual misconduct by their own clergy, one of the options often used was to bury the problem. They simply transferred the clergyman and threw a cloak of secrecy over the issue. No one cajoled the victim to avoid her making a scene or bought her off in any way. They simply denied the reality of the experience in the worst cases. Those in authority feared that the church and all the good deeds accomplished in its name would lose credibility. As a result of this fear, the church leaders colluded with the perpetrator. The net effect is that traumatic bonding, in the form of secrecy, persisted inside a supportive environment. These leaders committed betrayal by spirit.

This collusion often becomes quite extreme. In the famous Father Porter case, over 240 victims came forward. Instead of facing the issue, the church transferred Porter from one parish to another or from one state to another. To give you an example of how difficult it is to stop this extreme response, one Protestant denomination, after a series of painful situations, developed an abuse policy that outlined what should happen if someone reported sexual misconduct. A task force composed of leaders, victims, their attorneys, therapists, and perpetrators carefully thought through the process so it would be fair and helpful to everyone. Shortly after leaders approved it as the official policy, one of the best preachers in the denomination, known for his ability to raise funds, had a report of sexual misconduct filed against him. Church leaders handled it in a secretive way, basically discounting the victim. They handled it this way because of "special" and "unique" circumstances. They ignored the policy because of the power and visibility of the clergyman involved. It was business as usual.

That leaves the victim with one alternative: to go to court. But most victims do not wish to use the legal system. What they want is to have people hear them, to see things change, and to have resolution. Victims' advocates say that without significant court settlements, these large systems probably would not have changed their policies of denial and secrecy. The unfortunate result is that the victims place themselves in the adversarial legal system—which adds even more stress. In that arena, the goal is not resolution, but winning. Legal action often has the effect of intensifying betrayal bonds.

WHEN THERE ARE FAMILIAR ROLES OR SCRIPTS

Whenever we see Lucy with the football looking for Charlie Brown, we tend to smile, since we know we are going to revisit the old scenario. Lucy will have some good reason to entice Charlie Brown into taking another run at it. Charlie Brown will resist but will succumb to some new promise. Lucy will pull the ball away, and Charlie Brown will be flat on his back again. Lucy will then make some pronouncement that negates her promise. We have seen this script before. We smile because of Lucy's inventiveness and because Charlie Brown's susceptibility reminds us of our own.

It's from our families that we learn to have these Lucy–Charlie Brown relationships. Consider the case of Ken. When I met Ken, he

PEANUTS reprinted by permission of United Feature Syndicate, Inc.

was struggling with both depression and drug addiction. As a young adolescent, a man who was a close friend of his parents sexually victimized him. This man was like an uncle. His parents reacted much like the churches described earlier. They did not believe Ken and punished him severely for making the accusation. So it was for him in his family. Anytime he said something uncomfortable to the rest of the family, they scapegoated him. An example of this took place when he was in his early thirties and his wife related to his mother something Ken had said. Ken's mother, a raging alcoholic, ordered his brothers to beat him up, which they did. As a result of the beating, he was admitted to the emergency room with severe head trauma. These dramatic confrontations filled the family history. At one point one of his brothers attempted to drown him. When asked why he did not leave, Ken answered that this was his family. It was easier to medicate his pain by using drugs. The truth just brought him pain. Leaving would risk even more punishment.

Ken had a role and a script. Each scenario took a predictable course. He replicated this scenario in school and at work with punitive teachers and bosses. And he always told himself these events were his fault. Notice that Ken experienced betrayal by known and trusted people, that the family's reactions were extreme, and that there was a predictable cycle of events in which his role was very clear—he received the punishments for the excess of the family. He and Charlie Brown both knew their roles. Those roles support traumatic bonding.

One other trait was present. The roles in the family could quickly reverse. His mom, who ordered the beatings, would also rescue him from his brothers. His wife, who was trying to rescue him from the insanity of the family, would attack him for not being stronger. His brothers would befriend him after the attacks and plot against Mom. All of this added to the volatility and intensity of the family. Which brings us to the last major source of strength for trauma bonds.

WHEN THE ROLES OF VICTIM, VICTIMIZER, AND RESCUER SWITCH

Role switching is common in betrayal bonding. Domestic abuse serves as an excellent example. Police are often very slow to respond to domestic abuse situations; they have learned that these can be extremely dangerous for the officer. Here is how it works:

The 911 call comes. The intervening officer arrives at the scene. His first priority is to restrain the perpetrator so he can gain control of the situation. When the officer attempts to secure the perpetrator, the battered spouse attacks him. And who separates them, looking like the epitome of calm and reason? The original perpetrator. This dynamic routinely injures or kills. It is the same dynamic that worked in Ken's family.

Psychiatrist Stephen Karpman identified this switch in what clinicians call the Karpman triangle. There are three critical roles involved: (1) a victim who is exploited or violated; (2) the victimizer who exploits or violates the victim; and (3) the rescuer who wants to stop the transgression. In the case of domestic abuse, the intervening officer is the rescuer. The officer becomes the victim when the battered spouse, who becomes the victimizer, attacks him. The perpetrator then becomes the rescuer.[12] Figure 4.3 graphically shows the interaction of the three roles.

Traumatic bonding thrives when the system reverses its victim, victimizer, and rescuer roles. It makes the betrayal exponential because it adds insecurity, intensity, and complexity to the situation. The cycles, the uniqueness, and the reactivity in traumatic bonding become even more volatile, all of which add to the anxiety and the terror.

Remember the fundamental premise: Attachment deepens with terror. This occurs not only in domestic abuse; it happens in incest and sexual misconduct when the victim threatens exposure and becomes aggressive with the victimizer for the purpose of exploitation. When Congressman Ryan went to save the victims in Jonestown, they killed him. In Stockholm, the hostages were critical and abusive toward the rescuers. In the story at the beginning of this chapter, when Don and Jan were betraying Phil, the bank officers, in rescuing Phil, opened themselves to substantial lawsuits and federal penalties for betraying client confidence. These role reversals are what keep the dramatic momentum going. They are the stuff of which soap operas are made.

Figure 4.3. The Karpman Triangle

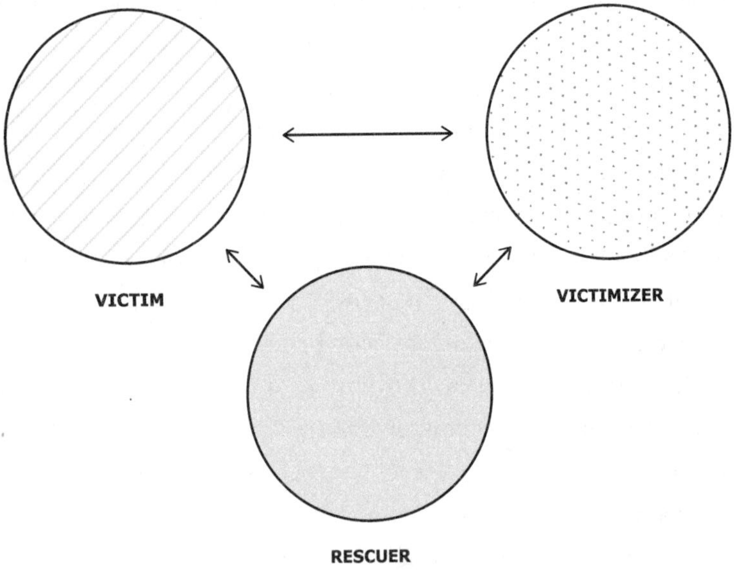

VICTIM   VICTIMIZER

RESCUER

Further, all three roles (victim, victimizer, rescuer) have important similarities. All three roles originate from shame and self-doubt. All three positions stem from a sense of being defective and unworthy. People in these dramas are never confident that anyone will fulfill their needs. Victims ally with the perpetrators in the hope of gaining acceptance and meeting their needs. Victimizers so fear that their needs will not be met that they feel they have to deceive and exploit the victims. And rescuers are trying to secure a place by being heroic, hoping that if they go to this extreme, the others will recognize their needs and meet them.

Ironically, all three roles identify with the victim in the other. The victim believes the perpetrator's story of victimization. The perpetrator identifies with the victim by making the promise—knowing exactly what the victim wants. The rescuer wants to protect the victim since the rescuer has an abuse history as well. The net result is that they all obsess about one other: The victim obsesses about the perpetrator, the perpetrator obsesses about the victim, and the rescuer obsesses about the crisis.

In each role the participants use magical thinking. The victim is naïve in repeatedly trusting that things will change. For Charlie Brown to think that Lucy is actually going to hold the ball for him is not logical, given the history. The victimizer is naïve in thinking the true intent will not emerge. Sooner or later the truth will come out. And the rescuer is naïve in thinking the rescue will actually work.

All three positions represent boundary failure. Victims fail to protect themselves; victimizers fail to limit themselves; and rescuers fail to define themselves. They become enmeshed with others when they're caught up in a crisis. They lose their sense of self. Because of this, their personal boundaries become too elastic.

There is a grandiosity in all this. Victims are grandiose in seeing themselves as beneficiaries of the promise; victimizers are grandiose in telling the story that contains the promise; and rescuers are grandiose by believing one intervention can do away with the past. Figure 4.4 summarizes these dimensions for all three positions.

The bottom line: The reason a person can be in all three roles in the same traumatic relationship is that the person shares the commonalities listed in the chart in Figure 4.4. All victimizers need to see that they also play victim and rescuer; all victims need to see how they rescue and victimize; all rescuers need to understand their own motivation for helping lest they become victims or worse, victimizers; and anyone who has been part of a betrayal bond needs to understand how all role reversals intensify insane loyalties. It is the history of all great bonding conflicts: the Hatfields and the McCoys, the Montagues and the Capulets of *Romeo and Juliet* fame, the wars between Mafia families—betrayal and counter-betrayal.

At the conclusion of this chapter is an exercise on your conflict history. As in earlier exercises, this activity will help you form a complete picture of your own relationships. Again, keep a record of your reactions to completing the inventory, as it will be of great assistance to you shortly.

Figure 4.4. Commonalities for Victim, Victimizer, and Rescuer

DIMENSION	VICTIM	VICTIMIZER	RESCUER
Shame	doubts personal value	doubts personal value	doubts personal value
Needs deficit	allies with perpetrator to meet needs	deceives and violates victim to meet needs	becomes heroic to meet needs
Abuse identification	sees victim in the perpetrator's story	identifies with victim in promise	wants to protect victim in others
Obsession	with perpetrator	with victim	with crisis
Magical thinking	naïve in repeatedly trusting	naïve in thinking he or she will not be caught	naïve in thinking rescue will work
Boundary failure	failure to protect self	failure to limit self	failure to define self

CONFLICT INVENTORY

Sometimes we can learn much about ourselves by studying the conflicts that we have had. List ten people below with whom you have had a significant conflict. Note what relationship you had with the person. After each person, write a two- to three-sentence description of your primary coping strategies. In what ways did you strategize to deal with the problems in the relationship? After each person, check the appropriate boxes as to whether you participated in the role of victim, victimizer, or rescuer.

NAME OF PERSON	PRIMARY COPING STRATEGIES	ROLES PLAYED (check each)
Example: A. John B. (my brother)	I was cold and withdrawn. Sometimes I would get angry and make threats. I tried to get his wife as an ally. Also, I told everything I knew to my parents so they would force him to see the light. I saw his boss in the store and told him what was going on.	(X) victim (X) victimizer (X) rescuer
Example: B. Bill (my husband)	I would agree to calm him down and try to keep the peace. I would let him get his way until things got too awful. Then I would have a temper tantrum and throw things.	(X) victim (X) victimizer ( ) rescuer
1.		( ) victim ( ) victimizer ( ) rescuer
2.		( ) victim ( ) victimizer ( ) rescuer

NAME OF PERSON	PRIMARY COPING STRATEGIES	ROLES PLAYED (check each)
3.		( ) victim ( ) victimizer ( ) rescuer
4.		( ) victim ( ) victimizer ( ) rescuer
5.		( ) victim ( ) victimizer ( ) rescuer
6.		( ) victim ( ) victimizer ( ) rescuer
7.		( ) victim ( ) victimizer ( ) rescuer
8.		( ) victim ( ) victimizer ( ) rescuer

9.		( ) victim ( ) victimizer ( ) rescuer
10.		( ) victim ( ) victimizer ( ) rescuer

What Is the Path of Awareness?

For Anita Hill, "family" began as her relationship with [Clarence] Thomas, who was not only a colleague, but a boss and a "father figure" to her and others. Thomas spoke of his supervisees as being like his "children," and how he often had fatherly feelings for them. For such a "father" to betray his "child"

IS COMMON IN OUR WORLD OF UNHEALTHY
FAMILIES. ANITA HILL ALSO HAS A GREATER
FAMILY—IN HER WORKPLACE, AND THEN FINALLY
IN HER GOVERNMENT, WHERE SHE AND WE
ENCOUNTERED THE UNHEALTHY FAMILY OF THE
SENATE AND ITS JUDICIARY COMMITTEE.
AND THIS COMMITTEE HAD A SECRET,
LIKELY ONLY ONE AMONG MANY MORE SECRETS
THAT IT TRIED TO KEEP FROM ITSELF
AND THE NATION.

—Charles Whitfield[1]

THE RANGE OF WHAT WE THINK
AND DO IS LIMITED BY WHAT WE FAIL TO
NOTICE AND BECAUSE WE FAIL TO NOTICE THAT
WE FAIL TO NOTICE THERE IS LITTLE WE
CAN DO TO CHANGE UNTIL WE NOTICE HOW
FAILING TO NOTICE SHAPES OUR
THOUGHTS AND DESIRES.

—R. D. Laing

"Exactly!" Tom's therapist exclaimed. "You don't feel loving, you feel bonded!" Tom and his therapist, Sam, had just spent the last hour of therapy going round and round. Tom had been divorced from his ex-spouse for over four years. They had three children together and a nightmare for a relationship. His ex-wife, Barbara, had been manipulative, cruel to him and the children, and very abusive in her frequent attacks of rage. Tom persisted in being calm and giving despite all this. His therapist was pushing him as to why. Tom had said he did not love her but somehow he connected to her. Sam was working to help him understand that he had a trauma bond.

In part, his therapist made sense. Barbara had always been volatile. Their courtship had regular episodes of angry dramatic exits alternated with incredible displays of devotion by Barbara. Sometimes Tom thought he was coerced into the marriage, although he could not quite put the idea into words. For Barbara, Tom's hesitancy to get married was not acceptable. It was going to happen. She waged a campaign to mobilize the goodwill of everyone around Tom. What they did not see were her outbreaks of rage. Finally she got pregnant and that was it.

About four months into the marriage, Barbara had an affair with her supervisor. From that point, things started unraveling. She started a campaign about how bad a husband Tom was. Consequently, Tom ended up defending himself, which angered him. Barbara had the affair and he was the one who was defensive! When he was ready to leave, she love-bombed him, and they ended up with a second child. Six years into the marriage and one more child later, he could not stand it anymore, and they separated. The divorce talks were interminable, and

Tom spent much of every day coping with the chaos Barbara created. Sam was helping Tom to see that he had not really left at all.

Tom could not figure it out. He did not feel loving toward her. He was no longer attracted to her. He did not respect her, nor did he trust her. Their history together verified over and over again that she would go to any lengths to get what she wanted and present a positive image to the outside world. She deliberately lied in therapy. However, when the children came to therapy and corroborated Tom's reality in front of the therapists, she looked contrite and aghast. Once out of the therapy office, she threw a fit before they got to the car. A reign of terror started, which let everybody know that what had just happened was not to happen again. For openers, she refused to let the children go to therapy again. Then there were outright lies. She told Tom's parents and sisters stories that were far from reality. The lies and the raging continued. Given this history, Tom could not understand how, or why, he was still so involved with her. He admitted to Sam that at times he felt overwhelmed with anger and despaired that his life was ruined. As long as he was actively a father to the children, he would have to pay the price.

Tom paid in many ways. He paid financially. His attorney in the divorce was upset because Tom conceded many points that he did not have to. He had some profound need to be "fair," which to outsiders looked absolutely self-destructive. After reading a draft of the divorce decree, Tom's secretary joked with him by asking if she could be married to him even for a little while.

Tom also paid in time. Barbara was on the phone three or four times a day—complaining, raging, cajoling, or asking for help or advice. He paid in disruption. Barbara moved into a house two blocks from Tom's. The idea was to make it more convenient for the kids. The net effect was that Tom could not have a meal with his children or spend an evening with them without Barbara having some reason to show up, often with her latest man in tow.

Sam pressed Tom to accept that this chaos was not about Barbara alone. True, she did awful things, but Tom participated as well. The two of them had a deep, negative attachment for each other. Tom was hooked into her as much as she was into him. Sam made a statement that to Tom was like a Zen koan: "Barbara is no longer your wife and yet she is not your 'ex' either." "So what is she then?" snapped Tom. Sam smiled back and said, "Barbara is your addiction."

THE PATH OF DENIAL

From 1985 to 1990, I directed a team of researchers who followed the recovery of over a thousand sex addicts. This group had a number of significant characteristics, beyond their sex addiction, that made them important to study. First, they had multiple addictions: alcoholism and drug addiction (42 percent); eating disorders, including anorexia (38 percent); and other forms of addictive compulsion, including working, spending, and gambling. Further, they had histories of trauma and abuse: sexual abuse (81 percent), physical abuse (72 percent), and emotional abuse (97 percent). Finally, many of them reported the type of traumatic bonding I've described in this book. From the data collected and with the help of a university computer, we were able to reconstruct the process by which trauma affects people. We began to understand the confusion and denial people like Tom have about their relationships. More important, we discerned the process by which people restored their lives. I learned a lot from the project. In fact, it started me in the direction of researching and developing the material for this book.

Here is what we learned. For most people, there was some original trauma. Remember, this does not have to be some earth-shattering event. It can be neglect, or it can be witnessing something traumatic such as incest or domestic abuse. When that original trauma occurs, we begin to see the first signs of compulsive behavior. Compulsive masturbation, for example, was common for many of the sex addicts in our study. Other forms of compulsion emerged as well. An abused child will learn, for the sake of her own survival, to focus on the emotional well-being of the abusing caregiver. The child will become "expert" at noticing and responding to the moods of her abuser. The child may, for example, become expert at caregiving as a way to soothe the parent or may feel compelled to become compliant as a way to lower the anxiety of the abuser. Yet another option exists, given that abuse intensifies the child's attachment to the abuser. The child may learn how to endure pain in order to maintain the bond with the caregiver. These compelling patterns form a working model for how the child will later deal with significant people in her life. As an adult, the working model becomes the template for all important relationships.

Tom was classic in this sense. He had an alcoholic father known for his rages. He remembers the screaming as his mother barricaded herself in the bedroom. He remembers the ambulance when she was injured. When he was eight, his father joined Alcoholics Anonymous, and the fighting stopped, but he was always afraid of his father's temper. He was also very good at consoling his mother. To use Sam's words, he was one of the world's best "at walking on eggshells and comforting the wounded." It was only after Sam and a clinic hypnotist helped Tom talk about the feelings he had as he watched these events that Tom accepted his internal terror.

Victims acclimatize to the terror. They distort, transform, reinterpret, dissociate, distance, repress, disown, or use any of a number of strategies to accommodate their reality. We call this denial. They also can have traumatic amnesia, which means there is no conscious recall of specific events. For example, Tom's brother and sister told him of specific events they witnessed of which he had no memory. Similarly,

Tom told them of events that he was absolutely sure happened to the three of them, that his siblings could not remember. That is when Tom first understood what Sam meant by repression.

Children are presented with what trauma researcher David Calof has described as the "universal bind." Do not see, hear, sense, feel, or address what is real. Instead, accept what is unreal and proscribed in the interest of your survival. Disbelieve the obvious and accept the improbable.[2] The bind is that the child is presented with only two options: (1) be overwhelmed with terror and not able to function, or (2) distort reality to survive. Because of the bind, distorting reality becomes part of the "working model" eventually used in adult relationships. Therapists Blizard and Bluhm describe it this way:

> These defenses are highly adaptive in childhood, because they permit the child to survive in an abusive family. In adulthood the defenses become maladaptive, because they prevent the survivor from accurately perceiving the presence or absence of abuse. By permitting the adult survivor to maintain a relationship with someone who resembles the original abuser, these defenses perpetuate the cycle of abuse.[3]

In Tom's case, Barbara combined the angry violence and intimidation of his dad with the compelling sadness of his mom. While an irresistible combination, Tom had to make up a narrative or story that made sense to him in order to stay connected to Barbara, but to outsiders his explanations were bizarre distortions and rationalizations. Combine this with Barbara's fictions and distortions, and reality became very elusive for anyone looking in from the outside.

With denial and repression in place, all the trauma solutions are available in the service of the trauma bond. Reactivity, arousal, blocking, splitting, abstinence, shame, and trauma repetition can be accomplished in the context of the relationship.

Reactivity comes with constant chaos, involvement, and betrayal. There is always something to induce the cycles of old to activate the victim, victimizer, and rescuer scenarios.

Arousal surges in the relationship with high risk, intensity, and sometimes violent sex. Anger, fear, and anxiety create a neurochemical cascade that makes sane relationships boring.

Blocking occurs when there is the honeymoon or "I have pushed you too far" phase. Seductive and pleasing efforts to make up for it are calming and provide temporary relief.

Splitting happens when the victim dissociates from the chaos or from obsessing about the partner. Internal "dialogues" with your partner would be an example.

Abstinence manifests in many ways, including the obvious: staying in the relationship without needs being met, or worse, living in deprivation because the chaos prevents you from taking care of yourself, so martyrdom seems functional.

Shame appears in the form of despair about yourself, in feeling defective because the victim has absorbed the shame of the perpetrator (carried shame), and in believing in your unworthiness.

Repetition cycles the "working model" of how relationships should work over and over again. Each recycle repeats the victimization of the past.

In short, you have an addictive relationship that results in compulsive involvement and compulsive relationship patterns. For Tom, being with Barbara put in place all the paths that people use addictively.

In addition, notice that the addictive relationship is woven with other addictive compulsive behaviors. Core to this process are: alcohol and drug abuse; sex addiction; eating disorders; compulsive working, spending, and gambling; and the compulsive seeking of high-risk situations (including violence and arrest). Very seldom will you find traumatic bonding without other addictions woven into the pattern on somebody's, if not everybody's, part. Conversely, seldom do you find addictions of any type without vulnerability to traumatic bonding. A complex constellation of out-of-control relationships and behaviors emerges. It's a cycle that results in a self-perpetuating system.

Sooner or later this system gathers enough momentum that a life crisis occurs. Something so bad happens that the victim can no longer simply go forward. Forgetting about the past and coping with the day is not enough. Those who have the courage decide to change, whatever the cost; it literally takes that kind of resolve to make the change. Figure 5.1 summarizes the role trauma plays in the evolution of the life crisis.

Figure 5.1. Role of Trauma in a Life Crisis

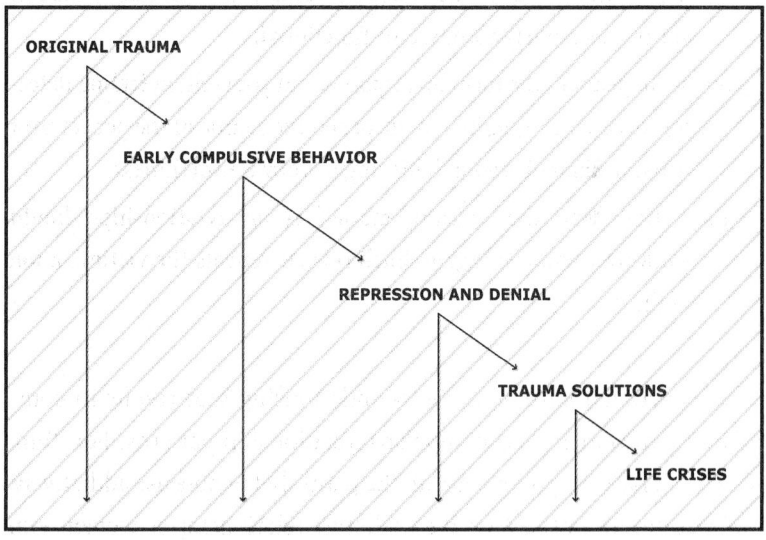

In Figure 5.1, note that the development of the survivor starts with the original trauma and then proceeds to early compulsive behavior.

This behavior may have a role in helping with the repression and denial that come into play. As the full force of the various trauma options becomes available, the chaos escalates to the point of life crisis. The arrows graphically show the sequence of the progression. Also notice that there is an arrow that points down. This represents how each dimension progresses. The original perpetrator may continue abusing. Those early compulsive behaviors will persist. The denial and repression continue and expand, as will the traumatic solutions they enable. All of this continues until it crashes under its own weight. The survivor can no longer keep up with all of it.

THE PATH OF AWARENESS

By reconstructing the path from the original trauma to the life crisis, we gained an important insight into recovery. People in our study recovered in stages, and the order of their recovery was almost the reverse of how people got into their life crises. Most had to experience some type of intervention to get out of the trauma-based system. If they were addicted to alcohol or gambling, they had to start a recovery program around that illness. If they were hooked into a destructive relationship, they had to do something about it. If they were dissociating, stuck in deprivation behaviors, or immersed in shame, they would seek treatment for it. To start, they had to focus on the trauma solutions, identifying the immediate source of the chaos. Their recovery was akin to putting up a tent in the wind—some pegs have to go in the ground before you can anchor the tent and raise the poles.

These early interventions create confusion about what is real. The survivors, in beginning these initial changes, also start to accept that the rationalization and distortions they have used or believed were part of the problem. And they were confused by that. Remember, a survivor has been asked to disbelieve the obvious and accept the improbable.

After the intervention, survivors were unsure of what reality really was. This created the window for the next stage—the stage in which denial and repression break. When survivors stop using the dysfunctional solutions they have used (i.e., high-risk behavior, medicating or anesthetizing, repeating the event), they can expect that:

memories of previous abuse will return

they will have intense reactions to what they do remember

they will have an expanded understanding of what happened in the past

they will see continuing aspects of those abusive patterns now

they will know how high the cost has been

they will be very fearful of what this means for them and their lives

After the intervention, those participating in the study asked several questions: What if this is all true? What does this mean about me? About my family? What will happen now if I say this out loud? How will people react? Will it be worse if I admit the truth? Is it safer to hide? As you've read this book, you may have asked yourself some of those same questions.

If you understand that this fearful reaction is the beginning of grief, it helps. Whenever there is significant loss—whether individually or collectively—the stages of human grieving are quite predictable. First, there is denial—"This cannot be true!" Then there is fear—"What if it is true?" This is followed by anger—"This is unfair!" Anger is followed by the wrenching pain of loss—"This hurts too much to bear." Finally, there is acceptance and an attempt to derive some meaning out of all that happened.

There are several things that make it different for survivors. First, grief is delayed. Most grief cycles begin with a current loss, such as the death of a loved one. Survivors have not been able to acknowledge the pain that has been accumulating. It is somewhat akin to running in front of a growing avalanche for years and never being more than a few inches in front of it. When you stop, the avalanche overwhelms you. When you no longer have the cushion of the trauma solutions, the pain envelops you all at once.

Second, the initial trauma may have distorted the relationship template used as an adult. The result is that survivors have a vulnerability most people do not have. They often are not able to discern when someone is being exploitive or abusive toward them. This interferes with their sense of loss, their outrage, and their pain.

Third, most people plunged into grief can be public about their loss. If a loved one dies in an auto accident, there is no mystery as to why the family members hurt. But when the loss is shrouded in pledges of secrecy and in shame and betrayal, getting support will require incredible vulnerability: "How could I have been so foolish? So trusting and accepting?" Worse, talking about the loss means disloyalty within the abusive system. Anger can help break the loyalty of the betrayal bond. For survivors, the typical anger at God most people in grief experience is coupled with anger toward the victimizer. This anger becomes an empowering emotion that helps to break the secrecy and dissolve the insane loyalties.

Finally, most people grieve because the loss is painful. Survivors must add another dimension to that pain. It starts when they realize that the people who abused them also were abused. Perhaps the abuse may even go back many generations. Survivors move beyond this realization to a new level of integrity when they acknowledge that they have also abused others. Maybe they did not do the same things, but they still victimized others. They are part of an unbroken chain, which can be incredibly painful to admit. We call this victimization consciousness, which means the victim understands the whole picture. She now grasps and accepts the whole complex series of relationships, solutions to trauma, and accumulated loss. With that acceptance comes a new sense of peace.

Figure 5.2.
Awareness of Victimization Consciousness

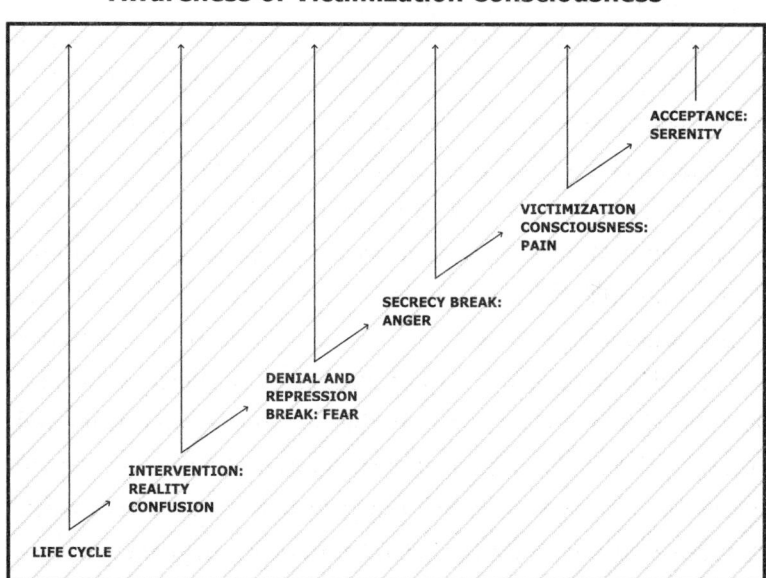

Figure 5.2 graphically represents this process of awareness and understanding. It is the reverse path of the denial that protects the abusive system and its web of solutions to the trauma. The arrows in the figure show the order in which things occur. Note also the arrows indicating that each phase of this path continues. You do not simply go through the phases and finish. Survivors will continue to make connections with their memories and their current circumstances.

Each stage of awareness will go through the process. With time, the survivor will acquire the skills to process through these realizations more rapidly. It will become more manageable; this is a promise.

It is important to examine each phase of the path of awareness from a traumatic bonding perspective.

DENIAL AND REPRESSION

Let's summarize the problem: Adults who are trauma-bonded to people who are harmful to them believe they have made that choice. Everyone around them can see how compulsive the relationship is except the person involved. The trauma-bonded person has also constructed a story that explains the initial involvement and rationalizes the continued involvement. The story has powerful reasons for what happened and powerful hopes for change. Sometimes this story is a variant of the perpetrator's story of promise but sometimes not. The critical factor is that this scenario, with its embedded conclusions, came from the victim, and for that reason it is particularly difficult to overcome.

In 1942, Anna Freud described this process as "identification with the aggressor." She meant that the victim will start to perceive the world from the point of view of the aggressor. Since then we have acquired a greater understanding of what goes into traumatic bonding. We know it has a profound neurochemical impact, and it creates a working model for other relationships. We understand the complex web of addictive and family systems that preserves this "identification." Yet at the core of the bonding is a story.

To breach the denial, the victim needs to step outside of the story and see it as others see it. In part that is how a therapist, therapy group, or support group can be helpful. It requires, however, courage and willingness. A helpful exercise is to write a brief narrative of your life story as if it were the story of someone else. Usually you start as if it were a fairy tale: "Once there was a little girl (boy) . . ." In writing, most victims start to have compassion for the character in the story that is themselves. They begin to see the faulty logic their character has used. When read by the victims to a support or therapy group, there is often a profound shift in the victims as they start to acknowledge the pain.

They would not have been able to achieve that understanding without looking differently at the story. Instructions for writing the story follow.

When Tom did this exercise, it was life changing. One of the toughest parts for him to acknowledge was that as a man, he was a victim. He told Sam, his therapist, that he always thought that as a man he should be in charge. It was extremely hard for him to admit that he was easily manipulated and that he did not protect himself well. Further, he felt afraid often because it always seemed that Barbara was a move or two ahead of him. Those admissions came hard for a man who was supposed to be in charge.

WRITE THE STORY

This assignment asks that you write your own story in your journal, but write as if it happened to someone else. Use third-person pronouns in your description: "Once there was a girl and she . . ." It may help you to visualize it as a movie or a fairy tale. Limit yourself to 750 words (about three pages). Focus on how the character in the story is thinking and feeling. You may wish to draw a picture or two with crayons to illustrate the story. After you have finished, do the following:

With your therapist or group, read the story out loud and show the pictures.

If you think of this as happening to someone else, what feelings do you have for the character?

What do you wish to tell the character?

Write in your journal about the realities you have not been willing to examine.

Record any patterns you see emerging throughout your life.

Record any common profiles of persons you recognize.

What Tom and other victims learn is that compulsive relationship patterns start early. They start as survival strategies for the child, but for the adult they become imprisoning patterns. Trauma specialists observe the following common compulsive relationship patterns:[4]

1. **Compulsive Helplessness**—The child is so focused on the adult and the abuse, she does not learn to master her environment or take care of herself well. Therapists refer to this uninvolved state as "learned helplessness," or "inattention." They irritate others because they do not notice what needs to be done. Adults with this pattern face constant chaos because they do not act for themselves and do not provide their basic needs. They seem oblivious until there is a crisis.

2. **Compulsive Focus on the Abuser**—For survival's sake, the child becomes an "expert" on the abuser. What the child wants or needs becomes subservient to the caregiver's moods. Thus the child loses the sense of self and identifies with the source of fear. As an adult, the person will obsess about anyone with power over her and do whatever she can to control what happens.

3. **Compulsive Self-Reliance**—As an alternative strategy to the previous two options, the child will become excessively self-reliant. No needs are expressed. No help is asked or accepted. All affection and closeness are avoided. As an adult the victim will use self-sufficiency as a defense against needing others.

4. **Compulsive Caregiving**—Priority is placed on the needs of the others, with feelings of martyrdom and resentment resulting. Self-sacrifice goes to the extreme. Care is supplied whether requested or not, whether needed or not. As adults, victims become burdensome and easily exploitable.

5. **Compulsive Care-Seeking**—Problems are presented so that care will be received. Relationships are defined by those who can

supply assistance. The victim expects others to assume responsibility for major areas of life. The only way anyone gets close to the victim is by providing help. As adults, victims will always present the latest problem as a reason to have a relationship.

6. **Compulsive Rejection**—Extreme negative reactions result from perceived unavailability of or lack of response by the caregiver or abuser. Often a generalized anger occurs on the principle of "I will reject you before you have a chance to reject me." Such emotional violence simply echoes a violent home life. In adults, this emotional volatility can become a way of victimizing others.

7. **Compulsive Compliance**—This is a placating stance in which being extremely agreeable provides protection from more abuse. No wish is challenged. Resistance is token. No boundaries exist. As adults, these people commit to things they do not wish to do, provide information they should not provide, and do things that are self-destructive, uncomfortable, or dangerous simply because someone asked them.

8. **Compulsive Identification with Others**—This person can easily be sold a "bill of goods." He or she has instant sympathy for even the most patent lies, tales of insanity, stories of hardship, and seduction strategies. Victims may even have the capacity to see through the seduction, but in the presence of the perpetrator they get carried away by the story. Their gullibility produces personal loss and constant chaos. They are especially irritating to others because they will never negotiate on their own behalf.

9. **Compulsive Reality Distortion**—The victim will persist in not seeing abuse as abuse. Excuses, rationalization, minimization, and other defenses combine to allow the endurance of more pain and exploitation. In part, this comes from the deep wish that the story or promise of the perpetrator be true. In adults, it means ignoring the obvious.

10. **Compulsive Abuse Seeking**—The victim sets up relationships to repeat the same patterns of abuse. This creates familiar binds, neurochemistry, and coping strategies. For a relationship to work, it must comply with the original abuse scenario. What can vary is the amount of risk and intensity. Adults may combine a number of abuse scenarios to get the desired effect.

At the core of every addiction is compulsive behavior. Compulsion means that you exhibit the behavior even though you know it is self-destructive. You cannot stop it on your own. Traumatic bonding is essentially a compulsive relationship with very definite patterns of compulsive behavior.

For successful recovery, the victim has to be able to break through denial and see the compulsive patterns for what they are. I've provided a compulsive relationship self-assessment as a way to start facing the reality of those compulsive patterns. It is structured on the ten dimensions described above. On those dimensions that you rate yourself high, you will be asked to describe events in childhood in which that dimension was evident. The goal of the exercise is to help you see each dimension as a coping strategy you needed at that time. Next to each of those childhood examples you will be asked to record a parallel adult event in which the same behavior is dysfunctional.

It is certainly possible for a person with little or none of these compulsive patterns in childhood to experience trauma bonding as an adult. As an adult, some situations are so terrifying that they can immediately precipitate these compulsive behaviors and alter a person's life. If you are in that situation, simply focus on the adult examples.

It may also happen as a result of this and the previous exercise that you will remember traumatic events you had forgotten. Expect traumatic repression to lift as you work on these issues. Simply record them and add them to your understanding. It means the process is working.

You will have feelings about them, which you should also record. But also note that your awareness is expanding, which is good news.

Please complete the compulsive relationship self-assessment before you continue reading this book.

COMPULSIVE RELATIONSHIP SELF-ASSESSMENT

Complete the following self-assessment by assigning yourself a number between one and ten in each compulsive dimension. A rating of one, on a scale of ten, would mean there was little or none of that behavior present. By contrast, a score of ten would mean that the behavior was constant (a daily experience). Once you have completed the scales, note those you have rated five or above. Next to these higher-rated scales, record a childhood event that describes how you coped with the compulsivity. Then record an adult event that shows the same pattern.

DIMENSIONS OF COMPULSIVITY	CHILDHOOD EVENT (COPING STRATEGY)	ADULT EVENT (DYSFUNCTIONAL PATTERN)
Example: A. Compulsive Self-Reliance 1 2 3 4 5 6 7 ⑧ 9 10	I refused any help with my homework from teachers, parents, or anybody. The result was that I often did poorly in school.	I insisted on doing my taxes myself and got audited. It took three years to get out of trouble with the IRS.
Example: B. Compulsive Compliance 1 2 3 4 5 6 ⑦ 8 9 10	I would rub Dad's back and sleep in his bed when I really hated doing it, but I feared I would be beaten.	I would sleep with Jim and give him a massage just to calm things down after he hit me.
1. Compulsive Helplessness 1 2 3 4 5 6 7 8 9 10		

DIMENSIONS OF COMPULSIVITY	CHILDHOOD EVENT (COPING STRATEGY)	ADULT EVENT (DYSFUNCTIONAL PATTERN)
2. Compulsive Focus on the Abuser 1 2 3 4 5 6 7 8 9 10		
3. Compulsive Self-Reliance 1 2 3 4 5 6 7 8 9 10		
4. Compulsive Caregiving 1 2 3 4 5 6 7 8 9 10		
5. Compulsive Care-Seeking 1 2 3 4 5 6 7 8 9 10		
6. Compulsive Rejection 1 2 3 4 5 6 7 8 9 10		
7. Compulsive Compliance 1 2 3 4 5 6 7 8 9 10		
8. Compulsive Identification with Others 1 2 3 4 5 6 7 8 9 10		
9. Compulsive Reality Distortion 1 2 3 4 5 6 7 8 9 10		
10. Compulsive Abuse Seeking 1 2 3 4 5 6 7 8 9 10		

What reactions do you have to seeing a profile of the areas of compulsive behavior in your relationships? Record these reactions in your journal. In scales you rated as eight, generate a list of examples from both childhood and adult life, so you are very clear as to how the patterns affect you.

TRAUMA BONDS AND CODEPENDENCY

Those readers who are familiar with addictions might wonder what the difference is between codependency and traumatic bonding. An additional risk could be that, out of denial, some might categorize a trauma bond as codependency.

The concept of codependency has been around for decades and was originally applied to those in a dysfunctional relationship with an addict. Codependency was the first model to understand what family members go through when living with addiction and trauma.

Building on this early model, we can now add what the attachment and trauma literature have discovered. As introduced earlier, this is the compulsive attachment model, which is based on the background of the variety of attachment issues resulting from our history with trauma and relationships. We now have more information and a more comprehensive model from which to understand the complexity of these relationships and what characteristics can be found embedded in families where there is trauma, addiction, and even mental illness. Not all who fit the compulsive attachment model are also in a trauma bond. At times, these are uniquely separate issues. This book's focus is primarily on traumatic bonding, the betrayal bond. For some, issues related to codependency, compulsive attachment, and traumatic bonding will all be present. For others, they will be separate. All of these issues can be heightened when abuse and fear are present.

PROBLEMATIC RELATIONSHIPS EXERCISE

As we have been discussing throughout the book, betrayal intensifies fear in relationships, which can lead to a trauma bond. Take a few minutes to complete this exercise as you examine the four most problematic relationships in your life.

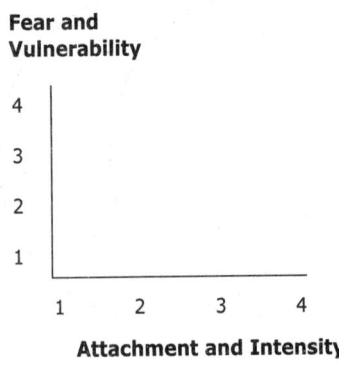

You can use this graph as a guide as you think about how fear and vulnerability can increase the feelings of attachment and intensity in the relationship.

Think of the four most problematic relationships that you have had in your life and answer these questions:

1. How much fear was there present in that relationship?
2. How vulnerable did you feel? (Feeling as though you could not leave due to financial issues, children, etc., feeling that you owed the person, feeling that they would self-destruct if you left, etc.)
3. What was the level of intensity in the relationship?
4. How compulsively attached would you say that you were?

For most people, the most problematic relationships are also those for which there is a trauma bond present forged through fear, intensity, and betrayal. As you reflect on these relationships, you might see a pattern of compulsive attachment.

Figure 5.3. Abuse and Addiction Populations

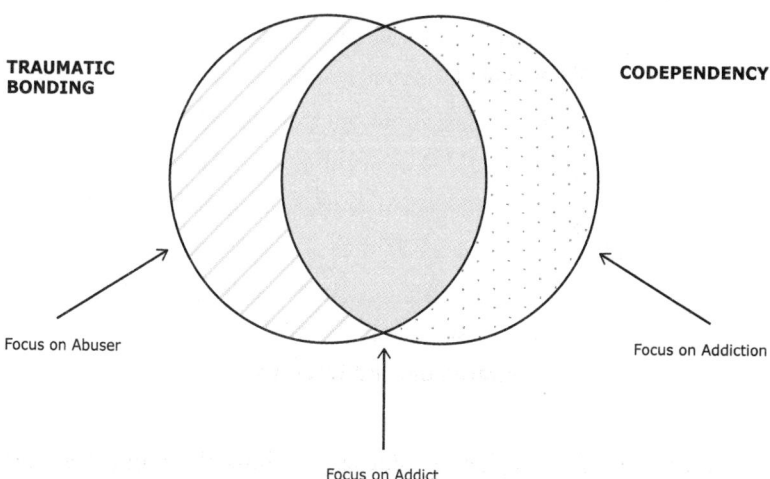

Figure 5.3 illustrates a way to look at two overlapping populations. One population focuses on the abuser. The other obsesses on the addiction. The two come together when the addict is also an abusive perpetrator. The overlap is extremely large, probably involving most of both populations. It is very important for codependents to understand the elements of trauma bonding. It is also critical for persons struggling with a traumatic bond to understand the nature of codependency. There is a rich set of resources and an extensive set of support groups that can help sort through denial and help manage reactive responses. Many survivors who have trouble with trauma bonding are addicts themselves. They can also participate in groups appropriate to the addictions they have.

THE TRANSITION FROM ANGER TO PAIN

Anger liberates the truth. But for many, true anger comes grudgingly. The loyalty rules still hold. You can ruin your life, and your abuser will shake his head in resignation. He will lock himself in a fortress of righteousness and denial, keeping at bay any realization of the role his abuse played in your life. Appropriate anger on the part of the victim can break through this denial and start a significant change process.

Yet there are all those rules about not upsetting people. "Children are to be seen and not heard." "If you cannot say something nice, don't say anything at all." Plus, there are all those sayings told to children to cajole them out of being upset: "Your face will freeze like that." "You are going to step on your lower lip and turn yourself inside out." Then there are family rules such as "We keep our business in the family," which means "You better never tell anyone what happened."

The worst, however, are the rules of terror and betrayal. The worst betrayal is to let people know what happened. A parent might say, "If you talk about this, they will take me away."

If you are a kid and already feel responsible for the abuse, this threat goes to your core: "What will happen to me if my parent is gone?" The most effective rules against anger are based in terror. Children know that to speak could mean a serious beating or even death. When you live with someone dangerous, you learn to keep the waters smooth. Thus there exists a web of rules against anger and a deep, almost preverbal, primitive fear of holding an abuser accountable.

Most victims need help expressing their anger. Therapists, therapy groups, and support groups can help immensely in that process. You can write letters that may or may not be sent, or talk to an empty chair. These are two ways you can reexperience those early scenes and share the feelings with others now that you could not share when you were a child.

If appropriate and safe, sharing the feelings with the abuser can often open up a path to healing and reconciliation. For those who are currently in a betrayal/trauma bond, anger becomes the source of resolve to change and to draw a line in the sand that says "no more."

One task that helps break through denial, overcome fear, and develop a fierce resolve is to examine the costs. Oftentimes for addicts, this is a core part of what is called a "first step." In the First Step of Alcoholics Anonymous and other related Twelve-Step programs, the addicts and codependents look at both powerlessness (efforts made to stop the behavior) and unmanageability (what my behavior has cost me). A similar inventory, the Compulsive Relationship Consequences Inventory, has been provided for you around traumatic bonding. Before completing this inventory, go back to the journal and paperwork you have already completed, including your work on seduction and betrayal, your conflict survey, and your Compulsive Relationship Self-Assessment. You will now be able to pull all that work together in terms of the impact these patterns have had on your life. Before proceeding to the remainder of the chapter, please complete the consequences inventory.

Compulsive Relationship Consequences Inventory

Every person who has experienced compulsive relationship behavior has had consequences because of that behavior.

You have probably had consequences. Sadly, people sometimes don't name what has happened to them as consequences, or they use their compulsive relationship behavior as a way to avoid feeling or admitting what has happened.

It is important that you look realistically at the consequences of your behavior in each of the categories listed. Put a check next to each of the things that you have experienced. In the space provided, record examples and dates if you can remember them.

Emotional Consequences: Examples and Dates

○   1. Thoughts or feelings about committing suicide _____
_____

○   2. Attempted suicide _____
_____

○   3. Homicidal thoughts or feelings _____
_____

○   4. Feelings of hopelessness and despair _____
_____

○   5. Failed efforts to control your relationship _____
_____

○   6. Feeling like you have two different lives—one public and one secret _____
_____

○   7. Depression, paranoia, or fear of going insane _____
_____

○   8. Loss of touch with reality _____
_____

○   9. Loss of self-esteem _____
_____

○ 10. Loss of life goals _____
_____

○ 11. Acting against your own values and beliefs _____
_____

○ 12. Strong feelings of guilt and shame _____
_____

○ 13. Strong feelings of isolation and loneliness _____
_____

○ 14. Strong fears for your future _____

_____

○ 15. Emotional exhaustion _____

_____

○ 16. Other emotional consequences _____

_____

Physical Consequences

○ 1. Continuation of relationship despite the risk to your health

_____

○ 2. Extreme weight loss or gain _____

_____

○ 3. Physical problems (ulcers, high blood pressure, etc.) _____

_____

○ 4. Physical injury or abuse by others _____

_____

○ 5. Involvement in potentially risky or dangerous situations __

_____

○ 6. Vehicle accidents (automobile, motorcycle, bicycle) _____

_____

○ 7. Injury to yourself from your relationship _____

_____

○ 8. Sleep disturbances (not enough sleep, too much sleep) ____

_____

○ 9. Physical exhaustion _____

_____

○ 10. Other physical consequences related to your sexual behavior such as venereal disease, HIV/AIDS, bleeding, etc.

_____

Spiritual Consequences

○ 1. Feelings of spiritual emptiness _____

_____

○ 2. Feeling disconnected from yourself and the world _____

_____

○ 3. Feeling abandoned by God or your Higher Power _____

_____

○ 4. Anger at God or your Higher Power _____

_____

○ 5. Loss of faith in anything spiritual _____

_____

○ 6. Other spiritual consequences _____

_____

Consequences Related to Family

○ 1. Risking the loss of partner or spouse _____

_____

○ 2. Loss of partner or spouse _____

_____

○ 3. Increase in marital or relationship problems _____

_____

○ 4. Jeopardizing the well-being of your family _____

_____

○ 5. Loss of family's or partner's respect _____

_____

○ 6. Increase in problems with your children _____

_____

○ 7. Loss of your family of origin _____

_____

○ 8. Other family or partnership consequences _____

_____

Career and Educational Consequences

○ 1. Decrease in productivity in work _____

_____

○ 2. Demotion at work _____

_____

○ 3. Loss of coworkers' respect _____

_____

○ 4. Loss of the opportunity to work in the career of your choice

_____

○ 5. Failing grades in school _____

_____

○ 6. Loss of educational opportunities _____

_____

○ 7. Loss of business _____

_____

○ 8. Forced to change careers _____

_____

○ 9. Not working to your level of capability _____

_____

○ 10. Termination from job _____

_____

○ 11. Other career or educational consequences: specify _____

_____

Other Consequences

○ 1. Loss of important friendships _____

_____

○ 2. Loss of interest in hobbies or activities _____

_____

○ 3. Few or no friends because of relationship problems _____

_____

○ 4. Financial problems _____

_____

○ 5. Illegal activities (arrests or near-arrests) _____

_____

○ 6. Court or legal involvement _____

_____

○ 7. Lawsuits _____

_____

○ 8. Prison or workhouse _____

_____

○ 9. Stealing or embezzling to support behavior _____

_____

○ 10. Specify other consequences _____

_____

As you think about the consequences you checked as you went through the last few pages, what new insights or thoughts came to you? Please record these in your journal. Record how it feels to know what the costs have been to you.

As you worked through the consequences inventory, you should have noticed a variety of emotions. You certainly should have felt anger, maybe enough anger that you determined to change your patterns.

Your anger can fortify you to take the actions you must to care for yourself. It will also empower you to overthrow the old rules of secrecy and betrayal and to be honest about what you see and feel. No more will you disbelieve the obvious and believe the improbable. In the future, your anger will make you intolerant of being exploited and used. Not only will it be okay to upset people, you may even find occasions when you *enjoy* upsetting them.

As you went through the various consequences you experienced, you also probably had feelings of sadness, loss, and regret. That means you started accessing the pain stage of your grieving process. Knowing your own hurt and expressing that hurt is critical to healing. First of all, the sadness moves the survivor beyond the anger. Sometimes those in trauma bonds hold on to the anger as a way to stay connected to the abuser. This anger stems from blame and rage and prevents the survivor from experiencing her pain. An example would be the divorcing couple who start off expressing their anger and telling the stories about why they are angry to all their friends. One partner, however, moves beyond that point and realizes that he, too, has significant responsibility for what happened. This partner learns from his experience and goes on to reconstruct his life. He even remarries. The other partner stays stuck in the anger and nine years later is still telling the blaming stories to anyone who will still listen. That partner has used anger to stay in the relationship and is probably too scared to accept the pain of the loss.

Let's return to Tom and Barbara's situation. Tom's therapist, Sam, explained to Tom how stuck anger could be a type of *negative intimacy* in a trauma bond. By blaming the other for the problems in his life, the blaming partner can prevent the actual acceptance of the loss of the relationship or the losses caused by the relationship. *Healthy anger* expresses limitations—i.e., what is acceptable and what is not. *Blaming anger* recycles the history of betrayal and all the intense feelings that are part of a trauma bond. It is a negative way to keep the old person around.

Sam gave Tom an assignment to help him. First, he asked Tom to make a list of people Tom had hurt in this process. Further, he wanted Tom to add to that list all those people whom Tom and Barbara had hurt together. When Tom was finished, he was stunned to realize that his responsibilities went far beyond just his compulsive relationship patterns. To admit, for example, that he had been compliant in things he did not want to do was not so bad. However, to admit that he also had been vengeful and victimizing to Barbara was extremely difficult to own, even with Sam's help. After all, Barbara was the one with the outrageous behavior. Tom had to admit that he had done dishonorable things as well and that the craziness he and Barbara created together had hurt many whom he loved deeply. Sam pushed Tom to understand his responsibility so he could understand his own role in his losses. (You may wish to make a list similar to Tom's in your journal. Record what feelings you have about harm you may have caused.)

To finally grieve means to accept that your life did not turn out the way you wanted, the way you deserved, or the way it should have. There is an existential reality we all must face that is best captured in the serenity prayer that is the heart of most Twelve-Step programs: *God, grant me the serenity to accept the things I cannot change, the courage to change the things I can, and the wisdom to know the difference.* Those who are trauma-bonded have to accept not only the reality of compulsive relationships but also the accumulated losses in their lives going back to whatever created the original working model for relationships.

Viktor Frankl observed that those who survived the concentration camps often had one essential characteristic: They were able to transform suffering into meaning. I believe survivors of any form of abuse have that essential task. Out of the indescribable pain comes clarity of belief and depth of purpose. They become people of substance, with no more tolerance for living in the lie. They know evil for what it is and arm themselves with rituals that keep the meaning close to their hearts. They have a high regard for that which connects and reject all that divides or hides. Inescapable pain creates enduring honesty and accountability. To take the position that "I am the way I am because of how my family was or because of how they abused me" is to miss the point. You are a participant. As with any addiction, you are powerless, but you have a responsibility to do something about it now. You are responsible for your behavior.

Consider the Greek story of Orestes. Atreus, the grandfather of Orestes, challenged the gods—always a mistake for the Greeks—and as a result his whole family was cursed. Atreus's daughter-in-law, Clytemnestra, murdered her husband, Agamemnon. This act trapped her son, Orestes, between the highest priority of the Greek code of honor, avenging his father's death, and the worst crime of the Greeks, killing his mother. In the end, he murdered his mother. His punishment was to be pursued by the Furies, frightening harpies who tormented him. Orestes was bound to lose either way. He was powerless.

Even though the gods were willing to excuse his solution, Orestes did not duck responsibility. At his trial, he pointed out to all the gods assembled that it was he, no one else, who killed his mother. All he asked for was to be allowed to do something to get the curse lifted. The gods, moved by his integrity, gave him tasks to perform. When Orestes completed those tasks, the Furies were transformed into the Eumenides, the three sources of wisdom. M. Scott Peck wrote about Orestes's non-victim stance:

> Being an inevitable result of the original curse upon the House of Atreus, the Furies also symbolize the fact that mental illness is a family affair, created in one by one's parents and grandparents as the sins of

the father are visited upon the children. But Orestes did not blame his family—his parents or his grandfather—as he well might have. Nor did he blame the gods or "fate." Instead he accepted his condition as one of his own making and undertook the effort to heal it. It was a lengthy process, just as most therapy tends to be lengthy. But as a result he was healed, and through this healing process of his own effort, the very things that had once caused him agony became the same things that brought him wisdom.[6]

Like Orestes, survivors cannot afford to blame others. The path of awareness brings them ultimately to acceptance of what their reality is, including their own part, and, like Orestes, they have to take action—which is the focus of our next chapter.

What Is the Path of Action?

> WE MUST ALWAYS HOLD TRUTH,
> AS WE CAN BEST DETERMINE IT, TO BE MORE
> IMPORTANT, MORE VITAL TO OUR SELF-INTEREST
> THAN OUR COMFORT. CONVERSELY, WE MOST
> ALWAYS CONSIDER OUR PERSONAL DISCOMFORT
> RELATIVELY UNIMPORTANT, AND INDEED,
> EVEN WELCOME IT IN THE SERVICE FOR TRUTH.
> MENTAL HEALTH IS AN ONGOING PROCESS OF
> DEDICATION TO REALITY AT ALL COSTS.
>
> —M. Scott Peck, *The Road Less Traveled*

Awareness is the first step toward action, and when we spend time reflecting, we can change our brains' capacity to heal and change. As we understand the brain to have plasticity, the ability to change and adapt, research is now showing that mindfulness actually has the ability to change the brain. This focus and paying attention, promotes neural plasticity, the change of neural connections in response to experience. How encouraging to know that we have the power to help our brains grow, heal, and become more resilient and adaptable!

As we are more attuned to ourselves, we are able to take responsibility as we are more aware and attuned to those around us. Within the scope of recovery, studies have shown the benefits of mindful awareness include improving the capacity to regulate emotion, to combat emotional dysfunction, to improve patterns of thinking, and to reduce negative mind-sets (p.22). Beyond that we improve our body's response to stress, improve immune function, and improve interpersonal relationships. Jon Kabat-Zinn has devoted his life to bringing mindfulness into the mainstream of modern medicine and defines mindfulness as, "the awareness that emerges through paying attention on purpose, in the present moment, and non-judgmentally to the unfolding of experience moment by moment" (p. 25). These practices help develop ways to deepen our understanding of how the mind functions.

You are learning to come to your own aid as you learn to be present and in reality. You can learn new emotional first aid tools and how to be in relationship with yourself and others in new ways. These new ways of interacting with ourselves and the world bring about healthy brain development and healing. Each new experience offers this hope.

> Experience involves the activation of neurons. In this manner, experience shapes the function of neural activity in the moment, and can potentially shape the continually changing structure of the brain throughout the life span. Recent findings from neuroscience in fact suggest that the brain remains plastic, or open to continuing influences from the environment, throughout life. This plasticity may involve not only the creation of new synaptic connections among neurons, but also the growth of new neurons across the life span. The capacity for attachment classifications to change beyond the early years of life may be related to this ability of the brain to continue to grow in response to experiences across our lifetimes (Siegel 2001).

A significant part of healing involves a process called integration. One powerful part of integration is forming a coherent narrative of our lives, understanding where we have been and what has happened in our lives as part of our journey and as part of making us who we are today. This process is often referred to as narrative integration, and it is central to healing and learning to relate differently in our lives and to establishing healthy relationship patterns. In his book *Mindsight* (2010), Dr. Daniel Siegel discusses narrative integration as part of the overall process of integration, which involves nine processes toward a healthier and more integrated self and how we are able to heal from trauma. As you have been working through the exercises in this book and reflecting on your story, this is the process you have been engaging in. You are integrating these experiences into your current story and using these experiences to grow and change.

In her book *The Gifts of Imperfection,* Dr. Brené Brown discusses the process of owning our stories and how it is one of the bravest things that we will ever do. She also shares how important it is to love ourselves as we go through the process. This book is designed to help navigate this process of narrative integration, owning our stories, and ultimately having the courage to write new and beautifully different chapters.

"So, do you want it to be different?" John asked his workshop class. Participants in the weeklong workshop on trauma bonding all vigorously nodded their heads. "If you do, you will have to give up compulsive rescuing!" John responded. As John gave examples about rescuing behavior—or, as he described it, "pathological giving"—various participants groaned or laughed in self-recognition. John talked about identifying specific behaviors as "bottom line" behaviors. These are behaviors you refuse to do any more. Instead of repeating these behaviors, you develop other coping strategies that are healthy.

A teacher from northern New York asked, "What is the difference between healthy nurturing or care and coming to the rescue? I would like to think I am a caring person." John responded by pointing out that if you attempt to help a butterfly break out of its cocoon, it may die. The butterfly needs the struggle to be strong. You can be supportive without doing for others what they can do for themselves. As a general rule, it is best to help only when help is truly needed. John added that from a trauma perspective, it is insane to help someone else exploit you. From an addiction perspective, rescuing may only add to the intensity and the insanity of old, addictive cycles of behavior.

To illustrate his point, John asked the participants to list all the payoffs to being a savior or hero. Then he asked them to list the actual costs and liabilities. He pulled the group together and made a common list of participants' payoffs and liabilities. Here are some of the comments on their payoff list:

> "I can avoid conflict by rescuing them so they will not be upset with me."
>
> "I want people to appreciate me and my efforts."

"I protect my own childhood wounds by overcompensating so others will not feel disappointed or hurt as I did. I end up blocking reality from them."

"I have a reservoir of resentment that excuses my sexual acting out."

"Feeling obligated keeps my shame intact and powerful because I am overextended and behind all the time."

"Rescuing supports my hero role in the family."

"Turmoil prevents success, which is my life script."

"Overextension by meeting the needs of others creates great martyrdom stories."

"Rescuing creates a one-up position from which I can avoid my feelings and intimacy."

"It is one more way for me to obsess about him/her."

Some of the comments from the liability list are:

"I lost my freedom and ended up owned by those saved."

"I wanted to prevent him/her from leaving but my helping became so much it forced him/her to leave."

"It never works and usually backfires."

"I set myself up to be exploited—and then was upset because I felt taken for granted."

"I lost money I could ill afford."

"Real issues were not addressed, and I could keep drinking."

"Keeps me in denial—even when it is dangerous for me."

"Feeling important falsely bolstered my sense of worth. Boy, was I surprised when the truth came out!"

John pushed the group to look at the implications of their work. He asked them to write out specific behaviors to abstain from, strategies needed to avoid those behaviors, and guidelines for positive caring behaviors. These activities were part of creating a recovery plan to overcome a pattern of traumatic bonding.

In creating this plan, a central decision must be made that depends upon the recovering person's current life circumstances. One path of action is for people who have been in exploitive relationships and have no reason to be in any further contact with the people who hurt them. Here the goal is not to repeat any of the old compulsive patterns in future relationships.

Another path of action is for those who have been in exploitive relationships and must have limited contact with the abusing person. Examples would be when there is involvement in ongoing legal action, when there are children common to both parties, or when there are professional duties that require periodic contact.

Finally, a path exists for both parties in a traumatic bond to fundamentally reconstruct the relationship in a healthy way. This will take an extraordinary amount of work, but in some cases it can be done. Usually these are marital or family relationships, but it can happen in professional settings as well.

All survivors should know all three paths since, more than likely, they will at some point in their lives need the skills involved in each.

The Path of No Contact

Sue fell in love with her counselor in treatment. She declared her love for him in a counseling session, and he admitted that he was both attracted to her and had feelings for her. At the time she was convinced that their meeting was a "cosmic" happening. With new doors opening up to her in sobriety, she felt sure that meeting him at that time was not an accident but destiny. After she left treatment, they were sexual for several months. She was in ecstasy. She had never met a man like him—so gentle, kind, handsome, and competent. There were some problems, however. He was married, with two small children, but his wife was a shrew. Then there was an intervention, and it turned out that he had other relationships—or women who thought they had a relationship with him. Sue was willing to stand by him through that, but then he cut off the relationship when she said that he had been inappropriate.

Sue was furious. In her heart she knew that if they could have just set aside the professional rules, rules that were so arbitrary, he would have married her. After all, they did not have sex while she was in treatment; they waited until she left the hospital. Sue believed she had been cheated of the one man with whom she could have been happy.

Sue persisted in this belief. Two different therapists tried to help her understand that she had been exploited. She quit both of them. She then accepted a job offer to move to Baltimore. It was there she met a therapist named Judy. It took almost two years of therapy before Sue fully accepted that what happened to her was exploitive.

One of the first things Judy insisted Sue do was join a Twelve-Step program to continue her recovery on her own addiction. Eventually, she also joined a therapy group of men and women. It was only later that she understood how important those relationships were to help see her through rough times. She discovered the most fundamental rule about trauma bonds: *Trauma bonds can be disrupted when healthy bonds are available.* It was a very powerful night when Sue gave some feedback to someone in one of her groups, telling her she was being exploited by the man she had been seeing.

So often in therapy we can see in others the issues we wrestle with in ourselves. Her therapist then asked Sue to explain how that felt to the other woman. While explaining, it became clear to Sue how the affair with her counselor was part of a life pattern; she had a history of one "cosmic" relationship after another. Each was characterized by an "impossible situation" and an exploitation of power and intimacy. Sue was also an incest victim, an impossible situation involving the exploitation of power and intimacy. Her support network became the emotional safety net she needed when she could finally admit the truth to herself.

Finding supportive, healthy relationships is the foundation of recovery. Usually this means establishing a relationship with a competent therapist. As with Sue, it often means participating in some form of therapy group. It means also participating in support groups that fit your circumstances. Support is the ground floor of any recovery effort. See the appendix for an extensive listing of support groups and resources for change.

One of the principal functions of a support network is to tell your story to a group of people who will understand what happened to you because it also happened to them. One of the few core strategies proven to help prisoners who have been tortured and sexually molested is the *testimony method*. Torture, especially sexual torture, is designed to break down a prisoner's identity. Political refugees, prisoners, inmates of concentration camps, and slaves have endured this process throughout history and down to the present day. People who specialize in helping these survivors with their trauma have found in recent years that the first part of recovery is to give a detailed description of what happened to a sympathetic audience. For this testimony to work it must go through a *reframing*. This reframing puts an individual story in a larger context, enabling other prisoners or captives to see their own story as part of a greater struggle.[1] By telling their story, they are "reunited" with other humans who care for them. It now means something to survive. That sense of survival begins a process of restoration to the human community. Healthy bonding can now occur.

Alcoholics Anonymous started on that principle. Carl Jung had written Bill W. and told him that change would probably not occur if alcoholics did not pass on their story. This principle has proved effective in an almost uncountable number of contexts and has shaped our culture in a significant way. Whether you are an incest survivor, a domestic abuse victim, or a victim of clergy sexual misconduct, there is a place to tell your story, receive support, and make meaning out of your experience.

The other contribution support networks can make concerns boundary development. Supportive people in the survivor's life can help the survivor draw a line in the sand that says: "I will not tolerate this any more in my life." With that limit set, the survivor begins reclaiming her- or himself.

Boundary development is critical for those who grow up unable to tell if abuse is present or not. *Figuring out what you do not want forces you to determine what you do want.* That means you have to know who you are and then value yourself enough to mean what you say. An old Buddhist saying suggests that to say "no" means you have to know what "yes" is. That process forms a sense of self—which is precisely what was lost in the trauma bond.

In Sue's case, and on her therapist's advice, she stopped dating altogether for a period. She needed time out from the roller coaster of instant and "cosmic" relationships. Understanding the cycle she was in and the role of victimization she played was transformative in her life. When she started dating again, she worked very hard to keep her boundaries: the types of men she saw, when and under what circumstances she saw them, and what she expected of them. Were they honorable men or "impossible situations"? At times she missed the intensity, but for the most part she was amazed at how much easier things were for her.

For trauma bonds to be disrupted, the survivor must be able to identify the cycles of abuse and the roles of victim, victimizer, and rescuer. This is how the relationship system and the roles of the survivor in that system can change. This will create a compassion for the self in much the way you may have experienced it when writing your story in the third person earlier in this book (see Chapter 5). That exercise created a "psychological distance" so that you could see yourself. This is similar to the way Sue could see the problem in another woman in her group easier than in herself. When Sue's perception shifted, she had a better sense of what it meant to "care *for* herself" and to take "care *of* herself."

Most therapists are trained to help the identification process with the use of metaphor. Metaphors become part of the story. Like medicine men and medicine women of earlier times, healers can sometimes help people on the journey more through a story or symbol that represents what needs to be done.[2] An extremely helpful example of a healing metaphor used within a trauma context is the concept of *remodeling*. When remodeling a home, you restructure it so it is more functional, more livable, and more attractive. You work also to preserve those parts that have special character and meaning. Therapist Rochelle Scheela has broken the remodeling metaphor down into six specific areas:[3]

falling apart: final acceptance that the home can no longer be sustained the way it is and that it has to be remodeled

taking on the remodeling: decision to personally do the work because the task is now unavoidable

tearing out: assessing the damage, understanding the original design, and sorting out what is salvageable

rebuilding: replacing damaged parts and adding new, more functional parts, but making them part of a seamless, attractive design

doing the upkeep: maintaining the whole home so it does not return to disrepair

moving on: decision to move on to more remodeling projects

Anyone who has remodeled knows that these steps seldom happen in an orderly fashion. A survivor may be rebuilding one area and tearing down another. Also, life is unpredictable enough that some more falling apart might occur.

For Sue, the actual remodeling took almost five years. In looking back, she wrote off the first two years as being in denial. To put it in remodeling language, she did not take on the task even though people around her were willing to help. At the end, however, she could hardly believe how different her life was. She was productive, focused, and in a happy relationship. She now joked about the days of "impossible situations" and "cosmic relationships." Getting to that point involved both tearing down and rebuilding. On the tearing down side, Sue had to abandon relationship rules that went back to childhood. Judy, her therapist, helped her with strategies for desensitizing around some of her original trauma with her father. Therapists today have access to technology, such as *eye movement desensitization*, which can help lower reactivity time. For Sue, the result was that she no longer had to manage her feelings by creating the exhilaration of "cosmic" connections.

Judy also insisted that Sue create a recovery plan. Similar to what participants did in the workshop described at the beginning of the chapter, Sue had to be very specific about relationship behaviors in which she would and would not engage. A recovery plan consists of three parts. *First, you must identify bottom-line behaviors.* These are the behaviors you simply do not do. For Sue, a bottom-line behavior was not to date anyone who had authority over her. *Second, you must create a boundaries list.* These are limits to be observed around activities and relationships that would put you at risk or that do not add to your recovery. For Sue, this meant that she agreed not to be sexual with anyone with whom she did not have a relationship for at least six months. If she decided she wanted to be sexual, she would talk to her therapy group before taking action. Sue understood that this was not punitive, but rather a way for her to lower potential intensity and preserve her perspective. *Finally, a recovery plan asks what kind of behavior you want in a relationship.* How will you know if a relationship is successful? One of Sue's criteria was "waking up each day feeling unafraid and happy."

At the conclusion of this chapter, there is a model recovery plan. Before exploring that, however, there are two other paths that need to be understood: first, the path of limited contact; second, the path of full relationship.

THE PATH OF LIMITED CONTACT

Sometimes there is no escaping contact. Children can be involved. There is a court process to complete. Both parties work in the same profession in the same city. You own property or businesses together. Finances have to be settled. Something will exist that requires you to see the person who has been problematic for you. The path of limited contact may be your only option.

Such was the case with Catherine, who left her husband, Fred, after thirteen years of marriage. They had three children together, ages thirteen, eleven, and three. Catherine was Fred's second wife. Fred was an attorney, and Catherine had been his secretary. They had an affair while Fred was still married. Catherine got pregnant, and Fred left his first wife, with whom he had two children.

There were warning signs for Catherine. She will always remember the night Fred's ex-wife dropped off the kids, looked at Catherine, and said, "You are in a world of trouble." When Catherine asked what she meant, the woman actually looked at her with some compassion and said, "I was his first secretary" and walked out the door.

There were many scary things about Fred. He was one of the best litigators around. He was known for ruthlessly defending his clients and liked being a "hired gun." He was incredibly smart and could anticipate his opponents' moves. He was a large man, over six foot four, and prone to raging. He felt his outbursts were okay, he would joke, as long as he did not "leave any marks." He was rough with sex and loved bondage scenes. He was intimidating, ruthless, handsome, smooth, and, as Catherine was to learn, totally without scruples.

The early years of the marriage were hectic. Two children right away kept Catherine very busy. As the years went on, Fred's drinking increased, and there was episodic violence. It became clear that sex and violence were fused for Fred. Their youngest child was actually a product of Fred's rape of Catherine. If that were not enough, during that second pregnancy Catherine discovered the following in the space of one week: Fred was using prostitutes for sadomasochistic sex; he had been involved with her very own sister; and he had been guilty of jury tampering and witness bribery for a client with underworld connections. She resolved to leave.

The nightmare of leaving made the marriage look like a holiday. She suddenly became Fred's "opponent." She faced a legal barrage. Every day there was another legal maneuver. Depositions, accusations, and motions became a way of life. There was conflict over custody. Arrogant, punitive faxes about problems he had with her parenting were routine. He had her own family almost convinced that she had an emotional problem. When he urged treatment, she started making up lies about him. That actually worked until her sister collapsed under the strain and owned up to her affair with him. Since Catherine was the "hero" in a family that had problems of alcoholism and violence, issues became layered upon issues. Her abusive father was absolutely on Fred's side until Catherine's sister came forward with her affair. There was one more ingredient: Fred's firm was representing Catherine's father's company in an extremely convoluted court case that, if it failed, would leave her parents impoverished at retirement.

Catherine felt like she was in a battle zone. The worst part was that Fred was good at not "leaving any marks," so she could not get court protection or prove anything. During the whole settlement period, she had to see Fred in court and had to deal with the children seeing Fred. Being in a group and having a therapist was lifesaving for Catherine. Her therapist explained how in trauma bonding the roles are so strong, you have to have help from people who care about you and who know the real situation. They can help debrief or *de-role* the victim from the intensity of the bond. She used the concept of *bookending*. For example, before a deposition she had to meet with two members of her group and have a therapy appointment scheduled immediately after. Catherine learned never to have scheduled contact with Fred without first getting a stress inoculation of support. She would literally get coaching from people in her network about what to expect and how to handle it. She also never talked to Fred without immediately calling someone to de-role.

With her therapist's and attorney's help, she established limits with Fred. These boundaries improved things, but Fred was very skillful at breaching those boundaries by creating ambushes. Catherine had to learn what many victims have found out: Boundaries are great when you can plan things out, but often you will need strategies to use "in the moment." This is where Catherine learned about the *stillness*. This exercise is based on a story about the Royal Navy. Sailors are instructed that whenever they hear a specific whistle it means something has happened so serious that everyone on the ship is in immediate danger. When that whistle blows, the sailors stop what they are doing, since they have only moments, look at what resources are around them, and do the right thing. It is called the *stillness*. For Catherine, this meant that when Fred created a situation that demanded an immediate response from her and tried to stampede her into a decision she might later regret, she had a right to the stillness. She would stop, center herself, and see what her options were before responding. She learned to tell Fred that she needed ten minutes to respond, ten minutes that would give her time to think or make a phone call. The metaphor of the still-ness was a gift to Catherine. She grew to appreciate a window of time, even if only seconds, so she could do the right thing.

At her therapist's recommendation, Catherine went to a residential facility for an intensive workshop intended for abuse survivors who struggled with addictive issues. It was a gift in many ways. For the first time it became clear to her how her working model for relation-ships was in part responsible for her involvement with Fred. Catherine started to make all kinds of connections about what happened in her original family and in her life with Fred. For example, it was no surprise that her father chose Fred's firm for his company. They had similar values and ways of operating.

In the workshop she also learned about the concept of *carried shame*. This means that the victim feels shameful and the perpetra-tor shameless.[4] Victims are set up in the exploitive system to devalue themselves as a defense against examining what the abuser is doing. They feel at fault because they are told they are responsible for what-ever problems there are. As long as they feel at fault, the abuser is in the "one-up" position.

Catherine learned a wonderful metaphor to help with the shame issue. Her instructor compared having boundaries to having a zipper.[5] Most people can control their zippers from the inside. If someone asks them for information they do not want to give, they simply do not give it. If asked to do something that feels uncomfortable, they say no. If told they are bad or responsible for something they did not do, they figure those comments are really about the other person, not them. People who have been tyrannized by terror and invaded often have the zippers on the outside. Anyone can access them. They simply unzip. Victims can be asked information they do not wish to reveal, and they reveal it. They commit to things they do not want to do. They feel responsible when they have done nothing. They can easily be invaded sexually, physically, and emotionally. The challenge for the victim is to get the zipper firmly back inside. This requires more than knowing when someone is being abusive. It means being able to say no without shame.

After the workshop, Catherine discovered how helpful it was to be away from all the stress so she could focus on the issues. Her therapist observed that the core to recovery was the ability to psychologically distance from the intensity. Catherine would not always be able to get away, so she needed to develop strategies to help her de-escalate the intensity on a daily basis. Her therapist now taught her the concept of *doing business*. She asked Catherine what she would do if she ordered an item that had to be picked up later. Catherine said she would call, find out when it would be ready, and then pick it up. Her therapist then asked if this would be an emotional event. Catherine, seeing where this was heading, laughed and said no. Her therapist then asked what would happen if she needed to know when the kids would be ready to be picked up from Fred's house. Catherine got the point and responded, "It's an international incident." Then her therapist invited Catherine to role-play such a call with Catherine being Fred and the therapist playing Catherine. It went like this:

> **Catherine:** What time will the children be ready?
>
> **Fred:** So we are going to try to be grown up enough to be on time!
>
> **Catherine:** All I need to know is what time they will be ready.
>
> **Fred:** As if you really cared about them.
>
> **Catherine:** I need the time, Fred.
>
> **Fred:** What are you going to do about the interrogatories I sent you?
>
> **Catherine:** My attorney will respond to that. What time will the children be ready?
>
> **Fred:** Three o'clock.
>
> **Catherine:** Three o'clock. Thank you.

All Catherine needed was the time. The rest was all intensity. Fred was expert at provoking responses. Catherine learned she could be expert at focusing on the "business" at hand. Or as she said to the therapist, "getting my zipper turned around."

Changing the abusive system requires a reframing of the interactions in the system. A therapist will ask a victim to revisit a specific scene of abuse. As the victim talks, the therapist becomes a coach, helping the victim understand the reactions that occur. The therapist then teaches the client how to manage her feelings more effectively. Clinicians call this *cognitive restructuring*, which means the victim creates a new map or working model for the relationship. Reframing is one of the strategies most often used. Reframing means you create a new way of looking at the interaction. For example: "When your father says those sarcastic statements and says he is only joking, he is wrong. He is being cruel and mean-spirited. He is trying to connect with you but doing it in a horrible way." Another example for Catherine was the conception of her third child. Her therapist insisted that Catherine start referring to the event as a sexual assault. The shift within Catherine with that reframe was astounding because she knew it was true.

Catherine's recovery plan included bottom-line behaviors for both Fred and her father. With Fred she would no longer share any emotions or friendly talk. They were designed to drag her back into the system. With her father she would no longer tolerate his sarcastic remarks, even by ignoring them. As one of her boundaries, Catherine decided to have her attorney address Fred on anything legal or financial. She personally would no longer respond. Among her relationship goals, Catherine put down that she would know she was in a good relationship when she could fully be herself. She felt she had lived in fear for so long that she had forgotten what it was like to be with people without being on guard.

FULL RELATIONSHIP

For many, the restoration of exploitive relationships would be impossible or pointless. If the clergyman who abused you was now in prison, it would be difficult, insane, and futile to seek him out for spiritual care. But what if it is your father who is in prison for sexual abuse of his children? Or what if it is your husband, with whom you've had five children, who is making extraordinary efforts to change his life? What criteria would you use? Here are some suggestions. First, if addictions are involved, they must be addressed. That means the abuser must willingly go to treatment and commit to a program of recovery. Second, the victim must be in therapy and in a support program for recovery. All members of the support network must be informed as to what is happening. Third, there must be a period of separation so that the victim can experience living independent of the abuser and can observe how the abuser lives when the two are separated. If those conditions are met, add these criteria:

a clear track record of non-abusing behavior

a verifiable commitment to therapy and Twelve-Step group attendance

a coordinated effort of joint therapy involving both partners

an acceptance by the abuser of the consequences of his actions

a clear and earnest effort to make amends to all who have been hurt

an agreement for zero tolerance of old behavior

Let's use the circle analogy once again. Can both parties remain in the circle of intimacy at the same time? For the victim, how does it feel to be in the other's presence?

There is an old Al-Anon piece of wisdom that says "Nothing major the first year." That means that after a year of recovery, things will look extremely different. Doing anything that is not reversible may be premature. Also, the victim has much to do to work on his or her own healing. Once that foundation is there, a new relationship might be negotiated. Remember, the principal problem trauma victims have is reactivity. During the initial phases of recovery, monitoring your reactivity to others is very important. The focus should remain on you, not the abuser.

Consider the story of Marge. She was married to a Protestant minister named Brad who served as pastor to 8,000 people in the wealthiest suburb in the city. He worked upwards of ninety hours a week. When the tension was high he would, on occasion, rage at Marge and the kids. Sometimes he was extremely punitive with the children, exacting consequences that far outweighed whatever the child had done. Sometimes in his anger he struck Marge, which she found shattering. Then he would make up to her and rationalize his angry outbreaks as a result of working too hard and trying to serve the Lord. She was proud of his work, but she also was lonely raising their children. And as time went on, she was progressively more scared. As a minister's wife, she knew that to get help in their denomination might mean the end of Brad's career. What would they do then? So she kept quiet, hiding behind the veneer of "everything is good in the minister's family."

The veneer fell off, however, when a friend called Marge and asked to meet with her. When they got together, the friend brought a woman who was called an advocate. The advocate worked in the bishop's office. They came to tell her that Brad had been having an affair with a parishioner. Brad had attempted to cut it off and the parishioner had gone to the bishop. Word spread quickly. Seven more women had come forward to the bishop. There was to be an intervention the next day. Before the intervention, they wanted to know if she knew about these women, how things were with her, and whether she would help them. Marge was stunned. She felt like a fool. On the other hand, this was the first time she felt she could tell anyone what life with Brad was like. She started sobbing as she told them about her pain.

Brad was admitted to an inpatient treatment facility for his sex addiction and cocaine abuse. Marge and the kids attended family week. They found out that Brad had a whole life none of them knew or could even guess at. To begin with, they had no idea about his cocaine use or that he took loose money donated on Sundays to support his drug habit. It was how he got himself through. His secret life was a fast life, a life enabled by wealthy parishioners, especially women.

Raised in a rigid farm family, Brad had been steadily and severely abused, both physically and sexually, since the age of five. The perpetrators of the abuse were farm hands. He had also experienced work abuse, working at least twelve hours a day every day he was not in school. Overwork and violence had long been part of his life.

After doing a family genogram in family week, everybody could see how the problems for both Marge and Brad went back for generations. Marge and the kids went to therapy when they returned from family week. Marge's therapist asked her to put a moratorium on deciding whether to divorce Brad or not. He had been sent by the church to an extended care facility. He remained there for eight months. When he returned, he found an apartment of his own. Marge was struck by how there was no pressure from Brad to move back in. It also became clear to her that he was committed to working on their relationship.

In fact, there was a lot about Brad that was different. He was patient and open with the kids. In family therapy he shared several stories in which he cried deeply in their presence. He clearly felt shame and remorse for what he had done. Marge was struck about how being with him now was like what it used to be when they were first together.

Brad also began taking the initiative in their relationship. He asked Marge to go a Twelve-Step couples retreat. Out of that retreat they joined a Recovering Couples Anonymous group, or RCA. It was in

RCA that Marge felt real healing begin for her and Brad. They met many couples who had been through similar dramas and who were committed to supportive relationships. They used the metaphor of the three-legged stool. The three legs represented "my recovery," "your recovery," and "our recovery as a couple."

On the retreat, the lead couple described relationships as a "blending of epics." Each couple had the task of blending families whose traditions and rules spanned many generations. If a family history was filled with trauma, addiction, and violence, it was virtually impossible not to repeat the sins of the previous generation. When the inevitable relationship crisis came, there was always the option to move on to another person. Yet if that were done, the process of blending would have to begin all over again. Better to face the issues with the person you are with and then see if the relationship works.

RCA couples were no strangers to the problem of intensity. One of the first things Brad and Marge had to do was to write a "fair fight" contract. If you care about someone, over time you will have conflict with them. But many couples never firmly establish how they will settle their issues. For Marge and Brad the impact was revolutionary. One of their rules was "no dramatic exits," which Brad would do often and Marge dreaded. Once he agreed to that, it freed her up to be honest with her issues. As a couple they learned that, as trauma survivors, they needed to contain their reactivity. And the "fair fight" contract helped them immensely.

Another RCA concept that was helpful was *couple shame.* Individuals have shame, and so do couples. Marge and Brad had a lot of shame about the public outcry over Brad's behavior. They were also profoundly embarrassed with their children about the chaos of their life. They recognized that both of them contributed to the problem and that they could get into deep despair about it. Fortunately, they had a wonderful sponsor couple who helped them not be so hard on themselves.

When Brad and Marge felt despairing, or without hope, they called their sponsor couple.

Conjoint couples therapy was also extremely helpful. They learned about intimacy and got help for when they had trouble negotiating the new rules for making decisions. The biggest lesson of all, however, was about blame. One of their therapists talked about the "no fault" system. They learned it was more important to find out how the problem happened than it was to blame each other for the problem. It was extraordinary progress when they could sit down and pinpoint the process that brought them to crisis and not be defensive or accusing. In fact, a relationship goal for each of them was to take responsibility for whatever they did that made things harder for the other.

They also negotiated boundaries. Marge did not want to talk about serious matters after nine o'clock at night. She was too tired by that time, and it was always counterproductive. Another bottom-line behavior for Marge was not to protect Brad from the consequences of his behavior. She learned to stay out of the way completely.

Brad and Marge had a number of tough years. Brad could not work as a minister, and money was extremely tight. Marge went back to school to study theology, which was very demanding. But they worked on their therapy and remained very active in their own recovery groups as well as RCA. Their children matured, went to college. and started families of their own.

Eleven years after the intervention on Brad, he was accepted back into active ministry. Marge finished theology school and was ordained into the ministry as well. For her, it was the realization of a forbidden dream. (Marrying Brad was as close to the ministry as she ever thought she'd get.) She and Brad began serving as assistant co-pastors of a small church in Northern California.

It was a powerful Sunday when the new co-pastors told their story. The people loved them, as did their children.

THE DIMENSIONS OF RECOVERY

Whichever path is yours—no contact, limited contact, or full relationship—key dimensions of recovery must be addressed. They are:

healthy bonds—must be available in the form of therapy and support groups

boundary development—critical to restoring the ability of the victim to take care of self

role development—allows new interaction beyond victim and victimizer

trauma resolution—diminishes the power of the original events and makes reactivity less of a problem

systems change—necessary to move into non-exploitive relationships

sense of self—the essential developmental process that has been disrupted and needs to be restored

key metaphors—critical for helping to develop a new "working model"

recovery plan—makes concrete the recovery changes

Figure 6.1 summarizes all eight dimensions of recovery in each of the specific paths. As already mentioned, it is important to notice the activities in each path because, more than likely, you may eventually need to use some of the strategies from all the paths as you move toward recovery. For example, you might be in "no contact" now but run into someone you need to "limit contact" with in the future.

Figure 6.1. Trauma Bond Recovery Paths

RECOVERY DIMENSION	NO CONTACT	LIMITED CONTACT	FULL RELATIONSHIP
1. Healthy Bonds	Establish support network to tell the story	Group or community can debrief or de-role victim	Group or community supports relationship
2. Boundary Development	Learn boundary setting strategies	Strategies for using boundaries in the moment	Negotiate new partnership/ relationship
3. Role Development	Identify roles of victim, victimizer, rescuer	Develop new working model for relationships	Identify relationship patterns of healthy intimacy
4. Trauma Resolution	Trauma desensitization	Psychological distance from intensity	Develop fair fight contract
5. Systems Change	Identify cycles of abuse	Reframe traumatic interactions	No fault system
6. Sense of self	Work for self-acceptance and self-care	Strategies for resisting carried shame	Strategies for resisting couple shame
7. Key Metaphors	Remodeling; write a story	Stillness; doing business; bookending	Three-legged stool; the blending of epics
8. Recovery Plan	Three recovery areas for no contact	Three recovery areas for limited contact	Three recovery areas for full relationship

Before going on to the next chapter, please complete your recovery plan carefully. Bring it to your therapist or support group and ask for feedback. It is important to complete this work before starting the activities of the next chapter.

RECOVERY PLAN FOR COMPULSIVE RELATIONSHIPS

Step One: *Finish the Story:* Return to Chapter 5 and the assignment "Write the Story." In that assignment you were asked to write your story using third-person pronouns and to write it as if it were a fairy tale: "Once there was a little girl . . ." is how you started. Now finish your work by adding a page or two describing how you would like to see the story end. When complete, take it to your support group and therapist and read it out loud. Record your experiences in your journal.

Step Two: *Establish Level of Contact:* List below those people who have been abusive in your life and who are on no contact, limited contact, or full relationship levels of contact. Remember, there is no right or wrong list—only what serves as the best match for you.

No Contact	Limited Contact	Full Relationship
1. _____	1. _____	1. _____
2. _____	2. _____	2. _____
3. _____	3. _____	3. _____
4. _____	4. _____	4. _____
5. _____	5. _____	5. _____

Step Three: *Bottom-Line Behaviors:* These are destructive behaviors from which you wish to abstain. Write very concrete descriptions of what you do not want to do.

Example: Sue

A. Date no one who has any authority or power over me.

1. _____

2. _____

3. _____

4. _____

5. _____

6. _____

7. _____

8. _____

9. _____

10. _____

Step Four: *Boundaries List:* These are behaviors to avoid because they put you at risk or they do not add to your recovery. Check them by seeing what "exceptions" you can find and rewrite accordingly.

Example: Catherine

A. I will not discuss legal or financial matters with Fred. He must always go through my attorney.

1. _____

2. _____

3. _____

4. _____

5. _____

6. _____

7. _____

8. _____

9. _____

10. _____

Step Five: *Relationship Goals:* These are behaviors that would constitute relationship health for you. Again, make the statements as concrete as possible.

Example: Marge

A. I will take responsibility and own explicitly behavior that has been harmful to my partner.

1. _____
2. _____
3. _____
4. _____
5. _____
6. _____
7. _____
8. _____
9. _____
10. _____

Further Steps on the Path to Recovery

THIS CONSISTENT PATTERN OF
HYPERAROUSAL ALTERNATING WITH NUMBING
HAS BEEN NOTICED FOLLOWING SUCH A VAST
ARRAY OF DIFFERENT TRAUMAS, SUCH AS
COMBAT, RAPE, KIDNAPPING, SPOUSE ABUSE,
NATURAL DISASTERS, ACCIDENTS,
CONCENTRATION CAMP EXPERIENCES,
INCEST, AND CHILD ABUSE.

—Bessel van der Kolk[1]

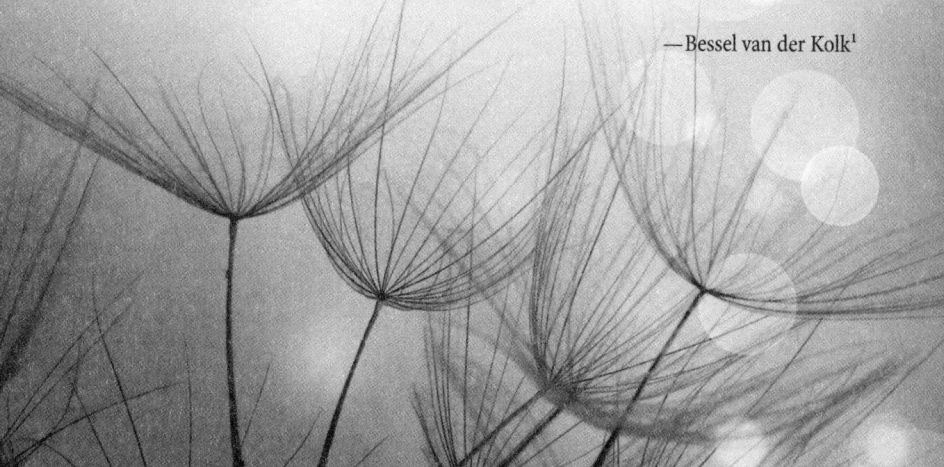

S itting in my office, Traci described her nightmare step-by-step. It was her last week of treatment before returning home. She was scared. She was a strong woman, pretty, in her early forties, with four children. Two years previously she had started an affair with her psychologist, a woman named Sandi. The psychologist had twenty years of experience in her field. She also was a highly respected teacher at a nearby university. Traci was very attracted to Sandi's charisma, intelligence, and wit. She continued in therapy while they were dating. Finally Sandi said that they needed to stop therapy because it was unprofessional. Then she suggested that they could move in together. Traci left her husband of fifteen years so she could be free to be involved with the therapist.

Sandi took over Traci's life, controlling everything from job to children. When Traci tried to break it off and moved to an apartment of her own, Sandi battered her front door down. Sandi also made direct threats on the lives of Traci's husband and children. The list of abuses over the two-year period seemed endless. I asked Traci what her reaction would be if Sandi busted through her front door again. With a tear rolling down her cheek she admitted, "To tell the truth, I can't wait to see her again."

Traci actually was on schedule. She was very clear about the nature of the abuses, the life consequences it caused, her own personal issues that were part of it, and the family dynamics with her husband and children. She had made much progress. So she was mystified as to why she still had these feelings for someone who had hurt her and her loved ones so badly. I told her that the feelings are normal. In the language of addictions we call them cravings; they do not go away simply because you understand. Many get to the point of understanding but get pulled back in by the emotional reactivity. The key is to dismantle the reactivity and the other trauma solutions that support traumatic bonding. The relapse prevention plan you just completed focuses specifically on the relationship life itself. Now we need to focus on how reactivity, arousal, blocking, splitting, deprivation, shame, and repetition are used in that relationship. Only then will you have sufficient distance to recognize that the feelings are not about reality. They are like the Sirens of the ancient Greeks, who seduced unwary sailors off course, where they crashed on the rocks hidden under the sea.

This chapter is organized around a series of exercises to help you with the emotional distance you need. Doing these exercises well will require much work and time. Groups who have used these activities will often spend up to two or three weeks on a single section. Take your time. There are rewards for doing these exercises thoroughly. The first is that a thorough relapse plan will, the more you work it, become a process of self-definition. Second, the plan will increase your self-knowledge and give you new skills to cope with stress and trauma. You will be tempted to skip to the next chapter and not return to these activities. If you do, you will experience what Traci and others have found: that it is not sufficient to simply understand. You will need skills to cope. You will also need your support group, journal, and therapist to make the most out of what is asked of you. Some of you might say that your life was relatively problem-free until you got into the specific relationship that prompted you to read this book. For some people that will be true, but all it takes is one trauma bond to bring terror to your life. Do the exercises anyway.

Traci returned home and started going to a therapist who worked hard with her on the activities you are about to do. Traci reported Sandi to the state board and has achieved a working relationship with her husband in which there is good co-parenting. She wrote me about her progress, and then mentioned she had recently read the novel by Mario Puzo called *The Last Don*. In the novel, there is a woman whose husband and family were murdered in front of her on her wedding night as retaliation for a gangland slaying. She stayed loyal to the family and even cooked for the father (the Don), until finally she went insane.[2] Traci's comment about this character was, "I did more than understand the plight of Rose Marie. I know what happened to her." Traci was telling me that understanding was not enough. The knowledge has to get to the core of who you are if you are to survive.

Two suggestions before you proceed. First, review your self-assessment scores from Chapter 2. Now that you are more clear about the problem, your assessment may shift. Second, if you get stuck, review the appropriate sections in the first two chapters to help you think about a specific trauma solution. Now to begin.

REACTIVITY RECOVERY PLAN

Survivors of terror tend to react in extremes. Their "alarm system" is set to hypersensitive. The result is inner turmoil, personal chaos, and relationship dysfunction. The other trauma solutions are an effort to manage this reactivity. By finding healthy ways to manage the internal reactions, you will be less vulnerable to those dysfunctional coping strategies.

Start by listing ways that you underreact and ways you overreact in the relationships you are concerned about. Give a description of what the reaction is, what the feeling is, and the behavior that results from it. Describe a specific event in which that happened. Then describe an appropriate response strategy and what probably would have happened had you done that.

UNDERREACTIONS

Example: Fear of telling Mother the truth about how I do not like her hitting the children. I keep quiet and my anger comes out at the children. Like when she slapped Jason last week.

Balanced response: I have to tell her clearly what my rules are and that I do not hit my children. If she hits them again, I will limit her contact with them. As long as I am with her, she will respect that, and I will have to ignore her comments. She might be open to talking about it. I will tell her how her hitting me has affected me. That might have a real impact.

OVERREACTIONS

Example: I get angry at Bill and feel hopeless about ever getting his attention. I love taking his car and doing something destructive to it. Last week I drove his car right through the garage door.

Balanced response: No more dramatic exits. No abuse of his car. I could tell him that I am angry and that we need to talk this through. If he is unwilling, I will take that as a sign as to how badly he wants us to be together. I will use the "fair fight" contract. Had I used the contract, Bill probably would have listened, and I would not have looked like such a fool.

1. Underreaction:

Balanced Response:

2. Underreaction:

Balanced Response:

3. Underreaction:

Balanced Response:

4. Underreaction:

Balanced Response:

5. Underreaction:

Balanced Response:

6. Overreaction:

Balanced Response:

7. Overreaction:

Balanced Response:

8. Overreaction:

Balanced Response:

9. Overreaction:

Balanced Response:

---

10. Overreaction:

Balanced Response:

Record your reactions in your journal and share with your group.

As we previously introduced, the "window of tolerance," as described by Dr. Daniel Siegel, is a term used to describe the zone of arousal in which a person is able to function and regulate most effectively. When people are within this zone, they are typically able to readily receive, process, and integrate information and otherwise respond to demands. We can think of the window of tolerance as a state where we feel capable, connected emotionally, physically, and socially, and can attend to our own needs as well as the needs of others.

At different times we can be triggered, and these triggers can lead to "flooding," or leaving, the window of tolerance. The triggers lead to distress and cues our nervous system to respond in primarily two ways. On the upper end we can find ourselves in a state of hyperarousal and on the lower end in a state of hypoarousal. Each of these states have their own unique emotional, physical, and social symptoms just as being in the window of tolerance does. Many people experience both. When this happens, the prefrontal cortex region of the brain shuts down, affecting the ability to think rationally and being in a state of dysregulation.

When this happens, we can learn to recognize when we leave the window of tolerance, and we can learn to return to our window of tolerance thorough developing habits of resourcing. When we recognize the symptoms of hyperarousal and hypoarousal, we can see the cues and we can learn what we need to do to reengage our window of tolerance and regulate our emotional state.

We can learn techniques to return to our window of tolerance through grounding, mindfulness, focusing on physical sensations, deep breathing, and so forth. Many of these techniques can be learned in therapy. As we learn to practice these skills, we actually widen our window of tolerance and become more resilient, learning to deal with stress in more adaptive ways. Use the worksheet on the next page to help you begin to identify your patterns related to the window of tolerance. It has been adapted from the work of Dr. Daniel Siegel, who introduced the concept of the window of tolerance. The worksheet will help you to identify common symptoms of hyperarousal, hypoarousal, your triggers, and tools to help you regulate.

This exercise is intended to help you identify your triggers as well as skills to help you when you recognize that you have left the window of tolerance. This is a very helpful exercise to work on with your therapist and/or share with members of your support group.

Anxiety	Feeling unsafe
Impulsivity	Nightmares
Emotional reactivity	Hypervigilance
Anger/rage	Overwhelmed
Insomnia	Rigidness

Difficulty concentrating	Panic
Addictions	Easily startled
Obsessive/compulsive thoughts and behaviors	Jumpy
Over-eating/restricting	
Disabled cognitive processing	

TRIGGERS: These are the memories, core beliefs, feelings, and body sensations which are connected to the past trauma and have the potential to move us out of the window of tolerance.

1. _____
2. _____
3. _____
4. _____
5. _____
6. _____
7. _____
8. _____
9. _____
10. _____

Warning signs of flooding:

Window of Tolerance

When we are in the window of tolerance we:
1. Are able to self-soothe
2. Stay emotionally regulated
3. Remain flexible
4. Are connected to ourselves (mind, body, emotions)
5. Are able to connect to others

Warning signs of flooding:

Tools for Regulation: What are behaviors that you can engage in to help regulate and return to the window of tolerance?

1. _____
2. _____
3. _____
4. _____
5. _____
6. _____
7. _____
8. _____
9. _____
10. _____

Fatigue	Shut down
Depression	Numb
Dissociation	
Not present	
Auto pilot	
Disconnection	
Memory loss	

**HYPOAROUSAL
FREEZE**

| Disconnected from emotions and body |
| Reduced physical movement |
| Aches and pains |
| Disabled cognitive processing |

AROUSAL RECOVERY PLAN

High arousal and intensity bring relief to painful feelings. Absorption in pleasure and high risk dilutes the hurt and pain.

This part of your recovery examines the role of high arousal in the relationship or relationships you are concerned about. First you need to notice what "arousal" addictions you use as part of this relationship.

If you have questions about this exercise reread Chapter 1.

AROUSAL ADDICTIONS

1. Sexual behavior (including sadomasochism, swinging, pornography, and public sex)

   _____

   _____

2. Drugs (including cocaine, crystal, crack, and amphetamines)

   _____

   _____

3. Caffeine, tobacco

   _____

   _____

4. High-risk behaviors

   _____

   _____

5. Gambling (including risky commodities trading and other financial trades or risks)

   _____

   _____

Now you need to look at the intensity of the relationship. In what ways does the relationship create emotional intensity? Chaos? Fear? Inconsistency? Roller-coaster career? High stakes and high risks? Threats? Make a list of the sources of intensity, and include an example for each.

Sources of Intensity:

1. _____

2. _____

3. _____

4. _____

5. _____

Write a plan of action for distancing from the intensity. Plans will vary by the level of contact you intend to have and the sources of intensity. Be very specific about the steps you will take.

Record your reactions in your journal, and share with your group.

BLOCKING RECOVERY PLAN

Survivors of abuse seek soothing. Anything to calm, medicate, or anesthetize anxiety can be used to block awareness and pain.

This part of your recovery plan examines the role of blocking strategies in the relationship or relationships you are concerned about. First you need to notice what satiation addictions are part of this relationship.

If you have questions about this exercise, reread Chapter 1.

SATIATION ADDICTIONS

1. Alcoholism

_____

_____

2. Compulsive eating

_____

_____

3. Compulsive working

_____

_____

4. Depressant drugs

_____

_____

5. Compulsive sex (sex as a way to calm down or go to sleep)

_____

_____

6. Compulsive spending (buying things to feel better)

_____

_____

7. Compulsive television watching (binge watching)

_____

_____

8. Compulsive social media use

_____

_____

Soothing Strategies:

1. _____

2. _____

3. _____

4. _____

5. _____

Write a plan for calming yourself in healthy ways. Be very specific about the steps you will take. For example: "Each weekday morning I will meditate for twenty minutes."

Record your reactions in your journal, and share with your group.

Splitting Recovery Plan

Survivors will split off from reality as a way to deal with their terror and pain. Dissociation (living in an unreal world) then becomes a coping strategy.

This part of your recovery plan examines the role of living in an unreal world in the relationship or relationships you are concerned about. There are many ways to create unreality. Addicts will use obsession and preoccupation as a vehicle to literally be in a trance. First you need to notice if addictive preoccupation was part of this relationship.

Preoccupation and Obsession Used to Escape Reality

Example: obsessing about next sexual episode with abusive partner

With drugs and alcohol

_____

_____

With sexual behavior

_____

_____

With food

_____

_____

With risk

_____

_____

With perpetrator's addictions (codependency)

_____

_____

With work

_____

_____

With social media or television

_____

_____

Have you used the following as a way to enter another "reality" and avoid what is happening around you and in the relationship?

Hallucinogenic drugs such as LSD and marijuana

_____

_____

Excessive religious or spiritual practice

_____

_____

Immersion in art and music

_____

_____

Compulsive book reading (as in romance or adventure novels)

_____

_____

Compulsive video and TV watching (e.g., bingeing on Netflix)

_____

_____

Living in daydreams

_____

_____

Rehearsing conversations in your head that you never seem to have

_____

_____

Having separate "parts" of yourself you do not let others know about

_____

_____

In trauma bonds, the relationship itself is an escape from reality. Victims will ignore friends, family, work, and values to be in a relationship built on deception.

The following diagram is an extremely helpful way to see how such a relationship "splits" reality. You will notice two columns, one for illusion and one for reality. Using the diagram, review the relationship or relationships you are concerned about in light of what you now know about seduction and betrayal. You will see how trauma bonding generated a life based on illusion.

ILLUSION VS. REALITY

ILLUSION	REALITY
First contact: The promise the victimizer made was in the form of a story, or kindness, or compassion for you, or a noble cause. What was that promise? _____ _____ _____	Your vulnerability: You had developmental or unmet needs, or unfinished business that made you vulnerable to the promise for which you would give up all. What was that vulnerability? _____ _____ _____
Validation: The victimizer validated the promise in some way so that you believed things are actually the way they were presented. How was your confidence gained? _____ _____ _____	First betrayal: The real intention becomes clear in early abuse or exploitation. What really happened? _____ _____ _____
Reseduction: The victimizer adds an explanation to the story so that the abuse is understandable. How did the victimizer revalidate the promise so you would stay? _____ _____ _____	More betrayal: The abuse and exploitation continue in a number of forms. What are the costs to you now because you have stayed? _____ _____ _____
Reframing: The victimizer interpreted costs to you as minimal and reframed them as necessary for the good of the relationship. What did the victimizer tell you to do about your losses? _____ _____ _____	Life crisis: Ultimately, reality asserts itself and you realize you can go no further. What loss was significant enough to make you face reality? _____ _____ _____

Find a different color pen than the one you used to finish this last section. Go back over the exercise and write in the empty spaces how you could have handled the relationship differently. After completing your comments, look at the other parts of this section, and compose a brief statement of "Ten Rules to Stay in Reality." Record your thoughts in your journal and read your "rules" to your group and therapist.

TEN RULES TO STAY IN REALITY

1. _____

_____

_____

2. _____

_____

_____

3. _____

_____

_____

4. _____

_____

_____

5. _____

_____

_____

6. _____

_____

_____

7. _____

_____

_____

8. _____
_____
_____

9. _____
_____
_____

10. _____
_____
_____

DEPRIVATION RECOVERY PLAN

"What are you doing to take care of yourself?" is one of the most often asked questions in recovery. Self-neglect is one of the common causes of relapse, and it is true that children whose parents neglected them have difficulty taking good care of themselves.

This part of your recovery plan looks at those areas of your life that have gone beyond neglect of yourself and become compulsive deprivation or even compulsive self-harm. First you need to identify forms of compulsive deprivation or self-harm that existed in the relationship(s) that you worry about.

COMPULSIVE DEPRIVATION AND SELF-HARM

1. Anorexia (self-starvation with food)

_____
_____

2. Sexual anorexia (aversion to sex)

_____
_____

3. Compulsive saving or hoarding

_____

_____

4. Compulsive cleaning

_____

_____

5. Cutting or hurting self

_____

_____

6. Hair pulling or skin picking

_____

_____

7. Body piercing or excessive tattoos

_____

_____

8. Compulsive exercising (excessive athleticism)

_____

_____

9. Compulsive debt (so much debt you cannot care for yourself) or compulsive saving

_____

_____

10. Compulsive working (working to the point of exhaustion and numbness)

_____

_____

RELATIONSHIP DEPRIVATION

Were you ever:

1. Asked to sacrifice in extreme ways?

   _____

   _____

2. Asked to endure extreme hardship?

   _____

   _____

3. Denied medical care?

   _____

   _____

4. Asked to work extreme hours?

   _____

   _____

5. Denied clothing?

   _____

   _____

6. Asked to deplete your own funds for the relationship?

   _____

   _____

7. Asked to give up significant friendships?

   _____

   _____

8. Asked to give up important family relationships?

   _____

   _____

9. Forced to live in inhospitable conditions?

_____

_____

10. Asked to give up a job or make self-destructive career decisions?

_____

_____

Review the above and make a list of what a healthy, caring human being would do for her- or himself.

1. _____

2. _____

3. _____

4. _____

5. _____

6. _____

7. _____

8. _____

9. _____

10. _____

11. _____

12. _____

13. _____

14. _____

15. _____

16. _____

17. _____

18. _____

19. _____

20. _____

Pick three from the list that you can do in the next week and three more you can do in the next month. Share with your group and therapist. Commit to a date by when you will have done them. Record your reactions in your journal.

Shame Recovery Plan

An injury to one's sense of self forges some bonds. The self-injury becomes part of the fabric of the relationship and further disrupts the natural unfolding of the self. When this involves terror of any sort, an emptiness forms at the core of the person, and the self becomes inconsolable. No addiction can fill it. No denial of self will restore it. No single gesture will be believable. Only a profound sense of the human community caring for the self can seal up this hole. We call this wound *shame*.

This part of your recovery agenda looks at how the relationship forced you to devalue the self and plans for self-restoration to the human community. Start by making a list of how the relationship devalued you. Think of times you felt unworthy, embarrassed, flawed, or ashamed. Make a list of ten sources of shame in the relationship.

Devaluation in the Relationship

Example: I did things to please my partner sexually—such as sending explicit, nude pictures of myself to a men's magazine—that deeply embarrassed me.

1. _____

2. _____

3. _____

4. _____

5. _____

6. _____

7. _____

8. _____

9. _____

10. _____

Share the list with your group and therapist. Note in your journal the feelings that accompanied each entry to the list. Ask your group what you need to do to build support for yourself.

REPETITION RECOVERY PLAN

Addiction to the trauma, or *repetition compulsion,* means that the victim seeks situations that duplicate the original trauma. The victim seeks similar situations to resolve the original trauma, in part to re-experience all the reactions to it and in part to live out the original "working model" for relationships created in the abuse experience.

The following exercise was given to me by Marilyn Murry, author of *Prisoner of Another War.*[3] I have modified it some for inclusion in this planning process. It is one of the best ways to understand repetition compulsion in your life and to change it. It does, however, require some effort. What follows are step-by-step instructions.

1. Find a large piece of newsprint. A standard size is 24" × 36" and can be found in tablet form at any office supply store. You will also need felt tip colored markers that you can write legibly with.

2. On the newsprint, draw a large oval that takes up most of the newsprint. About three-quarters of the way up, draw a dotted line across the oval as in the figure that follows:

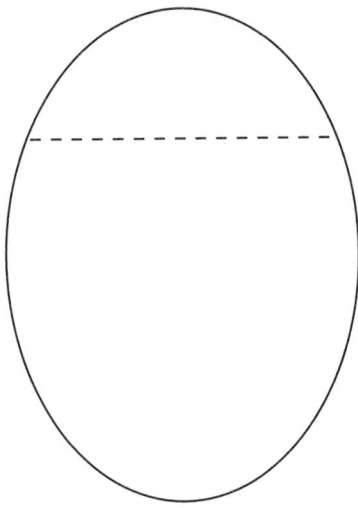

3. Outside of the oval and at the bottom of the page, write words that you think of when you think of your parents or original caregiver. Put the words you associate with Mom on the right and words you associate with Dad on the left. You only need five to ten words.

4. Now think of events in your life that were painful or difficult. Usually these are events in which there was profound disappointment, betrayal, or abuse. Think of times when you were embarrassed or let down, or when there was some upset or crisis that involved you. Starting with the earliest events you can remember from early childhood, draw a small symbol for each event and separate it by a small curve, as in the figure that follows. Do not use words—only symbols.

With all these events recorded, the bottom of your oval will start to look like a honeycomb. Keep adding events through the various phases of your life—preschool, elementary school, early teenage years, young adulthood, and adulthood to the present. Fill the oval up to the dotted line. The most recent should be near the top and the earliest at the bottom. Done well, this should take many hours to complete.

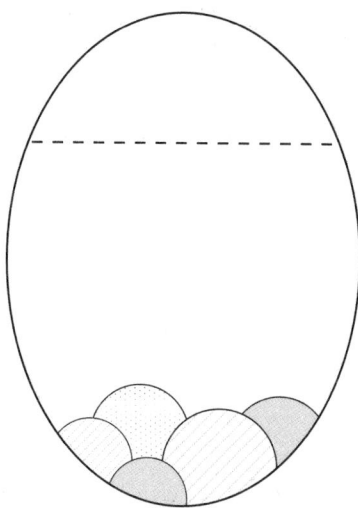

5. Before going on to the next instruction, spend time showing your work to your therapist or your sponsor. Ask this person to look for themes that are common to the events. Examples would be: "Many of the events represent some type of abandonment" or "The events seem to indicate extreme neglect." When you have these repeating themes clear, proceed to the next step.

6. Outside of the oval, in the upper-right corner, list what roles you played in the family (such as hero, scapegoat, etc.). Outside of the oval, in the upper-left corner, list family rules that affected you (such as "don't show feelings.").

7. On the basis of all this work, write what you believe your family's marching orders to you were. Write it in the form of a mission statement. This mission statement should accurately state what you perceived your family wanted you to do with your life. If you were the loyal kid, or the hero, what were you supposed to do in life? Record this mission statement in the top quarter of the oval, above the dotted line.

Your newsprint should end up looking like this:

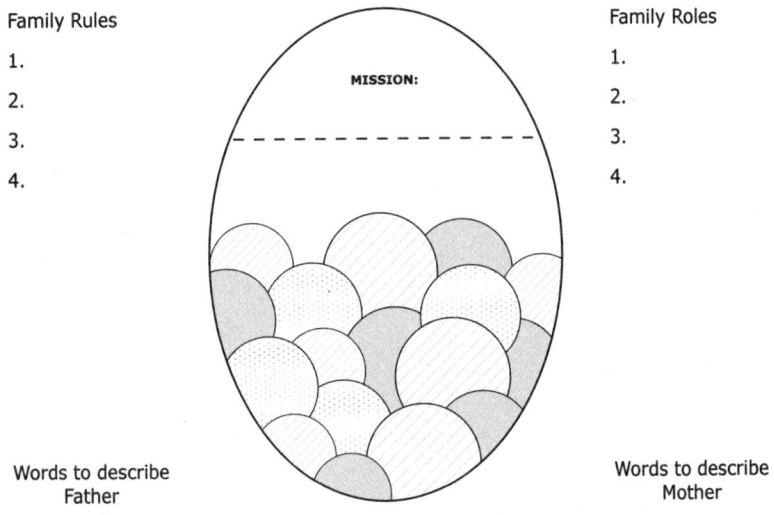

8. If you had the power to clone yourself—meaning the same you with no programming—what mission would you give yourself? Write that mission down. In your journal, respond to the following questions:

What does the mission given you by your family have to do with the trauma bond(s) in which you have been?

How did the original mission create repeated events throughout your life?

What are you willing to do in order to change the mission?

What steps would that take?

Who can help you with it?

How will you start?

Suggestion: In this task of changing the mission, there are two books designed to help you with that process. *The Artist's Way*, by Julia Cameron, and *First Things First*, by Stephen Covey. I highly recommend both of them.

What Are the Risks of Recovery?

To "own" one's shadow is the highest moral act of a human.

—Robert Johnson

Some of us cried out, "It's too great a task!"

—*The Big Book of Alcoholics Anonymous*

hysicists tell us that once an atom has touched another atom, there is a relationship between the two atoms that endures forever, no matter how far they are from each other. While the physics involved are quite complex, the physical relationship principles are quite simple. Once made, a relationship always exists. It seems that in human relationships, that principle exists as well. Once a person has been part of our lives, the ripples remain, even when we have no further contact. In that sense a relationship continues even though we may deliberately exorcise it from our conscious contact. Once you understand that principle, a shift will occur in all of your contact with others.

If the relationship was toxic, as in a traumatic bond, the relationship must go through a transformation, since it will be always with you. You do not need to be in contact with the person to change the nature of the relationship. You can change how you perceive it. You can change how it affects you. This is true of all human systems—intact or not.

Some time ago I was responsible for a family-centered treatment center that took in all members of the family down to age six. Typically, we had twenty or more families attend at once. We often did an exercise with them that we described as a set of skills to teach problem-solving. We started by having everyone line up against the wall according to age. We started with the youngest child and finished with the oldest adult. The youngest kids would then pick out new brothers and sisters from the older kids. These new "siblings" would then pick out new parents. We then taught the concepts of "brainstorming" and "win-win" problem-solving to these reconstituted families. Then, we gave the families a task or problem to solve. They were to spend the evening (three hours) doing something no one in this new family had ever done before. They typically went out and had a great time with each other.

When their therapists referred these families to us, they pointed out that the family members did not have skills in problem-solving, boundary setting, intimacy, or even play. Yet when you put these same people with other people's spouses and with other people's children, they had appropriate boundaries, solved problems, communicated effectively, could be vulnerable, and could have fun. In fact, when they returned from the exercise, the kids would ask, "Why can't our family have fun like this?" The adults, too, asked why it was so different. Their questions gave us the perfect opportunity to explain about systems and risk. It was not that they did not know how to be different with each other. They did know. It was more about risking being different.

So it is with traumatic relationships. Whether it be no contact, limited contact, or full relationship, there needs to be a shift. Your whole emotional and intellectual stance toward that person must be different. By this point you already have what you need to know. The problem of recovery is whether you are willing to risk the changes necessary. Those risks are as follows:

TO COMMIT TO REALITY AT ALL COSTS . . .

The movie *Mask* tells the story of a young man who had an illness that, among other things, "lionized" his face. His facial features were so distorted that they often repelled people. The movie tells the story of how he deals with other adolescents, his first girlfriend, other adults, his family, and ultimately his death. There is a point in the story when the boy, his mother, and their friends go to an amusement park and buy tickets to the fun house. In the fun house are the typical mirrors that distort appearance. The mirrors make you look fat or skinny or misshapen—only in the movie, the boy's face in the distorting mirror looks "normal." He calls his mother over to see. The poignancy of the scene comes with the two of them gazing at the handsome face he would have had without his illness.

In many ways, betrayal and exploitation are like being in the fun house. It makes the abnormal and the grotesque appear normal. Trauma distorts our perceptions just as sure as the mirrors in the fun house. Your task is to leave the fun house and face the reality without the distortion. This risk is the price of admission to recovery. You simply have to be willing to do it.

Scientists who studied trauma in rats made a startling discovery: Rats who received electric-shock treatment in little boxes returned to those little boxes when they experienced stress from other sources. Even though they received electrical shocks upon entering the boxes, they still returned to their boxes. It was a familiar, known way to return to their stress. Similarly, the trauma-bonded survivor will run back into the fun house of exploitation even though it will be destructive.

Recovery requires staying in reality.

Betsy was a woman who finally chose reality. For four years, she was in a sexual relationship with a clergyman who was also her therapist. She knew it was wrong and destructive. She even went to the extent of getting another therapist two years into the relationship. When that therapist asked for the name of who it was that was exploiting her, she could not give up the name and eventually dropped out of therapy. Time and time again she tried to leave but could not. She would run back to the minister, seduced by yet another story of how badly he was hurting. But finally she realized how crazy things were when she discovered that the clergyman and his wife were stalking her. She left therapy with the exploitive therapist. She told her support group and her children. It was the children that did it. When she saw how upset they were, she knew there was no going back. She had to make the break. When she came out publicly with her story, other women came forward. These other women joined her in reality. There was no going back for them, the congregation, and the small town where they lived. The price of admission? Reality.

THE MISPERCEPTIONS OF OTHERS

Once you have clarity about reality, you must be willing to risk that others will misperceive you. Survivors want others to understand them. They do not want anyone upset with them. Their childhood training taught them that "if you cannot say something nice, do not say anything at all." If they have tried to change in the past, they may even have had their lives threatened. They hold out a vain hope that they can write a letter to explain their actions or that they can have the "talk" that will gain them the acceptance of their actions. The fact is that they can give the perfect explanation, and others in the abusive system will not understand it, maybe not even believe it. Even those who truly do cherish the survivor will misperceive. Remember, they are back in the fun house. If survivors are making significant changes, the people around them will not like it. They will misinterpret the survivor's actions. They may even question the survivor's motivation and conduct. Count on it.

The problem is shame. Shame is part of our internal guidance system, which tells us what is appropriate. Survivors embedded in traumatic shame become so other-directed that they lose their sense of self. They feel like the exploitation is their fault. The victim then carries the shame of the abuser and is shameful. The abuser, however, remains shameless. The victim becomes more desperate for the approval of others. For the victim, shame ceases to be a tool for appropriate action and becomes a prison from which there is a loss of autonomy and freedom.

When Betsy reported what happened to her with her minister-therapist, it became public. Members of the church she had attended for twenty years shunned her. People whom she thought were her friends and part of her spiritual support network would not talk with her. The parish issued a letter asking for prayers for the man who had abused her. When it mentioned her name it simply referred to her as "the cause of the problem." The church that had been her home abandoned her when she told the truth. Fortunately, Betsy had her support group and her new therapist. She knew that the congregation's shunning her was not so much about her as it was about its members' own issues—including the church's feelings of betrayal and pain. Remember, others in the system will have to go through denial, fear, and anger before they get to the pain. That includes family members, friends, and other people on whom survivors might count. If you are committed to reality, you must accept that people will misperceive you.

To Have Boundaries . . .

If you are willing to have others misperceive you, then you must run the risk of drawing boundaries. Implementing the boundaries you have specified in your recovery plan will upset people. With time, however, you will learn that not only is it all right for you to upset people but you also may learn to enjoy upsetting them. Sometimes you may set exaggerated boundaries, meaning that they are more rigid than the situation calls for. It makes no difference. The learning is in having them. It makes up for the years of deficits caused by having no boundaries at all.

The deeper issue with boundaries is that they force an essential restructuring of the relationship with self. The autonomy that you lost to shame is regained in several ways. First, within the exploitive system, victims make promises to themselves that they do not keep. They will draw lines in the sand and say no more and then let people step over them with impunity. No one takes them seriously, which adds to their shame. When the victim starts insisting on maintaining limits and meeting her or his own needs, self-respect emerges. Here is a person who demands reckoning, a person of value.

Second, having boundaries clarifies values. They essentially are the answer to the question, "For what am I willing to fight?" Those values help define who the person is.

Finally, by successfully implementing boundaries, a new trust for yourself emerges. Victims learn that they do not have to have the zipper on the outside. They can and will take care of themselves, which creates a new sense of safety. For example, if one of the coping strategies for sexual trauma is to become celibate, having boundaries can be a revolution. You can be sexual and passionate if you know you will not let anyone exploit you. If you have good boundaries, no one can exploit you. By being trustworthy to yourself, you can give yourself over to passion. You know that you will take care of yourself. Perhaps the most important part of recovery is developing a trustworthy relationship with self.

TO SAY GOOD-BYE . . .

If someone does not respect your boundaries, you will have to leave. Many times I have witnessed incidents in which the victim gets to the point where she or he is ready to leave, only to have the abuser deliver the most compelling version of the seduction story. The abuser does not test the boundaries at that point, but once the victim is sucked back into the circle, the boundary abuse occurs again.

How can you change this? It is simple. State what is not acceptable, and indicate that the cost of crossing the line will be that you will leave. For some people that is all that is necessary. When the line is crossed, you have your answer about the value of the relationship and the state of health of the other person. The best thing for you—and in fact the other person as well—is to face the reality that the relationship cannot survive.

Saying good-bye is wrenching for survivors, who already grieve their many losses. Here the survivor must confront the deep desire for the seduction story to be true. There is more than exploitation or abuse at stake here. There is the loss of some dream or core hope that made the seduction story so irresistible. Usually that dream or hope has roots in some original wound for which the survivor has not yet fully grieved. So when it is time for good-bye, the grief will be overwhelming. The only choice you have to survive is to embrace the pain and experience the loss. In many ways the betrayal bond protected you against that pain.

You may not have to say good-bye, but you must be willing to do so. In fact, life as you know it may require a complete transformation for you to survive these relationships. Work, values, homes, friends, and even family relationships may have to substantively change for a successful recovery. What lengths are you willing to go to in order to be free? When you answer that question, you may have to face another risk: to be alone and be okay.

TO BE ALONE AND OKAY . . .

Behind grieving past losses lurks the fear of being alone. Yet it is the essential component of having a relationship with yourself. It is that sense of enjoying your own presence. We are not talking about narcissism here. We are describing the ability to be alone with yourself so you are clear about your own internal processes, your needs, and your creative expression. For those who fear abandonment, the shift to a positive regard for oneself and the desire for time with oneself is one of the key developmental changes that an abusive environment may have blocked. Instead of shame, the survivor moves into autonomy.

Theologian Henri Nouwen calls this transition the "conversion of loneliness into solitude."[1] Many people suffer terrible relationships because they fear being alone. They give themselves away piece by piece rather than face an empty house or apartment. They will accept partial relationships, as in:

the leftover attention from a workaholic spouse

the second-class status of mistress

the secret, clandestine affair

the partner to the addicted spouse

the illicit, exploitive relationship

the life of loving someone on the run

the partner of the inmate in prison

the long-distance relationship

Yet in these cases, something is not better than nothing. People who are not afraid to be alone can afford to demand relationships that work. They are not desperate while between relationships. Nor do they fill their lives with mindless television or mind-numbing addictions. They learn to be alone and be okay.

TO BE SPIRITUAL . . .

The following is a simple statement of what happens spiritually:

Crisis and pain force surrender.

We accept the realities we tried to flee.

The lesson will be repeated until learned. If ignored, the lessons become harder.

The lessons teach us about human limitation.

We believed we were more than other humans. We could escape the harm.

When we accept suffering, we reconnect with the deeper rhythms of the universe.

We cannot escape the inevitable message. Now it means too much.

We have lost too much, but we do have integrity.

Never again will we let things not matter. We are part of a larger purpose.

We know we have learned the lesson when our actions change.

Simple.

Nouwen describes three essential movements to a spiritual life. First comes the connection with self and the acceptance of your own brokenness. Then there is the acceptance of the community and a renewed trust of others. The ability to trust oneself and others clears the path to trusting a creator. That trust also means acceptance of a larger purpose, a purpose in which, at times, even bad things can happen to very good people.

For many survivors, the gateway to a spiritual life starts with a new relationship with oneself and with the growing network of relationships in the support community. To trust a higher purpose or power requires an essential trust of others. Trust of others really only comes with a deep trust of your own integrity. For example, will you follow through on enforcing the boundaries you have set? If you know you are untrustworthy, then it is difficult to take the next step of believing it possible that others can be trustworthy. Trusting a higher power, then, will remain elusive. Trust starts when you risk taking a stand. Then, somehow, it all matters. In the trauma bond, you were unfaithful to yourself, and so someone hurt you. By being true to yourself, you will heal. And out of that healing, a spiritual life emerges. It's amazing what betrayal can teach us if we are willing to learn.

TO BE HONEST . . .

If you have a solid spiritual life, you realize that nothing really disconnects you from others. Then it is a matter of courage to be yourself and to be honest about who you are. This means:

to admit the hard things about yourself

to be clear about hard things others must hear

to not mislead anyone

to not live a secret life

to abandon false fronts and false pride

to be clear about your intent

to tell the truth

to not hide from difficult moments

to give up being nice all the time

to state your needs and wants without shame

to not cover or lie for anyone

The truth does, in fact, make you free.

TO BE VULNERABLE . . .

The most important skill to acquire and use in recovery is the capacity to get a consultation. To get a consultation means to involve people in what goes on in your own interior world—the dumb thoughts, the scary thoughts, the garbled thoughts, the irrational fears, the angry, vengeful fantasies, the nightmares, and the unspoken desire. By sharing with others, you have an examined life. People know who you are. They also help you with their perspectives and ideas. They bring reality and problem-solving skills to your life. This process allows for integration of the darker side of yourself and acceptance of your humanness.

For the survivor whose vulnerability has been exploited, this risk may first appear insurmountable. It is from the sharing of stories, however, that trust starts to build. Common experience reduces the isolation of shame. Dr. Brené Brown, in recent years, has written and spoken beautifully on the concepts of vulnerability, shame, and connection. Her work would be a tremendous resource for you to explore these issues in greater detail. It is then that we can share the shadow side of ourselves, the nasty, mean-spirited side of ourselves, the side that others have victimized, the side whose motives for rescuing were not that wonderful, the side that has frightening fantasies. Failure to own that reality will keep us from the serenity we seek. Disowning our shadow will prevent integrity. Remember that others are mirrors for ourselves. What we love or hate in others reflects what we love or hate about ourselves. Dr. Carl Jung wrote that to acknowledge our skeletons is the only way we will be able to ultimately accept the "gold" of life. More important, he observed that the greatest gift you could give your children (and the next generation) is to acknowledge the shadow side of yourself. To do that means to be vulnerable.[2]

TO FIGHT . . .

Most survivors avoid conflict. In their past, anger and violence meant great danger. There were the rules about keeping the peace and saying nice things. The truth is that sometimes you will have to fight. To remove yourself from a trauma bond safely and with self-care might mean you have to insist on your rights. Do not accept a significant loss because it is easier not to fight for it. You may need to get help to coach you, to advocate for you, or even to represent you. But it is okay to get what is yours, what you need, or what others should do for you. It is also important to let go of being nice. It is always important to let others hear you. It is always important to protect yourself. It is always important to make sure you do not intentionally hurt others purely for the sake of hurting them. These are all good reasons to fight. Besides, the boundaries become clear in the process.

Remember that adversarial processes such as court action can also be traumatic. As I indicated earlier, anger can lead to negative intimacy. Your goal should be to take care of yourself and not to allow the bond to reseduce you.

Also, all intimacy has some struggle to it. There is no healthy relationship that does not have significant differences in it. That is why I like the "fair fight" contract that Recovering Couples Anonymous uses. Learning to handle differences safely is the most important skill a couple can have. It is more important than love, attraction, and common interests. Sustained intimacy will only last if the couple can learn to be separate and together. Working that through will happen over and over again. If it is a safe process, there will be joy. The same principles apply to raising children, having friends, and forging successful work relationships. And yes, it applies to relationships with therapists as well.

TO DEFINE SELF . . .

One of the most common reports from people emerging from a trauma bond is that they had not realized how much someone else regulated their values, lifestyle, and daily choices. The people in most of the situations described in this book probably said the phrase, "He (she) took over my life." Once out of the trauma bond, even the most simple things can become difficult. I had one woman describe for me how simply decorating her new apartment became a challenge.

She wanted the apartment to be a statement about who she had become, but it was a challenge—since even she was still unclear about that.

Sometimes the dilemmas are heartrending; they are more akin to the level of problem that Orestes faced. If you remember, Orestes had to choose between avenging his father's death—and consequently murdering his mother—and loyalty to his mother. I have seen too many situations such as that, situations for which there were no easy solutions.

Consider Tom, whose situation with his volatile wife, Barbara, I described in Chapter 5. One of Tom's core values was to be the best parent he knew how to be to his children. His divorce settled with a joint custody arrangement, which featured the children going back and forth between the two homes at biweekly intervals. While Tom got much better at limiting Barbara's intrusions in his life, she still caused what he called "emotional overhead." Just as a business has overhead costs, having to be a parent with Barbara cost Tom a certain amount of chaos. While he couldn't eliminate the chaos entirely, he knew he had to get some physical distance between Barbara and himself. When he received an extraordinary job offer, 1,500 miles away, he was elated. But what about the children? The older kids were old enough that he did not worry about his relationship with them. But the youngest was an ache in his heart. She did not want to move, and that meant staying with Barbara. So his choice was to pass on the offer and stay with the kids or be true to himself and accept the incredible offer he received.

He accepted the offer and learned much. He was like a new man. He felt more like himself than he had in years. He became CEO of the company. He remarried. Two of his children actually moved in with him while they went to college and graduate school; one of them was his youngest child.

Tom remained true to himself, and doing so paid off for him. The price? A soul-wrenching choice that offered no guarantees.

You may experience terrible choices on your recovery path. They will force you to define who you are and what you are all about.

Expect the difficult. Your journey will have ups and downs. It is all part of the process. Healing and recovery are worth it. In her book *When Things Fall Apart,* Pema Chodron stated, "We think that the point is to pass the test or overcome the problem, but the truth is that things don't really get solved. They come together and they fall apart. Then they come together again and fall apart again. It's just like that. The healing comes from letting there be room for all of this to happen: room for grief, for relief, for misery, for joy." Recovery allows space for all of life. It creates space for new narratives and new relationships.

TO TAKE RESPONSIBILITY FOR YOURSELF . . .

This risk reminds me of how monkeys are captured in Africa. Tribal peoples put out slotted cages filled with fresh fruit. The cages are anchored securely to the ground. Monkeys discover the cages, reach in and grab the fruit. Of course, they cannot retrieve the fruit because as long as the hand holds the fruit, it will not fit through the bars of the cage. The monkeys are then trapped. They could always let go of the fruit and escape, but they refuse to let go. Even as their human captors pick them up, they hold on.

Trauma bonds are similar. There is always something kind, noble, or redeeming about someone who has betrayed you. Victims of betrayal will hold to those good things even while the world crashes in around them. By holding on, they stay stuck, just like the monkeys. We do make our own prisons.

That is exactly how it was with Jack. He sat in my office, admitted for an addiction relapse and treatment because he was absolutely suicidal about a woman he had broken up with four months earlier. He was a very high-profile sports figure. He spent over a half-hour telling me how she was his dream woman. The sex was fabulous. She was his best friend. They each had children the same ages, who really got along well with one another. They had been together for two years. All of which was well and good, except that she had stolen thirty thousand dollars from him, embarrassed him countless times with violent outbursts at highly visible public events, alienated all of his friends, and kept him in constant turmoil with her dramatic exits. After their last breakup, she became involved with one of his closest colleagues and slept with him within the week. Jack was sad she would no longer take his calls. I told him he was lucky, and therapy began.

The scenarios of abuse in Jack's history and her history were there. He admitted that she terrified him most of the time. And he acknowledged that the relationship was over. Yet he had a thread of hope he could get her to therapy and retrieve the relationship. Like a monkey with fruit, Jack was holding on to the dream.

The bottom line is: *Your life is up to you. Take charge of it, or somebody else will.*

FROM SUFFERING TO MEANING . . .

There is a revolution occurring. Sometimes it is public and the battle lines are clearly drawn. Sometimes it is very personal and the lines are very intimate. The struggle goes on in courtrooms, corporate offices, legislatures, universities, and playgrounds. It affects employers, parents, spouses, teachers, judges, and members of the clergy. Many of us think it is a turning point for our species. The revolution is about relationships. Whether it is betrayal by seduction, terror, power, intimacy, or spirit, exploitation is simply no longer acceptable. We've surveyed centuries of damage, and we know better. We need to move toward a culture of mutuality and respect. We can build our relationships on the basis of our competencies, needs, and care. Men and women need to share power and privilege. All of us must commit to the nurturing of children. And we are accountable to each other for our behavior. There is no more room for terror in the human community.

Ecologically, we are now too numerous to continue to abuse the planet. We must deeply acknowledge our connections with all creatures. We must now respect that interdependence or we will suffer greatly. While most of us know that danger, the abuse of the earth still continues. Our consciousness must eventually outstrip the forces of exploitation. Similarly, we understand what trauma does. Violence simply begets more violence. War, child abuse, domestic violence, sexual harassment, and all manner of exploitation limit what we can be. In fact, one of the most astute observers about childhood over time, Lloyd deMause, writes, "The history of childhood is a nightmare from which we have only recently begun to awaken."3 Just as with our ecological awareness, the fact that we are awake does not mean the abuse has stopped.

I wish to applaud you, dear reader, for completing this book and meeting all its demands, for you have gone beyond awareness. You have committed yourself to stopping or changing an abusive relationship. In that, you have helped all of us. You have contributed in the only way any of us can make a difference. You were not one of those who found the risks too great a task. Good work.

As you finish this book, take a moment to rank yourself on the following scales. Think about where you were at the beginning of the book and where you would rank yourself now.

It is important to understand and become more aware of the impact of trauma on your life. The questions in this assessment will help you to clarify and understand behavior in your life and its possible connection to trauma.

Judith Herman is a psychiatrist, researcher, teacher, and author who has focused on the understanding and treatment of incest and traumatic stress. She is best known for her distinctive contributions to the understanding of trauma and its victims, as set out in her second book, the now classic study of the diagnostic category post-traumatic stress disorder (PTSD), *Trauma and Recovery*.

Herman discussed three states of healing from trauma. Herman states, "Recovery unfolds in three stages. The central task of the first stage is the establishment of safety. The central task of the second stage is remembrance and mourning. The central focus of the third stage is reconnection with ordinary life" (Herman 1997). In all stages, it is important to address the themes and dynamics related to one's history of trauma and how that has played out in traumatic bonding in relationships. This is the central theme of this book. As we grow in our ability to recognize these themes and dynamics and the unhealthy belief systems they support, we have a greater ability to take responsibility for them and an expanded ability to choose new, healthier responses and actions. We are able to regain control of our lives.

"Recovery can take place only within the context of relationships; it cannot occur in isolation. In her renewed connection with other people, the survivor re-creates the psychological facilities that were damaged or deformed by the traumatic experience. These faculties include the basic operations of trust, autonomy, initiative, competence, identity, and intimacy. Just as these capabilities are formed in relationships with other people, they must be reformed in such relationships. The first principle of recovery is empowerment of the survivor. She must be the author and arbiter of her own recovery. Others may offer advice, support, assistance, affection, and care, but not cure." (Herman 1997).

This assessment is designed to help facilitate the healing process and help you to become more aware of how specifically the trauma from your past or from a current trauma bond relationship is impacting you as you start to work through the stages of healing. As we become more aware of the impact of trauma, the more we are able to set in place a plan for healing and recovery. As you have been working your way through this book, the process of healing has more than likely already began for you, offering a deeper level of awareness and understanding.

Please respond to each of these from two different points in time, one where you think you were when you started this book, and second, where you believe you are now.

Cognitive Impairment: Traumatic experiences can impact our ability to think and problem-solve. This often includes having trouble concentrating and staying focused, forgetting things easily, being easily distracted, and having difficulty planning and organizing. The emotional flooding, which can occur following a traumatic event or through trauma responses, can lead to the areas of the brain that help us to think, problem-solve, and make decisions becoming compromised, which leads to difficulty gaining access to cognitive processes.

Low   **High**

1	2	3	4	5	6	7	8	9	10
1	2	3	4	5	6	7	8	9	10

Trauma Bonding: Traumatic bonding is being connected (loyal, helpful, supportive) to people who are dangerous, shaming, or exploitive. Those who experience trauma bonds often find that they help or stay in relationships with people who continue to harm or abuse them, seem to attract people who are incapable of caring for them, find they are attracted to untrustworthy people, and are loyal to people no matter what, even if they have betrayed them.

Low   **High**

1	2	3	4	5	6	7	8	9	10
1	2	3	4	5	6	7	8	9	10

Compartmentalization: Compartmentalization is an unconscious psychological defense mechanism used to avoid cognitive dissonance, or the mental discomfort and anxiety caused by a person's having conflicting values, cognitions, emotions, beliefs, and so forth, within themselves. As a result of traumatic experiences, survivors often feel conflicting emotions and struggle with confusing thoughts and beliefs. Those who compartmentalize find that they see certain behaviors that will bring trouble, but they do them anyway, have parts of their life that they keep hidden, repeatedly attempt to stop behaviors that are harmful, and may live a double, or secret, life.

Low									High
1	2	3	4	5	6	7	8	9	10
1	2	3	4	5	6	7	8	9	10

Traumatic Shame/Self-Perception: Traumatic shame is the sense of believing that you are unworthy and having self-hate due to traumatic experience. Trauma can leave deep changes in our belief system, which bring about distorted views of ourselves. We tend to think of an emotional wound as the original traumatic experience—as the "thing" that happened to us, but the wound is actually the dis-empowering belief that we developed as a result of the traumatic experience. These beliefs are disempowering and painful, and they become emotional wounds. Often, healing from trauma is difficult because we try to heal the original event but not the underlying traumatic belief that we hold about ourselves and the world. These feelings of unworthiness and self-hate can lead to ongoing cycles of trauma, abuse, unhealthy life patterns, and unhealthy decisions. Those who experience traumatic shame/self-perception often feel that they should be punished for their choices even more than they have been punished already; they believe they are unworthy of deserving a good life, and often feel unlovable and unworthy.

Low									High
1	2	3	4	5	6	7	8	9	10
1	2	3	4	5	6	7	8	9	10

Traumatic Sexual Harm/Degradation: Traditionally self-harm behaviors are those behaviors that included overt forms of self-injury, such as cutting, burning, pulling out hair, and physical harm to self. They can also be less obvious forms, such as eating disorders, alcohol and drug use, failing to take prescribed medications correctly, self-sabotage, perfectionism, and setting unrealistic goals, and there are many more. Anything with the intent to cause harm to self, whether physically, emotionally, or psychologically, is self-harm. Sexual self-harm behaviors are similar in that they involve sexual behaviors that cause physical and/or emotional harm. Those who experience traumatic sexual harm/degradation may feel shame by being aroused by pain, feel sexual when they are degraded, used, or treated poorly, and are aroused by sexual violence.

Low									High
1	2	3	4	5	6	7	8	9	10
1	2	3	4	5	6	7	8	9	10

Avoidance/Distrustfulness: Avoidance symptoms represent an effort to withdraw from certain situations that bring about body-level distress of trauma-related symptoms. There may be a significant amount of time and effort spent in avoiding the distressing memories, thoughts, people, places, or feelings associated with the traumatic event. The avoidance may also include feelings of detachment and diminished interest in significant activities. An overall feeling of distrustfulness of others can develop, which leads to isolation and potentially self-medicating behaviors such as self-harm behavior or addictive behaviors. Those who experience avoidance/distrustfulness often make sure that most people know very little about them, do not display many emotions, and may avoid people, places, and things that most people would enjoy.

Low									High
1	2	3	4	5	6	7	8	9	10
1	2	3	4	5	6	7	8	9	10

PTSD Reactions: Traumatic reactions involve experiencing current reactions to trauma events in the past and are the most frequently described trauma reactions. These reactions can include sudden feelings of panic and anxiety, nightmares, difficulty sleeping, sweating, having trouble eating or experiencing an upset stomach, irritability, anger, difficulty concentrating, and difficulty expressing positive emotions. Those who experience PTSD reactions may have sudden and vivid memories of painful experiences, startle easily by certain noises, sounds, or sudden actions, and spend a lot of time thinking about people who hurt or abused them.

Low									High
1	2	3	4	5	6	7	8	9	10
1	2	3	4	5	6	7	8	9	10

High-Risk Behaviors: High-risk behaviors are defined as behaviors with an uncertain outcome that entail negative consequences and commonly include the use of illicit drugs, heavy drinking, high-risk sexual behavior, and behavior where the more risky option is chosen rather than the safer option. There may be a repeated pattern of being drawn to activities where there is an element of danger. Those who experience high-risk behaviors may like to live "on the edge," be drawn to dangerous people and/or activities, and find that they may get excited or aroused when facing a dangerous situation.

Low									High
1	2	3	4	5	6	7	8	9	10
1	2	3	4	5	6	7	8	9	10

Substance Use: Many individuals who have experienced trauma will turn to drugs or alcohol as a way to numb their pain or to gain some measure of control in their lives. The use of substances can provide a temporary escape from the often distressing and at times debilitating symptoms of trauma. Those who use drugs and alcohol may do so as a way to cope or escape and find that they use them in excess when life feels too difficult.

Low									High
1	2	3	4	5	6	7	8	9	10
1	2	3	4	5	6	7	8	9	10

Dysregulated Eating: Dysregulated eating includes disturbances in behavior related to eating. These disturbances may affect health, growth, and/or development but not necessarily appearance and include binge eating disorder, bingeing and purging, overeating, obesity, and deprivation. Many times, behavior centering on food is used as a means to avoid difficult or distressing emotions. Those who experience dysregulated eating may be preoccupied with food and eating, eat excessively to avoid problems, and have attempted diets repeatedly.

Low									High
1	2	3	4	5	6	7	8	9	10
1	2	3	4	5	6	7	8	9	10

Over-Arousal and Avoidance of Emotional Arousal: Trauma can impact our ability to emotionally regulate, and often survivors experience a compromised regulatory capacity in which they may become over-aroused and/or under-aroused, or they may avoid emotional arousal. They may experience rapidly shifting states of arousal, which affect thinking and behaving. These shifting states are caused as their brains continue to flip them into hyperarousal or hypoarousal whenever they perceive a threat to be present. During hyperarousal and hypoarousal, the thinking brain becomes difficult to access, which makes it difficult to formulate coherent thoughts. When persons with a trauma background are in hyperarousal, they may experience anger or rage. When they are in hypoarousal, they may withdraw or shut down to avoid conflict. Whether they go into hyperarousal or hypoarousal, people with trauma backgrounds can learn to identify that they have left optimal arousal, where they perceive the world as safe, when they experience a "limbic hijack." Stated briefly, limbic hijack occurs when the person's limbic system, or primitive emotional control center in the brain, shuts down the thinking parts of the brain and directs them into the fight, flight, or freeze response. Those who experience over-arousal and avoidance of emotional arousal find that they will try anything to stop their feelings when anxious, have difficulty tolerating uncomfortable feelings, and may feel restless and unable to calm down.

Low									High
1	2	3	4	5	6	7	8	9	10
1	2	3	4	5	6	7	8	9	10

"Traumatic events, by definition, overwhelm our ability to cope. When the mind becomes flooded with emotion, a circuit breaker is thrown that allows us to survive the experience fairly intact, that is, without becoming psychotic or frying out one of the brain centers. The cost of this blown circuit is emotion frozen within the body. In other words, we often unconsciously stop feeling our trauma partway into it, like a movie that is still going after the sound has been turned off. We cannot heal until we move fully through that trauma, including all the feelings of the event" (Banitt 2012).

REFLECTIONS

The practice of ongoing reflection helps us to turn inward and navigate our inner world. It helps us to process and understand what we feel and think about our life experiences. This habit works to help build ongoing resilience and helps to build our capacity to connect in relationship. We encourage you to develop habits that allow for this inner reflection, whether it be through journaling, meditation, yoga, or time in nature, to name a few. Please take a few minutes to reflect on your process of awareness and healing through this book.

_____

_____

_____

_____

_____

_____

_____

_____

I have included a final metaphor at the end of this chapter to take with you on your journey. My best wishes go with you.

A Guided Imagery for the Journey...

The following is a guided imagery that has been used by thousands of recovering people. Once you learn the structure of it, you can use it over and over again to help you reclaim your priorities. You can have a friend read it to you or even ask your therapist to do it with you. Some have recorded it and then played the tape for themselves. A special version of this imagery can be found at *www.drpatrickcarnes.com*.

Guided imageries are not magic. They are metaphors that help you access your own wisdom. Each time you use the imagery, you will come up with new insights. This particular imagery is very easy to use because all you have to know are the directions of north, south, east, and west. Native Americans would use these directions as a way to inventory where they were in their life's journey. We can use the same process as well.

To do this you will need a sanctuary or safe place. Think of some location in your life that has been very peaceful and serene for you. Picture that as the site for this imagery. Now, simply follow the instructions.

Close your eyes and make yourself comfortable. Make sure nothing physical distracts you. If you are upset about anything, picture a box around it and set it aside. Tune in now to your own bodily rhythms—your breathing and your heart beating. Know that with each beat of your heart and each breath that you take, you are participating in the larger forces of the universe. Each heartbeat and each breath is therefore sacred.

Imagine a safe place. A place that has no demands. A place that always gives peace. Look around the safe place. Notice colors, sounds, and textures. What is it that makes this place so good for you?

You become aware of another presence in the safe place. You look to see who it is. It is a healer, a wise person who has come to support you in the safe place. Greet your healer. Your healer invites you to do an inventory of your life but wishes to do it in the manner of traditional peoples. Your healer then asks you to face the north and joins you at your side.

North is the direction of the winter winds. It is the direction of challenge, endurance, and courage. Your healer asks: "For what challenge do you need to be strong? What do you need courage to face?" Tell your healer what that is. Your healer then asks you to face the east.

East is the direction of the rising sun. It is the direction of beginnings. Your healer asks: "What do you need to start in your life? When is it time to begin?" Tell your healer what you must begin. Your healer then asks you to face the south.

South is the direction of the summer sun. It is the direction of nurturing, vitality, and growth. Your healer asks: "What do you have going on in your life that needs your attention, your nurturing, your cultivation? What do you need to grow or heal?" Tell your healer what you must have now in order to grow. Your healer then asks you to face the west.

West is the direction of the setting sun. It is the direction of endings. Your healer asks: "What do you need to bring to a close? To whom do you need to say good-bye?" Tell your healer what you have not been willing to end and that you know it is time now to end it. Your healer then asks you to gaze upward to Father Sky.

The sky is the direction of openness and possibility. It is the direction of creativity. Your healer asks you to picture yourself against the sky doing something that uses talents you currently do not use. Tell your healer about your unused talents. Your healer then asks you to gaze downward toward Mother Earth.

Mother Earth is the direction of gravity. It is the direction of stability. Your healer asks: "What is it that you need to remain stable?" Tell your healer what you need to remain grounded. Sit down with your healer. Your healer has a special message for you about your direction in life. What does your healer tell you?

As you talk, you become aware of another presence in the safe place. As you look to see who it is, you see that it is a child about five years old. As the child approaches, you realize the child is you at the age of five. Welcome the child. Ask the child how things are going. What concerns and fears does the child have? Allow the child to climb into your lap. Reassure the child. Even though the child has maybe suffered neglect, or harm, or abandonment, or even abuse, you are now here to protect the child. You will allow nothing to happen to the child. Hold the child close and comfort the child. As you hold the child in your arms, the healer now has something to tell you about the child. What does the healer say?

As you and the healer talk, the child becomes restless. The child gets up and asks if you and the healer would like to play. You and the healer agree. You take one hand, and the healer takes the other, and you leave the safe place. You walk out into a spectacular green meadow. At one end of the meadow is a playground with all kinds of play equipment: water slides, merry-go-rounds, jungle gyms, and swings. Picture yourself playing. Notice that you can have intense feelings and still play.

You realize it is time to leave. Tell the child and the healer you have to go. The child responds, "We know. But first we have a gift for you." The child runs and gets the gift and hands it to you. If it is wrapped, unwrap it. What is the gift? What does it look like? What does it mean? Thank the child and the healer. And when you are ready, open your eyes.

This imagery has helped many survivors sort out their needs. Once you have done it, simply remember what happens with each direction: with the north, cold winds; with the east, the day's beginning; with the south, growth due to the summer sun; the west, day's end; the sky, openness and creativity; and the earth, gravity and stability. After a while you will not need the script. You will be able to do it on your own.

As before, use your journal to record your imagery. What emerged for you with each direction? What happened with the healer and the child? How was it to play? What was the gift? Record what insights you have gained, and share with your therapist and group.

APPENDIX:
RESOURCES

GENERAL

Al-Anon Family Group Headquarters, Inc. (AFG), and Alateen
1600 Corporate Landing Parkway
Virginia Beach, VA 23454
(757) 563-1600
E-mail: wso@al-anon.org
www.al-anon.alateen.org

Alcohol and Drug Problems Association of North America
1555 Wilson Boulevard
Suite 300
Arlington, VA 22209
(703) 875-8684

Alcoholics Anonymous World Services
475 Riverside Drive
New York, NY 10163
(212) 870-3400
www.aa.org

AMEND (Domestic Violence)
777 Grant Street
Suite 600
Denver, CO 80203
(303) 987-3444
E-mail: tchatfield@amendcounseling.com
www.amendcounseling.com

Amnesty International of the USA (AIUSA)
5 Penn Plaza, 16th floor
New York, NY 10001
(212) 807-8400
Washington National Office
600 Pennsylvania Avenue, SE, 5th floor
Washington, DC 20003
(202) 544-0200
www.amnestyusa.org

BA (Batterers Anonymous)
1850 N. Riverside Avenue, No. 220
Rialto, CA 92376
(909) 312-1041
E-mail: jerrygoffman@hotmail.com
www.batterersanonymous.com

Co-Dependents Anonymous
P.O. Box 33577
Phoenix, AZ 85067-3577
(602) 277-7991
1-888-444-2359
E-mail: info@coda.org
www.coda.org

GAM-ANON International
P.O. Box 157
Whitestone, NY 11357
(718) 352-1671
E-mail: gamanonoffice@gam-anon.org
www.gam-anon.org

Gamblers Anonymous
P.O. Box 17173
Los Angeles, CA 90010
(626) 960-3500
E-mail: isomain@gamblersanonymous.org
www.gamblersanonymous.org

**National Catholic Council on Alcoholism and
Related Drug Problems (NCCA)**
1550 Hendrickson Street
Brooklyn, NY 11234–3514
(718) 951-7177
www.nccatodya.org

National Coalition Against Domestic Violence (NCADV)
One Broadway, Suite B210
Denver, CO 80203
www.ncadv.org

National Council for Couple and Family Recovery (NCCFR)
434 Lee Avenue
Saint Louis, MO 63119
(314) 963-8898

National Council on Alcoholism and Drug Dependence
17 Broadway, Suite 712
New York, NY 10010
www.ncadd.org

National Council on Sexual Addiction and Compulsivity (NCSAC)
1090 Northchase Parkway
Suite 200 South
Marietta, GA 30067
(770) 989-9754

Overeaters Anonymous
6075 Zenith Court NE
Rio Rancho, NM 87124–6424
(505) 891-2664
www.oa.org

Parents Anonymous
675 W. Foothill Boulevard
Suite 220
Claremont, CA 91711–3416
(909) 621-6184
www.parentsanonymous.org

Parents United International (PUI)
615 15th Street
Modesto, CA 95354–2510
(209) 572-3446
http://parents_united.tripod.com

Recovering Couples Anonymous (RCA)
P.O. Box 11029
Oakland, CA 95354
(781) 794-1456
E-mail: info@recovery-couples.org
www.recovering-couples.org

CULTS

Cult Awareness Network (CAN)
3055 Wilshire Boulevard, Suite 900
Los Angeles, CA 90010
E-mail: can@cultawarenessnetwork.org
www.cultawarenessnetwork.org

SEX ADDICTION

COSA
9337-B Katy Freeway
Suite 142
Houston, TX 77024
E-mail: info@cosa-recovery.org
www.cosa-recovery.org

Incest Survivors Anonymous
P.O. Box 17245
Long Beach, CA 90807-7245
(310) 428-5599

Incest Survivors Resource Network International (ISRNI)
P.O. Box 7375
Las Cruces, NM 88006
(505) 521-4260
(505) 521-3723 fax

Sex Addicts Anonymous (SAA)
P.O. Box 3038
Minneapolis, MN 55403
(612) 339-0217
E-mail: info@saa-recovery.org
www.saa-recovery.org

Sexaholics Anonymous (SA)
P.O. Box 3565
Brentwood, TN 37024
(615) 370-6062
E-mail: saico@sa.org
www.sa.org

Sex and Love Addicts Anonymous (SLAA)
Fellowship- Wide Services
1550 NE Loop 410, Suite 11B
San Antonio, TX 78209
(210) 828-7900
www.slaafws.org

Sexual Compulsive Anonymous (SCA)
P.O. Box 1585
Old Chelsea Station
New York, NY 10011
(212) 606-3778
1-800-977-HEAL
www.sca-recovery.org

Survivors of Incest Anonymous (SIA)
World Service Office
P.O. Box 190
Benson, MD 21018
(410) 893-3322
www.sawso.org

NOTES

NOTES

How the Book Came to Be:

1. Doidge, N. *The Brain That Changes Itself: Stories of Personal Triumph from the Frontiers of Brain Science.* New York: Penguin, 2007.

2. Smith, D. E. "Editor's Note: The Process Addictions and the New ASAM Definition of Addiction." *Journal of Psychoactive Drugs* 44, no. 1 (2012): 1–4.

3. Angres, D. H., and K. Bettinardi–Angres. "The Disease of Addiction: Origins, Treatment, and Recovery." *Disease-a-Month,* 54, no. 10 (2008): 696–21.

4. Hilton Jr., D. L. "Pornography Addiction— Supranormal Stimulus Considered in the Context of Neuroplasticity." *Socioaffective Neuroscience & Psychology 3,* no. 1 (2013): 20767.

5. Freyd, J. J. *Betrayal Trauma Theory: The Logic of Forgetting Abuse.* Cambridge, MA: Harvard (1996).

6. Herman, J. L., and M. R. Harvey. "Adult Memories of Childhood Trauma: A Naturalistic Clinical Study." *Journal of Traumatic Stress* 10, no. 4 (1997): 557–71.

Introduction: Why Read This Book?

1. *www.nbcnews.com/storyline/nfl-controversy/why-she-stayed-ray-rice-video -sheds-light-domestic-violence-n200266.*

2. J. Bain, *Ontario Medical Review* (January 1989): 20–49.

3. Alice Miller, *For Your Own Good* (New York: Farrar, Straus & Giroux, Inc., 1983).

4. Rachman, S. "Betrayal: A Psychological Analysis." *Behaviour Research and Therapy* 48, no. 4 (2010): 304–311.

5. Daire, A. P., L. Jacobson, and R. G. Carlson, R. G. "Emotional Stocks and Bonds: A Metaphorical Model for Conceptualizing and Treating Codependency and Other Forms of Emotional Overinvesting." *American Journal of Psychotherapy*, 66, no. 3 (2012): 259–278.

6. Schore, J. R., and A. N. Schore. "Modern Attachment Theory: The Central Role of Affect Regulation in Development and Treatment. *Clinical Social Work Journal* 36, no. 1 (2008): 9–20.

Chapter 1: What Trauma Does to People

1. ———. "Clinical Implications of Neuroscience Research in PTSD." *Annals of the New York Academy of Sciences* 1071, no. 1 (2006): 277–93.

2. Siegel, D. J., *Mindsight: The New Science of Personal Transformation.* New York: Bantam, 2010.

3. van der Kolk, B., *The Body Keeps the Score.* New York: Viking, 2014.

4. Levine, P. A., and M. Kline. *Trauma Through a Child's Eyes: Awakening the Ordinary Miracle of Healing; Infancy Through Adolescence.* Berkeley: North Atlantic Books, 2006.

5. Schwartz, M. F. "Sexual Compulsivity as Post-Traumatic Stress Disorder: Treatment Perspectives." *Psychiatric Annals* 22, no. 6 (1992): 333–38.

6. van der Kolk, B. "The Compulsion to Repeat the Trauma." *Psychiatric Clinics of North America* 12, no. 2 (1989): 389–11.

8. Doidge, N. *The Brain That Changes Itself: Stories of Personal Triumph from the Frontiers of Brain Science.* New York: Penguin, 2007.

9. Cozolino, L. *The Neuroscience of Psychotherapy: Building and Rebuilding the Human Brain (Norton Series on Interpersonal Neurobiology).* New York: W. W. Norton & Company, 2002.

10. Morton, P. M., M. H. Schafer, and K. F. Ferraro. "Does Childhood Misfortune Increase Cancer Risk in Adulthood." *Journal of Aging and Health* 24, no. 6 (2012): 948–84.

11. Brown, B. *I Thought It Was Just Me (but it isn't).* New York: Avery, 2007.

Chapter 2: Trauma Bonds and Their Allies

1. Martin Gilbert, *The Boys* (New York: Henry Holt and Company, 1997).

Chapter 3: What Does Betrayal Do to Relationships?

1. See Bessel van der Kolk, "The Trauma Spectrum: The Interaction of Biological and Social Events in the Genesis of the Trauma Response," *Journal of Traumatic Stress* 1 (1988): 286, and Bessel van der Kolk, "The Compulsion to Repeat Trauma," *Journal of Victims of Sexual Abuse* 12 (1989): 389. See also Andrine M. Lemieu, MA, and Christopher L. Coe, PhD, "Abuse-Related Post-Traumatic Stress Disorder: Evidence for Chronic Neuroendocrine Activation in Women," *Psychosomatic Medicine* 57 (1995): 105.

2. Amanda Vogt, "Cults Get Mainstream Makeover," *The Arizona Republic* 26 April 1997, sec. R, p. 2.

3. Two examples of this type of research can be found in Renee L. Binder, MD, "Why Women Don't Report Sexual Assault," *Journal of Clinical Psychiatry* 42, no. 11 (1981): 437, and Thomas G. Gutheil, MD, "Patients Involved in Sexual Misconduct with Therapists: Is a Victim Profile Possible?" *Psychiatric Annals* 21, no. 11 (1991): 661.

4. Dara A. Charney, MD, CM, and Ruth C. Russell, MD, CM, FRCP, "An Overview of Sexual Harassment," *American Journal of Psychiatry* 151, no. 1 (1994): 10.

5. Patricia A. Gwartney-Gibbs and Denise H. Lach, "Sociological Explanation for Failure to Seek Sexual Harassment Remedies," *Mediation Quarterly* 9 (1992): 365.

6. Mary De Young and Judith A. Lowry, "Traumatic Bonding: Clinical Implications in Incest," *Child Welfare League of America* LXXI (1992): 165–175.

7. For elaboration of this concept, see William L. White, *Incest in the Organizational Family* (Bloomington, IL: The Lighthouse Training Institute, 1986).

8. K. Lebacqz and R. G. Barton, *Sex in the Parish* (Louisville, KY: Westminster, 1991).

9. J. Seat, J. Trent, and K. Jwa, *Journal of Pastoral Care* 47 (Winter 1993): 363–370.

10. K. S. Leong, "Sexual Attraction and Misconduct between Christian Therapists and Their Clients," *Dissertation Abstracts International* 50 (1989), 4225B.

11. Barbara R. McLaughlin, "Devastated Spirituality: The Impact of Clergy Sexual Abuse on the Survivor's Relationship with God and the Church," *Sexual Addiction and Compulsivity: The Journal of Treatment and Prevention* 1, no. 2 (1994): 145–158.

Chapter 4: What Makes Trauma Bonds Stronger?

1. "Diagnostic and Treatment Guidelines on Domestic Violence" (Chicago: American Medical Association, 1992).

2. Mary De Young and Judith Lowry, "Traumatic Bonding: Clinical Implications in Incest," *Child Welfare League of America* LXXI (1992): 165–175.

3. Richard Irons, MD, and Mark Laaser, PhD, "The Abduction of Fidelity: Sexual Exploitation by Clergy—Experience with Inpatient Assessment," *Sexual Addiction and Compulsivity: The Journal of Treatment and Prevention* 1, no. 2 (1994): 119–129.

4. Richard Solomon, "The Opponent-Process Theory of Acquired Motivation: The Costs of Pleasure and the Benefits of Pain," *American Psychologist* 35 (1980): 691–712.

5. For a good summary of this position see McClelland in Richard Lyons, "Stress Addiction," *The New York Times*, 26 July 1983, sec. C, p. 1.

6. Thomas Wolfe, *The Bonfire of the Vanities* (New York: Farrar, Straus & Giroux, Inc., 1987).

7. Robert M. Post, MD, "Transduction of Psychosocial Stress into the Neurobiology of Recurrent Affective Disorder," *American Journal of Psychiatry* 149, no. 8 (1992): 999–1010.

8. Jerry Kroth, "Recapitulating Jonestown," *The Journal of Psychohistory* 11, no. 3 (1984): 385. See also Jose I. Lasaga, PhD, "Death in Jonestown: Techniques of Political Control by a Paranoid Leader," *Suicide and Life-Threatening Behavior* 10, no. 4 (1980), 210–213, Richard H. Seiden Hoyt, PhD, MPH, "Reverend Jones on Suicide," *Suicide and Life-Threatening Behavior* 9, no. 2 (1979): 116–119, and Albert Black Jr., PhD, "Jonestown—Two Faces of Suicide: A Durkheimian Analysis," *Suicide and Life-Threatening Behavior* 20, no. 4 (1990): 285–306.

9. William L. White, *Incest in the Organizational Family* (Bloomington, IL: The Lighthouse Training Institute, 1986): 108–109.

10. Bessel van der Kolk, "The Trauma Spectrum: The Interaction of Biological and Social Events in the Genesis of the Trauma Response," *Journal of Traumatic Stress* 1, no. 3 (1988): 273–290, and John Money, PhD, "Forensic and Family Psychiatry in Abuse Dwarfism: Munchausen's Syndrome by Proxy, Atonement and Addiction to Abuse," *Journal of Sex and Marital Therapy* 11, no. 1 (Spring 1985): 30–40.

11. For original research plus a review of this literature, see Leslie L. Feinauer, "Comparison of Long-Term Effects of Child Abuse by Type of Abuse and by Relationship of the Offender and the Victim," *The American Journal of Family Therapy* 17, no. 1 (1989): 48–56.

12. Stephen B. Karpman, MD, "Overlapping Egograms," *Transactional Analysis Journal* 4, no. 4 (October 1974): 16–19.

13. van der Kolk, B. *The Body Keeps the Score*. New York: Viking, 2014.

14. Rachman, S. "Betrayal: A Psychological Analysis." *Behaviour Research and Therapy* 48, no. 4 (2010): 304–11.

15. van der Kolk, B. "Post-Traumatic Stress Disorder and the Nature of Trauma." *Dialogues in Clinical Neuroscience* 2, no. 1 (2000): 7.

Chapter 5: What Is the Path of Awareness?

1. Charles Whitfield, "Denial of the Truth: Individual and Political Dysfunction in the Thomas-Hill Hearings," *The Journal of Psychohistory* 19, no. 3 (1992): 269–279.

2. David Calof, "Adult Survivors of Incest and Child Abuse, Part One: The Family Inside the Adult Child," *Family Therapy Today* 3 (1988): 1–5.

3. Ruth A. Blizard and Ann M. Bluhm, "Attachment to the Abuser: Integrating Object-Relations and Trauma Theories in Treatment of Abuse Survivors," *Psychotherapy* 31, no. 3 (1994): 383. See also K. Blum, M. Trachtenberg, and G. Kozlowski, "Cocaine Therapy: The Reward Cascade Link," *Professional Counselor* (January/February 1989): 27–30, 52.

4. For example of trauma-based compulsive-relationship behavior research, see Malcolm West, PhD, and Adrienne E. R. Sheldon, BA, "Classification of Pathological Attachment Patterns in Adults," *Journal of Personality Disorders* 2, no. 2 (1988): 153–159.

5. See Chapter 5 of Patrick J. Carnes, *Don't Call It Love* (New York: Bantam Books, 1991) for data on codependency.

6. M. Scott Peck, *The Road Less Traveled* (New York: Simon & Schuster, 1978), 51, 295.

Chapter 6: What Is the Path of Action?

1. For review of this literature and model of the testimony method, see Inger Agger, "Sexual Torture of Political Prisoners: An Overview," *Journal of Traumatic Stress* 2, no. 3 (1989): 305–318.

2. The classic book on that process is David Gordon, *Therapeutic Metaphors* (Cupertino, CA: Meta Publications, 1978).

3. Rochelle A. Scheela, "The Remodeling Process: A Grounded Theory Study of Perceptions of Treatment Among Adult Male Incest Offenders," *Journal of Offender Rehabilitation* 18, no. 3/4 (1992): 167–189.

4. The concept of carried shame is described in Pia Mellody, Andrea Wells Miller, and J. Keith Miller, *Facing Codependency* (San Francisco: Harper-Collins, 1989).

5. The zipper metaphor comes from M. Fossum and M. Mason, *Facing Shame: Families in Recovery* (New York: The Guilford Press, 1986).

6. Siegel, D. J. "Toward an Interpersonal Neurobiology of the Developing Mind: Attachment Relationships, " 'Mindsight,' " and Neural Integration." *Infant Mental Health Journal* 22, nos. 1– (2001): 67–4.

7. ———. *Mindsight: The New Science of Personal Transformation.* New York: Bantam , 2010.

Chapter 7: Further Steps on the Path to Recovery

1. Bessel van der Kolk, "The Trauma Spectrum: The Interaction of Biological and Social Events in the Genesis of the Trauma Response," *Journal of Traumatic Stress* 1, no. 3 (1988): 58.

2. Mario Puzo, *The Last Don* (New York: Random House, 1996).

3. Marilyn Murry, *Prisoner of Another War* (Berkeley, CA: Page Mill Press, 1991).

Chapter 8: What Are the Risks of Recovery?

1. Henri J. M. Nouwen, *Reaching Out* (New York: Doubleday & Company, 1975).

2. For an analysis of Jung around this issue, see Robert Johnson, "On the Teeter-Totter of Ego," *Parabola: Myth, Tradition and the Search for Meaning: The Shadow* (Summer 1997): 19–25.

3. Lloyd deMause, "The History of Child Abuse," *Sexual Addiction and Compulsivity* 1, no. 1 (1994): 77–91.

4. Herman, J. L., and M. R. Harvey. "Adult Memories of Childhood Trauma: A Naturalistic Clinical Study." *Journal of Traumatic Stress* 10, no. 4 (1997): 557–71.

5. Banitt, S. P. *The Trauma Tool Kit: Healing PTSD from the Inside Out.* New York: Quest Books, 2012.

BIBLIOGRAPHY

General References

American Medical Association. "Diagnostic and Treatment Guidelines on Domestic Violence." Chicago: American Medical Association, 1992.

Bain, J. *Ontario Medical Review.* (January 1989): 20–49.

Berry, J. *Lead Us Not into Temptation: Catholic Priests and the Sexual Abuse of Children.* New York: Doubleday, 1992.

Binder, Renee L., MD. "Why Women Don't Report Sexual Assault." *Journal of Clinical Psychiatry* 42, no. 11 (1981): 437.

Black, Albert Jr., PhD. "Jonestown—Two Faces of Suicide: A Durkheimian Analysis." *Suicide and Life-Threatening Behavior* 20, no. 4 (1990): 285–306.

Burkett, E., and F. Bruni. *A Gospel of Shame: Child Sexual Abuse and the Catholic Church.* New York: Viking, 1993.

Calof, David. "Adult Survivors of Incest and Child Abuse, Part One: The Family Inside the Adult Child." *Family Therapy Today* 3 (1988): 1–5.

Carnes, Patrick J., PhD. *Don't Call It Love.* New York: Bantam Books, 1991.

Charney, Dara A., MD, CM, and Ruth C. Russell, MD, CM, FRCP. "An Overview of Sexual Harassment." *American Journal of Psychiatry* 151, no. 1 (1994): 10.

deMause, Lloyd. "The History of Child Abuse." *Sexual Addiction and Compulsivity* 1, no. 1 (1994): 77–91.

Fortune, M. M. *Is Nothing Sacred? When Sex Invades the Pastoral Relationship*. San Francisco: HarperCollins, 1989.

Fossum, M., and M. Mason. *Facing Shame: Families in Recovery*. New York: The Guilford Press, 1986.

Gabbard, G. *Sexual Exploitation in Professional Relationships*. Washington, DC: American Psychiatric Press, 1989.

Gordon, David. *Therapeutic Metaphors*. Cupertino, CA: Meta Publications, 1978.

Gutheil, Thomas G., MD. "Patients Involved in Sexual Misconduct with Therapists: Is a Victim Profile Possible?" *Psychiatric Annals* 21, no. 11 (1991): 661.

Gwartney-Gibbs, Patricia A., and Denise H. Lach. "Sociological Explanation for Failure to Seek Sexual Harassment Remedies." *Mediation Quarterly* 9 (1992): 365.

Hoyt, Richard H. Seiden, PhD, MPH. "Reverend Jones on Suicide." *Suicide and Life-Threatening Behavior* 9, no. 2 (1979): 116–119.

Johnson, Robert. "On the Teeter-Totter of Ego." *Parabola: Myth, Tradition and the Search for Meaning: The Shadow* (Summer 1997): 19–25.

Karpman, Stephen B., MD. "Overlapping Egograms." *Transactional Analysis Journal* 4, no. 4 (October 1974): 16–19.

Kroth, Jerry. "Recapitulating Jonestown." *The Journal of Psychohistory* 11, no. 3 (1984): 385.

Lasaga, Jose I., PhD. "Death in Jonestown: Techniques of Political Control by a Paranoid Leader." Suicide *and Life-Threatening Behavior* 10, no. 4 (1980): 210–213.

Lebacqz, K., and R. G. Barton. *Sex in the Parish*. Louisville, KY: Westminster, 1991.

Leong, K. S. "Sexual Attraction and Misconduct Between Christian Therapists and Their Clients." *Dissertation Abstracts International* 50 (1989): 4225B.

McLaughlin, Barbara R. "Devastated Spirituality: The Impact of Clergy Sexual Abuse on the Survivor's Relationship with God and the Church." *Sexual Addiction and Compulsivity: The Journal of Treatment and Prevention* 1, no. 2 (1994): 145–158.

Mellody, Pia, Andrea Wells Miller, and J. Keith Miller. *Facing Codependency*. San Francisco: HarperCollins, 1989.

Nouwen, Henri J. M. *Reaching Out.* New York: Doubleday & Company, 1975.

Ochberg, Frank M., MD. *Post-Traumatic Therapy and Victims of Violence.* New York: Brunner/Mazel, 1988.

Ochberg, Frank M., and David A. Soskis. *Victims of Terrorism.* Boulder, CO: Westview Press, 1982.

Peck, M. Scott. *The Road Less Traveled.* New York: Simon & Schuster, 1978.

Post, Robert M., MD. "Transduction of Psychosocial Stress into the Neurobiology of Recurrent Affective Disorder." *American Journal of Psychiatry* 149, no. 8 (1992): 999–1010.

Puzo, Mario. *The Last Don.* New York: Random House, 1996.

Scheela, Rochelle A. "The Remodeling Process: A Grounded Theory Study of Perceptions of Treatment Among Adult Male Incest Offenders." *Journal of Offender Rehabilitation* 18, no. 3/4, 167–189.

Schoener, G. R., J. C. Milgrom, E. T. Luepker, and R. M. Conroe. *Psychotherapists' Sexual Involvement with Clients.* Minneapolis: Minneapolis Walk-In Counseling Center, 1989.

Shupe, Anson. *In the Name of All That Is Holy.* Greenwood, CT: Praeger Publishers, 1995.

Sipe, Richard A.W. *Sex, Priests and Power: Anatomy of a Crisis.* New York: Brunner/Mazel, 1995.

van der Kolk, Bessel. "The Trauma Spectrum: The Interaction of Biological and Social Events in the Genesis of the Trauma Response." *Journal of Traumatic Stress* 1, no. 3 (1988), 286.

———. *Traumatic Stress.* New York: The Guilford Press, 1996.

White, William L. *Incest in the Organizational Family.* Bloomington, IL: The Lighthouse Training Institute, 1986: 108–109.

Whitfield, Charles. "Denial of the Truth: Individual and Political Dysfunction in the Thomas-Hill Hearings." *The Journal of Psychohistory* 19, no. 3 (1992): 269–279.

Wolfe, Thomas. *The Bonfire of the Vanities.* New York: Farrar, Straus & Giroux, Inc., 1987.

Trauma Reactions

Agger, Inger. "Sexual Torture of Political Prisoners: An Overview." *Journal of Traumatic Stress* 2, no. 3 (1989): 305–318.

Briere, John. *Child Abuse Trauma: Theory and Treatment of the Lasting Effects.* Newbury Park: SAGE Publications, 1992.

Courtois, Christine. *Healing the Incest Wound: Adult Survivors in Therapy.* New York: W. W. Norton & Company, 1988.

Dolan, Yvonne. *Resolving Sexual Abuse: Solution-Focused Therapy and Ericksonian Hypnosis for Adult Survivors.* New York: W. W. Norton & Company, 1991.

Gilbert, Martin. *The Boys.* New York: Henry Holt and Company, 1997.

Grove, David, and B. I. Panzer. *Resolving Traumatic Memories: Metaphors and Symbols in Psychotherapy.* New York: Irvington Publishers, Inc., 1991.

Money, John, PhD, Charles Annecillo, ScD, and June Werlwas Hutchison, MMH. "Forensic and Family Psychiatry in Abuse Dwarfism: Munchausen's Syndrome by Proxy, Atonement, and Addiction to Abuse." *Journal of Sex and Marital Therapy* 11, no. 1 (Spring 1985): 30–40.

Murray, M. *Prisoner of Another War.* Berkeley, CA: PageMill Press, 1991.

van der Kolk, Bessel. "The Trauma Spectrum: The Interaction of Biological and Social Events in the Genesis of the Trauma Response." *Journal of Traumatic Stress* 1, no. 3 (1988): 273–90.

———. "The Compulsion to Repeat the Trauma." *Journal of Victims of Sexual Abuse* 12 (1989): 389.

Trauma Pleasure

Anderson, Nancy B., MA, and Eli J. Coleman, PhD. "Childhood Abuse and Family Sexual Attitudes in Sexually Compulsive Males: A Comparison of Three Clinical Groups." *American Journal of Preventive Psychiatry and Neurology on Medical Aspects of Sexual Addiction/Compulsivity* (Spring 1991).

Blum, K., M. Trachtenberg, and G. Kozlowski. "Cocaine Therapy: The Reward Cascade Link." *Professional Counselor* (January/February 1989): 27–30, 52.

Carnes, Patrick J. *Contrary to Love*. Minneapolis, MN: CompCare Publishers, 1989.

———. *Don't Call It Love*. New York: Bantam Books, 1991.

Earle, Ralph, and Crow, Gregory. *Lonely All the Time: Recognizing, Understanding and Overcoming Sex Addiction, for Addicts and Codependents*. New York: The Phillip Lief Group, Inc., 1989.

L'Abate, L., et al. *Handbook of Differential Treatments for Addictions*. Boston: Allyn & Bacon, 1992.

Milkman, H., and S. Sunderwirth. *Craving for Ecstasy: The Chemistry and Consciousness of Escape*. Lexington, Mass.: Lexington Books, 1987.

Schwartz, M. "Sexual Compulsivity as Post-Traumatic Stress Disorder: Treatment Perspectives." *Psychiatric Annals* 22 (1992): 6.

Sunderwirth, G., and H. Milkman. "Behavior and Neurochemical Commonalities in Addiction." *Contemporary Family Therapy* (Oct. 1991).

Wilson, Peter, ed. *Principles and Practice of Relapse Prevention*. New York: The Guilford Press, 1992.

Trauma Blocking

Blizard, Ruth A., and Ann M. Bluhm "Attachment to the Abuser: Integrating Object-Relations and Trauma Theories in Treatment of Abuse Survivors." *Psychotherapy* 31, no. 3 (1994): 383.

Buchanan, L., and W. Buchanan. "Eating Disorders: Bulimia and Anorexia." *Handbook of Differential Treatments for Addictions*. Boston: Allyn & Bacon, 1992.

Edwall, G., N. Hoffman, and P. Harrison. "Psychological Correlates of Sexual Abuse in Adolescent Girls in Chemical Dependency Treatment." *Adolescence* (Summer 1989).

Evans, K., and J. M. Sullivan. *Dual Diagnosis: Counseling the Mentally Ill Substance Abuser*. New York: The Guilford Press (1990).

Evans, S., and S. Shaefer. "Incest and Chemically Dependent Women: Treatment Implications." *Journal of Chemical Dependency Treatment* 1, no. 1 (1987).

Feinauer, Leslie L. "Comparison of Long-Term Effects of Child Abuse by Type of Abuse and by Relationship of the Offender and the Victim." *The American Journal of Family Therapy* 17, no. 1 (1989): 48–56.

Hagen, T. "A Retrospective Search for the Etiology of Drug Abuse: A Background Comparison of a Drug-Addicted Population of Women and a Control Group of Non-Addicted Women." *National Institute on Drug Abuse: Research Monograph Series* (1988): Mono 81.

Miller, B. A., W. R. Downs, and D. M. Gondoli. "Delinquency, Childhood Violence, and the Development of Alcoholism in Women." *Crime and Delinquency* 35, no. 1 (1989).

Rohsenow, D. J., R. Corbett, and D. Devine. "Molested as Children: A Hidden Contribution to Substance Abuse?" *Journal of Substance Abuse Treatment* 5, no. 1 (1988).

Root, M. "Treatment Failures: The Role of Sexual Victimization in Women's Addictive Behavior." *American Journal of Ortopsychiatry* (Oct. 1989).

Shaefer, M. R., K. Sobieraj, and R. L. Hollyfield. "Prevalence of Childhood Physical Abuse in Adult Male Veteran Alcoholics." *Child Abuse and Neglect* 12 (1988).

Sullivan, E. J. "Associations Between Chemical Dependency and Sexual Problems in Nurses." *Journal of Interpersonal Violence* 3, no. 3 (1988).

Trauma Splitting

Bliss, Eugene. *Multiple Personality, Allied Disorders and Hypnosis.* New York: Oxford University Press, 1986.

Braun, B. G., MD, ed. *The Treatment of Multiple Personality Disorder.* Washington, DC: American Psychiatric Press, 1986.

Briere, John. *Child Abuse Trauma: Theory and Treatment of the Lasting Effects.* Newbury Park, MA: SAGE Publications, 1992.

Foy, D. ed. *Treating PTSD: Cognitive-Behavioral Strategies.* New York: The Guilford Press, 1992.

Herman, Judith Lewis. *Trauma and Recovery.* New York: Basic Books, 1992.

Kluft, Richard, MD. *Childhood Antecedents of Multiple Personality Disorder*. Washington, DC: American Psychiatric Press, 1985.

———. "First Rank—Symptoms as a Diagnostic Clue to Multiple Personality Disorder." *American Journal of Psychiatry* 144 (1985): 293–298.

———. *The Natural History of Multiple Personality Disorder in Childhood Antecedent of Multiple Personality*. Washington, DC: American Psychiatric Press, 1985.

Lew, Michael. *Victims No Longer: Men Recovering from Incest and Other Sexual Child Abuse*. New York: Harper and Row, 1988.

Putnam, Frank W. *Diagnosis and Treatment of Multiple Personality Disorder*. New York: Guilford Press, 1989.

———. *Recent Research on Multiple Personality Disorder*. Psychiatric Clinics North America, 1991.

Ross, Colin A. *Multiple Personality Disorder, Diagnosis, Clinical Features and Treatment*. New York: John Wiley and Sons, 1989.

van der Kolk, Bessel. *Psychological Trauma*. Washington, DC: American Psychiatric Press, 1987.

Young, W. "Observations on Fantasy in the Formation of Multiple Personality Disorder." *Dissociation* 1 (1988): 13–20.

———. "Psychodynamics and Dissociation: All That Switches Is Not Split." *Dissociation* 1 (1988): 33–38.

Trauma Abstinence

Abramson, E., and G. Lucido. "Childhood Sexual Experience and Bulimia." *Addictive Behaviors* 16 (1991).

Buchanan, L., and W. Buchanan. "Eating Disorders: Bulimia and Anorexia." *Handbook of Differential Treatments for Addictions*. Boston: Allyn & Bacon, 1992.

Covington, Stephanie. *Awakening Your Sexuality: A Guide for Recovering Women*. San Francisco: HarperCollins, 1991.

Fossum, M., and M. Mason. *Facing Shame: Families in Recovery*. New York: W. W. Norton & Company, 1986.

Gil, Eliana. *The Healing Power of Play*. New York: The Guilford Press, 1991.

Goldfarb, L. "Sexual Abuse Antecedent to Anorexia Nervosa, Bulimia, and Compulsive Overeating: Three Case Reports." *International Journal of Eating* 6, no. 5 (1987): 675–680.

Irons, Richard, MD, and Mark Laaser, PhD. "The Abduction of Fidelity: Sexual Exploitation by Clergy—Experience with Inpatient Assessment." *Sexual Addiction and Compulsivity: The Journal of Treatment and Prevention* 1, no. 2 (1994): 119–129.

Maltz, W. *The Sexual Healing Journey: A Guide for Survivors of Sexual Abuse*. New York: HarperCollins, 1991.

Maltz, W., and B. Holman. *Incest and Sexuality: A Guide to Understanding and Healing*. Lexington, MA: Lexington Books, 1987.

Trauma Shame

Bradshaw, John. *Healing the Shame That Binds You*. Deerfield Beach, FL: Health Communications, Inc., 1988.

Carlsen, Mary Baird. *Meaning-Making: The Therapeutic Processes in Adult Development*. New York: W. W. Norton & Company, 1988.

Fossum, M., and M. Mason. *Facing Shame: Families in Recovery*. New York: W. W. Norton & Company, 1986.

Harper, James, and Margaret Hoopes. *Uncovering Shame: An Approach Integrating Individuals and Their Family Systems*. New York: W. W. Norton & Company, 1990.

Kaufman, G. *The Psychology of Shame: Theory and Treatment of Shame-Based Syndromes*. New York: Springer Publishing Company, 1989.

Trauma Repetition

Foy, D., ed. *Treating PTSD: Cognitive-Behavior Strategies*. New York: The Guilford Press, 1992.

Love, P. *The Emotional Incest Syndrome: What to Do When a Parent's Love Rules Your Life*. New York: Bantam Books, 1990.

Money, John. *Lovemaps: Clinical Concepts of Sexual/Erotic Health and Pathology,*

Paraphilia, and Gender Transposition in Childhood, Adolescence, and Maturity. New York: Irvington Publishers, Inc., 1988.

Schwartz, M. "Sexual Compulsivity as Post-Traumatic Stress Disorder: Treatment Perspectives." *Psychiatric Annals* 22, no. 6 (1992).

Trauma Bonds

De Young, Mary, and Judith Lowry. "Traumatic Bonding: Clinical Implications in Incest." *Child Welfare League of America* LXXI (1992): 165–175.

Feinauer, L. "Comparison of Long-Term Effects of Child Abuse by Type of Abuse and by Relationship of the Offender to the Victim." *The American Journal of Family Therapy* 17, no. 1 (1989): 48–56.

Graham, Dee L. R., with Edna I. Rawlings, and Roberta K. Rigsby. *Loving to Survive.* New York: New York University Press, 1994.

Gutheil, T. "Patients Involved in Sexual Misconduct with Therapists: Is a Victim Profile Possible?" *Psychiatric Annals* 21, no. 11 (1991): 661–665.

Herman, Judith Lewis. *Trauma and Recovery.* New York: Basic Books, 1992.

Lemieu, Andrine M., MA, and Christopher L. Coe, PhD. "Abuse-Related Post-Traumatic Stress Disorder: Evidence for Chronic Neuroendocrine Activation in Women." *Psychosomatic Medicine* 57, (1995): 105. Levine, Peter A. and Gabor Mate. *In an Unspoken Voice.* Berkeley: North Atlantic Books, 2010.

Morton, P. M., M. H. Schafer, and K. F. Ferraro. "Does Childhood Misfortune Increase Cancer Risk in Adulthood." *Journal of Aging and Health* 24, no. 6 (2012): 948–984.

Russell, D. "The Prevalence and Seriousness of Incestuous Abuse: Stepfathers vs. Biological Fathers." *Child Abuse and Neglect* 8 (1985): 15–22.

Seat, J., J. Trent, and K. Jwa. *Journal of Pastoral Care* 47 (Winter 1993): 363–370.

Terr, L. "Chowchilla Revisited: The Effects of Psychic Trauma Four Years After a School-Bus Kidnapping." *The American Journal of Psychiatry* 140, no. 12 (1983).

van der Kolk, Bessel. "The Trauma Spectrum: The Interaction of Biological and Social Events in the Genesis of the Trauma Response." *Journal of Traumatic Stress* 1, no. 3 (1988).

Vogt, Amanda. "Cults Get Mainstream Makeover." *The Arizona Republic*, 26 April 1997, sec. R, p. 2.

West, Malcom, PhD, and Adrienne E. R. Sheldon, BA. "Classification of Pathological Attachment Patterns in Adults." *Journal of Personality Disorders* 2, no. 2 (1988): 153–159.

INDEX

A

abandonment, 30
absentmindedness, 52. *See also* trauma, splitting
abstinence, 37, 55, 161, 162
    and fear, 133
    See also trauma, abstinence; trauma, effects
        over time
abuse, 24, 30, 42, 46
    cycles of, 121–122, 124, 125
    domestic, 124, 147–148
    emotional, 159
    history of, 136, 159
    intrafamilial, 142
    inventory, 137–141
    physical, 159
    relationship between frequency and impact,
        138–141
    role in betrayal bonds, 121
    seeking, compulsive, 172
    sexual, 56, 143, 159
    spiritual, 110
    by trusted family members or friends, 141
    See also Kaiser Permanente Adverse
        Childhood Experiences (ACE) Study;
        patterns, compulsive relationship
Abuse Inventory, 137–141
abuser
    compulsive focus on, 170
    limiting contact with, 195
    See also patterns, compulsive relationship
accident prone, tendency, 52. *See also* trauma,
    splitting
acclimatization, 38, 39
activities

high-risk, 44. *See also* trauma, arousal
    mental, 32
addict, 128
addiction, 24, 71, 72, 121
    assessment for, 45
    behavior, obsessing around, 52
    and brain plasticity, 32
    in clergy, 129
    and deprivation, 56
    differential diagnosis of, 49
    in families, 175
    "fantasy," 51
    and high arousal, 130
    as partner to dissociative process, 51
    relapse, connection with trauma work, 45, 49
    and resilience, 25
    and risk, 130
    role of, in domestic abuse, 124
    romance, 50
    sexual, 123, 129, 159, 162
    teaching concepts of, 45, 49
    traditional patterns of, 123
    to the trauma, 135, 241
    and traumatic bonding, 163
    treatment, 45, 49
    See also trauma, arousal; trauma, blocking;
        trauma, splitting
adrenaline, 35, 56, 95
affirmation, 61
agoraphobia, 53. *See also* trauma, abstinence
alcohol (alcoholism), 46, 164
    abuse of, 123, 162
    addictive disorders to, 51
    in clergy, 129

and lack of receptor sites in brain, 48
leading factor in relapse, 47
pressure to use before sex, 123
in sex addicts, 159
and threats and assaults to partners, 123
used to rationalize violence, 123
See also Dr. Jekyll and Mr. Hyde; trauma,
    blocking; trauma, splitting
Alcoholics Anonymous, 197
amnesia, 50, 52
    traumatic, 160
    See also trauma, splitting
anger, 158,
    and arousal, 162
    and betrayal bond, 166
    blaming, 185–186
    in compulsive rejection, 171
    as connection to abuser, 185
    and danger, 259
    directed at children, 222
    and fear, 4
    at God, 166, 182
    healthy, 185
    in hyperarousal, 271
    at injustice and exploitation, 3
    and insane loyalties, 166
    interfering with life functioning, 4
    as legacy of trauma, 2, 3
    and #MeToo movement, 3
    as motivation for action, 179, 184–185
    and negative intimacy, 260
    in process of grieving, 141, 165, 253
    as PTSD reaction, 269
    resulting from betrayal, 142
    and sadness, 185
    toward victimizer, 166
    transition to pain, 178–179
anorexia nervosa, 53, 56
    in sex addicts, 159
    See also trauma, abstinence
anorexia, sexual, 53. *See also* trauma, splitting
anxiety, 28
    and arousal, 162
    behaving to ameliorate, 48
    in children, 135
    and compulsive deprivation, 55
    disorders, 142
    and high drama, 131
    misuse of power, caused by, 103
    neglect, caused by, 36, 40

reduction, 47, 49
    rejection, caused by, 40
    and role reversal, 147
Applewhite, Marshall, 98–99
arousal, 27, 30, 37, 43–45, 51, 56, 64, 122, 161
    avoidance of emotional, 271
    and blocking cycle, 49
    and fear, 133
    hypo-, 223–224
    hyper-, 223–224
    and intensity, 131, 162
    over-, 271
    recovery plan, 228–229
    and relief cycle, 125–126
    sexual, 131
    See also trauma, arousal; trauma, effects
        over time; window of tolerance
arrest, compulsive seeking of, 163
asphyxiation, autoerotic, 62
assault, 35
    sexual, 124
associations, triggered, 39
attachment, 25, 29, 40
    compared with codependency, 72
    compulsive, 72, 73–74, 89, 177
    in domestic abuse, 147–148
    dysfunctional, 70
    increased by fear and vulnerability, 176
    and resiliency, 30
    in sexual misconduct, 147–148
    and terror, 147
attempts, suicidal, 59, 63
attorneys, 44, 56, 129, 143, 158, 201, 203, 205,
    206, 215
aversion and self-discipline, pattern of, 54–55
avoidance, 268–269
avoiding
    normal activities because of fears, 55
    reality, 50
    thoughts or feelings associated with trauma,
        52
    See also trauma, splitting
awake, difficulty staying, 48. *See also* trauma,
    blocking
awareness
    expanding, 173
    as first step toward action, 191
    full, 25
    mindful, benefits of, 191
    as reverse path of denial, 167

and understanding, 167
of victimization consciousness, 167
See also Siegel, Daniel; Mindful Awareness
Research Center; *Mindsight*

B

"bait and switch," 3
battle fatigue, 39
behavior(s)
addictive, 135, 162
addictive cycles of, 193
blocking, 49
bottom-line, 193, 200, 206, 211, 214
compulsive, 159, 162, 163, 172
high-risk, 269–270
positive caring, 194–195
responsibility for, 187
self-abusive, 135
self-destructing, 57, 59, 63, 158
sexually compulsive, 30
belief(s)
about self and world, 29
about uniqueness, 67
clarity of, 187
betrayal, 1, 24, 27, 30, 44, 58, 64, 67, 70, 72, 73,
87–113, 121
acceptance of, 110–111
bonds, 11, 137, 166
bonds, signs of, 9–10
catastrophic, 2
covenant of, 126–127
cycles, 123
definition of, 2
effects of, 142
by family members, 142
by intimacy, 104–106
most common forms of, 142
by power, 100–104
rules of, 178
by seduction, 89–97
sexual, 131
by spirit, 107–110, 143
by terror, 97–100
in TV, 120
and vulnerability, 166
See also trauma, bonds; trauma, repetition;
trauma, shame
bibliotherapy on shame, 61
bind, universal, 161
binge/purge cycle, 53, 58. *See also* trauma, shame

bingeing, 47
blocking, 37, 161
and fear, 133
and honeymoon phase, 162
recovery plan, 229–231
See also trauma, effects over time
bondage, 124
bonding, 29, 40
betrayal. *See* bonds, betrayal
and fear, 133
healthy, 67
and resiliency, 30
traumatic, 25, 30, 64, 67–70, 110, 126, 132,
136, 142, 143, 147, 157, 159, 161, 163,
172, 175, 176, 195, 266
unhealthy, 73
bonds, 30, 37
betrayal, 6, 11, 16, 44, 97, 111, 120, 121, 123,
137
healthy, 196, 212
payoffs of, 68
teaching concepts of, 67
traumatic, 132, 142, 143, 146, 147, 159, 163,
167, 168, 172, 175, 177, 179, 195, 220,
249, 265, 266
See also trauma, effects over time
The Bonfire of the Vanities (Tom Wolfe), 131
bookending, 203
borderline personality disorder, 39, 41
Boston University Medical School, 24
boundary (boundaries)
development, 198, 212
failure, 149
to have, 253–254
healthy, 72
list, 200
self-protective, 136
violations, 24
See also recovery, risks of
brain
changes in abused children, 40
development, 30
fear, effects of on, 40
mindfulness, effects of on, 191
plasticity, 31, 32, 191, 192
traumatic experiences, effect of, 38
breathing, controlled, 42. *See also* trauma,
reactions
Brown, Brené, 58, 192–193. *See also The Gifts of
Imperfection*

Brown University, 130–131
bulimia, 53

C

Calof, David, 161. *See also* bind, universal
cancer, 42
caregiving, compulsive, 170. *See also* patterns,
 compulsive relationship
care-seeking, compulsive, 170–171. *See also*
 patterns, compulsive relationship
caretaking, compulsive, 72–73
Catholic Church, 69, 107
cautious of surroundings, extremely, 41. *See also*
 PTSD, reactivity
CDC (Centers for Disease Control), 42
Center for Culture, Brain, and Development
 (UCLA), 25. *See also* Siegel, Daniel
child
 abuse, 74, 125
 molestation, 35
childhood patterns, 63
children
 abused, 40
 and cancer, 42
 traumatic bonding in, 135
clergy(man), 44, 56, 104, 107, 108, 109, 127,
 129, 143, 144, 198, 207, 251, 263, 127
codependency, 67, 72, 73
 and trauma bonds, 175, 177
compartmentalization, 267
compartmentalizing, 50, 52. *See also* trauma,
 splitting
comfort, seen as frivolous, 55
compliance, compulsive, 170. *See also* patterns,
 compulsive relationship
compulsion(s)
 in clergy, 129
 layers of, 123
 definition of, 172
 repetition, 62
 in sex addicts, 159
 See also reenactment; trauma, repetition
Compulsive Relationship Consequences
 Inventory, 179–188
concentrating, difficulties, 52. *See also* trauma,
 splitting
Conflict Inventory, 151–153
conflict, approach/avoidance, 30
confusion, 52. *See also* trauma, splitting
connection

extremes as dysfunctional balance
 mechanism, 57
loss of, 26–27
neural, 32
to our bodies, 27
to others, and shame, 58
of trauma issues with dissociative or
 addictive patterns, 53
contracts
 "fair fight," 210
 no contact, 68
coping, 30, 50
cortisol, 56
couple shame, 210
crisis, life, 163, 164, 234
cults, 67, 71, 98–99, 110, 133–135
cycles
 abuse, 67, 71, 121
 bipolar, 39
 disruption of systemic, 64
 in domestic abuse, 121
 shame, 57

D

danger, 44, 45
 and sexual attraction, 132
daydreaming, excessive, 50, 52. *See also* trauma,
 splitting
debtor, compulsive, 53. *See also* trauma,
 abstinence
deception, 70
Dederich, Charles, 134. *See also* Synanon; cults
defenses, 34–35, 161, 170, 171, 204, 267
degradation, traumatic sexual, 268
denial, 160, 161, 164, 178
 breaking of, 165
 and repression, 168–169
depression, 28, 57, 67
deprivation
 addictive, 56
 behaviors, 164
 compulsive, 53–55, 56, 57
 patterns of, 57
 recovery plan, 236
 role in other addictions, assess, 57
 See also self-care; self-esteem; trauma,
 abstinence
desensitization
 hypnotic, 42. *See also* trauma, reactions
 systematic, 42. *See also* trauma, reactions

detachment, strategies for, 68
diaries, 43. *See also* trauma, reactions
diets, attempting repeatedly, 55
Disclosure, 101
dissociation from experience, 50, 51, 164. *See
    also* trauma, splitting
dissociative identity disorder. *See* disorder,
    multiple personality
disorder(s)
    addictive, 51
    borderline personality, 39, 41
    codependency personality, 57
    dissociative, 50
    DSM, 53
    multiple personality, 50, 51–52
    obsessive compulsive, 2, 62, 64
    sexual aversion, 53, 55
    See also trauma, splitting; trauma,
        abstinence
distortions, 102, 161, 164, 251
    compulsive reality, 171. *See also* patterns,
        compulsive relationship
    See also patterns, compulsive relationship
distress when exposed to reminders, 41. *See also*
    PTSD, reactivity
distrust of others, 41. *See also* PTSD, reactivity
diuretics, to avoid weight gain, 55
Doidge, Norman, 32
doing business (therapy concept), 205
downers. *See* drugs depressants
Dr. Jekyll and Mr. Hyde (Robert Louis Stevenson,
    1895), 51. *See also* alcoholism
dreams, troubling, 39, 41. *See also* PTSD,
    reactivity
drinking, excessive, 47. *See also* trauma,
    blocking
drugs
    abuse of, 123, 162
    addiction in the clergy, 129
    addiction in sex addicts, 159
    addictive disorders to, 51
    depressant, 46, 47, 48. *See also* trauma,
        blocking
    marijuana, 51, 52
    hallucinogenic, 51
    pressure to use before sex, 123
    psychedelic, 51, 52
    stimulant, 44, 45
    used to rationalize violence, 123
    See also trauma, arousal

Dugard, Jaycee, 7
dysfunction, emotional, 191

E
eating
    compulsive, 47
    dysregulated, 270
education, level of, 32
EMDR, 43, 200. *See also* trauma, reactions
emotion(s)
    capacity to regulate, 191
    normal, 59
endorphins, 56
entitlement, 128–129
    in the clergy, 129
escape, 50. *See also* trauma, splitting
exercise, compulsive, 47
exhibitionism, 51, 124
experiences
    avoidance of good, 60
    high-risk, 43
    painful, 63
    processed as extremes, 58
    trauma, 64
    See also trauma, arousal; trauma, repetition
exploitation, 24, 67, 70, 121, 125
    sexual, 134
eye movement desensitization reprocessing.
    See EMDR

F
fantasizing, 52, 67. *See also* trauma, splitting
fantasy, 50, 51, 52
    addictive responses, 50, 53
    sustaining, 96
    See also betrayal, by seduction; trauma,
        splitting
Fatal Attraction, 67, 71, 101
Father Porter case, 6, 143
fear, 30, 40
    and arousal, 161
    attachments, effects on, 176
    intensified by betrayal, 176
    and bonding, 133
    of depending on people, 60
    in domestic abuse cycle, 122
    and deprivation, 55
    and high arousal, 44
    and human attachment, 133
    increasing amounts of, 132–135

and intensity, 130
mechanism to manage, 56
and reactivity, 133
role in betrayal bonds, 121
and sexuality, 44
in trauma bonds, 70
in TV shows, 120
See also trauma, arousal
feelings
of being unworthy, unlovable, immoral, or
sinful, 60
recognition of, 24
Fifty Shades of Gray series, 70-71
fight, flight, or freeze response, 29
fight, to, 259-260. *See also* recovery, risks of
flashbacks, 39, 40, 41, 52. *See also* PTSD,
reactivity; trauma, splitting
flight-or-fight response, 30, 38
flooding, 223. *See also* window of tolerance
focus, how to retain, 53. *See also* strategies,
clinical for trauma splitting
food and eating
abuse of, 123
compulsive, 124
disorders in sex addicts, 159
loss of interest in, 55
preoccupation with, 48
See also trauma, blocking
For Your Own Good, 18
forgetfulness, 52. *See also* trauma, splitting
Frankl, Viktor, 109-110, 186
Freud, Anna, 168
friendships, 27, 32
future, dim outlook on, 60

G

gambling
addiction to, 164
addictive disorders to, 51
compulsive, 43, 44, 45, 51, 162
Game of Thrones (TV show), 120
gaming, 50. *See also* trauma, splitting
Germany, 18
The Gifts of Imperfection, 192-193
Gone Girl, 7-8, 67
grandiosity, 149-150
grief
beginning of, 165
delaying of, 165
resulting from betrayal, 2

support, 68
grieving, 141
stages of, 165
grounding, 224
gullibility, 171. *See also* identification with other,
compulsive

H

harassment, sexual, 97, 100-102
harm, traumatic sexual, 268
Harvard, 131
healing, 24-25, 27. *See also* window of tolerance
and brain plasticity, 31, 191
and healthy boundaries, 72
and independent worth, 72
and integration, 192-193
and reconciliation, 179
steps for, 73
Heaven's Gate (cult), 98-99
helplessness, compulsive, 170. *See also* patterns,
compulsive relationship
Herman, Judith, 264-265. *See also* PTSD;
Trauma and Recovery
Hill, Anita, 102, 155-156
histrionism, 129
hobbies, as way to numb out, 47
Holocaust, 109-110, 129
"honey-moon" stage, 122
honesty, 258. *See also* recovery, risks of
Horgan, John, 129-130. *See also* terrorism
hostage situations, 67
House of Cards (TV show), 120
hypervigilance, 39

I

idealization of others, 41. *See also* overreaction
ideation, suicidal, 57
identification
with aggressor, 168
compulsive, with others, 171
illness, 32
mental, 175, 187-188
impairment, cognitive, 266
incest, 46, 67, 71, 97, 98, 102
and attachment, 147-148
and covenant of betrayal, 126
organizational, 104
typical family cycle, 125
insomnia, 39
integration, 192-193

internal, 27
lack of, experiences into personality, 49
narrative, 192–193
neural, 25
strategies for, 53
See also Mindsight
intensity, 131
interpersonal relational trauma, 23, 24, 27, 28, 29, 72, 73
intimacy, 131–132
and high intensity, 121, 130–132
negative, 185, 260
IRA (Irish Republican Army), 130
ISIS, 129–130

J

Jones, Jim, Rev., 69, 115–116
job(s)
termination, 35
underachieving, 55
Johns Hopkins University, 107
Jonestown, 6, 115–116, 129, 133–134, 148
Jung, Carl, 197, 259
"Just Like a Pill" (Pink), 72

K

Kabat-Zinn, Jon, 191. *See also* mindfulness
Kaiser Permanente Adverse Childhood Experiences (ACE) Study, 42
Karpman, Stephen, 147
Karpman triangle, 147–148
kidnapping situations, 71
Kolk, Besel van der, 24, 25–26, 30, 136

L

Levine, Peter, 8, 26
living
double life, 50, 52
in extremes, 39
See also trauma, splitting
loneliness, 255–256. *See also* recovery, risks of
loss
of autonomous action, 24
and resilience, 25
love
bomb, 99, 121
confusion about, 121
See also cults
loyalty, misplaced, 67, 70, 71, 74, 136–137, 150
and anger, 166

See also attachment, compulsive; role reversal
luxuries, seen as frivolous, 55

M

Maleficent, 8
marriage
problems, 28
toxic, 36
#MeToo movement, 3, 101, 102
meaning
from pain, 186
from suffering to, 263–272
from victimization, 42
See also Frankl, Viktor; trauma, reactions
memories, sudden "real," 41. *See also* PTSD, reactivity
Mercy General Hospital, 101
Middle East Media Research Institute, 130
Miller, Alice, 18
Mindful Awareness Research Center, 25. *See also* Siegel, Daniel
mindfulness, 27
and brain plasticity, 191
definition of, 191
and window of tolerance, 224
See also Kabat-Zinn, Jon
Mindsight, (Daniel Siegel, 2010), 25, 192
misconduct, sexual
and attachment, 147–148
in religious denominations, 143
misperceptions of others, 252–253. *See also* recovery, risks of
model(s)
codependency, 72, 73, 175
compulsive attachment, 72, 73, 175
recovery plan, 201, 212
working, for relationships, 160, 161, 186, 204, 206, 212, 213, 241
trauma, 73
modeling, covert, 43. *See also* trauma, reactions
money hoarding, 55
multiple personality disorder, 50, 51–52, 53
Murry, Marilyn, 241

N

narcissism, 128
in clergy, 129
narrative, personal, 32
writing, 168–173

National Center for Child Traumatic Stress
Complex Trauma Network, 24
needs, social and emotional, 29
neglect, 30, 36, 42, 56. *See also* Kaiser
Permanente Adverse Childhood
Experiences (ACE) Study; trauma,
abstinence
neuroimaging, 23
neuroscience, 27, 32, 72
integration with attachment theory, 5
non-deserving, beliefs about being, 57
norepinephrine, 56, 135

O

obesity, 124
obsession, 51, 52, 56
in domestic abuse cycle, 122, 123
in victim, victimizer, rescuer roles, 149
obsessive compulsive disorder, 62
and catastrophic betrayal, 142
in clergy, 129
See also trauma, repetition
OCD, 2, 62, 64
opioids, endogenous, 135
options, alternative "high," 45
Orestes, story of, 187–188
outbursts, angry, 41. *See also* overreaction;
PTSD, reactivity
overeating, compulsive, 46. *See also* trauma,
blocking
overreaction, 27, 41, 222–225. *See also* window
of tolerance

P

pain
acknowledging the, 168–169
endure, 160
honesty, and accountability, 187
physical, 59
as stage in grieving process, 185
passion, 131
path
of awareness, 164–168,
of denial, 159–164
of full relationship, 207–211
of limited contact, 201–206
of no contact, 195–201
patterns
abuse, 121
addictive, 30

compulsive relationship, 170–172
healthy relationship, 192
of thinking, 191
See also integration
peace, 167
Peck, M. Scott, 187–188, 189
physicians, 44, 56, 129
play activities
as healing, 57
seen as frivolous, 55
People's Temple, 133–134. *See also* Jonestown
personality, shame-based, 57
Pink (singer), 72
pornography, 48–49, 50
posttraumatic embitterment disorder (PTED),
3, 4
posttraumatic stress disorder. *See* PTSD
Post-Traumatic Stress Index, 74–82
poverty obsessions, 53, 54. *See also* trauma,
abstinence
power, 123
disequilibrium of, 102–103
prefrontal cortex and response to threats, 23
preoccupation, 51, 52
artistic or mystical, 50, 51
with children of certain age, 64
with long-gone aggressor, 67
See also trauma, splitting
Presumed Innocent, 101
Prisoner of Another War, 241
"The Prevalence of Clergy Sexual Advances
Toward Adults in Their Congregations,"
107
procrastination, extreme, 50, 52. *See also*
trauma, splitting
prostitution, 43, 44, 108. *See also* trauma, arousal
purpose
attention on, 191
depth of, 187
larger, 257
PTSD, 2, 24, 28, 38, 39–40
effects of catastrophic betrayal in, 142
reactivity, 41
reactions, 269
teaching concepts of, 42. *See also* trauma,
reactions

R

rage, 67
rape, 35, 67, 104, 124

rationalization, 164, 171. *See also* patterns, compulsive relationship
reaction, extreme, 121
  of community, family, or social structure, 143–144
reactivity, 64, 133, 161, 162, 210, 212, 220
  in the context of a relationship, 161
  emotional, 220
  modulation of, 135
  as principal problem of trauma victims, 208
  PTSD, 41
  recovery plan, 221–227
  time, 200
  traumatic, 103
  in traumatic bonding, 147
  See also eye movement desensitization
reading, as way to numb out, 47
reality
  altered, 51
  to commit to, at all costs, 250–252. *See also* recovery, risks of
  ten rules to stay in, 235–236
recall important details of experiences, inability to, 52. *See also* trauma, splitting
recollections, recurrent and intrusive, 41. *See also* PTSD, reactivity
Recovering Couples Anonymous (RCA), 209–211
recovery, 164
  and denial, 172
  dimensions of, 212–213
  groups, 27
  plan, 195, 200–201, 212
  plan for compulsive relationships, 213–215
  risks of, 249–275
re-creation of experience, abreactive, 64
reenactment, 62, 63, 64. *See also* trauma, repetition
reframing, 197, 206
  of trauma experiences, cognitive, 42
  See also trauma, reactions
regulation, emotional, 23, 26–27, 38
  and overcoming passivity and fixed reactions, 31
relapse
  connection with trauma issues, 57
  prevention, implementation of, 42, 45, 49, 57
  See also trauma, abstinence; trauma, arousal
relationship(s)
  abusive, 63
  creation of new working model for, 206

dysfunctional, 71, 175
  compulsive, 121, 168, 170
  compulsive, self-assessment, 172, 173–175
  destructive, 164
  and emotional regulation, 31
  and formation of beliefs about self and world, 29
  goals, 206
  problematic, exercise, 176–177
  problems, 28
  recovery plan for compulsive, 213–216
  resilience and longevity, effects on, 25
  templates, 135, 160, 166
  and trauma bonds, 176
  unhealthy, 67
relaxation, deep muscle, 42. *See also* trauma, reactions
religiosity, excessive, 51. *See also* trauma, splitting
rejection, compulsive, 171. *See also* patterns, compulsive relationship
remodeling, 199
repetition, 37
  compulsion, 241–245
  cycles, 162
  and fear, 133
  recovery plan, 241–245
  systemic, 68
  trauma, 161
  See also trauma, effects over time
repression, 160–161, 164
  breaking of, 165
  traumatic, 172
rescuing, compulsive, 193
resilience, 24, 25, 30, 67
  and brain plasticity, 191
resolution, 144
responses
  addictive, 46
  all-or-nothing, 135
  phobic, 53
  See also trauma, abstinence; trauma, blocking
restructuring, cognitive, 64, 206
risk, 44, 70
  addiction to, 130–131
  in domestic abuse cycle, 122–123
  forced for unwanted pregnancy, 123
roles and scripts, 121
  familiar, 144–146
  reversal, 146–150

and traumatic bonding, 146
role development, 212
role-playing, 43, 123. *See also* trauma, reactions
Ryan, Leo (Congressman), 134, 148. *See also*
    Jonestown; Jones, Jim, Rev.

S

sadomasochism, 43, 44. *See also* trauma, arousal
Sandy Hook Elementary School, 17–18
satiation, 46, 47. *See also* trauma, blocking
saving, compulsive, 53. *See also* trauma,
    abstinence
say good-bye, 254–255. *See also* recovery, risks of
Schore, Allan, Dr., 5
seduction, 70
    history of, 111–113
    strategies, 171
    in TV shows, 120
self, definition of, 260–262. *See also* recovery,
    risks of
self-care, 27, 56. *See also* neglect; trauma,
    abstinence
self-dialogue, guided, 43. *See also* trauma,
    reactions
self-doubting, 142
    resulting from betrayal, 2
    and roles, 148
self-esteem, 29, 56
    damaged, 2, 142
    See also neglect; trauma, abstinence
self-hatred, 57, 59
self-help groups, 68
self-monitoring, 43. *See also* trauma, reactions
self-mutilation, 57, 59
self-neglect, 53. *See also* trauma, abstinence
self-perception, traumatic, 267–268
self-regulation, 24
self-reliance, compulsive, 170. *See also* patterns,
    compulsive relationship
self-soothing, 24, 30
self-starvation. *See* anorexia nervosa
serotonin, 135
setups, systemic, 67
sex
    abuse of, 123
    addictive disorder to, 51
    addicts, 159
    anonymous, 44
    derogatory comments during, 123
    forced involvement in unsafe or group, 123

high-risk, 43, 44, 45, 123
offending, 43, 44. *See also* trauma, arousal
performance enhancers, 123
public, 124
supercharged, 44
violent, 162
sexuality, difficulties in, 40
shame, 37, 44, 55, 57, 58, 59, 64, 67, 70, 95, 99,
    133, 135, 161, 162, 164
    carried, 204
    recovery plan, 240–241
    and roles, 148
    traumatic, 267
    and vulnerability, 166
    See also betrayal, by terror; trauma, bonds;
        trauma, effects over time; trauma,
        repetition; trauma, shame
Siegel, Daniel, 25, 27, 192, 225. *See also* Center
    for Culture, Brain, and Development
    (UCLA); Mindful Awareness Research
    Center; *Mindsight*; window of tolerance
situations, all-or-nothing, 45
sleeping, excessive, 46, 47. *See also* trauma,
    blocking
sleeplessness, periods of, 41. *See also* PTSD,
    reactivity
social media, excessive use of 47. *See also*
    trauma, blocking
sociopath, 128
soldiers, 39
Somatic Experiencing, 26. *See also* Levine, Peter;
    The Meadows
spacing out, 52. *See also* trauma, splitting
spender, compulsive, 53, 159. *See also* debtor,
    compulsive
spiritual practice, excessive, 51. *See also* trauma,
    splitting
spirituality, 256–257. *See also* recovery, risks of
splitting, 37, 49, 50, 161, 162
    and fear, 133
    recovery plan, 231–235
    See also trauma, effects over time; trauma,
        splitting
startled more easily than others, 41. *See also*
    PTSD, reactivity
Stevenson, Robert Louis, 51
stillness (Royal Navy exercise), 203
Stockholm, 148
    syndrome, 6–7
story, writing the, 168–173

storytelling, therapeutic, 42. *See also* trauma,
  reactions
strategies
  clinical, for trauma abstinence, 57
  clinical, for trauma arousal, 45
  clinical, for trauma bonds, 67
  clinical, for trauma reactions, 42
  clinical, for trauma repetition, 64
  clinical, for trauma shame, 61
  clinical, for trauma splitting, 53
  coping, 50, 193
  "good cop, bad cop," 98
  incremental "use," 57
  relapse prevention, 57
  thought-stopping, 42
  trauma resolution, 45
  used by victims to accommodate reality, 160
stress, 28, 42, 55
  management techniques, 42
  See also Kaiser Permanente Adverse
    Childhood Experiences (ACE) Study;
    trauma, abstinence; trauma, reactions
substance use, 270
success avoidance, 53, 55. *See also* trauma,
  abstinence
support
  groups, 32, 168, 178, 198
  twelve-step, 45, 49. *See also* trauma, arousal;
    trauma, blocking
surgery, cosmetic, 123
Survivor (TV show), 120
survivors
  and integrity, 166
  of sexual abuse, 39, 40, 41–42, 50
  vulnerability in, 166
swapping (sexual partners), 124
symptoms, physical, 39
Synanon, 134. *See also* cults
system, "no fault," 211

T

taking responsibility for self, 262–263. *See also*
  recovery, risks of
tasks, sustained, steady, 45
technology
  excessive use of, 47
  and seduction, 89–91
  See also trauma, blocking
televangelists, 108
television, binge-watching, 50. *See also* trauma,

  splitting
terror, 55, 97–100, 103, 121, 122, 133
  acclimatization to, 160
  and attachment, 147
  facing children, 135–136
  and role reversal, 147
  rules of, 178
terrorism, 129–130
testimony method, 197
The Meadows, 26, 95, 110. *See also* Somatic
  Experiencing
therapy, 27, 32, 168
  art, 62
thinking, magical, 149
Thomas, Clarence, 102, 155–156
thoughts
  intrusive, 39, 60
  suicidal, 59
threats
  flexible response to, 23
  suicidal, 59
ties, abusive/conflictual, 67
Tollefson, William, 137. *See also* loyalty,
  misplaced
trauma
  abstinence, 53–57, 64, 161, 162
  by accumulation, 36, 38
  and addictive patterns, 30
  arousal, 43–45, 64, 161
  attachment to, 38
  "Big T," 28
  blocking, 46–49, 161
  bonds, 25, 30, 64, 67–70, 110, 126, 132, 136,
    142, 143, 147, 157, 159, 161, 163, 172,
    175, 176, 195, 266
  characteristics of, 28–31
  definition of, 25–27
  effects on the brain, 37–38
  effects on resilience, 24, 25, 26
  effects over time, 37, 38–64
  history of, in sex addicts, 159
  and intense emotions, 23
  inability to recognize, 34–35
  interpersonal relational, 23, 24, 27, 28, 29,
    72, 73
  "Little t," 28
  neurobiological impact of, 26
  pleasure, 44–45
  primary reactions, 38–64
  psychobiological impact of, 26

psychological impact of, 26
reaction, 37, 39–43, 64
and recovery, 31–37
reenacting of experiences (re-creation), 30, 61, 62, 135–136
and relationship dynamics in children, 30
repetition, 62, 161
resolution, 212
resolution strategies, 49
shame, 57–60, 161, 162
splitting, 49–53, 64, 161, 162
traces of, 26, 27
and translation of experience into language, 23
vulnerability to, 28–29
Trauma and Recovery (Judith Herman), 265
traumatic brain injury, 32
Traumatic Stress Index worksheet, 83–84
trigger, 30
trust, break in, 58
TV
reality shows, 120
as way to numb out, 47
Twilight series, 70–71

U

UCLA School of Medicine, 25
UMass Lowell, 129–130
uniqueness, beliefs of, 68, 121, 126–130. *See also* betrayal, covenant of; bonds, betrayal
underachieving, 53. *See also* trauma, abstinence
underemployment, 55
underreaction, 222–223, 226–227
unreality, 50. *See also* trauma, splitting
unworthiness, beliefs about, 53, 57. *See also* trauma, shame

V

vacations, routinely skipping, 55
victim(s)
de-role from intensity, 203
victimizer, and rescuer commonalities, 150
of violent crimes, 39

victimization consciousness, 166–167
video games, 47
violence, 24
compulsive seeking of, 163
compulsive sexual, 123
domestic, 15, 56, 67, 71, 73–74, 99, 104, 124
and pleasure, 44
statistics on interpersonal, 125
against women, 13–14
visualization, 61, 64. *See also* re-creation of experience, abreactive
vomiting to avoid weight gain, 55
voyeurism, 124
vulnerability, 28, 106, 110, 234, 258–259
and constancy, 132
effects on attachment, 176
exploitation of, 259
and fear, 176
and passion, 131, 132
and trauma bonding, 102–103, 136, 163
See also recovery, risks of

W

war, 39, 48, 67
The War of the Roses, 7, 67, 71
window of tolerance, 27, 225–227. *See also* Siegel, Daniel
warmth and intention, 92–94
Wolf of Wall Street, The, 131
workaholism, 53. *See also* trauma, abstinence
work environment, toxic, 71
working
to avoid feelings, 48
compulsive, 47, 159, 162
working model for relationships, 160, 161, 168, 186, 204, 206, 212, 213, 241

Y

yoga, somatic experiencing trauma-informed, 43

Z

Zweig, Elliot, 130. *See also* Middle East Media Research

ABOUT THE AUTHORS

Patrick J. Carnes, PhD, is an internationally known authority and speaker on addiction and recovery issues. He has authored more than twenty books, including the bestselling titles *Out of the Shadows: Understanding Addiction Recovery; Betrayal Bond (first edition); Don't Call It Love; The Gentle Path Through the Twelve Steps;* and *The Gentle Path through the Twelve Principles.*

Dr. Carnes' research provides the architecture for the "task model" of treating addictions that is used by thousands of therapists worldwide and many well-known treatment centers, residential facilities, and hospitals. He founded IITAP (International Institute for Trauma and Addiction Professionals), which has trained more than 2000 therapists in sixteen countries, providing CSAT (Certified Sex Addiction Therapist) training and certification as well as cutting-edge information for addiction professionals.

He helped to develop assessments critical to the diagnosis and treatment of sex addiction, such as the Sexual Addiction Screening Test (SAST) and the Sexual Dependency Inventory (SDI), as well as assessments in trauma and financial disorders.

Dr. Carnes is the founding architect of the Gentle Path program and co-founder of Willow House, specialty programs for sexual and trauma disorders for men and women at The Meadows in Wickenburg, Arizona, where he currently serves as a Senior Fellow.

Most recently, in 2017 and 2018, Dr. Carnes served as a visiting professor of Brain Science at the University of Alberta Medical School and as a Fulbright Scholar focusing on genotypes in sex addiction.

Dr. Carnes graduated in 1966 from St. John's University, Collegeville, Minnesota, with a bachelor of arts. He received his master's degree in 1969 from Brown University, and a doctorate in counselor education and organizational development from the University of Minnesota in 1980.

Dr. **Bonnie Phillips** is an Assistant Professor in the Graduate Counseling Program at John Brown University's Little Rock campus. Her course work includes, among others: Sexuality, Addictions, Group Therapy, Marital Therapy, Brief Therapy, and Crisis and Trauma Counseling. She is a Licensed Professional Counselor in the state of Arkansas and specializes in working with individuals, couples, families, and groups who struggle with addiction and trauma.

Bonnie received her master's degree in Marriage and Family Therapy in 1995 and her PhD in Marriage and Family Therapy from the University of Louisiana at Monroe in 2004. She is a Licensed Professional Counselor in Arkansas and is a Certified Sexual Addictions Therapist and Supervisor, Certified Multiple Addictions Therapist, trained in EMDR, and is currently undergoing certification in Somatic Experiencing. She has been a guest speaker at several national conferences including the International Institute for Trauma and Addictions Professionals conference.

Dr. Phillips has practiced individual, couple, family, and group therapy in a variety of settings including outpatient, residential treatment, and intensive outpatient working with adolescents and adults. Most recently, she has been teaching and working in private practice in Little Rock. She worked for three years full time for Dr. Patrick Carnes and continues to work with him, consulting on several projects.